T0110515

STRATEGIC MEDIA PLANNING AND BUYING

This book explores media planning, media buying and the advertising land-scape in India. It provides a comprehensive look into the essential aspects of media strategies for brands and businesses to effectively reach their intended audiences and consumers.

The book cuts through and demystifies complex media jargon and theories to provide an understanding of the key concepts for developing a media mix that will yield results for businesses. It discusses media research and theories and offers marketers suggestions on how to use both traditional and digital media effectively to build brands. The first section of the book introduces the basics of media theory, including data collection methodologies and their application. The second section covers the fundamentals of planning a media strategy and advertising plans and campaigns based on the goals of the company or brand. The third section discusses the practical nuances of planning – like media mix selections, media vehicle selections and media buying across all types of media.

This book will be of interest to students and researchers of business and management studies, media and communication studies as well as to marketing and media professionals working in different sectors of business.

Basant Rathore is Senior VP, Strategy, Brand and Business Development at the Jagran Group, India. He has worked at media agencies like Ogilvy, Mudra, Mindshare and Madison. An alumnus of MICA, Ahmedabad, he has conducted over 30 media workshops. Over the last decades he has been a visiting faculty at MICA, IIMC, XIM Bhubaneshwar, IMT Ghaziabad and Flame University, among others.

STRATEGIC MEDIA PLANNING AND BUYING

Integration of Traditional and Digital Media

Basant Rathore

Routledge
Taylor & Francis Group

LONDON AND NEW YORK

Designed cover image: Basant Rathore

First published 2024
by Routledge
4 Park Square, Milton Park, Abingdon, Oxon OX14 4RN

and by Routledge
605 Third Avenue, New York, NY 10158

Routledge is an imprint of the Taylor & Francis Group, an informa business

British Library Cataloguing-in-Publication Data
A catalogue record for this book is available from the British Library

ISBN: 978-1-032-49982-6 (hbk)
ISBN: 978-1-032-72457-7 (pbk)
ISBN: 978-1-032-72453-9 (ebk)

DOI: 10.4324/9781032724539

Typeset in Sabon
by SPi Technologies India Pvt Ltd (Straive)

To my wife Shikha and my daughters Ahana and Mahikka for their patience with me during the process of writing the book. And to all my students over the last 2 decades, who have helped me learn along with them.

CONTENTS

FIGURES

TABLES

FOREWORD

The advertising profession has seen ups and downs like no other business. The variables by which it is impacted are innumerable. The opening up of the economy in the early 1990s propelled the profession, while a recession in the mid-1990s pulled it back. The first wave of the tech boom left advertising unimpressed, but a decade later, the second wave of the tech boom was embraced by the industry. Along with these ups and downs, the profession has had a tumultuous journey to where it stands now. Just technological advancement wasn't enough for a field that began as a pure play creative vocation. In the early days, ad executives balanced the demands of external clients and pressures of internal creativity with equal fervour. The only thing that an ad agency sold was creative and allied services. Media was limited to just print, with newspapers and magazines dominating the scene.

Winds of change came, first with the commercialization of the state-owned terrestrial broadcaster Doordarshan, and then with the subsequent satellite TV revolution from the private sector. During those days, the remuneration model for advertising agencies was a 15% commission based on the money an advertiser spent on media. This commission was actually paid by the media owners to the advertising agency for letting them publish/broadcast a particular advertisement. All business was routed via advertising agencies, and media owners didn't entertain advertisers directly. Then came the first tremors of economic recession in 1997 and coincidentally the entry of Media AOR (Agency on Record) in India. And for the first time officially, clients got their hands on the elusive 15%!

Over a period of time, the media business unbundled completely to become a standalone business. Yet, despite this, the agency remuneration model remains tenuously stretched on fees + bonuses. Rarely have these creative and media consultants been able to command the fee levels which other business service consultants command. Basant Rathore is a rare professional who has stood by his conviction that advertising (more specifically media planning) is a knowledge-based service which requires an in-depth understanding of human behavior, and how one could place a piece of communication in the consumer's mind. I wish this kind of a text cum reference book was available at the time when I came into advertising media planning back in 1988.

In a fast-changing media landscape, this book fills an important gap in the knowledge-driven media industry and presents a holistic view on how media could be leveraged to build brands. The book is relevant for media and marketing professionals, who, in order to reach out to their consumers with their product/brand communication, have to navigate the dynamic media jungle replete with concepts, jargon, research and data. Often, the front-end glitz, scale and glamour of the media world obliterate the hours of work required on the back end to achieve strategic soundness. It is this strategic soundness that the book lays emphasis on.

India is one of the most complex media markets in the world, with a huge demographic variance and linguistic and cultural differences. In such a market, this book enables a practitioner to anchor media thinking within a sound strategic framework. The book covers understanding media basics, about media research, about the dimensions of media strategy, about tactical planning, about media buying and about building media brands. At the same time, it discusses current thinking and new developments in media planning from around the world.

The book serves as an essential 'Reference Book' for a lot of traditional or internet entrepreneurs who spend big money on media chasing subscribers/users/customers/downloads as they brace themselves to become the next 'unicorns'. It's time new-age entrepreneurs spend that much more time and rigour in getting their media right (beyond the big splash of jackets in newspapers, and the big-ticket events), because media is often the last link between them and their eventual consumers. And, as all of us know, how important it is to get the 'last mile' right. This book will equip them to think business when it comes to media.

What I'm also particularly enthused about is the fact that no practicing professional has ever attempted to express his/her lifetime learnings so eloquently grounded in a strong strategic framework, replete with theoretical constructs and practical applications, and yet providing leeway for individual creativity in media. This is a must-have on the shelf for every media and marketing student and professional.

Amit Ray
Founder Partner, Media First Consulting. Estd. 2011

PREFACE

I was first thrust into a classroom full of eager students at MICA in Ahmedabad long ago in 1999 to take a session on media planning when one of the visiting guest faculty from Mumbai missed his flight. I was fairly new to the media business then (just 3 years into work), so I thought of introducing students to the real world of media which was far removed from the international context presented in the prescribed textbooks. So for every session I conducted, I made it a point to simplify the concepts, give their application in the Indian context, and give real-world examples so that students could maximize their learning.

Subsequently over the years, whenever I went back to teach at communication and business schools, I would often see students struggling to adapt the international context (of textbooks) to the Indian media environment. What I noticed was a significant difference between the exciting Indian media environment and the 'not-so-exciting' classroom discussions on theories and applications. During this time, I also conducted several workshops for professional media salespeople and marketers, and they too faced the same challenges as students.

I soon realized that there was a persistent gap between academia and the real world of media. I've seen this gap exist over the last 2.5 decades even as I've straddled the media world, first as a media planner, and then as a media marketer. With media spends projected to grow to INR 90,000 cr in 2022, India is one of the fastest-growing markets in the world. It seems a bit anachronistic for this knowledge gap to exist in such a large and vibrant industry. This gap was the single most important factor which really got me started on the book.

There were three core thoughts while writing the book:

- To ensure that the concepts of media are simplified for easy understanding
- To create content with an Indian context so that it's relatable for students
- To contemporize the content, which was important as the media scenario continues to evolve by the day

The book is an essential guide for media and marketing students. It is also relevant for brand managers who, in order to reach out to their consumers and achieve brand goals, have to collaborate with their media partners. At the same time for media planners and buyers, the book could serve as an important primer to keep them abreast with the latest thinking in media.

The first module of the book covers basic concepts used in media with examples from the Indian context. It introduces media research, details research concepts and data collection methodologies, and explains the utility and applications of the data.

The second module in the book talks about the fundamentals of planning media strategy. It talks about how to identify target audiences and discusses market identification and prioritization, how one should schedule advertising, and how one arrives at the intensity of advertising. In the process, they also demonstrate the use of research data. The module has been capped with a discussion on the principles of strategy planning and debates issues like privacy, context, content marketing, frequency capping, and the latest in media thinking.

The third module discusses the practical nuances of planning like media mix selection, media vehicle selections, and media buying across all types of media. It also discusses the budget-setting process and the media briefing requirements. Additionally, it also has a chapter on media marketing which discusses how to manage a media brand as a marketer.

The book leads you on to revisit essential concepts, to appreciate research, to construct media strategy, and to understand the tactical aspects of planning and buying, yet would inspire you enough to blend individual creativity to leverage media for brand building.

ACKNOWLEDGEMENTS

A heartfelt word of thanks to each of the following who have been extremely generous with their time and valuable inputs.

Amit Ray: For being my earliest and longest-standing media mentor, and for very graciously agreeing to write the Foreword.

Aman Jain: The young digital whiz who very patiently took me through a day in the life of a digital media planner.

Anannya Paliwal: For sharing his view on digital planning.

Alok Kapase: For helping with inputs on digital planning.

Ashit Kukian, Kartik Kalla, and Varsha Ojha: The dynamic senior leadership team of Radio City who helped me with inputs on how the radio industry is structured, and shared their vision on building radio brands.

Bharat Gupta: For sharing a view on how one manages and builds a news media brand in the digital world.

Bhupinder Sahota: For his creative insights and views on design and aesthetics. For the constant encouragement and support.

Deepak Pandey: For his incisive understanding of the newspaper distribution models.

Gautam Chhatwal: For being ever so helpful with some images for the book.

Mahendra Mohan Gupta: For always inspiring me to take on challenges. His unrelenting focus on simplifying complexity has had an influence on me. Thank you, Sir, for the valuable lessons.

Mubin Khan: For the constant support and for always being a call away.

Naveen Chaudhary: For helping me find my way through the publishing world.

Nripendra Singh: For all the discussions we've had on media and the way forward, and for some vital content inputs.

OM Logics Team: For running me through what it means to run a digital media agency and its transformation to future-readiness during the pandemic.

Payal Singhal: For sharing her views on digital planning.

Prashant Kashyap: My colleague for his constant encouragement while writing, and his extremely valuable inputs on understanding consumers, markets, and cultures.

R K Agarwal: For the faith that he reposed in me. Just interacting with him over the past decade has been like a mentorship in practice. His guidance has been extremely valuable.

Sachin Kamat: For being the constant friend and guide in all things advertising, media and life.

Sandeep Menon: For writing an absolutely stunning and insightful piece on the conjunction of data technology, budget content, and how powerful stories are essential to engage with communities.

Sanjay Gupta: For all the learnings I've gleaned about the importance of content and how brand building with content at its core works beautifully for news media brands. His insights on everything about the media business have been extremely useful.

Sarbani Bhatia: For talking me through how a strong technology back end is critical for media organizations.

Satish Mishra: For sharing insights on how the production piece works in a print organization.

Shailesh Gupta: For allowing me to create a vision for the brand and backing me all through to implement it. His constant presence and encouragement has defined my professional journey.

Shantamoy Ray: A consummate professional and a dear friend, who helped with graphic and design inputs for the book.

Swati Vishwanathan: For talking me through the exciting world of branded content and partnerships on digital media.

V Sudarshan: For being the bouncing board on all issues pertaining to research in India, and for helping with several inputs.

Vinod Shrivastava: My colleague, with whom I've spent hours discussing the challenges involved in building media brands. Additionally, his inputs on the industry were a huge plus.

Vishal Rupani: For introducing me to a few firebrand digital media planners and buyers.

Vivek Malhotra: For being very generous with his time and inputs while talking about brand building on news channels.

Shikha Rathore: My wife, for her constant encouragement, and for being very patient all through and allowing me the liberty to encroach on her time over the last couple of years while writing the book.

1

BASIC CONCEPTS

Humans and Memory

It's often said that 90% of what human beings learn is incidental learning, and advertising is almost always incidental learning. We must remember that advertising does its job in the human mind, and the human mind does its job using memories.

Memory Formation and Traces

Memories are formed by repeated exposures. Do you remember when you had to learn a poem as a kid? We did it by repeating it multiple times. Similarly, brands too form neural networks in our minds. So when I say Nike, it triggers a certain visual element in your mind. For some, it triggers athletes, for some it triggers shoes, and so on. Similarly, every brand has a neural network in our brain – somewhat akin to a 'brand room'. Rooms that are lit up and furnished regularly are top of mind. The tracks of these neural networks get deeper when one keeps stimulating these networks.

Types of Learning

There are two ways of learning – high involvement learning and low involvement learning. High involvement learning is activated at will; for instance, when you say, 'I have to study this' or 'I have to focus on this'. So, one either concentrates hard or repeats it to oneself. That's high order, high involvement learning. Low involvement learning is picking up things subconsciously or implicitly. Research says that information that enters the memory through

DOI: 10.4324/9781032724539-1

low involvement processing goes into long-term memory. So think of low involvement processing if you want to create brand associations in the minds of consumers.

How to Lay Down a Memory

One can lay down a memory by saying that this piece of information is very important, and I would memorize it by repetitive rehearsal. Another way is, say, by driving home through the same route every day. One subconsciously registers the colour of homes on the way, or knows where an unpainted speed breaker is on the road, or where there are potholes, or where there's a Pan shop on the next bend. That's how we give directions. Those are all parts of low involvement process, and you never set out to read or learn that there are five potholes on the way to my home, or there's a big speed breaker ahead and I need to slow down before I get there. So those are the things that incidentally get into your mind. And then the other is to say, 'let me focus on it', 'this event is important to me', 'I want to understand what Trump is doing during elections in the US', and so on. These learning-forming memories are also applied to advertising. They are the same physiological processes whereby advertising memories are laid down by repetitive exposures.

Human Memory Is Fallible

Dr Carmen Simon, a cognitive neuroscientist, says that human memory is fallible. She says that we forget about 90% of what we've learnt in 48 hours. Thereafter, the 'metaphorical' 10% remains in our memories over time. Therefore, for your message to be remembered, it's important that one understands how the brain decodes messages and how it creates memories. In other words, as media people, we must talk to the human being rather than to a person dryly labelled as a 'consumer'. Dr Simon lays out five simple principles in marketing to the brain (Simon, 2015):

- The brain is cognitively a lazy organ. Therefore, marketing content has to be very easy to process. If we make it complicated, it needs more cognitive energy. Already marketing communication is incidental learning, and if we expect to summon greater cognitive energy, then we're asking for too much. So keep your message simple.
- Memory is aided by familiarity. Therefore, try to create familiarity for your brand through repetitive exposures.
- Break the pattern regularly because we humans become habituated very quickly. Too much familiarity may create something called a blind spot. Therefore, keep an element of surprise. The term used by Dr Carmen is that we must become 'choreographers of contrast'. While you have a singular

message to give to your audiences, if you rotate creative work and tell the story in different ways, we could keep the interest alive.

- Uncertainty gives a dopamine spike. This essentially means that the anticipation of eating chocolate releases more dopamine than the actual act of eating. The anticipation of planning for a trip spikes more dopamine than the actual trip. Therefore, keep an element of unexpected outcome from your commercial message.
- Reward the brain with complexity. Essentially, Dr Carmen is saying, keep things simple, and then reward the brain with complexity. So move from simple communication and add a layer of complexity. Don't instead try to simplify complexity.

Put the Human First

All this has an implication on how you frame your media strategy, how you look at content creation, how you look at maximizing the apertures available to innovate and stand out of the clutter, and how you build engagement bridges with your consumers. An understanding of the human ahead of the numbers is critical in today's complicated media world. Let's put the human first.

Learning about advertising is always incidental. Your challenge as a media planner is to make an impact on the mind of the consumer for whom advertising is not central to his/her existence. The challenge is to make an impact despite ad avoidance, clutter, and the massively fragmented media landscape. This learning forming memories also explains why multimedia works better in stimulating a brand's neural network in our minds.

What Is Media Planning?

A textbook definition I've found quite compelling is what I read in *Advertising Media Planning* by Jack Z Sissors and Roger B Baron, which said, "What are the best means of delivering advertisements to prospective purchasers of my brand or service?" (Sissors & Baron, 2012, p. 3). I find this an overarching definition of media planning because essentially I see media as the last link in the marketing chain that takes the message to the consumer in the anticipation of driving a desired action. The definition does not restrict one to just optimizing budgets or reaching an audience; rather, it unshackles one's mind to look at media neutrally, while at the same time aligning clearly with the marketing task at hand. In so much as this is true, media is in great measure a part of marketing. Hence, the media planner must understand product, brand, pricing, distribution, competition, marketing strategy, audience, advertising effects, communication, creativity, the media landscape, and the infinite opportunities it allows one to leverage for a brand. And when the planner looks at all this, he/she becomes an integral part of the marketing team and echoes the same passion as the brand managers do. I've often seen that when a planner aligns with the marketing strategy, the thinking process is very focused and goal oriented. This is what makes the task of media planning so exciting.

The Evolution of Media Planning

The evolution of media happened in parallel with the evolution of marketing itself. When marketers adopted the marketing concept of segmenting-targeting-positioning, it had an impact on media planning. When marketers asked for accountability, media aligned itself even more closely with the marketing function to ensure that they play a role in moving the needle towards a desirable consumer action. Now, when marketing increasingly seems to be driven towards being performance-led, it's media again which has reinvented the way it works. And finally, with the expansion of media, it became a full-blown discipline having to navigate amongst thousands of options before finalizing the plan. I've always seen it from the lens of a portfolio manager whose sole objective is to maximize returns. He/she studies the macroeconomic environment, categories, and companies and their strategies, to eventually place bets on a few who would yield the desired ROI. Likewise, a media planner's agenda is to ensure that the marketing ROI is achieved. In the process, the planner too navigates thousands of options before placing budgets across media and media channels to drive the desired consumer response.

The Evolution of the Media Planning Agency in India

In its early days, the media function was an insignificant part of the advertising agency. We had the state-owned Doordarshan and All India Radio channels, newspapers in different geographies, magazines across a few broad genres, and cinema halls and outdoor sites. Media fragmentation, as we know it now, didn't exist. Therefore, media choices were fairly straightforward, and hence there wasn't much 'sophistication' in media planning. This was pretty much true of the 70s and the 80s.

In the early 90s, the satellite TV revolution began in India, with Zee TV being launched in 1992. Soon thereafter, several other satellite channels were launched, offering a completely different set of alternatives to the content given out by Doordarshan. This period was also marked by the economic liberalization programme, which ushered us into an era of consumerism. These twin forces played a huge impact in shaping the economy, the marketing and advertising industry, and the media discipline in India. Since then, the media department became a critical part of the full service agency.

Soon enough, the mid-90s saw a recessionary period in the economy which forced large advertisers to ask the question of ROI. In a full-service agency structure, the media planning function and the creative function resided in the same agency. Large advertisers like Unilever (Hindustan Levers, back then) worked with different agencies for different brands, and in a full-service agency concept, the media planning and buying too was fragmented amongst different agencies. This, however, didn't allow a large advertiser like Unilever to leverage the benefits that one could get by buying media at scale. Thus started the agency unbundling process with the creation of buying AORs, or Agency of Record. The AOR consolidated the buying function across all brands of Unilever to drive benefits of buying media at scale. In that arrangement, the erstwhile media department at the full-service agency still made media plans for respective brands. Called 'shadow plans', these were sent across the central AOR (Fulcrum), which combined all the plans and negotiated centrally with media owners to get the best buy.

This AOR arrangement continued for a couple of years, and then India saw the entry of the global giant Carat Media, which offered the full stack of media planning, buying, and implementation services to advertisers. This marked the beginning of the complete unbundling of the agency service. The media department of the full-service agency was no longer a necessity in agency structures, as advertisers started assigning separate creative and media agencies. The full-service agencies restructured themselves and floated their media departments as new entities. Since then, media has become an independent business in India.

The Sequence of Events in the Media Process

If you look at the broad working of a media agency (refer to Figure 1.1), the process begins with the media brief, which is followed by planning and media buying. Negotiations are done with media to finalize deals, and then the approved plan goes to implementation. After the campaign is over, a post evaluation is done to understand whether the media plan delivered against a certain predefined benchmark or yardstick. This is because all planning is done on historical data and what we have at the planning stage is estimated

FIGURE 1.1 Sequence of events in the media process.

Source: Created by the author.

reach and campaign frequency numbers. The post evaluation answers questions of whether the plan deliveries were in line with the estimations, which markets overdelivered or underdelivered, learnings for the future, etc.

Therefore, the sequence begins with a media briefing, followed by media planning and media buying (which often take place simultaneously). Once the plan is finalized and approved by the advertiser, the plan is implemented through the scheduling department. Once the plan has been implemented, the planner conducts a post-buy analysis to assess whether the plan worked as desired.

Media Consumer Interface

Marketing literature is awash with models on how advertising works. Amongst the most popular of these is the 'Hierarchy of Effects', which essentially says that consumers move through different stages of information processing before they act. Several models talk about this with different degrees of variations – all albeit around the three pillars of Cognitive-Affective-Conative (Wijaya, 2012). However, there have been several debates regarding these models. Vakratsas and Ambler (1999, cited in Wijaya, 2012) have reviewed over 250 papers on these models and have concluded that there's little evidence of the existence of an advertising hierarchy of effects.

Irrespective of the merits and demerits of theories of how advertising works, the one thing that's at the start of all consumer conversation is exposure to communication. It's only after an exposure to some communication that a chain reaction of "effects" takes place.

Exposure must take place. Exposure must take place before Awareness. Exposure in media means "Open eyes facing a medium" (Sissors & Baron, 2012, p. 56).

Exposure in print is different from that of a TV or other media. Essentially, it is a consumer in front of a media vehicle. That vehicle could be anything from a digital tablet to a mobile, a laptop screen, a newspaper, a magazine, or a TV screen. Also, when we say 'exposure', we mean exposures to vehicles and not to the ads.

This is also an important determinant of audience estimations. Exposure across different types of media:

a) Press: People who have read the publication
b) TV: People who have watched a TV programme
c) Radio: People who have listened to a programme
d) Cinema: People who go to cinema halls
e) Outdoor: People who pass by a site
f) Internet: People who visit a site

This is largely about vehicle exposure, and it gives us the starting points for audience size estimations for various types of media vehicles. Why do audience size estimations become important? They are important in understanding the size of the audience delivered by the vehicle. It helps profile vehicles on various types of demographic parameters – and eventually it provides a currency that helps compare across media vehicles. Alongside, it also helps us understand media consumption habits of various target groups.

Basic Concepts Used in Media Planning

In media, a few basic concepts set the ground rules for all further media thinking. Most of these concepts are in the core area of defining measurements and from the perspective of evaluating the effect of a media plan or from the perspective of comparing various kinds of media. The foremost concept is that of reach.

Reach

Reach is defined as the total number of different people who have been exposed to a campaign at least once. The stress is on the word "different" – therefore, if one person has been exposed to your campaign two times, we don't count him/her as two people reached. If you do so, then you would be grossly overestimating reach. Normally from a campaign point of view, reach is expressed in percentage terms, but the absolute figure of the total number of different people reached is also relevant at times – more so when people make inter-media comparisons.

From a media vehicle point of view, reach is the total number of different people exposed to or reached by the vehicle concerned. So when a newspaper says that its reach is 1,00,000 – it means that 1,00,000 different people read the newspaper. Expressed as a percentage, it would take the population base of the town and arrive at a % reach figure. For instance, say in Delhi the population base is 25 million and the readership of Newspaper X is 5 million – the reach of Newspaper X will be 20%. Likewise for a TV channel which says that its reach is 20% – it means that 20% of the universe has viewed the channel during a specified period of time.

Interest in the concept of reach was initiated somewhere in the United States, where there was a popular magazine named *Life*. The publishers found that the issues of *Life* were selling so quickly that people had to borrow copies. The publishers rightly felt that the reach of the magazine was much beyond the physical number of copies sold by them. They then commissioned some research to find out the audience size of an issue of *Life*. This audience size was then termed as reach. From there the basic thinking about the concept of reach was started.

However, at that point in time when the media discipline was still evolving, the debate was centred on how many times a person should be in the audience of a vehicle to be considered as reached by the vehicle. After a lot of debate and discussion, it came to pass that one exposure to a vehicle was counted as reach. The rationale was that whether an ad in a media vehicle was seen or not, there was a great difference between those who were exposed even one time and those who were not exposed at all (Sissors & Baron, 2012, p. 111).

As stated earlier, reach stresses on 'different' people. Therefore, whenever the term *reach* is used, it always implies 'unduplicated reach'.

However, reach is *vehicle exposure* and not advertising exposure. When a media plan says that it reaches 70% of its intended audience, it means that 70% of the audience was exposed at least once to the combination of media vehicles used in the media plan. It does not mean that 70% of the audience was exposed to the advertising you placed in the vehicle. Some people may have not read the page where your ad was published, or some people may have been out of the hearing range when your radio spot was being aired, or some people may have left the room, or may have been on the phone, or reading something when your ad was played out on TV.

With the rise of digital platforms, there's talk of sharp targeting, impressions, personalization at scale, click through rates, and so on. However, despite several other data points being available, reach continues to be amongst the most important criteria in taking decisions regarding a media plan, and reach maximization continues to be an important planning goal.

Cumulative Reach

Closely related to the concept of reach is cumulative reach. Cumulative reach is the reach of a medium over a defined period of time. For instance, when a TV channel says that it has a cumulative reach of 30% amongst males NCCS AB, 25+ yrs, it means that at least 30% of the defined target audience tuned into the TV channel for at least a minute or more in the last one month. Likewise, cumulative reach of a newspaper will be the total number of different people who have read the newspaper in the last one month. For a website, it would mean the total number of different people who visited the site at least once in the last one month. Likewise for other media like radio, outdoor, etc. Usually, the terms *reach* and *cumulative reach* are used interchangeably, but this is incorrect. Cumulative reach is also referred to as 'Cumes' in media jargon.

Frequency

Stated simply from the perspective of a media plan, frequency is the average number of times people have been exposed to your campaign. Most often the term *frequency* is also used interchangeably with 'Average Frequency' or 'Opportunity to See' (OTS). So when a media plan is evaluated, people look at two basic metrics (apart from other numbers): reach delivered by the media plan, and the frequency or Avg Frequency or Average OTS delivered by the plan. In planning terminology, people say, 'This plan has a reach of 70% and an Avg OTS of 5' – it really means that in the defined target group in the defined markets, this plan will reach out to 70% of the target group, and on an average each person would have been exposed to the campaign around five times. Now, it is very much possible that some members of the target group would have received more than five exposures, some would have received fewer than five exposures, and some would not have been exposed to the campaign even once. But this is an average figure – the average number of times people are exposed to the campaign is five times.

Let me illustrate this through a simple example:

Suppose there is a print plan of 10 insertions. The defined target group is, say, SEC AB, Males, 25+ yrs in a market like Delhi. The total number of SEC AB, Males, 25+ yrs in Delhi is hypothetically 1500 people.

Given that there are 10 insertions released in a combination of newspapers in Delhi, the maximum number of times one can be exposed to the campaign will be 10. It is also possible that some people within the defined target group might not be reading any of the newspaper taken in the plan, and will hence not be reached by the campaign at all – in other words, they get zero exposures. Likewise, there will be some people who have received 2 exposures, some who have received 6 exposures, and so on. Let's put this into a frequency distribution table. This is nothing but a simple table which says how many people have been exposed at various levels of frequency.

The resulting frequency distribution table (Table 1.1) shows us the number of people exposed at various levels of frequency. There are 150 people who get 0 exposures, 180 people who get 3 exposures, 100 people who get 7 exposures, and so on. Overall, 1350 people have been exposed to the campaign. Therefore the reach of this plan will be

$$\frac{\text{Total Number of People exposed to the campaign at least once or more}}{\text{Universe of Defined TG}} \times 100$$

$$\frac{1350}{1500} \times 100 = 90\%$$

Therefore, this campaign reaches 1350 people out of the total universe of TG of 1500 people in Delhi. Expressed in percentage terms, it means that the

TABLE 1.1 Frequency distribution

Frequency of Exposure	Number Exposed
0	150
1	300
2	200
3	180
4	160
5	140
6	120
7	100
8	80
9	60
10	10
Total	1500

Source: Created by the author.

plan reaches 90% of the audience at least once or more. Always remember, reach is always an unduplicated figure. In the aforementioned frequency distribution, the 80 people who have been exposed to the campaign 8 times are different from the 200 people exposed to the campaign only 2 times.

Now, let's move to the next step of calculating the Average Frequency/ Average OTS of the same plan. Before we do this, I will introduce you to an intermediate concept termed as Gross Impressions, or Gross OTS. To put it in simple terms – one person being exposed to the campaign once is counted as one impression. The total number of impressions delivered by the plan are added up to represent Gross Impressions. Just to simplify in the aforementioned frequency distribution table (Table 1.1): if 200 people have got 2 exposures, then that results in 400 impressions (200 x 2); likewise, if 80 people have got 8 exposures, they have been delivered 640 impressions (80 x 8); and so on. Table 1.2 illustrates these calculations.

The above plan delivers 5280 Gross Impressions or Gross OTS. One person getting one exposure is 1 impression. Therefore 300 people getting one exposure is 300 impressions, 200 people getting 2 exposures is 400 impressions, and so on. The campaign has generated 5280 Gross Opportunities to See.

The Plan Reach we've already seen above was 1350 people. What this means is that the campaign has been seen 5280 times by 1350 people. And on an average, each person reached has been exposed to the campaign 3.9 times (5280/1350).

Expressed as a formula:

$$\frac{\text{Gross Impressions or Gross OTS Delivered by a Plan}}{\text{Total Number of different people reached by the plan}}$$

$$= \text{Average Frequency or Avg OTS of the Plan}$$

TABLE 1.2 Frequency distribution and Gross OTS

Frequency of Exposure	Number Exposed	Gross Impressions/ Gross OTS
0	150	0
1	300	300
2	200	400
3	180	540
4	160	640
5	140	700
6	120	720
7	100	700
8	80	640
9	60	540
10	10	100
Total	1500	5280

Source: Created by the author.

It is akin to distributing 500 toffees randomly amongst 100 kids. Some may get more and some may get less, but on average each kid has an average opportunity to eat 5 toffees.

So this is how the two most critical metrics of a media plan are calculated. Yes, in real terms there are more complexities involved in terms of duplications amongst publications, TV programmes, and so on, but the core of the concept remains the same. We will explore each of these complexities as we progress deeper into the subject in subsequent chapters. But reach will always be unduplicated and will always mean the total number of different people reached by a campaign, and Average Frequency will always mean the average number of times each person reached has been exposed to the campaign.

Gross Rating Points (GRPs)

Gross Rating Points (GRPs) form a very important part of the lexicon in media planning. Simply stated, GRPs are an indicator of media weight delivered by a media plan. Whenever a plan is made, it is evaluated to see whether it is reaching the required number of people at the desired frequency levels. There are separate software tools (which we will discuss later) which help a planner evaluate a media plan. Apart from some other things like a frequency distribution, the plan throws up two major indicators – Plan Reach and Average Frequency. Plan Reach is the percentage of target group the media plan reaches at least once. Average Frequency is the average number of times the audience gets to see the campaign. As explained in the previous frequency example, different people get exposed at different levels of frequency depending upon their media consumption habits. To evaluate a media plan, we use a broad metric called Average OTS or Average Frequency to establish the average number of times the target audience has been exposed to the campaign. Together the product of reach and frequency is called GRPs. Stated as a formula:

$$\text{Reach} \times \text{Frequency} = \text{GRP}$$

The Significance of GRPs

GRPs are significant to the extent that they tell us about the media weight delivered by a plan. The number of people the plan has reached and the number of times they have been reached are important metrics that are used to assess the intensity of the plan. GRPs are necessarily a duplicated figure as it is a product of Plan Reach percentage and Average Frequency. It is used to compare various plans. Different plans result in different Plan Reach and Average Frequency numbers and GRPs help a planner compare between the different plan options created. On their own, GRPs don't mean anything. Two plans with 400 GRPs each could be remarkably different in terms of their impact in the marketplace. One plan could be delivering a reach of 80% and an Average Frequency of 5, while the other plan could be delivering a reach of 40% and an Average Frequency of 10. The media vehicles used to make these two plans could be very different, the costs of buying these two plans could be very different, their frequency distributions could be very different, and they might achieve different objectives for the brand in question. Therefore, when making comparisons between plans, one should not go purely by the GRP numbers; instead, one must look at the reach and frequency delivered by the plan and also the frequency distribution.

GRPs are used as a common unit for planning future advertising. It is common in planning terminology to use GRPs as a reference point for evaluation of competition and plan construction. One can evaluate competition and say that the competing brand is doing an average of 1000 GRPs per month; and therefore given the brand objectives, a plan is made in which the brand does either more or less than competitive benchmarks.

Also, a lot of times, GRPs are used as a unit to ascertain results. Some large brands have their own brand tracking studies which deliver amongst other things, brand awareness indicators like Brand Top of Mind Recall and Spontaneous Recall. Sometimes, in sophisticated media planning, comparisons are made between GRP input and the resultant brand awareness. Trends are analysed, and some important decisions regarding the intensity of advertising and scheduling pattern are taken on the basis of the trends between GRPs delivered in a market and the resultant brand awareness levels.

An important thing while looking at GRPs is that because they are dependent on the Plan Reach % and Average Frequency delivered by a plan, it is always relevant to the market for which the plan has been evaluated. It might be unfair to compare an 800 GRP plan for Delhi vs a 1000 GRP plan for Chennai. Since the reach % is based on the population of the market, we cannot have a simple average of GRPs. In this case, the average GRPs delivered by the brand will have to take into account the differences in population of the two markets, and the Average GRP will be a weighted average GRP rather than a simple average. In the same example, assume, the target group is defined as SEC AB, Males, 25+ years. Say the size of this population in Chennai is 25 L and in Delhi it is 30 L. In this case, the average GRPs for Delhi + Chennai will be:

$$\frac{(800 \times 30) + (1000 \times 25)}{30 + 25} = 891$$

A simple average would have given us 900 GRPs for Delhi + Chennai. But because the population bases are different, we must take that into account.

While its popular use is largely with reference to TV planning, GRP is a concept that can be uniformly applied to other media as well. For any plan that we can evaluate and get a Plan Reach and Average Frequency, GRPs can be calculated and used. The concept holds just as well for print planning and other forms of media wherever metrics for plan evaluation are available. Therefore, GRPs, though largely used in the context of TV planning, are equally relevant across other types of media as well.

While GRPs are a resultant of Plan Reach percentage and Average Frequency, in TV planning typically, another way to calculate GRPs is the summation of TVRs of the programmes used in the plan. The TVR (Television Rating Point) of each programme (which we shall discuss later) is an indicator of the reach percentage of a programme.

GRP as a Summation of TVRs

Let's take a simple example to illustrate this. Assume the population of a town is 13.69 lakh people. There are two TV programmes that I use in a Media Plan – Programme A and Programme B. Programme A has a TVR of 32.4 while Programme B has a TVR of 8.3. In absolute size, this audience translates to 4.44 lakhs for Programme A and 1.13 lakhs for Programme B. We also have additional information that there are 47,000 people who view both the programmes. Table 1.3 illustrates the calculation of GRPs.

GRP as the Product of Plan Reach and Frequency

Table 1.4 illustrates an example of calculating GRPs as a product of reach and frequency.

TABLE 1.3 GRPs example

Base Population	1369000	Reach/TVR
Programme A	444000	32.4
Programme B	113000	8.3
GRPs (sum of TVRs)		**40.7**

Source: Created by the author.

TABLE 1.4 GRPs as product of reach and frequency

Reach of TV Plan	=	Reach of Programme A + Reach of Programme B – Duplication 444000 + 113000 – 47000 510000
% Reach of the Plan	=	(510000/1369000) × 100 37.25
Avg Frequency of the Plan	=	Gross Impressions delivered by Plan / Plan Reach in absolutes (444000 + 113000)/510000 1.09
GRPs	=	Plan Reach % × Avg Frequency 37.25 × 1.09 **40.7**

Source: Created by the author.

Critiques of GRPs argue that it's a simplistic measure and not very relevant in the fragmented media world of today. However, proponents of GRPs argue that the critics are misreading GRPs as an indication of 'effectiveness' as opposed to being an indication of 'media pressure or intensity'. In fact, in a cross platform, fragmented media world, the relevance of metrics like reach, frequency, and GRPs cannot be undermined, and in fact assume greater significance (Fulgoni, 2015).

Duplication

Duplication is a relatively simple concept. As consumers of media we read multiple publications, view multiple programmes on TV, listen to multiple channels on radio, surf across numerous websites, and so on. Therefore, there is this reality that the readers of one publication could also be the readers of another publication. This is called duplication between publications. Normally it is expressed in percentage terms. For example, say the readership of Publication A in Delhi is 4,44,000 people, and the readership of Publication B in Delhi is 1,13,000 people. However, there are 47,000 people who read both Publication A and Publication B in Delhi – and this is the duplication between the two publications. In percentage terms, one might say that 10.6% of Publication A's readers also read Publication B, and 43.7% of Publication B readers also read Publication A. Likewise on TV, there could be 2 programmes which could have some common viewers, two radio stations which could have common listeners, or two websites which could have common visitors.

The implication on planning is fairly simple. When one makes a media plan which has a high duplication within the vehicles chosen, then necessarily we are reaching out to the same audience over and over again. Such plans are likely to build higher frequency and lower reach. When a media plan has vehicles which have either no duplication or very low levels of duplication amongst them, such plans build more reach and less frequency. To revisit the definition of reach, it is the total number of 'different' people reached by the plan. But if in the plan there are vehicles which have very high levels of duplication amongst themselves, each vehicle would add more of the 'same' audience, and the plan would result in higher frequency.

To give an actual example (as illustrated in Tables 1.5a and 1.5b), the duplication between a TV programme T and another programme H is far

TABLE 1.5A Calculation of reach and frequency after accounting for duplication

Universe of Defined TG	1369	Plan	Cumulative Reach
Programme	Viewers		
Programme T	444		
Programme P	100		
People who watch both	20		
Plan Reach when we take one spot in Programme T:			
Universe of Defined TG	1369	**Plan**	**Cumulative Reach**
Programme	**Viewers**		
Programme T	444	1 Spot in Programme T	444
Programme P	100		
People who watch both	20		
Plan Reach when we take another spot in Programme P:			
Universe of Defined TG	1369	**Plan**	**Cumulative Reach**
Programme	**Viewers**		
Programme T	444	1 Spot in Programme T	444
Programme P	100	1 Spot in Prog T + 1 Spot in Prog P*	524
People who watch both	20	Plan Reach %	38.3%

Source: Created by the author.

* Reach = Reach of Spot in Prog T + Unduplicated Reach of Spot in Prog P
Reach = 444 + (100 − 20) = 524

TABLE 1.5B Calculation of reach and frequency after accounting for duplication

Universe of Defined TG	1369	Plan	Cumulative Reach
Publication	Viewers		
Programme T	444		
Programme H	113		
People who watch both	47		
Plan Reach when we take one spot in Programme T:			
Universe of Defined TG	1369	**Plan**	**Cumulative Reach**
Publication	Viewers		
Programme T	444	1 Spot in Programme T	444
Programme H	113		
People who watch both	47		
Plan Reach when we take another spot in Programme H:			
Universe of Defined TG	1369	**Plan**	**Cumulative Reach**
Publication	Viewers		
Programme T	444	1 Spot in Programme T	444
Programme H	113	1 Spot in Prog T + 1 Spot in Prog H*	510
People who watch both	47	Plan Reach %	37.3%

Source: Created by the author.

* Reach = Reach of Spot in Prog T + Unduplicated Reach of Spot in Prog H
Reach = 444 + (113 – 47) = 524

higher than the duplication between programme T and another programme P. Therefore, if to the base plan of Programme T, we add Programme H, then the incremental reach that we get is lower than what we get if we add Programme P to the base plan of Programme T.

Figures 1.2 and 1.3 illustrate this visually through Venn diagrams.

The operating rule, is: the higher the duplication between vehicles in a plan, the higher the skew towards frequency; and the lower the duplication between vehicles in a plan, the higher the skew towards reach. Reach build-up would be slow for plans with highly duplicated vehicles, while it would be high for plans with less duplicated vehicles. This also leads us to another concept called Audience Accumulation.

Audience Accumulation

In an ideal situation, an advertiser would like to reach out to everyone in his relevant target group and then repeat with as many exposures as possible. However, in the real world, people consume media in different degrees and consume media combinations of different types. At the same time, with so many options available, the number of the audience reached by a particular

Plan reach (%)

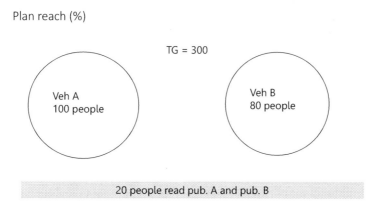

FIGURE 1.2 Reach calculation.

Source: Created by the author.

Plan Reach (%)

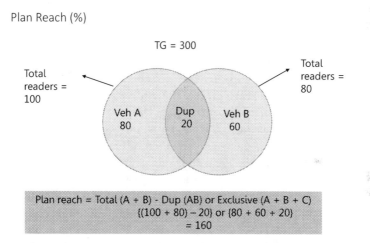

FIGURE 1.3 Reach calculation.

Source: Created by the author.

vehicle is very small. This is a result of what we call media fragmentation. Today, the single largest media vehicle will not cover more than 6–8% of the total audience available. At the same time, the advertiser would like to reach out to as many people as possible. Given this, audience accumulation becomes significant. It means that we choose combinations of media vehicles that help us build reach and cover a larger part of the audience. Therefore, if one spot in an IPL match gives me a reach of 4%, we choose more spots in other IPL matches and build reach to cover, say, around 20% of my audience. However, even that is not enough. To this we add a couple of mass reach channels, say a Star Plus, Colors, and Zee, and get the reach to 70%. Further, we add a couple of news channels and movie channels, and we perk up the Plan Reach to 80%. At this point in time, one might decide that putting more money in TV might not really be giving me incremental reach. Therefore, let's add another medium to this and push the Plan Reach curve up further. Although there is no single source of research that can give you the reach of a TV plan and a print plan put together, but simple judgement helps in taking such calls. Plan Reach can be pushed higher by using a combination of media. There are a couple of crude models available to estimate this combined reach, but then they do provide a broad sense of the numbers. This process of building reach is called audience accumulation. We can build reach in a media plan:

a. By placing more insertions in the same media vehicle. The audience for a media vehicle is not static. With each passing episode of a Programme X, there are different people who tune in to the channel and help accumulate audiences. For instance, say the reach of an average episode of Programme X is 4%. But the cumulative reach of five episodes could be 15%. It is very much possible that some people have watched only episodes 2–5, while some may have watched only episode 5, while other people may have watched all five episodes. Likewise, with each passing day, a newspaper brings in new readers, and that builds audiences. The average issue readership for a newspaper, maybe say a 1,00,000 people, over a period of a week might accumulate audiences to the tune of 2,00,000 people. Some people read the paper once a week, some may have read four issues in a week while some may have read all seven of that week's issues. Likewise, it works for other media like radio, cinema, outdoor, and Internet. Every medium has the ability to build audiences over a period of time.

b. By placing insertions in different vehicles. As previously explained, placing ads in different vehicles will also help accumulate audiences and build reach. An ad in a *Times of India* issue combined with an ad in *Dainik Jagran*, and *Dainik Bhaskar* will produce more reach. The governing factor here, as explained earlier, is something called duplication. When the duplication between two vehicles is high, audience accumulation happens at a slow pace. This is because higher duplication means that the same set of people are being reached again, and fewer new people are being reached by the campaign. When fewer new people are being reached by the campaign, reach build happens at a slow rate. Contrast this with a plan comprising media vehicles with minimal duplication. Here, because of low duplication, it means that each media vehicle reaches a newer set of people who have not been reached before and therefore help in building higher reach.

c. By placing ads in different types of media. A TV plan combined with a press plan will help extend the reach curve and build audiences as compared to only a TV plan. Not just on the numbers front, but even from a campaign effectiveness and impact point of view, multimedia works better.

A huge number of studies across the world have indicated that multimedia works better in more than just one medium. More on this when we discuss the concept of Media Mix.

Chapter Summary

The way humans form memories is essential to the understanding of how advertising and media work. Memories are formed by repeated exposures. The longer and better the exposure, the deeper the memory track it leaves on our minds.

Media planning

What are the best means of delivering advertisements to prospective purchasers of my brand or service?

Source: Advertising Media Planning by Jack Z Sissors
and Roger B Baron

Media is the last link in the marketing chain that takes the message to the consumer in the anticipation of driving a desired action.

The discipline of media evolved with marketing. Marketing's adoption of segmenting-targeting-positioning had an impact on media planning. With demands for accountability gaining currency, media aligned ever so closely with marketing to deliver brand goals. And now with media occupying a central place in our daily lives, it has become a full-blown discipline having to navigate amongst thousands of options before finalizing the plan.

The journey of the discipline in India from the heady days of Doordarshan and AIR to now has been a fascinating one. The advent of the satellite channels in the early 90s served the perfect launch pad for media evolution in India. The recession of the mid-90s brought about the birth of Media AORs as a response to leverage scale and optimize budgets. This eventually led to the birth of media agency as an independent business.

There are a few basic concepts which are important for media practitioners as well as for marketers who deal with media agencies. Here's a quick recap:

Reach: The total number of different people who have been exposed to a campaign at least once.

Cumulative reach: The reach of a medium over a defined period of time.

Frequency: The average number of people who have been exposed to your campaign. It's also known as Average Frequency or Average Opportunity to See (OTS).

Gross Rating Points (GRPs): The product of reach and frequency is called GRPs. It indicates the media weight delivered by a plan.

Impressions: One person being exposed to an advertisement once is one impression.

Duplication: The number or percentage of people who are exposed to two media vehicles in the same media plan. If the inter-duplication between vehicles in a media plan is high, the plan would tend to generate higher Average Frequency. Conversely, if the inter-duplication between vehicles in a media plan is low, the plan would tend to generate higher reach.

Further Reading

"C-Suite Marketing: Carmen Simon on Brain Science, B2B Marketing, and Memorable Communication", https://www.itsma.com/carmen-simon-on-b2b-marketing-and-memorable-communication/

Fulgoni, Gian, "Is the GRP Really Dead in a Cross-Platform Ecosystem? Why the Gross Rating Point Metric Should Thrive in Today's Fragmented Media World," *Journal of Advertising Research*, Vol. 55, No. 4, 2015.

Sissors, Jack Z., and Roger B. Baron (2012), *Advertising Media Planning*. McGraw-Hill, chapters on "Introduction to Media Planning", "The Relationship between Media, Advertising and Consumers", and "Advanced Measurements and Calculations".

Simon, Carmen, "#inbound15 live blog: Dr. Carmen Simon's 'The Neuroscience of Memorable Content'", October 2015, (https://www.inturact.com/blog/inbound15-live-blog-carmen-simons-the-neuroscience-of-memorable-content) and https://www.marketo.com/webinars/deliver-memorable-virtual-presentations/

WARC, "Understand the Brain to Deliver Marketing Effectiveness", https://www.warc.com/NewsAndOpinion/news/Understand%20the%20brain%20to%20deliver%20marketing%20effectiveness/40695

Wijaya, Bambang Sukma, "The Developments of Hierarchy of Effects Model in Advertising", *International Research Journal of Business Studies*, Vol. 5, No. 1, February 2012.

2

MEDIA RESEARCH

Need for Research

As planners, we have to rely on a lot of databases for taking a call in terms of which vehicles to include in your media plan. The obvious choice would be to place your advertisements in vehicles or in media channels that are seen or read by a large number of people. So reach is a basic requirement. Besides this, one would also want to be sure whether we're reaching the right kind of audience. Therefore, one also needs to know the profile of these audiences. For instance, what kind of people are watching cricket? What kind of people are watching daily soaps? What kind of people read the *Times of India*? What kind of people read the *Grehlakshmi*? Therefore, the primary requirement is that you need to know the absolute audience size and their profile. Besides this, one would like to understand the intensity with which your audience engages with different kinds of media – how frequently they refer to the medium, how much time they spend on it, and so on. To create a media plan, one needs to understand the media consumption pattern of the audience, the profile of the audience, and the size of the audience.

Across any type of media, there are numerous options for an advertiser to choose from. Some of the basic questions in the advertiser's mind are:

Which medium will deliver more audiences?
Which medium is appropriate given the media consumption habits of my target group?
Which vehicle within this medium will deliver relatively more than others?

DOI: 10.4324/9781032724539-2

What gives me a better value for money in terms of a media buy?
What are the media consumption habits of my target group?

These and a lot more questions come to the mind while trying to create a media plan. There are a host of questions related to media and vehicle selection, market selection, and the target group size, location, and media habits. Answers to some of these questions help in creating a good media plan. And most of these questions need to be answered through research.

In fact, apart from applying a lot of qualitative judgement in various phases of the planning process, media planners also take a look at some hard numbers, and a few decisions are taken on the basis of pure research numbers. However, it is important to understand the nuances of research so that one is very clear in terms of what is a reader, a viewer, a unique visitor, a listener, and so on.

Some of the Key Uses of Research in the Media Planning Process:

a) Sharper identification and definition of the target audience
b) Understanding the psychographics of the target audience
c) Understanding media consumption habits of the audience
d) Market identification and prioritization
e) Media scheduling decisions
f) Media weight setting decisions
g) Media mix selections
h) Vehicle selection
i) Profiling of vehicles
j) Understanding competitive media expenditure patterns
k) Creation of a common currency on which typically buying is done

What Kind of Research Is Available and Used in India?

In India, syndicated research is done largely for TV, print, Internet, radio, and cinema. Within this, the most in-depth research is conducted for TV, print, and digital. For the other media, measurement is done at a macro level due to the inherent difficulties involved in measuring media like cinema, radio, and outdoor. Also, between print, TV, and digital, they collectively account for about 90% of the advertising spends.

Most of the industry research in India is syndicated research, which is governed by a body comprising users. The major continuous syndicated studies available in India are:

a) Indian Readership Survey (IRS)
b) Television Audience Measurement by BARC

c) Radio Audience Measurement (RAM)
d) Advertising Expenditure Data on TV, Print, Digital and Radio
e) Target Group Index (TGI)
f) Audit Bureau of Circulations (ABC)
g) Census of India

Apart from these, there are a host of ad hoc studies which take place from time to time. For the purpose of research and for use in media planning/marketing, most of these studies have created some definitions/terms that are used in common parlance. I will introduce you to some of these key terms and their definitions and usage, and later we will move to covering in detail each of the aforementioned research studies.

Key Research Terms

Socio-Economic Classification (SEC)

The Market Research Society of India (MRSI) created an SEC classification in 1988 to classify all households on the basis of their socio-economic status, and it has created eight Urban SEC classifications:

- A1
- A2
- B1
- B2
- C
- D
- E1
- E2

These classifications are based on the occupation and education of the Chief Wage Earner of the household. This SEC system was defined to reflect the purchase behaviour patterns of households. Earlier, the only way one could do this was on the basis of monthly household income. However, income levels were not seen as good enough to create homogenous sets of people from an attitude/purchase behaviour pattern. Look at it this way – a small 'Paanwala' and a Junior Executive in a company could both be at a similar income level, but the purchase behaviour patterns would differ sharply. After much deliberation, the two critical parameters for defining SECs – occupation and education – were used to classify all households. A household is classified into one group based on the occupation and education of the Chief Wage Earner of the household. If a household is classified as SEC A1, then all individual members of the household belong to SEC A1. It is a household-level classification system.

SEC Classification Grid

Table 2.1 displays the urban socio-economic classification.

SEC is an important system and is used widely across India while identifying and defining target audiences. You would typically come across media people defining audiences as 'Males, SEC ABC, 25+ yrs' or 'Females, SEC AB, 20+ yrs', and so on. Most research tools and software use this as a standard definition, and plan evaluations are based on such definitions.

A large part of the urban Indian households were in SEC C, D, and E. However, all of the above were for the urban population.

A large part of India's population lives in rural areas. For this, the Market Research Society of India developed a classification system, and based it on two parameters – education of the Chief Wage Earner, and the type of house. Based on these two parameters, the rural households were classified into four groups:

- R1
- R2
- R3
- R4

Table 2.2 shows the rural socio-economic classification.

The SEC classification system had been in place for over 2 decades in India. While it was an important method of segregating audiences into various homogenous groups, over a period of time, a lot of industry watchers have believed that it is time to review this system and that some changes are required to make it more relevant. At the same time, rapidly changing occupation profiles, and new jobs and designations, rendered the existing occupation profiling criteria redundant. It was becoming difficult to collect data on an ambiguous occupation profile criteria. Therefore, there was an urgent need to draw up a new system of profiling households in India.

New Consumer Classification System (NCCS)

A new method of classifying households was created in 2011. It is based on two variables:

- Education of the Chief Wage Earner
- Number of 'consumer durables' (from a predefined list of 11 items) owned by the family

TABLE 2.1 Urban socio-economic classification grid

Occupation	Chief Wage Earner's Education						
	Illiterate	Literate but No Formal Schooling/School up to 4 Years	School 5–9 Years	SSC/HSC	Some College (Including a Diploma) but Not Grad	Graduate/Post-Graduate: General	Graduate/Post-Graduate: Professional
	1	2	3	4	5	6	7
Unskilled Workers	E2	E2	E1	D	D	D	D
Skilled Workers	E2	E1	D	C	C	B2	B2
Petty Traders	E2	D	D	C	C	B2	B2
Shop Owners	D	D	C	B2	B1	A2	A2
Bus/Ind with no. of Employees: 0	D	C	B2	B1	A2	A2	A1
44570	C	B2	B2	B1	A2	A1	A1
10+	B1	B1	A2	A2	A1	A1	A1
Self-Employed Prof.	D	D	D	B2	B1	A2	A1
Clerical/Salesmen	D	D	D	C	B2	B1	B1
Sup Level	D	D	C	C	B2	B1	A2
Off/Execs – Jr	C	C	C	B2	B1	A2	A2
Off/Execs – Mdl/Snr	B1	B1	B1	B1	A2	A2	A1

Source: MRUC.

TABLE 2.2 Rural socio-economic classification grid

Education	Type of House		
	Pucca	Semi Pucca	Kuchha
Illiterate	R4	R4	R4
Literate but no formal school	R3	R4	R4
Up to 4th Std	R3	R3	R4
5th–9th std.	R3	R3	R4
SSC/HSC	R2	R3	R3
Some college but not grad.	R1	R2	R3
Grad/PG (General)	R1	R2	R3
Grad/PG (Professional)	R1	R2	R3

Source: MRUC.

The list of 11 durables is as follows:

- Electricity connection
- Ceiling fan
- LPG stove
- Two-wheeler
- Colour TV
- Refrigerator
- Washing machine
- Personal computer/laptop
- Car/jeep/van
- Air conditioner

Therefore, during the survey, a household was asked which of these 11 items they own. Additionally, the education of the Chief Wage Earner is captured. Then a cross tab is created between the education of the Chief Wage Earner and the number of items owned by the household to determine in which socio-economic category the household would fall into. Table 2.3 depicts the NCCS grid.

Therefore, if some household has 6 of the 11 durables, and the Chief Wage Earner is a SSC/HSC level, then the household will be categorized as B1. Likewise, if a household has 9+ items and the Chief Wage Earner is a Graduate/Post-Graduate Professional, then the household will be categorized as A1. Unlike the earlier SEC system where we had different variable and grids for urban and rural homes, the NCCS is common for all homes irrespective of the fact whether it is urban or rural.

TABLE 2.3 New consumer classification system

No. of Durables	Chief Wage Earner's Education						
	Illiterate	Literate but No Formal Schooling/ School up to 4 Years	School 5–9 years	SSC/HSC	Some College (Including a Diploma) but Not Grad	Graduate/ Post-Graduate: General	Graduate/ Post-Graduate: Professional
	1	2	3	4	5	6	7
None	E3	E2	E2	E2	E2	E1	D2
1	E2	E1	E1	E1	D2	D2	D2
2	E1	E1	D2	D2	D1	D1	D1
3	D2	D2	D1	D1	C2	C2	C2
4	D1	C2	C2	C1	C1	B2	B2
5	C2	C1	C1	B2	B1	B1	B1
6	C1	B2	B2	B1	A3	A3	A3
7	C1	B1	B1	A3	A3	A2	A2
8	B1	A3	A3	A3	A2	A2	A2
9+	B1	A3	A3	A2	A2	A1	A1

Source: MRUC.

The NCCS had certain advantages over the previous SEC system:

- It was considered discriminatory enough to define target audiences.
- It was a single system for urban and rural India.
- It was less subjective as occupation was not used as a variable.
- Data collection was simple. Based on two inputs from the household (education of the Chief Wage Earner, and the number of consumer durables owned), one could classify a household.

However, within 5 years, industry experts felt that the NCCS system needed to be upgraded, or else it would become redundant. As years passed by, one saw that more and more households started getting classified in the upper A, B, and C categories, and the number of households in categories D and E started decreasing. This was happening because over the last 7–8 years, product penetrations increased, electrification across India improved, several government policies like the Ujjwala Scheme ensured that more households got access to cooking gas, and so on. As a result, the classification isn't discriminatory enough. As of this writing, the Market Research Society of India is working on devising a new method that has longevity, is a good discriminator, and is based on parameters that can be easily measured. Table 2.4 shows the current split of urban Indian households as per the NCCS.

Chief Wage Earner (CWE)

The Chief Wage Earner is the member of the family who makes the highest contribution to the household expenditure. The CWE's education is used

TABLE 2.4 Percentage distribution of urban households across NCCS

	Urban
Population 12+ years (mn)	377
NCCS A1	5.9%
NCCS A2	9.6%
NCCS A3	13.2%
NCCS B1	12.3%
NCCS B2	13.4%
NCCS C1	14.9%
NCCS C2	12.4%
NCCS D1	8.8%
NCCS D2	5.7%
NCCS E1	2.8%
NCCS E2	0.9%
NCCS E3	0.3%

Source: Indian Readership Survey, 2019 Q1, MRUC.

as one of the parameters to classify the household in a certain socio-economic category.

Urban and Rural

The media definition for urban and rural markets is the same that is used and defined by the Census of India. According to the Census of India 2011, the following criteria were adopted for treating a place as urban:

1. *Statutory towns*: All administrative units that have been defined by statute as urban, like Municipal Corporation, Municipality, Cantonment Board, Notified Town Area Committee, Town Panchayat, Nagar Palika, etc., are known as statutory towns.
2. *Census towns*: Administrative units satisfying the following three criteria simultaneously are treated as census towns:

   • A minimum population of 5000
   • At least 75% of the male working population engaged in non-agricultural pursuits
   • A density of population of at least 400 per sq km

3. Apart from these, the outgrowths of cities and towns have also been treated as urban.

All areas not identified as urban, are classified as rural. Sixty-nine per cent of India's population is in the rural areas. Table 2.5 gives the urban-rural split of population by state.

   Urban Agglomeration: As per the Census of India 2011, an urban agglomeration is a continuous urban spread constituting a town and its adjoining outgrowths (OGs), or two or more physically contiguous towns together with or without outgrowths of such towns. An urban agglomeration must consist of at least a statutory town, and its total population (i.e. all the constituents put together) should not be less than 20,000 as per the 2001 Census. In varying local conditions, there were similar other combinations which have been treated as urban agglomerations satisfying the basic condition of contiguity. Examples include Greater Mumbai UA and Delhi UA.

   Outgrowth: As per the Census of India 2011, an outgrowth (OG) is a viable unit such as a village or a hamlet or an enumeration block made up of such village or hamlet and clearly identifiable in terms of its boundaries and location. Some of the examples are a railway colony, a university campus, a port area, a military camp, etc., which have come up near a statutory town outside its statutory limits but within the

TABLE 2.5 Population and urban-rural split by state

Zone	State	Population (mn)			% Split	
		Total	Rural	Urban	Rural	Urban
	All India	**1210.19**	**833.09**	**377.11**	**69%**	**31%**
North	Haryana	25.35	16.53	8.82	65%	35%
	Himachal Pradesh	6.86	6.17	0.69	90%	10%
	Jammu & Kashmir	12.55	9.13	3.41	73%	27%
	NCT of Delhi	16.75	0.42	16.33	3%	97%
	Punjab	27.70	17.32	10.39	63%	37%
	Rajasthan	68.62	51.54	17.08	75%	25%
	Uttar Pradesh	199.58	155.11	44.47	78%	22%
	Uttarakhand	10.12	7.03	3.09	69%	31%
	Chandigarh	1.05	0.03	1.03	3%	97%
North Zone Total		**368.59**	**263.28**	**105.31**	**71%**	**29%**
East	Assam	31.17	26.78	4.39	86%	14%
	Arunachal Pradesh	1.38	1.07	0.31	77%	23%
	Bihar	103.80	92.08	11.73	89%	11%
	Jharkhand	32.97	25.04	7.93	76%	24%
	Manipur	2.72	1.90	0.82	70%	30%
	Meghalaya	2.96	2.37	0.60	80%	20%
	Mizoram	1.09	0.53	0.56	48%	52%
	Nagaland	1.98	1.41	0.57	71%	29%
	Odisha	41.95	34.95	7.00	83%	17%
	Sikkim	0.61	0.46	0.15	75%	25%
	Tripura	3.67	2.71	0.96	74%	26%
	West Bengal	91.35	62.21	29.13	68%	32%
East Zone Total		**315.65**	**251.50**	**64.16**	**80%**	**20%**
West	Chhattisgarh	25.54	19.60	5.94	77%	23%
	Goa	1.46	0.55	0.91	38%	62%
	Gujarat	60.38	34.67	25.71	57%	43%
	Madhya Pradesh	72.60	52.54	20.06	72%	28%
	Maharashtra	112.37	61.55	50.83	55%	45%
	Dadra & Nagar Haveli	0.34	0.18	0.16	53%	47%
	Daman & Diu	0.24	0.06	0.18	25%	75%
West Zone Total		**272.94**	**169.15**	**103.79**	**62%**	**38%**
South	Karnataka	61.13	37.55	23.58	61%	39%
	Kerala	33.39	17.46	15.93	52%	48%
	Tamil Nadu	72.14	37.19	34.95	52%	48%
	Telangana	35.00	21.40	13.61	61%	39%
	Andhra Pradesh	49.66	34.92	14.74	70%	30%
	Puducherry	1.24	0.39	0.85	32%	68%
	Andaman & Nicobar Islands	0.38	0.24	0.14	64%	36%
	Lakshadweep	0.06	0.01	0.05	22%	78%
South Zone Total		**253.01**	**149.16**	**103.85**	**59%**	**41%**

Source: Census of India 2011.

revenue limits of a village or villages contiguous to the town. While determining the outgrowth of a town, it has been ensured that it possesses the urban features in terms of infrastructure and amenities such as pucca roads, electricity, taps, a drainage system for disposal of waste water, educational institutions, post offices, medical facilities, banks, etc., and is physically contiguous with the core town of the UA. Each such town together with its outgrowth(s) is treated as an integrated urban area and is designated as an urban agglomeration.

The Census of India also classifies all towns and villages as per their population into various classes:

a) *Class I UAs/Towns*: The UAs/Towns which have at least 1,00,000 persons as population are categorized as a Class I UA/Town.

- *Million Plus UAs/Cities*: Out of 468 UAs/Towns belonging to the Class I category, 53 UAs/Towns have a population of one million or higher each. Known as Million Plus UAs/Cities, these are the major urban centres in the country.
- *Mega Cities*: Among the Million Plus UAs/Cities, there are three very large UAs with more than 10 million persons in the country, known as Mega Cities. These are Greater Mumbai UA (18.4 million), Delhi UA (16.3 million), and Kolkata UA (14.1 million).

b) *Class II UAs/Towns*: The UAs/Towns which have a population between 50,000 and 99,999 are categorized as Class II UA/Towns.

c) *Class III UAs/Towns*: The UAs/Towns which have a population between 20,000 and 49,999 are categorized as Class III UA/Towns.

d) *Class IV UAs/Towns*: The UAs/Towns which have a population between 10,000 and 19,999 are categorized as Class IV UA/Towns.

e) *Class V UAs/Towns*: The UAs/Towns which have a population between 5,000 and 9,999 are categorized as Class V UA/Towns.

f) *Class IV UAs/Towns*: The UAs/Towns which have a population of less than 5000 are categorized as Class VI UA/Towns.

Table 2.6 gives the breakdown of towns by Town classes as per the Census of India.

Table 2.7 gives the breakup of villages by village classes as per the Census of India.

As per the Census, India is divided into 28 states and 8 union territories. Refer to Figure 2.1 for states and their respective capitals. Further, each state is further subdivided into districts. There are a total of 718 districts in India. Each district is further subdivided into Tehsils. There are a total of 5564 Tehsils in India. Different states use different names for Tehsils – some call it Taluka, Mandal, Circle, CD Block, Sub Division, etc.

TABLE 2.6 Townclass distribution in India

Class	Population	Total Number of			Population
		Urban Agglomerations	Towns	UA + Towns	(mn)
Class I	1,00,000 +	298	170	468	264.7
	Mega Cities	3	0	3	48.8
	Other Million +	44	6	50	111.9
Class II	50000–99999	100	374	474	32.2
Class III	20000–49999	75	1298	1373	41.8
Class IV	10000–19999	1	1682	1683	24.0
Class V	5000–9999	0	1749	1749	12.7
Class VI	<5000	0	424	424	1.7
Total Urban Population		474	5697	6171	377

Source: Census of India 2011.

TABLE 2.7 Village class distribution in India

Village Population Size	No. of Villages	Population (mn)
<200	82151	8.2
200–499	114732	39.7
500–999	141800	103.3
1000–1999	139164	197.5
2000–4999	96428	288.8
5000–9999	18652	123.9
10000+	4681	72.4
Total Rural	597608	833.7

Source: Census of India 2011.

Household

As defined for the purposes of media research, a normal household is a group of persons who normally live together and take their meals from a common kitchen unless the nature of their work prevents any of them from doing so. Persons in a household may be related or unrelated to each other. There may be one-member households, two-member households, or multi-member households. The link in understanding whether it is a household or not is a common kitchen. Table 2.8 shows that, as per the Census of India, there are a total of 248 million households in India.

Householder

The Householder is defined as a person who takes the decision on purchase of day-to-day household products such as groceries, toothpastes, soaps,

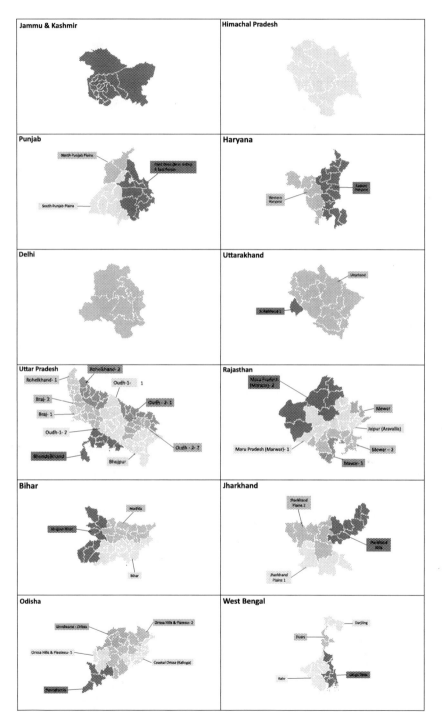

FIGURE 2.1 SCR maps by state.

Source: Created by the author.

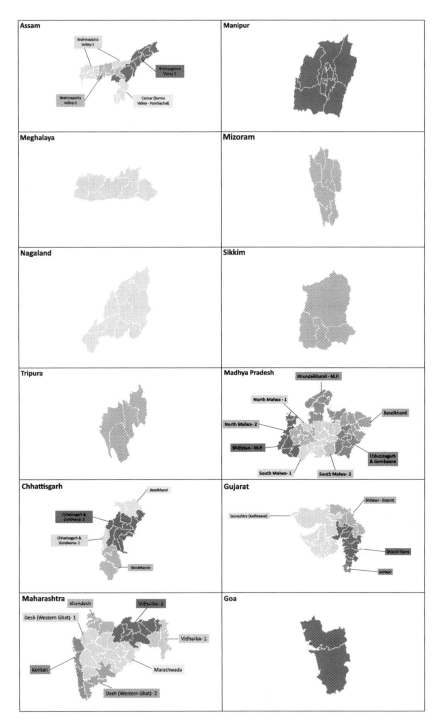

FIGURE 2.1 (Continued)

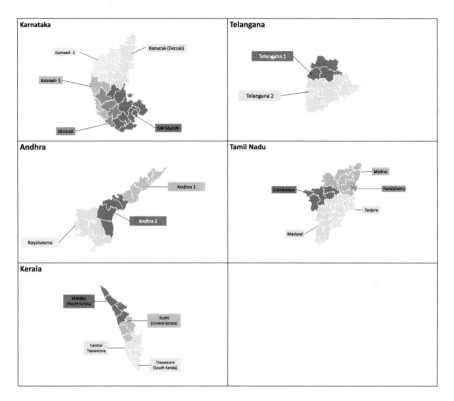

FIGURE 2.1 (Continued)

detergents, etc., with respect to what to purchase, when to purchase, and how much to purchase. This person has to be staying in the household and can be a male or a female.

- The Householder need not always decide on the brands
- The Householder need not always physically go to the shop to buy these products; the Householder may only be suggesting the requirements while someone else implements them

Literates

A person aged 7 years and older who can both read and write with understanding in any language was taken as literate. A person who can read but cannot write is not literate. It is not necessary that to be treated as literate, a person should have received any formal education or passed any minimum educational standard. Literacy could also have been achieved through adult literacy classes or through any non-formal educational system. People who are blind and can read in Braille were also treated as literates. All children of

TABLE 2.8 Zonewise-statewise distribution of households

	State	HHs (mn)			% Split	
		Total	Rural	Urban	Rural	Urban
	All India	**248.41**	**168.08**	**80.33**	**68%**	**32%**
North	Haryana	4.84	3.03	1.80	63%	37%
	Himachal Pradesh	1.48	1.31	0.17	89%	11%
	Jammu & Kashmir	2.10	1.55	0.56	74%	26%
	NCT of Delhi	3.41	0.08	3.33	2%	98%
	Punjab	5.49	3.34	2.14	61%	39%
	Rajasthan	12.65	9.46	3.19	75%	25%
	Uttar Pradesh	33.23	25.56	7.67	77%	23%
	Uttarakhand	2.05	1.42	0.63	69%	31%
	Chandigarh	0.24	0.01	0.23	3%	97%
North Zone Total		**65.48**	**45.77**	**19.71**	**70%**	**30%**
East	Assam	6.39	5.41	0.98	85%	15%
	Arunachal Pradesh	0.27	0.20	0.07	74%	26%
	Bihar	18.87	16.83	2.04	89%	11%
	Jharkhand	6.24	4.72	1.52	76%	24%
	Manipur	0.56	0.38	0.17	69%	31%
	Meghalaya	0.55	0.43	0.12	79%	21%
	Mizoram	0.22	0.11	0.12	48%	52%
	Nagaland	0.39	0.28	0.12	70%	30%
	Odisha	9.61	8.07	1.54	84%	16%
	Sikkim	0.13	0.09	0.04	72%	28%
	Tripura	0.85	0.61	0.24	72%	28%
	West Bengal	20.31	13.78	6.53	68%	32%
East Zone Total		**64.37**	**50.91**	**13.46**	**79%**	**21%**
West	Chhattisgarh	5.63	4.35	1.28	77%	23%
	Goa	0.34	0.13	0.21	37%	63%
	Gujarat	12.19	6.75	5.44	55%	45%
	Madhya Pradesh	15.02	11.04	3.98	74%	26%
	Maharashtra	24.30	13.16	11.13	54%	46%
	Dadra & Nagar Haveli	0.08	0.04	0.04	47%	53%
	Daman & Diu	0.06	0.01	0.05	21%	79%
West Zone Total		**57.62**	**35.49**	**22.14**	**62%**	**38%**
South	Karnataka	13.30	7.92	5.38	60%	40%
	Kerala	7.84	4.14	3.69	53%	47%
	Tamil Nadu	18.46	9.51	8.95	51%	49%
	Telangana	8.36	5.22	3.13	62%	38%
	Andhra Pradesh	12.57	8.97	3.60	71%	29%
	Puducherry	0.30	0.09	0.21	31%	69%
	Andaman & Nicobar Islands	0.09	0.06	0.04	62%	38%
	Lakshadweep	0.01	0.00	0.01	23%	77%
South Zone Total		**60.93**	**35.92**	**25.01**	**59%**	**41%**

Source: Census of India 2011.

age 6 years or less were treated as illiterate by definition, irrespective of their status of school attendance and the capability to read and write. Table 2.9 gives the distribution of literates by state.

Socio-Cultural Regions

At the time of independence, when the Indian sub-continent had to be divided politically and administratively into a number of units (states and districts), it was important that such a division should be made so that each such unit was homogeneous in composition.

Therefore, territories were then grouped not by geographical contiguity alone. Based on a number of socio-cultural parameters, the State Re-organisation Commission (1954) drew up the district and state boundaries. These form the basis of the socio-cultural regions (SCRs):

- Linguistic homogeneity
- Geographical contiguity
- Financial, economic, and administrative homogeneity
- Rationalization of culture and lifestyles, making each one unique from other districts
- Caste and class considerations

Based on these criteria, India was divided into 94 SCRs. Figure 2.1 gives the state-wise division of SCRs.

Overview of Media Research in India

Print Research in India

Print research in India is done at a fairly extensive level through the Indian Readership Survey (IRS), which is conducted by the Media Research Users Council (MRUC). Apart from providing information just for the print medium, the IRS provides a lot of information about other media and population demographics and, most importantly, also covers information about product penetration and usage patterns across most large categories. This is a fairly comprehensive study, and its usage is widespread across the media planning and marketing industries.

Indian Readership Survey

In 1995, the MRUC commissioned the Operations Research Group to conduct an All India Readership Survey – this resulted in the first Indian Readership Survey (IRS, 1995). Subsequently, in 1997, it was decided to

TABLE 2.9 Literate population by state

Zone	State	Population (mn) Total	Literates (mn)
	All India	1210.19	778.45
North	Haryana	25.35	16.90
	Himachal Pradesh	6.86	5.10
	Jammu & Kashmir	12.55	7.25
	NCT of Delhi	16.75	12.76
	Punjab	27.70	18.99
	Rajasthan	68.62	38.97
	Uttar Pradesh	199.58	118.42
	Uttarakhand	10.12	7.00
	Chandigarh	1.05	0.81
North Zone Total		**368.59**	**226.21**
East	Assam	31.17	19.51
	Arunachal Pradesh	1.38	0.79
	Bihar	103.80	54.39
	Jharkhand	32.97	18.75
	Manipur	2.72	1.89
	Meghalaya	2.96	1.82
	Mizoram	1.09	0.85
	Nagaland	1.98	1.36
	Odisha	41.95	27.11
	Sikkim	0.61	0.45
	Tripura	3.67	2.83
	West Bengal	91.35	62.61
East Zone Total		**315.65**	**192.36**
West	Chhattisgarh	25.54	15.60
	Goa	1.46	1.15
	Gujarat	60.38	41.95
	Madhya Pradesh	72.60	43.83
	Maharashtra	112.37	82.51
	Dadra & Nagar Haveli	0.34	0.23
	Daman & Diu	0.24	0.19
West Zone Total		**272.94**	**185.46**
South	Karnataka	61.13	41.03
	Kerala	33.39	28.23
	Tamil Nadu	72.14	52.41
	Telangana	35.00	20.70
	Andhra Pradesh	49.66	30.74
	Puducherry	1.24	0.97
	Andaman & Nicobar Islands	0.38	0.29
	Lakshadweep	0.06	0.05
South Zone Total		**253.01**	**174.43**

Source: Census of India 2011.

make IRS a continuous study, with reports being generated every 6 months. The first set of reports was based on the sample covered in the first round of 6 months (fieldwork, July–November 1997). The next report was based on the annual sample (combined for both the rounds, July 1997–June 1998). From then on, the Moving Annual Total method was used to generate the 6-month IRS report. From 2010 onwards, IRS started reporting data on a quarterly basis. This again used the rolling quarter method, where the oldest quarter was dropped and the newest quarter added (to complete the data for 4 quarters) and then presented. The following are the key information areas covered by the IRS:

- Readership of print publications for a wide range of local, regional, and national newspapers and magazines.
- Reach and consumption of other media – television, radio, digital, and cinema.
- Demographic profiling.
- Consumer durable ownership and FMCG usage.

Sampling

All research is conducted with a certain objective and a certain population/target audience in mind. Sometimes the population size is small or the study itself demands it – in which case it might make sense to cover everyone. This is called a Census or Complete Enumeration. But most often, the population sizes are large, and it becomes practically impossible and extremely expensive to cover everybody in the population. Here, a carefully chosen sample is picked up which reflects the characteristics of the population. This exercise is called sampling.

Sampling is the technique of selecting a suitable sample, or a representative part of a population for the purpose of determining parameters or characteristics of the whole population. Put simply, a small sample of people is pulled out of a universe, and that sample would adequately represent the universe. For instance, when we go to buy rice, we randomly grab a handful of rice and try to make a judgement on the quality of rice in the entire bag. Similarly, in research, we select a certain set of people from a population, observe their behaviour, and project it to the population. Remember, in either case, the sample has to be representative of the population. Therefore, the bag of rice has to be mixed well enough before we pull out a sample.

Sampling is done to draw conclusions about the population. It is of course cheaper to observe a sample rather than to observe the entire population or do a Census. In addition, sampling helps save time, for at times the population size may just be too large to cover, or it might be inaccessible.

IRS Sample Size and Methodology

The estimations made and provided in the IRS are based on random sampling methodology, and all such estimates operate within 20% (approximate) sampling/non-sampling error level for any reporting breaks with 90% confidence level for 10% incidence.

The level of sampling variation (margin of error) is what the survey designers have agreed to accept (indicated by the survey's reporting standard) for any survey estimate. The IRS reporting standards define that the estimates be reported within 20% margin of error at 90% confidence level for an incidence of 10%.

A 90% confidence level means that if a survey were to be conducted 100 times, on 90 occasions the variation would be within the range defined by the reporting standard. Please note that this means that in 10% of the cases, the estimate may well be beyond the defined range.

All estimates based on a sample survey are subject to 'sample variation'. The following are the major errors that could be in any sample survey:

- *Sampling errors*: Sampling errors take place because instead of measuring the entire population, we study only a smaller sample. The findings from the sample are projected to reflect the population. It's usually expressed as a standard error or as 'margin of error'. This is an error that is part of all research that use a sample to study a population.
- *Survey design errors*: These errors crop up as a result of the survey design. In the case of IRS, the household selection frame is the electoral roll. The accuracy and representativeness of the electoral roll will have an impact on sample selection and thereby lead to an element of error known as survey design error.
- *Non-sampling errors*: These are errors that happen when the respondent gives a wrong answer or an incomplete answer, or he/she misunderstands the question. Sometimes an error comes in if the interviewer has not followed the specified norms in selecting the respondent, or the responses are not captured properly, or they are entered incorrectly.

  IRS 2019 Q4 covered a sample of 327,661, across India. The urban sample was 2,14,357 households and the rural sample was 1,13,304 during 2019 Q4.

Geographical Areas Covered and Reported by IRS

In IRS 2019 Q4 reporting units are as follows:

- All India – Urban/Rural
- States

- Socio-cultural regions (SCRs)
- Ninety-four independent and 101 clustered districts are reported. Districts not reported individually are grouped into clusters based on population, literacy, and urbanization percentage.
- Population strata
- All 5 lakh+ population towns
- Two towns with a population of 2 to 5 lakh
- The four big metros – Delhi, Mumbai, Kolkata, and Chennai – which are reported at zone level

How Is the Data Collected?

All interviews for IRS have been conducted using the DS-CAPI (Dual Screen CAPI) methodology. This methodology brings significant reductions to non-sampling errors in the survey. Devices used are tablets for both main as well as dual screen.

IRS covers data at two levels:

- *Household data*: The household data is collected by interviewing the Householder or the Chief Wage Earner. Information in the household section is focused on all household details viz. household composition, durables owned, household items purchased, and other key demographic variables.
- *Individual data*: Individual data is collected from a systematically randomly selected person who is 12 years or older and stays in the household. The Individual Questionnaire is mainly focused on capturing readership of publications, TV viewing, radio listening, mobile usage, Internet usage, cinema viewing habits, and personal usage of selected products.

Information Areas Covered by the IRS

One of the major outputs of the IRS is to give out readership estimates for newspapers and magazines. The IRS defines readership as:

a) *Average Issue Readership (AIR)*: AIR of any publication is the number of people who claim to have read the publication within a time period equal to the periodicity of the publication preceding the day of interview. Therefore, if a respondent has read a newspaper 'yesterday', then he/she is said to be an average issue reader, and will be counted in the Average Issue Readership of the publication. Similarly, for a weekly magazine, if the respondent has read the magazine in the last one week, he/she would be counted in the Average Issue Readership of the magazine.

b) *Total Readership (TR)*: Total Readership is the number of people who claim to have read a publication during:

- The last month in the case of dailies
- The last month in the case of weeklies
- The last quarter in the case of fortnightlies
- The last 6 months in the case of monthlies
- The last 1 year in the case of bi-monthlies/quarterlies

Therefore, if someone has read Newspaper A in the last 30 days, then he/she would be counted in the Total Readership of Newspaper A. In the case of a monthly magazine, if someone has read it in the last 6 months, then he/she would be counted in the Total Readership of the magazine.

The other areas of information covered by the IRS are at two levels – household level, and individual level.

Information Areas – Household level

- Household demographics like NCCS, Householder details, Chief Wage Earner details, occupation and education of family members, family structure (nuclear, joint, etc), presence of children, number of working members
- Housing details – owned/rented, type of house, presence of exclusive toilet, access to water and electricity
- Detailed durable ownership of the household, from ceiling fan, to microwave oven, to a TV, to washing machines to a digital camera, to a four-wheeler
- Entertainment/media access: whether the household owns a television, radio, DVD, laptop or PC, telephones and broadband connection at home, mobile phone at home, and numbers of these.
- Ownership of means of transport
- Usage of household FMCG products purchased such as Biscuits, Edible Oil, Tea etc.

Information Areas – Individual level

- Education, occupation, marital status, presence of kid(s).
- Mode of transportation to work/school/college.
- Individual media consumption of print, TV, Internet, mobile, and radio. This covers usage of media, frequency of usage, time spent on the medium, etc.
- Individual lifestyle questions which are around things like travel, banking, insurance, mode of transport, etc.
- Information is also captured on usage and consumption of FMCG products like shampoos, conditioners, soft drinks, chocolates, etc.

IRS covers about 29 consumer durable categories and 38 consumer goods categories. In the case of durables, it captures information like owned in working condition, brands, type, and first acquired. In the case of consumer goods, it captures information like usage, frequency of purchase, pack size, brands purchased, pack type, quantity purchased, and frequency of consumption. Besides this, it captures the last 30 days of media access, which is an essential guide to understand how people consume media.

Uses of IRS

The following are the primary uses of IRS:

- For creating and evaluating print media plans
- To understand readership size and profile of publications
- To understand cross-media consumption patterns
- To understand consumption patterns of media like radio and cinema
- To understand product category penetrations (for over 50 product categories) across markets, demographic segments, and pop-strata
- To help in arriving at target audience decisions
- To understand media consumption habits to target audiences
- For demand estimation across a range of product categories
- To understand the demographic and socio-economic profile of India's population
- To link brand/category consumption/usage to media usage
- To help in market identification and market prioritization

TV Research in India

TV research in India is conducted by the Broadcast Audience Research Council (BARC). BARC India is a joint industry company founded by stakeholder bodies that represent broadcasters, advertisers, and advertising and media agencies. BARC has been mandated by the Indian Broadcasting Foundation (IBF), the Indian Society of Advertisers (ISA), and Advertising Agencies Association of India (AAAI) to conduct and manage the TV rating system in India.

Establishment Survey

Before beginning the sampling process, BARC conducts an establishment survey to understand the size of the TV viewing universe and to get an understanding of its audience from a demographic, socio-economic, and geographic perspective. This establishment survey is done on a large sample size of about 3,00,000 respondents (about 68% urban and 32% rural). It covers about

4300 towns and villages and captures information like TV ownership, connection type, language preferences, and other media consumption. A separate listing study is done to create a random pool of TV-owning households which could be used to recruit panel homes or the Currency Panel. All 5 L+ population towns (barring Srinagar) are part of the sample. The rest of the sample is distributed proportionally across town classes based on the Population Proportionate Sampling method.

Currency Panel Homes

BARC has a panel of 44,000 TV-owning homes to capture viewership data. BARC has a system of rotating panel homes to avoid panel fatigue and also to possibly remove bias (if any), as well as to ensure that the panel is adequate enough to capture the changes in TV viewing habits over a period of time. The panel includes all people in the family 2 years and older.

A remote is given to the panel member home. Each member of the home has a specific button assigned. When they view TV, they are supposed to press the button assigned to them. When they stop watching, they press the button assigned to them again.

The panel home members are also trained to use this remote. The training of the panel homes happens in two stages. The first visit to the panel home is usually made within the first week after installation. During this visit, the trainer explains to the panel household members how to use the remote, checks the equipment, etc. A second training is usually scheduled after 10–12 days of installation. During this second visit, the trainer checks on button-pressing behaviour, the On and Off status of the TV, and whether the remote buttons are correctly assigned to different family members of the panel home. The training largely focuses on teaching button pressing behaviour and to ensure that household members keep the meter on while watching TV.

In addition to panel homes (which is referred to as Currency Panel), BARC also recruits another panel known as the Out-of-Home Panel. A fair amount of TV is viewed outside the home. So BARC does a listing of all eateries in India which have a seating capacity of more than 24. From this, a OOH Panel of around 1050 is selected. BARC also conducts a footfall analysis to understand the number of people who visit the eatery, and this has an impact on the reach and impressions.

Data Capture

TV viewership data is captured in the following manner:

> *Watermarking ID for channels*: Every TV channel embeds a unique watermarked code in the audio component. This code consists of the Channel

ID and the time stamp. Each channel has its own unique code. The watermark is an inaudible audio code made available to TV broadcasters that subscribe to BARC. A master list of TV station watermarked IDs is stored on the BARC India server and downloaded to BAR-O-Meters for the identification and measurement of TV station viewing.

Bar-O-Meter at Panel Homes: It is a device like a set top box, installed on each TV set in the panel household.

Data capture: The Bar-O-Meter system continuously and passively captures TV viewing events in real time, recording the time and duration of channel tuning events and capturing the viewership events of individual members ages 2+ that have pressed their viewer ID button to confirm their presence in the audience. It sends the data to the BARC central server.

Individual identification: A remote is given to the Panel member home. Each member of the home has a specific button assigned. When they view TV, they are supposed to press the button assigned to them. When they stop watching, they press the button assigned to them again.

Data Processing

Data is collected for every second of viewing, but as per international standards, it has to be converted to minutes – only one channel is eligible to receive viewing credit for each clock minute. While individuals can view multiple channels within a single clock minute, only one channel will be assigned the viewing in each clock minute. To assign this viewing, the following rules are applied.

- *Rule 1: Only one channel watched.* In this case, it's very straightforward. The viewing for that particular clock minute is assigned to the channel viewed.
- *Rule 2: Multiple channels watched with different viewing durations.* In this case, the viewership is assigned to the channel with the higher viewing duration. For example, if in the clock minute one watched 45 seconds of Channel A and 15 seconds of Channel B, the viewership for the entire 1 minute will be attributed to Channel A because it has a higher viewing duration.
- *Rule 3: Multiple channels watched with two or more channels having the same maximum viewing duration.* There are two scenarios for this rule:
  - *Rule 3a*: If one of the channels continues to be viewed in the next clock minute, then the viewership is attributed to that channel. For example, during a clock minute, say a person watched 30 seconds of Channel A and 30 seconds of Channel B. If the person continues to watch Channel B into the next clock minute, then the viewership of the clock minute is attributed to Channel B.

- *Rule 3b*: However, continuing the above example if viewing doesn't continue for either Channel A or Channel B in the next clock minute, then viewership is attributed using a random allotment algorithm.

However, in an ad break, it is possible that two spots within the same minute could have different ratings. This usually happens when some part of the ad is aired in the previous clock minute and the balance part of the ad is aired in the next clock minute. For instance, if the ad duration is 45 seconds, and 15 seconds happen in minute 1 and 30 seconds in minute 2, the spot TVR would be a weighted average of TVR of the two minutes, i.e.:

$$\text{spot TVR} = \left(\left(15^* \text{ minute 1 TVR}\right) + \left(30^* \text{ minute 2 TVR}\right)\right) / 45.$$

Data Reporting

Data is reported for the following markets and demographics:

- 6 Mega Cities: Mumbai, Delhi, Kolkata, Chennai, Bangalore, Hyderabad
- Pop Strata: 10–75 L towns, < 10 L Urban, Rural
- State Groups:

  - PHCHPJK, Raj, UP/UT, Delhi (*PHCHPJK = Punjab, Haryana, Chandigarh, Himachal Pradesh, and Jammu & Kashmir)
  - West Bengal, Orissa, Bihar/Jharkhand, Assam/North East
  - Maharashtra/Goa, Gujarat/Daman & Diu/Dadra & Nagar Haveli, Madhya Pradesh & Chhattisgarh
  - Andhra Pradesh/Telangana, Karnataka, Kerala, Tamil Nadu/Pondicherry

- Gender: Males/Females
- Age Groups: 2–14 yrs, 15–21 yrs, 22–30 yrs, 31–40 yrs, 41–50 yrs, 51–60 yrs, 61 yrs+
- NCCS Groups: NCCS A, NCCS B, NCCS CDE

Key Terminologies Used by BARC

REACH'000 (Reach in Thousands): This is defined as the number of viewers who watched at least one minute of the content.

Impressions'000 (Impressions in Thousands): Number of individuals in 000s of a target audience who viewed an "Event", averaged across minutes.

Event: A programme or a 30-minute slot on a channel is called an 'Event'.

Rating% (Ratings Percentage): This is man-minutes spent viewing the content, expressed as a percentage of maximum possible man-minutes, and averaged per minute across total duration of the content. This is also called TRP.

ATS(Viewer): This is the average time spent (ATS) *by individuals who viewed the event.*

ATS(Universe): This shows ATS *across all target individuals*, irrespective of whether they viewed the content or not.

AMA '000 – INDIVIDUALS: Number of individuals in 000s of a target audience who viewed an 'Event', averaged across minutes. Also known as TVT.

Uses of TV Research Data

TV data from BARC is used primarily for the following purposes:

- To construct and evaluate TV plans
- To optimize TV plans
- To understand TV viewing patterns across markets
- To understand TV viewing preferences across different kinds of audiences

Digital Research in India

There are two research products that help measure digital audiences in India – Comscore, and Google Analytics. While Comscore is a third-party research agency that manages a panel of homes and gives out audience estimates across different websites and apps, Google Analytics is a service that lets an individual site owner get a deeper insight into how the audience interacts with that particular website.

Comscore

Comscore has a methodology which is termed Unified Digital Measurement (UDM). It has two components:

- Global Person Measurement – these are measurements based on a panel of respondents recruited online
- Global Machine Measurement – these are server-centric data collected by tagging websites

It's called a Unified Digital Measurement system because the methodology takes inputs from both a site census and a panel of users, to arrive at different audience metrics.

Data Capture

At the Panel Level

Recruited and registered panel members are required to download and install the 'meter' on their PC/mobile/tablet. This is basically an application that is downloaded and installed on the computer. This application then contacts Comscore servers to download other components of the 'meter' in the background without disturbing the panellist. This is a software known as Client Application or 'meter'. This meter is able to 'see' user-level activity on the computer. The meter monitors TCP/IP traffic and all traffic between the Internet and the user's computer. This includes applications on the computer that use Internet – such as browsers, email programs, instant messaging applications, as well as user interaction with the keyboard and mouse. Besides this, the meter measures system idle information, browser setting information (homepage and default search engine), Internet connection speeds, and active applications and browser tabs. Additionally, there are functions that help identify which household member is using the computer at a particular point in time.

The meter captures internet activity done by any application on the user's machine that uses the Internet. If the machine uses the Internet through the wi-fi connectivity of a handheld device, it would still measure the machine. If the PC's wi-fi is used for accessing the Internet on a handheld device, the meter can capture the data transfer activity. The user types the URL in his browser window, the browser contacts the relevant web server, it retrieves the result, and it displays the result on the screen. The meter will measure the URL visited. In some cases, the URL request is routed to the meter. The meter contacts the relevant web server – retrieves the result – gives it to the browser – that gets displayed on the screen. These are called routable requests.

Comscore also measures internet traffic on mobiles and tablets. The panel members download and install a 'meter' (an app) on their devices. They sign up a registration questionnaire, which has their demographic and device details. The meter captures all Internet activity through the device such as URL visited, auto refreshes, usage of apps, start and end time of app usage, and application installs.

Sometimes, the same desktop is used by different members of the family. Comscore is able to identify individual family members through the "Who are you?" self-identification popups while the machine is being used. At the time of panel recruitment, on multiple user desktops, the panel home lists out members of the family who access the same desktop. Based on this information and the self-identification popups, Comscore is able to attribute site visitation to the specific member identified.

Site-Centric Measurement

Each website has tags placed on its pages. A tag is a 1x1 transparent graphic image which is used to track an event. An event could include a visit to a website or a page within a website. Each time a page has been served, a tag call is made and that event is logged on the tag host server. The tag call captures:

- URL
- IP address of the computer that retrieved the image
- Timestamp of when it was retrieved
- Type of event (page view, ad impression, video, etc.)
- ISP
- Geography
- Operating system
- Device
- Type of browser
- Third-party cookies

Each Publisher, ad network, or content creator places these tags on their content and ads on the top of the page. Tags could be placed on websites and apps, as well as on video assets. Comscore uses cookies and tagging to collect site-centric data from participating websites. Tags can be applied on mobile sites, apps, websites, etc.

Arriving at Audience Estimates

ComScore has developed proprietary techniques for integrating panel and census data to produce the audience estimates. Besides, to ensure accuracy in measurement, Comscore also deploys several proprietary techniques to filter out invalid traffic.

The Site census data gives total cookies. The Site census also gives the total page view count. The panel data gives out cookies per person data. These two datasets are combined to find out the Total Unique Viewers of a site (Census Cookies/CPP). This is then further adjusted with a Cookie Deflation Factor ('Cookie Deflation Factor', or CDF, is a metric, derived based on panel observations, which allows Comscore to convert cookie counts into person counts).

Some Key Terminologies

Unique Visitors: The estimated number of different individuals that visited the website during the month

% Reach: The number of site visitors divided by the total Internet universe and expressed as a percentage.

Total Page Views: The total number of pages viewed on the website in a given month. This is the same as Total Impressions (1 page view = 1 impression).

Total Minutes: The total minutes spent by the visitors on the site in a given month

Total Visits: The total number of times a unique person visits the website during the given month with at least a 30-minute break between two visits.

Average Daily Visitors (000): The estimated average number of individuals visiting any website per day in a given month.

Data Reporting

Periodicity of Reporting: Monthly

Markets: Very recently, in March 2021, Comscore for the first time started reporting data for state clusters. Up till now, Comscore reported data for India overall, and there were no individual marketwise breakups available. The need for state-level clusters was felt because content consumption in India is heavily skewed towards digital. Nine of the top 10 newspapers in India are in regional languages, and increasingly digital campaigns are being created in regional languages for specific geographies. Comscore now provides data for various state clusters, as illustrated in Table 2.10.

TABLE 2.10 Comscore data by state cluster

State Cluster	% of Unique Visitors
Maharashtra & Goa	14.2
Uttar Pradesh	10.4
West Bengal, Sikkim, & Odisha	9.4
Andhra Pradesh & Telangana	8.9
Tamil Nadu & Pondicherry	8.5
Karnataka	7.4
Gujarat	7.0
Punjab, Haryana, Jammu & Kashmir, & Ladakh	6.1
Rajasthan	4.6
Delhi	4.6
Madhya Pradesh	4.3
Bihar	4.0
Kerala	3.8
Chhattisgarh & Jharkhand	3.0
Assam & North East	2.8
Himachal Pradesh & Uttarakhand	1.0
All India	100.0

Source: Based on Comscore December 2020 data.

For media planners, this granular data would be of tremendous help in planning for defined geographies, while for media marketers, it would help create content and focus marketing efforts to build their audience base.

>*Audience*: Data is collected for people 6+ years, and for gender. So no NCCS-level variables are captured.
>*Devices and Platforms*: One could look at Comscore data for

- Mobile app only
- Mobile web only
- Mobile web and app Jointly
- Desktop only
- Desktop + mobile

Additionally, Comscore reports data across platforms like iPhone, Android, all other smartphones, iPads, Android tablets, and all other tablets.

Client-Focused Dictionary

This is the taxonomy used in reporting traffic on Comscore. It defines the hierarchy of relationship between different entities belonging to the same publisher. The following are the key components of the client-focused dictionary:

>*Property (P)*: This is the highest classification reported by Comscore. So for instance, if there's a website www.xyz.com, it would report the full domain, any pages within the domain (for example, www.xyz.com/cricket), any apps of xyz.com, and any channel or sub channel under xyz.com. It represents the full domain, pages, and applications that are owned by one publisher.
>*Media Title (M)*: A media title is an editorially and brand-consistent collection of content in the digital landscape that provides the marketplace with a view of online user behaviour. This may represent a domain, a group of domains, an online service, or an application. Under this, there are other classifications including Channel, Sub-channel, Group, and Sub-group.

Google Analytics

Google Analytics allows you to make an in-depth analysis of how your website is performing in terms of number of users, their profile, the time they spend on the site, and other engagement metrics.

Google Analytics Reports

There are five kinds of standard reports – Real-Time, Audience, Acquisition, Behaviour, and Conversions.

> *Real-Time Reports*: These reports enable you to monitor your website on a real-time basis – it's a live report with information on:

- How many people are on your site right now
- To which geographical locations those people belong
- The source of traffic – whether the audiences reached your site organically, or through search, email, social media, etc.
- The page of your website the users are currently active on.
- The device people used to access your site – via desktop, mobile, or tablet
- The 'event' or buttons (like download, video play, ad click, etc.) being used on the site
- Whether people have completed any 'goal' (such as filling up a form, or voting, etc.) on your website

> *Audience Reports*: These are reports that give more granular details on your audience. The key information one gets from this report are:

- An overview of your audience in terms of number of unique users, page views, sessions, bounce rate, etc., at a weekly, daily, or monthly level.
- Number of unique users who have visited your site in the last 1 day, 7 days, 14 days, and 28 days.
- The lifetime value of a user in terms of revenue/user, transactions/user, or sessions/user. This is particularly useful if you have an ecommerce engine built into the site.
- Performance of the various versions of your app.
- Performance of your website across different cohorts.
- An understanding of individual user behaviour on the website.
- The age/gender of users.
- Interest and affinity categories of your users.
- Language and location of your website visitors.
- The ability to drill down into audience behaviour – how many times a user visits the site, session duration, intervals between sessions, etc.
- The devices, operating systems, and network operators through which users have visited your website.

> *Acquisition Reports*: These are reports that enable one to understand which marketing activities/channels have helped in acquiring new users for the website.
>
> *Behaviour Reports*: These reports allow one to understand the performance of individual pages within a website, how visitors have moved

from one page to another, how users navigate the site, and which content is being consumed on the site. They tell you on which page visitors land, and which pages help drive better conversions.

Conversion Reports: Goals are a set of pre-decided objectives that the site manager could put in place. It could be a registration page being filled, or a download, or a revenue goal, and so on. These reports help you assess how well your site is able to achieve its targeted objectives.

Uses of Digital Research

The following are the primary uses of digital research:

- To make and evaluate digital plans
- To understand digital media usage patterns of audiences across devices and geographies
- To understand the size and profile of digital media entities
- To develop a deeper understanding of how audiences interact with a website, the content they consume, how they navigate through the site, how they reach the site, etc. – all parameters that would help the web publisher create a better user experience

Radio Research in India

Radio has been an important medium in the Indian media ecosystem for a long time. Earlier in the era of government controlled AIR and Vividh Bharti channels, radio was considered an important medium to reach out to targeted cities at a low cost. In the early part of the 2000s, radio was privatized, and since then FM radio stations have become very popular. Currently, between just the private FM operators, there are about 386 stations across 91 cities. Add to this the 420 stations of AIR covering just about every nook and cranny of the country. However, given the nature of the medium, its usage varies depending upon device and location (some people listen at home, some listen on the go, some listen from different devices), rendering a huge measurement challenge. Given this, and the fact that the medium has been largely played a supporting role in the media mix, not much research investment has gone behind it. There are two primary sources of information on radio currently being used in India:

- Radio Audience Measurement (RAM)
- The Indian Readership Study (IRS), which also captures data on usage of radio

Let's take a look at both these sources.

Radio Audience Measurement (RAM)

RAM was launched in in 2007. It measures listenership of radio stations based on a panel of listeners. RAM is currently being conducted in Bengaluru, Delhi, Mumbai, and Kolkata. RAM conducts an establishment survey in all four cities. It identifies 3000 individuals aged more than 12 years who own an FM radio device through this survey. Such individuals are selected in each of the four cities using random sampling. Face-to-face interviews are conducted using a structured questionnaire through systematic random sampling in each city. The Establishment Survey helps estimate the radio universe size, and apart from giving information about consumption of radio, it also serves as the framework for panel recruitment.

A panel of 600 listeners in each city is recruited for the purpose of monitoring radio listenership. These selected individuals form the panel for the purpose of radio audience measurement. RAM uses the diary method to measure listenership for providing listenership data on a weekly basis. In the diary method, the selected individuals are supposed to write the details of channels and duration for which they listen to FM radio channels on a weekly basis. The diary has a schedule of 15-minute time bands, and the respondent has to tick the channel he/she listened to in that time slot. Only one station can be ticked for each 15-minute timeslot.

- The ticked station has to be listened to for at least 5 minutes in that 15-minute timeslot.
- In case more than one station is listened to, then the station which was listened to for more than 8 minutes will be ticked

Data Provided by RAM

- Listenership of radio stations
- Time spent by listeners
- Profile of radio listeners
- Daypart analysis of listenership
- Reach/frequency of radio plans
- Station loyalty
- Average audience (the audience for each individual quarter hour, added up and divided by the total number of quarter hours)
- TARP %: represents the audience, as a percentage of the universe, listening to any quarter hour over the defined time period. Table 2.11 gives an illustration of calculation of TARP:
- Exclusive audience: represents the percentage of a stations audience that does not listen to any other station, in the defined time period

TABLE 2.11 Radio TARPs calculation example

Timelot	Universe				
	Person 1	*Person 2*	*Person 3*	*Person 4*	*Person 5*
9:00–9:15	1	1			
9:15–9:30			1	1	1
9:30–9:45		1			
9:45–10:00					
10:00–10:15	1			1	
10:15–10:30			1		
Total Time					
(No. of people in Universe(5) x No. of timeslots(6) X Duration of timeslot (15) = 450					
Actual Time Listened					
No. of Timeslots listened (9) x Duration of each timeslot (15) = 135					
TARP %	(Actual Time Listened/Total Time) x 100 = 135/450 x 100 = 30%				

Radio Listenership Data Captured by Indian Readership Survey (IRS)

The IRS captures data on radio listenership and is by far one the most robust sources of data on the medium. It broadly captures the following information on radio:

- Radio listenership in last 1 month, 1 week, and yesterday
- Radio station listenership in last 1 month, 1 week, and yesterday
- Devices used to listen to radio (mobile, radio/music system/transistor, car stereo, radio through computer)
- Frequency of listening to radio
- Places of listenership of radio
- Time spent listening
- Daypart listenership

Cinema Research in India

Cinema too is used largely as a support medium and doesn't get heightened advertiser attention. The only source of authentic data on cinema is once again captured by IRS. The following is the data on cinema viewership through IRS:

- Cinema viewership in Hall in last 6 months and last 1 month
- Frequency of visiting cinema theatre

- Language of cinema watched
- Place where cinema was watched – multiplex, single screen, video parlour

Audit Bureau of Circulation (ABC)

The ABC was set up in 1948 to certify the circulation of newspapers and magazines for the benefit of both publishers and advertisers. The circulation figures acted as a common currency for trading in advertising space. The certification process involves a detailed audit by empanelled auditors on printing, distribution, financial, and production records of member publications as per the guidelines prescribed by the Bureau. The Bureau issues certificates for 6-monthly audit periods – January to June and July to December.

ABC's membership today includes 562 dailies, 107 weeklies, and 50 magazines, plus 125 advertising agencies, 45 advertisers, and 22 new agencies and associations connected with print media and advertising. It covers most of the major towns in India.

For every member publication, the ABC issues a certificate of circulation, and also an area breakdown of the circulation. So, if a publication has sold 60,00,000 copies during July–December 2019 and has 182 publishing days, then the average qualifying sales is 32,967 (60,00,000/182). Qualifying sales represents all sales above the NRR as well as compliant with all prescribed audit guidelines framed by the Bureau. This figure of 32,967 is then the average daily circulation of a publication. So when a publisher says that their circulation is 32,967, they imply that they, on an average, sell 32,967 copies of the publication daily.

Besides the circulation numbers, the certificate also mentions single copy sales, combo sales, institutional sales, subscription sales, and non-subscription sales. If a newspaper has a variant, it gives the breakup of the figures for the main edition and the variant edition. It also mentions number of copies sold at different cover prices. The certificate also mentions non-qualifying sales, i.e. any free or complimentary copies. Figure 2.2 shows a sample of an ABC certificate, and Figure 2.3 shows a sample of the area breakup of circulation.

Along with the information just presented, the ABC also gives a detailed Area Breakup statement or a Distribution statement. This gives the breakup of the average qualifying sales by states, districts, and towns.

TAM

TAM, a joint venture between Kantar Media and Nielsen, is India's only integrated media monitoring agency. It monitors advertising and content across 600+ TV channels, 900+ publications, 90+ FM radio stations, and 3000+ web publishers. It provides the following services:

Audit Period : January - June 2021

This Certificate is issued subject to the provisions of the bye-law dated 10th July1957 made by the Bureau's Council of Management in exercise of the powers conferred on it by Articles 42 and 43 of the Articles of Association of the Bureau.

MULTI EDITION

Certificate
Number
xxx / xxxx

Audit Bureau of Circulations
Wakefield House,Sprott Road, Ballard Estate, Mumbai - 1.

ABC Certificate of	: xxxxxxxxxxxxxx
Address	: xxxxxxxxxxxxxxxxxxxxxxxxxxxxxxxxxxxxxxxxxxxxxxxxxxxxxxxxxxxxx
Published/Estd	: A EDN, BB EDN, CCC EDN
Language	: ENGLISH **Frequency** : **DAILY EXPT SUN**
Cover Price	: **Single copy :** RS. 5.00 / 6.00 / 8.00 / 10.00. STUDENT EDITION (VARIANT) RS. 3.00 / 6.00.
Auditors	: xxxxxxxxxxxxxxxxxxxxxxxxxxx, xxxxxxxxxxxxxxxxxxxxxxxxxxxxxxxxxxxxxx

	JANUARY - JUNE 2021		
Edition(s)	Total Qualifying Sales	No. of Publishing Days	Average Qualifying Sales
A	4,02,39,650	154	2,61,296
BB	22,51,333	154	14,619
CCC	23,67,804	154	15,375
	4,48,58,787		
Average Total Qualifying Sales			2,91,290

Jul-Dec 2020 : 2,52,559 (154 ISSUES)	Jan-Jun 2020 : 1,43,327 (154 ISSUES)

Qualifying sales represents all sales above the NRR as well as compliant with all prescribed audit guidelines framed by the Bureau.

	Average Copies
A. Non subscription sales	
• Single copy sales	1,36,944
• Combo sales	Nil
B. Subscription Sales	
• Subscription copy sales (Single)	1,29,387
• Subscription copy sales (Joint)	Nil
• Subscription copy sales (Institutional)	Nil
C. Institutional Sales	**24,959**
Total Qualifying Sales :	**2,91,290**

DATED : 22-10-2021

Details of Variant copies in the same market place :-

Average Qualifying Sales

	Main Edition	Student Edition (Variant)	Total
A edition	2,49,572	11,724	2,61,296
BB edition	12,844	1,775	14,619
CCC edition	14,028	1,347	15,375

AUTHORISED FOR ISSUE BY THE COUNCIL OF THE BUREAU

xxxxxxxxxx xxxxxxxx
Secretary General
This certificate is the COPYRIGHT property of
Xxxxxxxxxx xxxxxxxxx
and the AUDIT BUREAU OF CIRCULATIONS

FIGURE 2.2 Specimen ABC Certificate.

Source: Audit Bureau of Circulations India.

Audit Bureau of Circulations
Wakefield House, Sprott Road, Ballard Estate, Mumbai - 1.

Certificate Number
XXX / XXXXX

ABC Certificate of : A EDN , BB EDN , CCC EDN

Language : ENGLISH **Frequency** : DAILY EXPT SUN

PART A - Qualifying Sales

	Average Copies	Average Copies
A. Non Subscription Sales		1,36,944
Single copy sales :		
• Sold to the distribution trade above the NRR*		
0 to 10 % above the NRR*	Nil	
10.1 % to 20 % above the NRR*	61	
Over 20 % above the NRR*	1,36,883	
	1,36,944	
• Incentives offered to the readers		
At NIL incentive on the cover price	1,36,944	
Upto 50% incentive on the cover price	Nil	

* Net Realisation Rate (NRR) is the term used for value per issue of newspaper in waste based on predetermined waste rate of Rs. per kg. fixed by the Council .

1,36,944

Combo sales	Nil	
B. Subscription Sales (Single, Joint, Institutional)		1,29,387
• At full cover price	Nil	
• Upto **50% inducement on the cover price	27	
• Upto **90% inducement on the cover price	1,29,360	
Total :	1,29,387	

(**Including discount on cover price, gifts etc. offered to subscribers aswell as delivery charges to the trade)

Subscription Categories

• General	1,29,387	
• School	Nil	
• Institutional	Nil	
• Others	Nil	
Total :	1,29,387	
C. Institutional Sales		24,959
• Airlines	6,623	
• Body Corporates	Nil	
• Educational Institutions	Nil	
• Hotels	1,598	
• Libraries	Nil	
• Others	16,738	
Total :	24,959	

ADDITIONAL INFORMATION

Break up of average qualifying sales by cover price individually for each edition/printing centre as per relevant publishing days. This is for information purpose only and is not to be reproduced / used for any publicity / promotion.

	Student Edition (Variant)		Main Edition			
Edition / Printing Centre (cover price)	Rs. 6.00	Rs. 3.00	Rs. 8.00	Rs. 6.00	Rs. 5.00	Rs. 10.00
A edition Ave copies (publishing days)	17,257 (103)	27,931 (1)	2,35,798 (153)	13,722 (153)	2,41,764 (1)	15,677 (1)
BB edition	3,305 (81)	5,685 (1)	-	12,842 (153)	-	13,053 (1)
CCC edition	3,183 (63)	6,753 (1)	-	14,033 (153)	-	13,278 (1)

FIGURE 2.2 (Continued)

PART B - Non Qualifying Circulation

Copies not qualifying for certification (as sold below the Net Realisation Rate) and / or sales not meeting the precribed audit guidelines

(Circulation figures for information only, Not to be used for any publicity / promotion)

	Average Copies	Average Copies
Non Qualifying Sales		**14,545**
Single copy sales (Non Subscription)		
• 0 to 10 % below the NRR*	1,121	
• 10.1 % to 20 % below the NRR*	501	
• Over 20 % below the NRR*	321	
• Others	Nil	
	1,943	

* Net Realisation Rate (NRR) is the term used for value per issue
of newspaper in waste based on predetermined waste rate of
Rs. per kg. fixed by the Council .

Subscription copy sales (Single)	11,925	
Free & Complimentary copies	677	

AUTHORISED FOR ISSUE BY THE COUNCIL OF THE BUREAU

xxxxxxxxxxxxxxxxxxxxxxxxxxxxx
Secretary General
This certificate is the COPYRIGHT property of
Xxxxxxxx xxxxxxxxxxxx
and the AUDIT BUREAU OF CIRCULATIONS

FIGURE 2.2 (Continued)

- Set Top Box Return Path Data (RPD) for DTH and MSO
- Ad monitoring across media
- Sports measurement (in stadia and on screen)
- PR/buzz measurement

The Advertising Information System division of TAM Media Research is called Adex. It was set up in 1970 to monitor and keep a record of all advertising on TV and print. It now captures advertising across media including radio and digital.

AUDIT BUREAU OF CIRCULATIONS

MULTI EDITION

Details of Distribution and Territorial Breakdown of circulation

Name of the Publication : XXXXXXXXXX , A EDITION, BB EDITION & CCC EDITION

Average Circulation for the audit period : January/June 2021 : 291,290

No.	
XXX	XXXX

Section A — Statewise distribution in India and outside India

	Main Edition	Variant	Total
1. In the town(s) of Publication			
A	231,685	10,041	241,726
BB	2,388	556	2,944
CCC	6,360	623	6,983
2. In the State(s) in which the town(s) of publication are situated :			
KARNATAKA	25,242	1,688	26,930
3. In Other States			
SOUTHERN ZONE			
Andhra Pradesh	2,310	484	2,794
Kerala	-	-	-
Lakshadweep	-	-	-
Puducherry	-	-	-
Tamil Nadu	6,875	1,101	7,976
Telangana	-	-	-
WESTERN ZONE			
Chhattisgarh	-	-	-
Dadra & Nagar Haveli	-	-	-
Daman & Diu	-	-	-
Goa	388	-	388
Gujarat	-	-	-
Madhya Pradesh	-	-	-
Maharashtra	1,196	353	1,549
NORTHERN ZONE			
Chandigarh	-	-	-
Delhi	-	-	-
Haryana	-	-	-
Himachal Pradesh	-	-	-
Jammu & Kashmir	-	-	-
Punjab	-	-	-
Rajasthan	-	-	-
Uttar Pradesh	-	-	-
Uttarakhand	-	-	-
EASTERN ZONE			
Andaman & Nicobar Islands	-	-	-
Arunachal Pradesh	-	-	-
Assam	-	-	-
Bihar	-	-	-
Jharkhand	-	-	-
Manipur	-	-	-
Meghalaya	-	-	-
Mizoram	-	-	-
Nagaland	-	-	-
Orissa	-	-	-
Rest Of India	-	-	-
Sikkim	-	-	-
Tripura	-	-	-
West Bengal	-	-	-
Outside India	-	-	-
TOTAL	276,444	14,846	291,290

Section B — Townwise distribution (250 copies or more) in various States

	Main Edition	Variant	Total
A EDITION			
KARNATAKA			
Bangalore District			
Anekal	514	-	514
Bangalore	231,685	10,041	241,726
Dist. Total	232,199	10,041	242,240
Kolar District			
Bangarapet	658	-	658
Other Places	210	98	308
Dist. Total	868	98	966
Mandya District			
Mandya	258	-	258
Other Places	260	-	260
Dist. Total	518	-	518
Mysore District			
Mysore	4,965	-	4,965
Other Places	524	-	524
Dist. Total	5,489	-	5,489
Tumkur District			
Adityapatna	505	-	505
Tumkur	808	-	808
Dist. Total	1,313	-	1,313
ANDHRA PRADESH			
Anantapur District			
Anantapur	911	174	1,085
Guntakal	279	-	279
Hindupur	170	174	344
Other Places	650	136	786
Puttaparthi	300	-	300
TAMIL NADU			
Dharmapuri District			
Dharmapuri	762	16	778
Other Places	276	109	385
Krishnagiri District			
Hosur	1,842	753	2,595
Krishnagiri	3,554	114	3,668
Other Places	441	109	550
BB EDITION			
KARNATAKA			
Bagalkot District			
Other Places	544	62	606
Dist. Total	544	62	606
Belgaum District			
Belgaum	1,607	304	1,911

P.T.O.

FIGURE 2.3 Area breakdown statement of circulation.

Source: Audit Bureau of Circulations India.

No.	
XXX	XXXX

-2-

XXXXXXXXX, A EDITION, BB EDITION & CCC EDITION

SECTION 'B'
Town-wise distribution (250 copies or more) in various States

	Main Edition	Variant	Total
Other Places	439	10	449
Dist. Total	2,046	314	2,360
Bellary District			
Bellary	820	24	844
Hospet	402	-	402
Other Places	241	45	286
Dist. Total	1,463	69	1,532
Bijapur District			
Bijapur	747	31	778
Dist. Total	747	31	778
Chitradurga District			
Chitradurga	370	-	370
Dist. Total	370	-	370
Davanagere District			
Davanagere	721	-	721
Other Places	285	6	291
Dist. Total	1,006	6	1,012
Dharwad District			
Dharwad	1,204	-	1,204
Hubli	2,388	556	2,944
Other Places	16	-	16
Dist. Total	3,608	556	4,164
Haveri District			
Other Places	367	89	456
Ranibennur	418	295	713
Dist. Total	785	384	1,169
Uttara Kannada District			
Karwar	404	-	404
Other Places	287	-	287
Dist. Total	691	-	691
GOA			
North Goa District			
Other Places	194	-	194
South Goa District			
Other Places	194	-	194
MAHARASHTRA			
Kolhapur District			
Other Places	433	62	495
Pune District			
Other Places	156	26	182
Pune	276	238	514
Sangli District			
Other Places	122	16	138
Solapur District			
Other Places	209	11	220

	Main Edition	Variant	Total
CCC EDITION			
KARNATAKA			
Chikmagalur District			
Chikmagalur	265	-	265
Other Places	228	-	228
Dist. Total	493	-	493
Dakshina Kannada District			
Mangalore	6,360	623	6,983
Other Places	961	168	1,129
Puttur	256	32	288
Dist. Total	7,577	823	8,400
Hassan District			
Hassan	1,104	379	1,483
Other Places	151	-	151
Dist. Total	1,255	379	1,634
Kodagu District			
Madikeri	306	-	306
Other Places	337	-	337
Dist. Total	643	-	643
Shimoga District			
Other Places	362	-	362
Shimoga	1,265	-	1,265
Dist. Total	1,627	-	1,627
Udupi District			
Kundapura	215	77	292
Other Places	488	-	488
Udupi	1,736	62	1,798
Dist. Total	2,439	139	2,578

FIGURE 2.3 (Continued)

TV Adex

All TV channels are recorded at the ops centre, where the recordings are monitored as per defined SOPs. The data is coded and scrutinized for accuracy and then made available to users via a cloud-based software. The TV Adex covers all advertising across 974 TV channels. It captures the following details:

- Super category: There are 682 individual product categories for which data is collected. These are grouped into 28 Super categories for ease of analysis. For instance, the Super category Hair Care constitutes individual product categories like anti-lice, hair care range, hair conditioners, hair dyes, hair oils, hair wash powders, other hair dressing, and shampoos.
- Product group: These are 628 individual product categories, as mentioned previously
- Name of advertiser
- Product: Name of brand, sub-brand, or variant
- Ad theme: The theme of the ad (for example: Ishaan Khattar-drone Delivery-match Time Pe Pyaas Hatao)
- Name of channel and the broadcasting network to which it belongs
- Name of programme
- The genre and language and theme of the programme
- Date, month, and year of telecast of the spot
- Time of airing of the programme
- The duration of the programme in minutes
- The time at which the spot was telecast
- The total number of ads telecast during the programme
- The sequence/position of the particular spot
- The sequence of the ad break in which the spot was telecast
- The position in the ad break in which the ad break was telecast
- The number of ads in the break in which the spot was telecast
- Language and duration of the ad
- Estimated cost of the ad

Print Adex

It captures advertising data across 809 publications across 15 languages. All copies (either physical/e-paper) are collated at the centre in Vadodara, where the advertising data is coded, checked for quality control, and then made available via cloud-based software. It captures the following details:

- Super category: There are 682 individual product categories for which data is collected. These are grouped into 28 Super categories for ease of analysis. For instance, the Super category Hair Care constitutes individual product categories like anti-lice, hair care range, hair conditioners, hair dyes, hair oils, hair wash powders, other hair dressing, and shampoos.

- Product group: These are 628 individual product categories, as mentioned previously
- Name of advertiser
- Product: Name of brand, sub-brand, or variant
- Ad type: Whether the ad is a display ad or a financial ad. All commercial ads are called display ads. Financial ads comprise audited/unaudited financial results, public issues, balance sheets, and fixed deposits
- Parent publication and publication group: The name of the Parent Brand. For example, if it is *Times of India* Mumbai edition and *Times of India* Delhi edition, then *Times of India* is the parent publication. Bennett and Coleman will be the publication group.
- Name of publication
- Supplementary: Has the ad been published in the main issue or in the supplement?
- Date and page number of the published ad
- Title of the page of the newspaper/magazine in which the ad has been published
- The position (solus, ear panel, island, skybus, centrespread, etc.) and language of the ad
- Type of ad: colour or black-and-white
- Location: Whether the ad is on the Front Page, Back Page, or Inside Page
- On which side has the ad been published – left-hand or right-hand side
- Pub nature: Newspaper or magazine
- Periodicity and genre of the publication
- Zone, state, and edition of the publication
- Whether it's a creative promotional ad (such as whether the ad is a contest, exchange offer, discount, etc.)
- Whether there was any innovation in the ad (like a text wrap, French window, etc.)
- Whether is ad in on a festival like Diwali, Ponpgal, and so on
- The name of the creative agency
- Size of the ad in column centimetres and square centimetres
- An estimate of the cost of the ad
- Date, month, and year of the published ad

Digital Adex

The Digital Adex Service covers 3000+ digital publishers, and OTT services including YouTube and Apps. It tracks around 46,000 advertisers with over 73,000 brands. Information is tracked across devices (mobile/desktop/tablets), and it captures all types of ads – display banner, video, or text. Since

April 2020, the Digital Adex has started capturing display ads on Facebook. It captures the following information:

- Just like Print and TV Adex, it captures super category, product group, advertiser, product, day, date, time, ad theme, and name of web publisher
- Digital channel in which the ad appeared: Desktop display, desktop video, In APP display, In App video, mobile display, mobile video
- Type of Creative: banner, HTML5, video
- The name of the YouTube publisher's channel in which the ad was placed
- Whether the ad was a pre-roll, mid-roll, or post-roll, and whether the video was skippable or not
- Transaction method: ad network, direct, programmatic
- An estimated spend on the ad
- Impressions

Radio Adex

Radio logs are collected from radio stations and put through the TAM software for scrutiny, coding, and validation. Post that, data is released via the software.

Uses of Adex

It is used for the following purposes:

- To understand spending patterns of advertisers across categories
- To estimate share of spend
- To understand scheduling patterns of brands
- To understand category advertising trends
- To track competition

The Way Forward on Media Research

Digital has blurred all sorts of boundaries – not just geographical boundaries, but boundaries between individual media as well. The same media content gets repurposed, repackaged, and redistributed across different platforms and devices – in a sense, extending the long tail of media content.

With the long tail now accounting for a significant share of time and attention, we have a situation where a large part of media consumption will go unmeasured. Add to this the fact that these new platforms are spawning new media behaviour. This creates questions of measurement that need to be tackled very differently from our traditional methodologies.

On the other hand, marketers have broken out of silos – they are planning idea-driven, cross-platform campaigns that frequently mix traditional media with PR activities, sponsorships, events, product placements, and other forms of promotion. But research is still operating in silos of individual media. We have TV research separately, we have print research separately, and so on for each individual media. And seldom are all these 'siloed' media on the same page. As a result, while a unified media strategy is being created, media plans for each medium are made separately and evaluated separately. So for a campaign which uses TV, print, and radio, there are three different plan evaluations – one for each medium. So you would have a TV Plan reach and frequency, a Print Plan reach and frequency, and a Radio Plan reach and frequency – but what about the campaign reach and frequency? Yes, some people use modelling methods and make assumptions on inter-media duplications to arrive at campaign reach and frequency across media. However, that is not enough.

The economics of yesterday were created for measuring eyeballs, reach, and awareness. Today, marketers have moved towards targeting multiple niches and in a dialogue mode with consumers. The media currency was created for trading, but that will increasingly become a smaller part of the overall game. Research will need to emerge out of silos and create metrics for 'decision making', rather than just 'trading'.

At one end of the spectrum, we see people consume media seamlessly, and they move from one medium to another effortlessly, sometimes even multi-tasking media – they watch TV and use social media on their phones or tablets simultaneously. At the other end of the spectrum, marketers are looking at the consumer as one entity and are increasingly focusing on integrated campaigns. However, the media that connects the marketer to the consumer is completely silo-driven and fragmented. Planners necessarily need to look at picking and buying multiple media simultaneously, as in an idea-driven media planning world, the idea will have to reign supreme – the platforms may become irrelevant. That means they will also need to make the apples-and-oranges comparisons between different media types. And that's the entire media research challenge.

What we really need is a common currency across media. In the absence of this, one might be spending inefficiently on media through buying wasteful frequency that also ends up irritating consumers. At the same time, advertisers want to measure the entire campaign rather than parts of it.

Media consumption habits have changed dramatically over the last decade, and during the Covid pandemic, digital media consumption grew at an unprecedented pace. In the current scenario, marketers are trying to gauge the total impact of their campaigns, but the current research silos do not support this. Media owners need data that shows their media in a good light, and hence they favour metrics that strengthen their case. It's a long road ahead to a true cross-media measurement that is fair to all media, transparent, and future proof. Despite the huge need for cross-media research, we are still trying to get on top of our game in traditional individual media-centric research, and the media research silos are only digging deeper. A 'media research renaissance' movement is needed on a war-footing.

Chapter Summary

India probably has the world's most complex media market. We have over 900 TV channels, over 400 large/medium newspapers, hundreds of magazines, over 300 radio stations, thousands of outdoor/ambient media sites, and millions of websites. At the same time, there are linguistic zones within the country, and planners have to manage national plan deliveries and supplement media plans with regional options in areas which are either undercovered by the plan or need extra media weight.

To create a media plan, one needs to understand the media consumption pattern of the audience, the profile of the audience, and the size of the audience. Besides this, one would like to understand the intensity with which the audience engages with different kinds of media – how frequently they refer to the medium, how much time they spend on it, and so on. When it comes to allocating budgets, one needs to understand which media would be most cost efficient, and which would give them a better value for money spent. Answers to most of these questions come through media research.

Some of the Key Uses of Research in the Media Planning Process:

a) Sharper identification and definition of the target audience
b) Understanding the psychographics of the target audience
c) Understanding media consumption habits of the audience
d) Market identification and prioritization
e) Media scheduling decisions
f) Media weight-setting decisions
g) Media mix selections
h) Vehicle selection
i) Profiling of vehicles
j) Understanding competitive media expenditure patterns
k) Creation of a common currency on which typically buying is done

Key Research Available in India:

a) Indian Readership Survey (IRS)
b) Television Audience Measurement by BARC
c) Radio Audience Measurement (RAM)
d) Advertising Expenditure Data on TV, Print, Digital and Radio (Adex)
e) Target Group Index (TGI)
f) Audit Bureau of Circulations (ABC)
g) Census of India

Key Terms Used in Media Research:

a) *New Consumer Classification System (NCCS)*: A new method of classifying households was created in 2012 and is based on the education of the Chief Wage Earner and the number of consumer durables owned by the household. The population of India is divided into 12 groups, ranging from NCCS A1 to NCCS E3.

b) *Chief Wage Earner (CWE)*: The Chief Wage Earner is the member of the family who makes the highest contribution to the household expenditure.

c) *Urban and Rural*: According to the Census of India 2011, the following criteria were adopted for treating a place as urban:

- Statutory towns: All administrative units that have been defined by statute as urban like Municipal Corporation, Municipality, Cantonment Board, Notified Town Area Committee, Town Panchayat, Nagar Palika, etc.
- Census towns: Administrative units satisfying the following three criteria simultaneously:

  - A minimum population of 5000
  - At least 75% of the male working population engaged in non-agricultural pursuits
  - A density of population of at least 400 per sq km

Apart from these, the outgrowths of cities and towns have also been treated as urban. All areas not identified as urban are classified as rural.

d) *Household*: A normal household is defined as a group of persons who normally live together and take their meals from a common kitchen unless the nature of their work prevent any of them from doing so.

e) *Householder*: A person who takes the decision on purchase of day-to-day household products such as groceries, toothpastes, soaps, detergents, etc., with respect to what to purchase, when to purchase, and how much to purchase.

f) *Literates*: A person aged 7 years and above who can both read and write with understanding in any language was taken as literate. A person who can read but cannot write is not literate. It is not necessary that to be treated as literate, a person should have received any formal education or passed any minimum educational standard.

g) *Socio-cultural regions*: India is divided into 94 SCRs based on linguistic, geographical, financial, economic, and administrative homogeneity, as well as geographical contiguity, rationalization of culture and lifestyles making each one unique from other districts, and caste and class considerations.

Print Research in India

Print research in India is done at a fairly extensive level through the Indian Readership Survey (IRS), which is conducted by the Media Research Users

Council (MRUC). IRS 2019 Q4 covered a sample of 3,27,661, making it the world's largest sample study. Apart from providing information just for the print medium, the IRS provides a lot of information about other media and population demographics, and, most importantly, also covers information about product penetration and usage patterns across most large categories. This is a fairly comprehensive study, and its usage is widespread across the media planning and marketing industries.

The utility of IRS goes beyond just readership numbers and making print plans. It can be used to understand cross-media consumption patterns which could be used to arrive at a media mix decision. It can be used to understand the spread of target groups across the country and their media habits. From a market planning standpoint, the data could be used to identify market potential, create scenarios for demand estimations, and help in market identification and prioritization. It reports data for all towns with a population of 5 Lakh and above and reports data for 94 independent and 101 clustered districts. Large metros like Mumbai, Delhi, Kolkata, and Chennai are reported at a zonal level.

TV Research in India

TV research in India is conducted by Broadcast Audience Research Council (BARC), which is a joint industry company founded by stakeholder bodies that represent broadcasters, advertisers, and advertising and media agencies. BARC has a panel of 44,000 TV-owning homes to capture viewership data, and India is one of the largest metered markets in the world. Data is captured using a watermarking ID technology with meters installed in the panel homes.

Data from BARC is used to create optimized TV plans, to understand TV viewing patterns across markets, and to understand TV viewing preferences across different kinds of audiences. It reports data across the mega cities – Mumbai, Delhi, Kolkata, Chennai, Bangalore, and Hyderabad. It also reports data for state groups – PHCHPJK, Raj, UP/UT, Delhi, WB, Orissa, Bih/Jha, Assam/NE, Mah/Goa, Guj/D&D/DNH, MPC, AP/Tel, Kar, Ker, and TN/Pondy.

Digital Research in India

There are two research products that help measure digital audiences in India – Comscore, and Google Analytics. While Comscore is a third-party research agency that manages a panel of homes and gives out audience estimates across different websites and apps, Google Analytics is a service that lets an individual site owner get a deeper insight into how the audience interacts with that particular website.

Comscore has a methodology, termed Unified Digital Measurement (UDM), which has two components:

- Global Person Measurement – these are measurements based on a panel of respondents recruited online
- Global Machine Measurement – these are server-centric data collected by tagging websites

Google Analytics allows you to make an in-depth analysis of how your website is performing in terms of number of users, their profile, the time they spend on the site, and other engagement metrics. There are five kinds of standard reports – Real-Time, Audience, Acquisition, Behaviour, and Conversions.

Digital research is useful in constructing digital plans, understanding digital media consumption, and gauging the size and profile of digital media entities.

Radio Research in India

Radio has been an important medium in the Indian media ecosystem for a long time. However, given the nature of the medium, its usage varies depending upon device and location (some people listen at home, some listen on the go, some listen from different devices), rendering a huge measurement challenge. Given this, and the fact that the medium has been largely played a supporting role in the media mix, not much research investment has gone behind it. There are two primary sources of information on radio currently being used in India:

- Radio Audience Measurement (RAM)
- The Indian Readership Study (IRS)

RAM was launched in in 2007. It measures listenership of radio stations based on a panel of listeners. RAM is currently being conducted in Bengaluru, Delhi, Mumbai, and Kolkata. It gives out data on radio station listenership, daypart listenership, time spent, and profile of listeners.

The IRS captures data on radio listenership, and is by far one the most robust sources of data on the medium. It gives data on radio listenership, daypart listenership, time spent listening, devices used to listen, and the frequency of listening to radio.

Cinema Research in India

The IRS captures data on cinema viewership frequency, language of cinema watched, and places where cinema was watched.

Audit Bureau of Circulation (ABC)

The ABC was set up in 1948 to certify the circulation of newspapers and magazines for the benefit of both publishers and advertisers. The circulation figures acted as a common currency for trading in advertising space. The certification process involves a detailed audit by empanelled auditors on printing, distribution, financial, and production records of member publications as per the guidelines prescribed by the Bureau. The Bureau issues certificates for two 6-month audit periods – January to June and July to December.

TAM Adex

The Advertising Information System division of TAM Media Research is called Adex. It was set up in 1970 to monitor and keep a record of all advertising on TV and print. It now captures advertising across media including radio and digital. It monitors advertising and content across 600+ TV channels, 900+ publications, 90+ FM radio stations, and 3000+ web publishers.

Adex is used to understand spending patterns of advertisers across categories, and understand their spending patterns. It is primarily used to track competitor ad spends and plays a useful role while trying to benchmark media weights for a plan.

The Way Forward on Media Research

The emergence of digital media has blurred all sorts of boundaries – not just geographical boundaries, but boundaries between individual media as well. The same media content gets repurposed, repackaged, and redistributed across different platforms and devices – in a sense extending the long tail of media content. Large parts of this long tail will go unmeasured. Add to this the fact that these new platforms are spawning new media behaviour. This creates questions of measurement that need to be tackled very differently from our traditional methodologies.

While media research is very silo-driven, marketers have broken out of silos – they are planning idea-driven, cross-platform campaigns that frequently mix traditional media with PR activities, sponsorships, events, product placements, and other forms of promotion. The challenge for media research is to break out of their silos and create metrics for 'decision making' rather than just 'trading'.

Media consumption habits have changed dramatically over the last decade, and during the Covid pandemic, digital media consumption grew at an unprecedented pace. In the current scenario, while marketers are trying to gauge the total impact of their campaigns, the current research silos do not support this. Media owners need data that shows their media in good light, and hence they favour metrics that strengthen their case. It's a long road ahead to a true cross-media measurement that is fair to all media, transparent and future proof. Despite the huge need for cross-media research, we are still trying to get on top of our game in traditional individual media-centric research, and the media research silos are only digging deeper. A 'media research renaissance' movement is needed on a war-footing.

Further Reading

Analytic Pillars of RAM, https://Tamindia.com

BARC India Universe Update (July 2018), https://barcindia.co.in

Census of India, 2011.

Comscore Media Metrix Desktop Description of Methodology, Unified Digital Measurement, September 2020, https://Comscore.com

Comscore: State Level Clusters in India, March 2021.

Department of Land Resources, Government of India, https://dolr.gov.in/document/statewise-tehsils-or-taluks-india

Description of Methodology, BARC India, September 2020, https://barcindia.co.in

"Establishing Principles for a New Approach to Cross-Media Measurement, An Industry Framework", World Federation of Advertisers, https://wfanet.org

Glossary of Terms and FAQs, https://barcindia.co.in

Google Analytics, https://analytics.google.com

A Guide to ABC Audit, October 2019, Audit Bureau of Circulation.

IRS, 1995: https://mruc.net/studies

IRS Release Notes, MRUC.

Media Glossary, MRUC, page 44.

Pitch Madison Advertising Spend Report 2019.

Tam Credentials, Tam Media Research Pvt Ltd.

3

EFFECTIVE FREQUENCY AND EFFECTIVE REACH

In a fast-fragmenting media world marked by rising clutter and ad avoidance, media planners are increasingly looking at cross-channel/cross-platform planning just to be able to communicate with their target consumers. In these times, the question 'How much frequency is enough?' is a complex one, and one which has no ready answers. Different researchers and practitioners have postulated different theories, yet there doesn't appear to be a single solution. With the ever-changing media landscape, and the rules of marketing constantly changing, the frequency playbook is a dynamic one. Throughout the history of media planning there's been a standing debate about what works better – a high reach strategy or a high frequency strategy.

Effective Frequency as a concept has been one of the most dominant concepts in the history of media. Numerous media scholars over a period of time have worked on the subject, and it has also been the most debated subjects in the short history of media. Let's take a look at the concept of Effective Frequency in a bit of detail.

What Is Effective Frequency?

Put simply, Effective Frequency is the level of frequency at which communication takes place. The dominant belief behind this is the fact that contact with advertising is incomplete and fleeting, and therefore repetition is necessary to ensure a minimum physical perception. The thinking, therefore, is that repetition builds advertising effectiveness. But systematic hammering over a period of time may be wasteful. Therefore, it is important to know the threshold level of repetitions. This threshold level is the level of Effective Frequency.

DOI: 10.4324/9781032724539-3

Numerous media scholars have debated endlessly about what this threshold level should be. Some say it is 3, some say 5, some say 2, and some even say 1. But the argument is still incomplete. My belief is that there is no quick-fix solution for this, and there is nothing known as the magic Effective Frequency level. The Effective Frequency level will vary from brand to brand, and at times even for the same brand, it can vary at different times of the year, or at different times in its lifecycle. Therefore, more than anything else, it is important to understand the factors that could influence the Effective Frequency level.

Factors that Influence the Effective Frequency Level

There are numerous factors that could have a bearing on the level of Effective Frequency. For the sake of simplicity, we could divide them into three broad types – Marketing Factors, Media Factors, and Creative Factors.

Marketing Factors

1. **Marketing objectives:** The marketing objectives could fall in the continuum between modest and very ambitious. Given this, the level of Effective Frequency would vary from low to high on the same continuum. However, how much is low and how much is high is again a subjective decision, and we will come to that later during the course of this chapter.
2. **Stage of product Life cycle of the brand:** At what stage the brand is in its lifecycle too has a bearing on the level of Effective Frequency. A brand in its growth phase would require a relatively higher Effective Frequency as compared to a brand which is in a mature phase of its lifecycle.
3. **Strength of brand in the market:** How strong the brand is in terms of its market position also has a bearing on the level of Effective Frequency. Typically weaker brands require a relatively lower Effective Frequency than stronger brands.
4. **Category salience:** Brands in categories which are highly salient will require a relatively lower frequency as compared to brands in categories with low salience. High salience categories typically have many brands; and all of them combined do a category sales role in some manner, and consumer awareness levels about the category are much higher. Categories with low brand salience typically have fewer brands being promoted, and consumer awareness levels are relatively lower. Therefore, brands in these categories need a higher level of Effective Frequency.

Creative Factors

1. **Impact of advertising:** High-impact advertising requires a lower Effective Frequency as compared to brands with average impact advertising.

2. **Communication task:** A tougher communication task will require a relatively higher Effective Frequency as compared to brands with a simpler communication task. For example, if the communication is about changing attitudes and habits of people, it would be a relatively more difficult task as compared to another brand which is trying to reinforce existing habits and attitudes.
3. **Complexity of message:** A simple message will require a relatively lower Effective Frequency as compared to brands with a complex message. For the lay consumer, it is simpler to understand, for instance, the benefits of a cold cream versus how microprocessors work in a computer.

Media Factors

1. **The level of media clutter:** If the level of clutter in media is high, brands will require a higher Effective Frequency level to be seen and heard versus a situation where the clutter levels are not so high. For instance, during the Diwali season in India, where consumer purchasing is at its peak, there are many brands being advertised, and the clutter levels are extremely high. In such a situation, individual brands in order to be seen and heard sufficiently well need to advertise at a relatively higher Effective Frequency level.
2. **The level of category clutter:** If there are many brands active in a category, they would require a relatively higher Effective Frequency as compared to categories with fewer brands. If the category clutter levels are higher, then to register impact, brands will require a higher Effective Frequency.
3. **Recent level of support:** Typically, planning in India is done on a 4-week cycle. Therefore, brands which advertise on a continuous basis keep changing the Effective Frequency levels during the course of their campaign. For instance, if I have a 3-month campaign for a certain brand, then one would keep a relatively higher Effective Frequency in month 1, bring it down marginally in month 2, and bring it further down in month 3. This works on the understanding that advertising effects have a carryover effect – advertising done in month 1 will also have some effect during month 2, and so on.

What Is Effective Reach?

Put simply, Effective Reach is the level of reach at the Effective Frequency level. How does one really use this concept? To illustrate this through an example, let's get back to the Frequency Distribution table that we had discussed in the previous chapter.

Suppose there is a Print Plan of 10 insertions. The defined target group is, say, SEC AB, Males, 25+ yrs, in a market like Delhi. The total number of SEC AB, Males, 25+ yrs in Delhi is, say, 1500 people.

Given the fact that there are 10 insertions released in a combination of newspapers in Delhi, the maximum number of times one can be exposed to the campaign will be 10, and it is also possible that some people within the defined target group might not be reading any of the newspaper taken in the plan, and will hence not be reached by the campaign at all – in other words, they get zero exposures. Likewise there will be some people who have received 2 exposures, some would have received 6 exposures, and so on. Let's put this into a frequency distribution table, as shown in Table 3.1. This is nothing but a simple table which says how many people have been exposed at various levels of frequency.

Here, if through whatever method, the advertisers/planners conclude that for the communication to be effective, the target audience must be exposed to the campaign at least two times. In other words, the Effective Frequency level for the campaign is set at 2. This would mean that members of the target group who have received two or more exposures to the campaign have been effectively communicated to. This is also the reason why typically Effective Frequency is referred to as 2+ – implying people who have received two or more exposures. In this particular case, the people receiving or more exposures are shown in Figure 3.1. If the Effective Frequency was set at 5+, the numbers would be as depicted in Figure 3.2.

History behind Effective Frequency

In the early 60s, media planning was struggling with the basic concepts of quantitative media analysis. At that time, a lot of the thinking went behind trying to figure out different ways of estimating reach and frequency.

TABLE 3.1 Frequency distribution

Frequency of Exposure	Number Exposed
0	150
1	300
2	200
3	180
4	160
5	140
6	120
7	100
8	80
9	60
10	10
Total	1500

Source: Created by the author.

Effective Frequency 2+

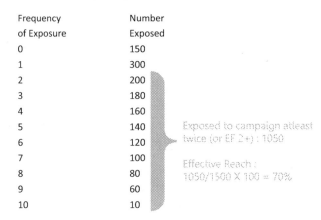

Frequency of Exposure	Number Exposed
0	150
1	300
2	200
3	180
4	160
5	140
6	120
7	100
8	80
9	60
10	10

Exposed to campaign atleast twice (or EF 2+) : 1050

Effective Reach : 1050/1500 X 100 = 70%

FIGURE 3.1 Effective frequency at 2+.

Source: Created by the author.

Effective Frequency 5+

Frequency of Exposure	Number Exposed
0	150
1	300
2	200
3	180
4	160
5	140
6	120
7	100
8	80
9	60
10	10

Exposed to campaign atleast 5 times (or EF 5+) : 510

Effective Reach : 510/1500 X 100 = 34%

FIGURE 3.2 Effective frequency at 5+.

Source: Created by the author.

However, as we know, the notion of reach and Average Frequency was not of much help, given the fact that different patterns of media exposure might result in the same reach and Average Frequency. Later, with the advent of computers, media planners were able to work with frequency distributions. This not only told them how many people were exposed, but how many were reached at various levels of exposure.

During this time, in 1972, Herbert Krugman came up with a three-exposure theory which described a sequence of consumer responses to television advertising. In simple terms, he said that the first time a consumer sees an ad, he asks, 'What is it?'; the second time, his response is 'What of it?'; and the third exposure is either a reminder or the beginning of disengagement.

While Krugman was talking of a cognitive response to advertising, the magic number three carried an instant appeal. Later, Colin McDonald's research too substantiated this claim of three exposures. Subsequently, the book on Effective Frequency by Michael Naples in 1979, lent a lot of respectability to the concept, and it played a huge role in how media planning was done and evaluated. The key conclusions in Naples's book were (Naples, 1979):

- One exposure has minimal effect on the target consumer
- That media planning should prioritize frequency over reach
- The optimum frequency should be 3 within a purchase cycle
- Increasing frequency beyond 3 would build advertising, but would do so at a diminishing rate

This created a thumb rule of 3, which continued to hold forth till as late as the early 90s, when John Philip Jones came up with his theory of advertising effectiveness.

How Does One Arrive at an Effective Frequency Number?

There is no one universally right way to arrive at the level of Effective Frequency. At the Effective Frequency Conference organized in 1982 by the Advertising Research Foundation, Joseph Ostrow of FCB agency presented a reckoner (Ostrow, 1982). There are numerous models used by different agencies across the world that help them arrive at a certain number. Each model is slightly different from the other. However, the operating logic behind each model is similar – it is based largely on the factors that influence the levels of Effective Frequency as discussed earlier in this chapter.

Ostrow's model assumed a base Effective Frequency of 3, and then it was up-weighted or down-weighted based on marketing, creative, and media factors. The model works on the following three factors:

1. Marketing Factors
   a. Established brands vs new brands
   b. High market share vs low market share
   c. Well-known brand vs less well-known brand
   d. High brand loyalty vs low brand loyalty
   e. Long purchase cycle vs short purchase cycle
   f. Infrequent use of product vs frequent use of product

2. Copy Factors

    a. Simple copy vs complex copy
    b. Uniquely differentiated copy vs ordinary copy
    c. Continuing campaign vs new campaign
    d. Product sell copy vs image sell copy
    e. Single-copy campaign vs multiple-copy campaign
    f. New message vs older message
    g. Large ad units vs smaller ad units

3. Media Factors

    a. Low advertising clutter vs high advertising clutter
    b. Compatible editorial environment vs non-compatible editorial environment
    c. High attentiveness vs low attentiveness
    d. Continuous advertising vs flighted advertising
    e. Few media used vs many media used
    f. Opportunities for media repetitions vs few opportunities for repetition

For each parameter if we need a lower frequency, we subtract 0.2 or 0.1 from the base frequency of 3. For example, if the brand is established, then we need lower frequency, so we subtract either 0.2 or 0.1 from the base frequency of 3 depending on how established the brand is. Similarly, as we move towards factors where we need a higher frequency, we add either 0.1 or 0.2 to the base frequency of 3 depending upon how strong the factor is. So if a brand was new, had a low market share, was less well known, had a low loyalty, had a short purchase cycle, and was a daily use product. In this case, the marketing factors would add a value of 1.2 to the Effective Frequency (0.2 for each factor).

Similarly, we evaluate the creative factors and assign scores. Assume those factors add up to a value of 0.8. Similarly, we evaluate the media factors and say, these factors add a value of 1.0 to the Effective Frequency. Combining the values of the three factors, we get an Effective Frequency of 5 (base frequency of 3 + 1.2 from marketing factors + 0.8 from creative factors + 1.0 from media factors).

Now, one could say that some of these variables are subjective in nature and ask how one evaluates what rating to give such variables. Yes, there is an element of subjectivity and individual judgement involved, but the correct way to arrive at this is to have a joint discussion with the Account Planning team and the advertiser to arrive at some sort of consensus on the scale. This would still be largely based on judgement and would still be subjective, but at least it would have all the decision-making constituents on the same page as far as objective setting is concerned.

Usually, Effective Frequency levels are set for a 4-week period. This is primarily because that's taken as a planning cycle. Therefore, if someone has a 3-month campaign, the levels of Effective Frequency could be moderated in month 2 and further down in month 3.

How Do We Find Effective Reach?

In an ideal situation, the advertiser would like to reach 100% of the target audience at the Effective Frequency level. But given the media consumption habits of the target audience, and given the reality of 'diminishing returns', one has to arrive at an 'optimized level of reach'. Plan optimizers are used to arriving at the optimum reach at the desired Effective Frequency level. If we assume the Effective Frequency is set at 5+, and the optimized reach at this level is, say, 35%, it means that in the concerned market, at a 5+ Effective Frequency level, 35% is the optimum reach possible. If we want to reach, say, 50% at 5+, then we will have to travel down the diminishing returns curve. What this means is that beyond 35%, for every incremental reach percentage, we need a higher percentage of incremental GRPs. This essentially means one needs to spend more to buy more GRPs, but the percentage of incremental reach at 5+ will be lower because diminishing returns in this market will set in at 35%. Therefore, one needs to make a call between getting 100% reach and not travelling too far down the diminishing returns curve. If we travel too far down, then we're building inefficiencies in the plan. There are several ways in which one tries to extend the diminishing returns curve while planning campaigns – one way is to add a different medium, because a new medium will duplicate less than the current medium will with itself. This is also a strong argument for a media mix. We'll discuss more of this when we discuss media target setting.

Coming back to Effective Frequency, typically, the levels are set for 4 weeks and it typically is used for one medium at a time. We do not have multi-media optimizers, and a print plan is evaluated separately and a TV plan is also evaluated separately.

How Is Effective Reach Different from Ordinary Reach?

Effective Frequency is the level at which communication takes place, and Effective Reach is the reach at the level of Effective Frequency. Reach, as discussed in the basic concepts chapter, is the total number of different people reached by the campaign at least once.

While a plan may have reached 90% of its intended target audience, it may have effectively reached only 50% of its target audience. This would depend on the Effective Frequency level identified for the campaign. Assume that the Effective Frequency identified for the campaign is 3+, and that only

50% of the target group have been exposed at this level. Then from a media perspective, 50% of the target audience have been effectively communicated to. The balance 40% people to have been reached, but not sufficiently enough for them to understand the communication. Plan optimization techniques help maximize reach at the level of Effective Frequency.

If Effective Frequency is defined as 1+ for a campaign, then Effective Reach and ordinary Plan Reach are the same.

But What Was the Debate around Effective Frequency?

While Krugman came up with a three-exposure theory which was further strengthened by

Colin McDonald's research and Michael Naples's book on Effective Frequency, the concept of Effective Frequency was not challenged till the early 90s, when John Philip Jones came up with his theory of advertising effectiveness. Before proceeding further, it might be pertinent to take another look at what Krugman actually meant (Krugman, 1972):

- Krugman believed that there's nothing called a fourth, fifth, or sixth exposure. He believed that these are all repeats of the third exposure.
- Krugman spoke of exposure from a psychological point of view, noting that the first exposure gets a 'What is it?' kind of response from the consumer, the second exposure gets a 'What of if?' kind of response from the consumer, and the third exposure actually just serves as a reminder to the consumer. If the consumer finds the message relevant, then the third, fourth, and all subsequent exposures keep serving as reminders. If the consumer doesn't find it relevant, then he/she would 'put it out of their minds' till such time it is of use to them.
- He said that the advertising world believed in the myth that if one doesn't repeat the message often, consumers would forget it.

Therefore, Krugman simply said that there are three levels of exposure in psychological terms and not media terms – curiosity, recognition, and decision. What Krugman calls 'frequency' is not what media planners would call 'frequency'.

A closer look at Naples's book on Effective Frequency however, clearly stated that three exposures are what are the most effective (Naples, 1979). His key conclusions were:

- One exposure of any message had little impact generally, and worked only in some minor cases
- With one exposure being ineffective, media planners should focus on increasing frequency rather than reach

- That though two exposures to a message should be good enough between purchase intervals, the optimal number should be three exposures. If one optimized a media plan for higher frequencies, it would build advertising effectiveness, but would do so at a diminishing rate.

John Philip Jones took a very serious look at this entire idea called effective frequency and through his work on how advertising works. According to Jones, Naples's book was largely based on the findings of Colin McDonald's research, and that research according to him was a small-scale experiment done once in one market, and therefore was not conclusive enough for the media industry to wholeheartedly embrace the three-hit theory as the golden rule in media planning. This opened up arguments across the media planning world, and there were numerous unending debates. To put this issue onto centre stage, the Advertising Research Foundation organized an Effective Frequency Research Day in November 1994 in New York.

Proceedings of the Advertising Research Foundation Seminar, New York, November 1994

As per the International Federation of the Periodical Press 1994, key papers presented were as follows:

1. Colin McDonald presented a paper on his understanding of effective frequency.
2. Donald Evanson presented a study of media plans which proved that the usage of Effective Frequency in media planning was declining.
3. Jim Spaeth presented a study based on Nielsen household panel data and concluded that converting low brand loyal users to heavy brand loyals should be the central aim of media planning.
4. Erwin Ephron argued that weekly reach maximization and targeting the exposure closest to the purchase occasion are the most effective. These were the cornerstones of the recency theory that he postulated.
5. Leo Bogart, in his argument, rejected the idea of following a single model for all kinds of ad campaigns, and called for more research to be conducted on the issue.
6. Mark Maiville spoke about how consumers processed information and the value of advertising repetition from a cognitive psychology perspective.
7. Paul Dyson of Millward Brown suggested that brands should consider pre-testing to understand advertising efficiency. He spoke about base probability as 'the probability that an individual will recall the brand

being advertised after seeing the ad once', and how each ad must be pre-tested to find its own base probability.

8. Hugh Cannon and Ronald Kaatz suggested using 'Effective Response' as against Effective Frequency.

Therefore, from the 60s to the early 90s, the entire scene on the usage of Effective Frequency was very chaotic and full of confusion. A part of this was the absence of large-scale single source research which conclusively proved a point. It was only after Jones published his book in 1995 that the industry started questioning things and started looking at newer ways to look at advertising and its effects.

The Aftermath of Effective Frequency Research Day

Colin McDonald acknowledged that one exposure can be effective in a *majority* of circumstances and not a *minority* of circumstances, as Naples said in 1979. The bottom line is that McDonald now believes that one exposure opportunity to see within a purchase cycle can potentially have a beneficial sales effect for most typical brands. He also acknowledged that both his theory and Krugman's theory were misinterpreted in the context of Effective Frequency. Naples also acknowledged that Jones's STAS (Short Term Advertising Strength) measure was the way forward for the industry. Jones's theory of STAS and the way forward on recency theory by Erwin Ephron then paved the way forward for the industry.

Jones suggested that Effective Frequency should be applied in exceptional and not normal circumstances. He gives three examples:

- Effective Frequency should be used for new brands and new campaigns. However, he cautions that this should be only a temporary strategy to initiate the campaign, and not a permanent strategy for the brand.
- Effective Frequency should be used for highly seasonal brands. Since the sales window is short, the advertiser could focus on the Effective Frequency strategy despite the fact that it would produce diminishing returns.
- Effective Frequency should be used for campaigns that target building up a consumer base in a very short window, for example publication subscription campaigns.

Jones had done a lot of work with single source data, and his research covered 78 American brands across 12 product categories for 2000 households covering over 1,00,000 purchase occasions. Later this was revalidated with similar research in Germany, and these findings were also validated by some other independent researchers, including McDonald.

According to Jones, the best-known response curves hypothesized for advertising response curves were:

1. *Diminishing Returns Response function*: The first dose of advertising boosts sales response, and all additional doses have a diminishing effect. Figure 3.3 shows what the graph looks like.
2. *S-Shaped Response Function (threshold effect)*: This curve describes the Effective Frequency 'threshold'. From the first to the third dose of advertising, the sales response increases and peaks at 3, which is the 'threshold' or Effective Frequency. Thereafter, the response curve declines in a pattern of diminishing returns. Figure 3.4 shows how the graph looks.

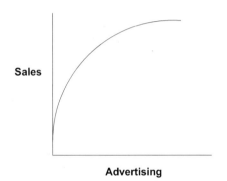

Diminishing Returns Response Function

FIGURE 3.3   Diminishing returns response curve.

Source: Created by the author.

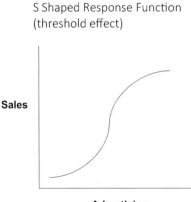

S Shaped Response Function
(threshold effect)

FIGURE 3.4   S-shaped response curve.

Source: Created by the author.

According to the findings of Jones's study, the prevailing pattern of response for repeat purchase packaged goods follows a pattern of diminishing returns. The greatest sales effects come from advertising one day before the purchase, fewer sales come from advertising 2 days before, fewer still 3 days before, and so on. Jones's STAS is essentially a measure intended to show whether an ad is being responded to, in the sense that it makes a purchase which follows it more likely.

What Is STAS?

STAS is defined as the brand share of category purchases when there has been advertising OTS during the previous 7 days (Stimulated STAS), compared with the brand share when there has been no advertising during the previous 7 days (Baseline STAS), presented as an index (Jones, 1995a, 1995b, 1995c). A positive STAS Index (greater than 100) means that the ad campaign is 'working' and is helping generate repurchase. A negative STAS Index (below 100) means that the campaign is not working, or that the competitors are doing a better job.

Based on this, Jones's key conclusions were:

- A positive STAS is important for a brand's long-term success. In Jones's study, 70% of the brands had a positive STAS and 30% had a negative STAS.
- Since the response curve is sharply diminishing, two or more than two exposures to advertising added hardly anything more to the sales effect generated by the first exposure. Therefore, he said 'One is enough'. This became an important finding for the continuity theorists who championed the recency argument.

Another researcher, Walter Reichel of A:S Link, did similar research, and his core finding was similar. He too says that advertising exposures one day before the purchase result in higher brand shares of category purchase.

These findings provided a support for continuity scheduling, the theory of which says that it is important for a brand to 'be there' at the time when it is relevant to the consumer – and this is what 'recency' is all about.

The Recency Theory

The theory rests on a simple premise that since consumers are in the market every day to buy products, the goal of media planning should be to influence these daily purchases. Therefore, the theory postulates that planners should focus on continuity of advertising and maximizing reach.

Erwin Ephron has been at the forefront of research on the recency theory, and according to him, recency is based on a couple of very simple premises (Ephron, 1995):

- Consumers buy products because of an inherent need, and things happening in their lives, not just because of advertising. If the toothpaste tube has got over, or it's about to, that's when the consumer starts thinking about buying toothpaste, and likewise for most other products. Certain things happen in everyday life that trigger the need to buy. And, advertising works best when there are people ready to buy. Therefore, targeting the message becomes important. From a recency standpoint, there are two important considerations – which consumers are ready to buy, and when are they in the market? If we get this right, then a single exposure to the consumers will work.
- The closer the message to the moment of purchase, the higher the chances of it influencing brand sales. Therefore, timing of advertising becomes critical.

Therefore, *when* a person gets a message is more important than *how many* messages he gets. This is because advertising just before the purchase brings about a higher brand share, and because purchases are happening every day, it is important that media focuses on continuity of advertising. And it makes better sense to reach three people rather than one person three times, and recency approach favours Reach Maximisation. Therefore, the three key recency arguments are:

1. Timing of the message is critical.
2. Continuity of advertising presence. More weeks make better sense than more media weight.
3. Reach over frequency. Because one exposure before purchase is enough, it is important to reach out to many more people and influence that many more brand choices. It is important, however, to get the timing right.

Implications on Planning

Recency impacted the traditional way of planning and thinking about media. The key areas of change are:

1. *Shorter planning interval*: The planning cycle was generally taken as 4–6 weeks. Most media plans were optimized to deliver a certain level of reach and frequency during this period. Recency changes this thought a little bit. As per this, weekly planning should be the unit of planning. A 4-week planning cycle worked towards accumulating reach and had a variable

pattern of delivery during each week. A weekly planning schedule would help minimize weekly fluctuations in media deliveries.

2. *Reach maximization*: While traditional thinking was to understand Effective Frequency for a brand, and then optimize reach at the level of EF, in contrast, recency favours reach over frequency. As per the theory, since one exposure is enough, it is important to reach out to as many different people as possible. While earlier planning media weights were reflected in terms of 4+/50 (Optimize plan to deliver a 50% Effective Reach at a 4+ Effective Frequency), the recency theory could well say 1+/90 (optimize plan to deliver a 90% Effective Reach at a 1+ Effective Frequency). This, coupled with weekly planning, marked a major change. One needs to maximize reach every week versus reaching people at a certain EF level over a 4-week period.

3. *Message dispersion*: How does one maximize or accumulate reach? By reducing duplication in the media plan. The less duplication the vehicles in the plan have, the higher the reach build. We discussed this in the earlier chapter on basic concepts when we discussed the topic of duplication. By scattering the brand message across various types of media, and by scattering the message across different vehicles within the selected media, reach maximization could be achieved. So for instance, in TV planning, one would look at spreading the message throughout the day across different dayparts, and try to maximize reach. In Print, one would try to cycle though the various sections of the newspaper, or in magazines, one would try to cycle through various genres, in radio through various dayparts, and so on. The underlying thought is to minimize duplication within the media plan, and maximize reach. All media selection no doubt will continue to be based on the target audience's media consumption habits and intensity. This thought was a major departure from the EF approach, where a certain degree of duplication was necessary – after all, you had to reach one person say three or four times for him to understand the message.

4. *Continuity*: Since consumers are there in the market every day, it is important that advertising focus on continuity. More weeks of advertising should be favoured over fewer weeks of higher intensity. How this works is that one needs to find out weekly brand purchases and identify the most important weeks which account for a significantly large portion of the sales, and try to cover those weeks with the objective of maximizing reach. However, it is important that a certain minimum weekly weight is arrived at. Therefore, maximize reach and continuity are the two important tenets from a media weight setting point of view.

According to recency theorists, this theory applies across most products. Though there are a lot of arguments in terms of whether one exposure will be enough, whether a continuity pattern of ours might get marginalized with concentrated bursts of competitive advertising, what the impact of the purchase cycle is, can this approach work with premium brands targeting a niche audience, how do I manage my SOV goals, what if I am into brand building, what about a brand launch situation, and so on. There are a lot of arguments and counter arguments doing the rounds, but the most effective approach as outlined by Jones (1997) is:

- Aim to cover a substantial proportion of the brand's target group once every week with as little duplication as possible. 'Substantial proportion' is a judgement call.
- To achieve this, determine the optimum number of weekly GRPs and establish the best media and dayparts to use in order to minimize audience duplication. These procedures require expert knowledge of the media consumption of audiences.
- Run your weekly advertising pattern for as many weeks as the budget permits. If there are any gaps, try scheduling in such a manner that the gaps in advertising are taken during off-seasons, or months will lower sales.

This was about recency as an approach and how it holds a counterpoint against the Effective Frequency theorists.

However, is recency the best fit solution to everything that defines media planning? Numerous experts have done work in this area and have suggested alternate ways to look at it. One of the foremost thinkers in this has been Simon Broadbent, director of BrandCon Limited, a brand consultancy. His books include *The Advertising Budget* and *Accountable Advertising*, and his work has influenced ad thinking over three decades. He came up with the concept of Adstock Modelling. This has implications on most aspects of media strategy – in particular the impact on scheduling and media weight setting.

But How Much Is Too Much?

Advertising Frequency is important to drive recall, but when you cross the fine line, it leads to ad avoidance, ad blocking, and, of course, wasting of money. The fine line is reached at a point when you start descending into diminishing returns for your brand. So you must know where to stop. It's a bit tricky, like our brain getting a signal 15 minutes later that you've overeaten. So we've got be a bit ahead to ensure that you've not overeaten. And this comes through discipline and practice rather than by looking over the shoulder of your fellow diners (competing brands). In times where mass media is increasingly fragmenting with linear TV acknowledging the power of digital TV (through OTT and alternative screens), it's important to remember the fine line, and more so when consumers are in control of their time, attention, and place of their media consumption. Cross the line too often, and you risk being avoided and losing all the gains your made before crossing the line. A good starting point is to work with media partners that have a quality environment and a great engagement quotient with their constituency of audiences.

As you have seen earlier in the chapter, there are no set rules to identify a precise effective frequency level, as there are both objective and subjective influences. Media has seen a huge level of fragmentation with the arrival of digital platforms, several new content players in the legacy media space, the huge prevalence of ad avoidance, and consumers multitasking while consuming media, the rising phenomenon of customized and dynamic targeted creatives – several factors have made connecting with audiences that much more difficult – all of these changing the way one would look at a frequency number. Post the Effective Frequency Day in 1994, new researchers have done some interesting work on frequency, and maybe, one could look at some broad guidelines emerging from these newer studies.

- A Nielsen Digital Brand Effect study (Australia, 2017) suggested an optimal frequency of 5–9 for campaigns that seek to generate awareness. However, for campaigns trying to drive intent and brand favourability, they could look at a frequency of 3–6.
- Research by Simulmedia (US, 2017) suggested that the optimum level of frequency is 5, after which every subsequent dollar spent would diminish in terms of efficiency.
- Another interesting study by Catalina Solutions (US) suggested that for FMCG categories, the highest Return on Advertising Spend (ROAS) was achieved after a single exposure. It also highlighted that the drop in ROAS is negligible as we move from one to five exposures. This finding is fairly consistent with the recency argument that suggests that a single exposure, closest to the moment of purchase, is the most effective.
- Research by Jennifer Lee Burton, Jan Gollins, Linda E. McNeely, and Danielle M. Walls examined the impact of frequency on purchase intentions. The research concluded that 'consumers who had seen an advertisement 10 or more times had higher reported purchase intentions than those in categories with less advertisement exposure'. The big conclusion from this study was that 'if a media planning goal is to maximize purchase intentions, media planners should strive for an average frequency of beyond 10 exposures'.

There are several other studies and pieces of research on the subject, each prescribing a certain number. Some studies show that fewer ads are more effective, while others suggest that a higher frequency is more effective. In fact, steering clear of another magic number or a golden rule, this is the time to think of media frequency not from the perspective of 'how many exposures', but 'what would it take for us to engage better with our target audience'. In fact, Erwin Ephron, the proponent of the recency argument, did have a change of heart in 2010. After seeing the impact of digital technology on how people consumed media, and with rising ad avoidance, he felt that a 'single exposure' might not be good enough, and it would need more than one exposure to be able to 'eventually' reach the consumer – and this calls for frequency.

However, excessive frequency can cost money besides just irritating your audience, therefore consider your experiences with frequencies and their impacts across campaigns to arrive at a better judgement of the frequency required that's best to help you achieve the brand task at hand. A higher frequency is required to break through the excessively high media clutter, to break open the threshold of ad avoidance by people, to be able to sufficiently engage with the consumers just enough to achieve the communication task. But go too high, and you risk losing all the gains made. In fact, with digital platforms gaining currency (which brings 'retargeting' capability), planners have been talking of fixing a lower and an upper cap on frequency – Frequency Capping.

The Issue of Frequency Capping

Typically, Effective Frequency is set as 2+, or 4+, and so on. But there are times when planners would also want to define the range of Effective Frequency, say 2–6. This would mean the Effective Frequency defined for the brand is a minimum of two exposures and also a maximum of six exposures. This is largely used to help control overexposure and waste. A plan optimized to deliver 2+ vs a plan optimized to deliver an Effective Frequency of 2–6 will be different both from channel/programme selection and in the plan cost and GRPs required. In the aforementioned frequency distribution example, if the Effective Frequency is set at 2–6, then Figure 3.5 illustrates this.

While, typically, Effective Frequency is used for TV planning, the concept holds just as well for other measured media like print, radio, etc.

In the digital world, programmatic leads you to 'the more, the merrier' kind of impression targeting. How often have we been bugged by banners that stalk us? Smart marketers have begun something called 'frequency capping' that limits the number of times an impression is delivered to the same consumer. AI takes this a notch higher by customizing frequency caps for each user, eventually improving retargeting, and efficiently using budgets. The jury is still out on its impact, though. In the hyper-competitive, dashboard-led, frantic marketplace, usually frequency is pushed lower in the hierarchy of media decision making – after all, customer irritation can be dealt with by customers themselves.

Effective Frequency 2–6

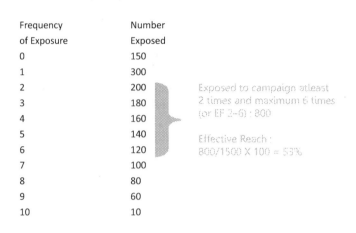

Frequency of Exposure	Number Exposed
0	150
1	300
2	200
3	180
4	160
5	140
6	120
7	100
8	80
9	60
10	10

Exposed to campaign atleast 2 times and maximum 6 times (or EF 2–6) : 800

Effective Reach : 800/1500 X 100 = 53%

FIGURE 3.5 Effective frequency with a frequency cap.

Source: Created by the author.

Data privacy calls for respecting the consumer. And respect we must. Yes they want to buy our products – and advertising will be an important force in helping them make their choices. However, what will increasingly become important in a 'direct-to-consumer' media world is the quantity (frequency) and quality of creative messaging that accompanies the micro targeting capabilities that we've developed. And in this world, one can't but emphasize enough the value of optimal frequency. To do enough justice to this, the industry would need a common language/currency across media platforms. This would enhance media efficiency, but most importantly improve the experience for consumers. In a rapidly changing landscape, cohesive measurement solutions will just be as important as the opportunity the landscape throws up.

As we move from an attention-surplus era to an attention-deficit era, the relationship between reach and frequency seems to have changed. While reach has got more importance, frequency has a dire need to be redefined. In simpler times, we determined optimal frequency for a creative message. Now with multiple, dynamic creative messages from the brand, frequency ought to be redefined. What a journey frequency has seen – from being central to planning, to the famously infamous Effective Frequency Day, and now seeking relevance in an altogether new way!

Chapter Summary

Effective Frequency is one of the earliest theoretical models followed by media planners. It began in the 1960s with Krugman's thinking. This was followed up by Colin McDonald's research and then by Michael Naples's 1979 book. In an era with little research data and an underdeveloped media market with limited options, the Effective Frequency formula appeared simple enough to follow.

Put simply, Effective Frequency is the level of frequency at which communication takes place. It was believed that contact with advertising is transient, and therefore one needs to repeat the advertising message for people to understand. But systematic hammering over a period of time may be wasteful. Therefore, it is important to know the threshold level of repetitions. This threshold level is the level of Effective Frequency.

Several models of Effective Frequency were created in the 70s and 80s to identify the right Effective Frequency for brands. Of the several models, the one created by Joseph Ostrow was very well recognized. All models of Effective Frequency acknowledged the role played by marketing factors, creative factors, and media factors in arriving at the ideal Effective Frequency for a brand's campaign.

Once the Effective Frequency level for a campaign is arrived at using one of the available models, the next step in planning was to identify how many people should one reach at the level of Effective Frequency. We all remember that reach is the total number of different people exposed to the campaign at least once or more. However, if the Effective Frequency for a campaign has been set at 4, then Effective Reach is the number of different people who have been exposed to the campaign at least four times.

However, media thinkers pursued the concept, and new findings by John Philip Jones in the early 90s questioned the basics of McDonald's research. According to Jones, the prevailing pattern of response for repeat purchase packaged goods follows a pattern of diminishing returns. The greatest sales effects come from advertising 1 day before the purchase, fewer sales come from advertising 2 days before, fewer still 3 days before, and so on. This set the stage for a completely new way of thinking about media. Following up on Jones's work, Erwin Ephron came up with the recency idea, which suggested that one should focus on maximizing reach and continuity.

As the media revolution unfolded with expansion of newspapers, magazines, hundreds of new TV channels, FM radio stations, and then the digital explosion, the question of frequency became important all over again. Consumer attention spans were short-lived, audiences were now fragmented across several media options, and ad avoidance was made easy through remotes, DVRs, and ad blocking technology. In such a scenario, would one exposure be enough? How many exposures are now required to break through the media clutter and catch consumer attention? Would too high a frequency start irritating consumers? These and several other questions are now under deliberation by media researchers and thinkers around the world. Different researches have thrown up different conclusions adding to the confusion. Some studies show that fewer ads are more effective, while others suggest that a higher frequency is more effective. In fact, steering clear of another magic number or a golden rule, this is the time to think of media frequency from the perspective not of number of exposures, but of what it would take for us to engage better with our target audience.

Over the years, the relationship between reach and frequency has changed. With a lot more research data available and the precision targeting capabilities afforded by the digital platforms, frequency is being looked at all over again. No other concept has had so much discussion and debate as much as the frequency question. While there are no uniformly accepted answers, brands around the world are using several ways to figure out what the most optimal frequency is for them to engage sufficiently well with their consumers.

Further Reading

Broadbent, Simon, "How Do Advertising Effects Decay", in his book *When to Advertise*, 1999.

Burton, Jennifer Lee, Jan Gollins, Linda E. McNeely, and Danielle M. Walls, "Revisiting the Relationship between Ad Frequency and Purchase Intentions", *Journal of Advertising Research*, Vol. 59, No. 1, 2019.

Chadwick, Michael, and Richard Frampton, "Is It Time to Move on from Frequency?", *Admap Magazine*, March 2019.

Ephron, Erwin (1995), "More Weeks, Less Weight: The Shelf-Space Model of Advertising", *Journal of Advertising Research*, Vol. 35, No. 3.

Hansen, Flemming, and Lotte Yssing Hansen, "Advertising Half-Lives for FMCG Brands and Markets", Copenhagen Business School (CBS), *Admap*, June 2002.

Jones, John Philip, "Keeping the Brand in the Window", in his book *When Ads Work*, 1995a.

Jones, John Philip, "The History of Single Source Research" in his book *When Ads Work*, 1995b.

Jones, John Philip, "The Short-Term Effect of Advertising, Passing through the Gate", in his book *When Ads Work*, 1995c.

Jones, John Philip, "What Does Effective Frequency Mean in 1997?", *Journal of Advertising Research*, Vol. 37, No. 4, July/August 1997.

Krugman, Herbert E, "Why Three Exposures May Be Enough", *Journal of Advertising Research*, Vol. 12, No. 6, 1972.

Naples, Michael J, *Effective Frequency: The Relationship between Frequency and Advertising Effectiveness*, McGraw-Hill, 1979.

Naples, Michael J, "Effective Frequency – Then and Now", *Journal of Advertising Research*, Vol. 37, No. 4, July/August 1997.

Ostrow, Joseph W, "Setting Effective Frequency Levels," in *Effective Frequency*, New York: Advertising Research Foundation, 1982.

Proceedings of Advertising Research Foundation Seminar, New York, November 1994, pp 193, *International Federation of the Periodical Press* 1994.

Sloane, Chris, "The Evolution of Effective Frequency", *Admap Magazine*, March 2019.

Sumner, Phil, "There Are No 'Golden Rules' for Optimal Frequency", *Admap Magazine*, March 2019.

White, Stephen, European Media Management "How Effective are your Frequency Models?" *Admap*, November 1999.

4

MARKETING STRATEGY AND MEDIA

Media is the last link of the chain in the marketing process leading up to the consumer. It is therefore absolutely critical that media planners take into account the marketing situation. Every marketer has a certain objective to achieve, and it is important that one should therefore look at aligning media goals and objectives with the marketing goals. In order to fully appreciate and implement this, it is vital for the media planners to understand the marketing situation of the brand in question. Amongst the most critical things that one must be completely aware of should be the brand, its functioning, and the needs of the consumer that it satisfies. What are the advantages that our brand has over its competitors? What is the distribution setup of the brand, and how strong is it versus other competing brands? How does the brand strength vary from market to market, and why? What are the price points? How does the consumer think about the category and the brand, and how does he/she decide to buy brands in this category? These and several other pieces of marketing-related information can be of tremendous help to the media planner. Each of these has implications for some element of the strategic media planning decisions. For example, in the edible oil category, there are some markets like Gujarat where consumers buy oil in bulk typically for 6 months or the entire year, while in other markets like Assam, frequency of purchase of edible oil is higher as they buy smaller pack sizes. This has implications on the pack sizes that the marketer introduces in different markets. From a media standpoint, it has clear scheduling and media weight implications.

Some of the key areas of marketing information and their implications on the media strategy decision variables are covered in this chapter.

DOI: 10.4324/9781032724539-4

Market Situation

a. *Brand and category sales, market shares, and growth patterns.* This is important to understand the relative strength of the brand. Category sales give an indication of market share movements. Growth rates across different markets are helpful in identifying priority markets. Information on all these factors is an important input while taking an important strategic call on which markets to advertise in. It helps in competitive benchmarking, in media weight setting, and in market prioritization.

b. *Geographic distribution of brand and category sales.* This is a very critical input required for market prioritization. Brand and category sales data across different markets are used as inputs in creating useful market planning indices like the Brand Development Index and the Category Development Index. Sales contribution data is juxtaposed against brand market shares to arrive at market priorities. Sometimes, sales contributions by different markets for both brand and category are also used to create a market prioritization grid. The strategic decision on where to advertise often hinges on brand and category sales across different markets.

c. *Market size.* Market size is an important input that helps in market identification and prioritization. It helps in analysing market potential and puts the overall media activity level into perspective. Usually, brands in the early growth stages look at the market size as a key input to market planning. They tend to focus on states where the market size is huge as compared to smaller states.

d. *Sales seasonality.* A critical input for media scheduling decisions, it plays an important role while taking a strategy decision on when to advertise. There are significant differences in sales seasonality patterns across categories. Brands often tend to mirror their sales seasonality and try to allocate heavy media weights when the sales are at their peak, and a lower media weight when the sales are low. Sometimes, promotional requirements or competitive action also could influence media scheduling decisions.

e. *Pricing effects.* It is important to understand the category dynamics of price changes. What happens to sales when there is a price rise vs the effects of a drop in price? How price sensitive is the market? How do different markets respond to price changes? These responses are critical inputs in categories which have frequent price changes. This has implications on media scheduling decisions, market prioritization, media weight setting, and media mix decisions.

f. *Distribution channels and strength in different markets.* Again, an important input required in the market prioritization process. Particularly in a country like India where different sales channels co-exist, and with a huge diversity in markets, distribution strength plays a huge role in which markets the brand is advertised. Across categories, we see examples of brands which are very strong in one particular region but don't have a great distribution network in other regions. A classic example is the tea category. Consumers across different parts of the country have different tea drinking habits and tastes, and brands have been quick to address these differences. For example, a brand named Wagh Bakri tea is immensely popular in Gujarat. While it is available in other parts of the country, the brand's following is much greater in its 'home' market, Gujarat, as compared to other states. There are examples of this kind in the edible oil, spices, and several other categories. If the distribution network is strong in a particular market, then it makes eminent sense to allocate higher media weights to these markets. At the same time, in markets where the distribution network is not strong enough, they are often pushed down in the order of market priorities.

Consumer Understanding

a. *Demographic profile*: This helps understand and identify the key consumer groups, and it forms the basis of evaluating and selecting media. Once the audience is defined in demographic terms, media planners look at the media habits of the defined audience as well as at their geographical spread. Audience media habits play a huge role in selecting the media mix and media vehicle selections. The geographical spread of audiences is an important input in market planning. This is also of some use in scheduling decisions.

b. *Psychographic profile.* Psychographics are the quantitative investigation of a consumer's personality, lifestyle, and values.

- Personality is a trait – a characteristic in which one person differs from another in a relatively permanent and consistent way – and personality is a combination of traits, e.g. reserved vs outgoing, conservative vs experimenting, etc.
- Lifestyle refers to how people live, how they spend their money and how they allocate their time (activities, interests, opinions)
- Values are enduring beliefs that a given behaviour or outcome is desirable or good. Types of Values are materialism, health, hedonism, technology (progress), youth, home, etc. Their usage is for understanding consumption patterns, market segmentation, new product ideas, and probably even creative insights.
- Psychographics go a step beyond a cold demographic definition of a target audience. A psychographic analysis gives us an inside peek into the mind of the consumer and gives a little more edge to the 'gut feel'-led decisions in the media process. Psychographics are of particular importance in media mix, media vehicle, and media scheduling decisions.

c. *Buyer behaviour*. How the consumer buys in this category gives a greater understanding of the consumer purchase behaviour. There are markets where consumers buy in bulk, while there are markets where consumers buy smaller packs and are more frequently seen in markets. Some consumer groups are highly price sensitive, while for others, price sensitivity is not an issue. It's important for the media planner to understand why buyers behave the way they do. What are the considerations that go in the mind of the consumer before making the purchase decision? A clearer understanding of buyer behaviour helps in taking better media decisions – be it media selection, timing and placement of ads, or even the intensity and frequency of advertising. These are critical qualitative inputs that help sharpen and fine-tune the media strategy. Erwin Ephron says that there is a small window preceding each purchase, and that the job of advertising is to influence that purchase, and the media planner's job is to put the message in that window. Therefore, timing and placement of the advertising is of critical importance.

d. *Brand users vs influencers vs decision maker*. Information about the brand's user vs the influencer vs the decision maker is a critical input that helps media planners decide to whom the communication should be targeted. There are times when all three of these are different people. In such cases, usually planners define the primary audience and a secondary audience. Given the rise of digital, the word 'influencer' now has a larger context. Brands rope in influencers to tell their 'followers' to think favourably about them. For example, if a washing machine is targeted at a young urban working couple, then both the husband and the wife would be targeted as users. In several categories, kids play a huge influencer role – be it in terms of selecting a colour for the car, or a brand of mobile phone, or which brand of ketchup should be bought. Therefore, this information about users, influencers, and decision makers gives a little bit more insight into the consumer involvement with the brand and the category, and it helps in identifying the target audience that receives the communication. In turn, this has implications on the media mix and vehicle selection decisions.

e. *Buying cycles*. It's important to understand purchase intervals or buying cycles of a brand. Some brands are bought every month, while others are bought less often, and there are several brands that have no defined purchase cycle. For example, edible oil might be on the monthly shopping list for most homes. From a media standpoint, this has clear media scheduling implications, and one could look at targeting buyers during the first and last weeks of the month. However, there are markets like Gujarat where edible oil is bought in bulk, as compared to some states in the North East, where they buy smaller packs. This implies that one must know during what time of the year bulk buyers buy, and time advertising accordingly. It wouldn't make sense to advertise all year round in such markets. It also means that in markets where smaller pack sizes are sold, the consumers are in the market more frequently, and therefore, one needs to follow a continuous scheduling strategy here. Therefore, as you can see, buying cycles have a huge impact on advertising scheduling decisions.

f. *When and how the product is used.* Apart from giving us a slightly better understanding of the brand and category usage patterns, it also gives an idea of the role the brand plays in the consumer's life. It allows us to look at various possible 'apertures' to target the consumer. These apertures are small windows of opportunity from the time when the consumer thinks about buying to the actual act of buying. It could also mean 'when' the consumer thinks about the category and its benefits. Targeting these 'when' moments and placing a message in this aperture is like the 'sweet spot' of media scheduling. This has implications on the media scheduling, media mix, and media vehicle selection decisions.

g. *Geographical distribution of consumers.* The geographical distribution of the target audience plays an important role in market prioritization. If the brand's objective is to convert medium users into heavy users, then the media planners would identify the medium users of the category and analyse their spread across different markets. Based on the geographical distribution (apart from considering other factors), of the selected audience, markets with a higher concentration of the audience would be ranked higher on priority and vice versa. Post this, media selection decisions are made based on the markets to be targeted thus.

Understanding the Brand

a. *Brand benefits/USPs.* What is the competitive edge our brand has over the others? This is a critical input in understanding the inherent strength of our brand. Is the benefit so powerful that once a consumer buys into it, the conversion rates are very high? If the answer to this is in the affirmative, it means the brand can do with relatively lower media weights. Some large brands also conduct research and some of them work on something called a 'Brand Pyramid', which talks about how the consumer moves from Awareness to being a Regular/Loyal brand user, and what the conversion rates are at each step. This could also help in identifying the media task for the brand. Digital media gives us the flexibility to target anywhere in this 'funnel'. Should we focus on getting as many people as possible to sample the brand, or should we focus on building loyalty initiatives? This is a critical input that helps in sharpening the 'gut feel' decisions in the media planning process.

b. *Brand History.* It is important for media planners to understand the brand's historical growth path. It allows us to delve deeper into the reasons for brand success or failure across different types of markets. This input helps in market planning and in the media strategic planning process. This data works as an important background information while taking key strategic decisions with respect to whom to target in which market, competitive benchmarking, and the media weight setting process.

c. *Consumer perceptions of the brand.* This is information that one typically gets from any custom research done on the brand. This helps us understand the positive and negative aspects of the brand, and works largely to aid in the qualitative decision making when it comes to media mix and vehicle selection decisions. For instance, when the cola companies got into a pesticide controversy in India, suddenly they all felt a rising wave of negative consumer perceptions about the brands. The foremost thing that came to their minds was 'How do we reassure the consumer about our purity and safety?', or 'How do we regain the trust of our consumers?'. Here, the goals of marketing and communication drastically changed from what they were always doing. They felt that they needed 'credible' media sources to communicate their new brand message of reassurance to their consumers. Suddenly, the cola companies, which were mainly into cricket and youth-related TV channels, changed tracks to news channels and to newspapers which were supposed to carry values of credibility. Also, they provided a so-called 'serious' environment for a message of this kind. This was a typical case of some brands getting into a controversy and changing tracks to address the negative perceptions about a brand. However, in the regular course of things too, at times some brands have perception issues in the market, and these need to be tackled by advertising. In terms of media, this has implications on media scheduling, media weight setting, media mix, and media vehicle selection decisions.

d. *Position in the lifecycle.* Every brand has a lifecycle – new, growth, maturity, and decline stages. Where the brand is in its lifecycle determines largely the overall marketing and therefore the media objectives. A brand in its growth stage would be largely focused on increasing consumer base and increase market share. This could have implications on market prioritization, as well as overall media objectives in terms of reach maximization. Contrast that with a brand in its maturity stage, which would focus more on retaining market shares and probably think of brand extensions and overall extension of the brand franchise. Media objectives here would be slightly different, and the brand probably would look at reinforcing messages rather than trying brand saliency building measures.

Understanding the Competitive Environment

a. *Category and brand advertising spending trend.* This is a critical input in understanding what competition is doing in terms of media. While doing a competitive analysis, media planners examine media mix chosen by competing brands, their scheduling patterns, and frequency and intensity of their media presence. They try to identify patterns of competitive behaviour across different markets. They analyse which markets the competing brands focus on. An analysis of Share of Voice trends is done and is seen with respect to their relative market shares across different markets. This analysis of competitive spending patterns serves as a critical input in deciding the media weight for the brand. It also serves as an important input in media mix and media vehicle decisions. Competitive spend tracking is a basic hygiene analysis done by planners before taking any major media strategy decision. Also, competitive tracking is done on a regular basis to keep a constant watch on the competing brands so that one could make course corrections depending upon competitive action.

b. *Our relative strength in media.* Are there some properties in media that our brand owns vs our competitors? For example some brands would like to own Cricket as a property, while some go with Bollywood and films, while some others go with game shows, and so on. What are some properties of our on which we can leverage our brand? How are we placed competitively in media compared to other brands? An understanding of this also helps in media weight setting, media scheduling, media mix, and media vehicle selection decisions.

Marketing Strategy Plans are about setting objectives that will help solve existing problems and take advantage of opportunities, determining how the product should be sold, the target audience, the role of various elements of the marketing mix, and how much should be spent. It is absolutely important for the media planner to be completely in sync with the marketing strategy and objectives of the brand in order to do justice to the brand and deliver true value. This is simpler stated than done. Given the reasons of confidentiality, there are times when it is not possible for marketers to share a lot of information with media agencies. However, an attempt must be made from both sides to get a clear understanding of the marketing objectives of the brand. If this is done, then the media objectives should also be completely in sync and work single-mindedly towards helping achieve the marketing objectives. Marketing objectives help give an overall sense of direction to the final media strategy and plan.

At times the sales strategy has implications on the media strategy. For example, if a sales promotion is being planned, the implication on media is that one would require quick reach and frequency buildup. In a situation of special pricing being announced, the implications on media are about building high reach in a short span of time. If some trade schemes have been announced, then those would require concentrated media inputs in relevant markets. If the marketing objective is to increase share with special effort directed only to the existing customer base, then the media objective would focus on the core target segment in the existing markets and increase frequency of exposure to advertising.

At a macro level, it is important for a media planner to align media objectives with the marketing objectives to deliver value to the plan. Various elements of the marketing strategy plan have clear implications on various elements of the media strategy decision variables. It is important, therefore, for a media planner to understand the marketing background for taking media decisions. This also underlines the importance of media briefing. More about this later when we discuss media briefing.

Chapter Summary

The process of media planning is closely intertwined with the marketing strategy of a brand. Media could be seen as an extension of the marketing team. It's the last link in the marketing chain before the brand eventually reaches the consumer. Therefore, it is very important that the marketing team and the media team are on the same page when it comes to understanding the brand and achieving marketing objectives. It's important to align media objectives with marketing objectives.

Some of the key areas of marketing information and their implications on the media strategy decision variables are:

- Brand and category sales, market shares, and growth patterns
- Geographic distribution of brand and category sales
- Market size
- Sales seasonality
- Pricing effects
- Distribution channels and strength in different markets
- Demographic profile of target consumers
- Psychographic profile of target consumers
- Buyer behaviour
- Brand users vs influencers vs decision makers
- Buying cycles
- When and how the product is used
- Geographical distribution of consumers
- Brand benefits/USPs
- Brand history
- Consumer perceptions of the brand
- Position in the lifecycle
- Category and brand advertising spending trend
- Our relative strength in media

Marketing objectives help give an overall sense of direction to the final media strategy and plan. At times the sales strategy has implications on the media strategy. In cases of sales promotion, one would look at a quick reach and frequency buildup. In cases of special price announcements, media would look at building high reach quickly. In cases of large mature brands, the focus would be on maintaining market shares with lowered media weights. In case of brands in the growth stage, media intensities would need to be kept high. When competitive pressures are high, media intensity needs to be readjusted. Various elements of the marketing strategy plan have clear implications on elements of media strategy.

Further Reading

Sissors, Jack Z, and Roger B Baron, *Advertising Media Planning*, McGraw-Hill, 2012.

5

MEDIA STRATEGY PLANNING DECISIONS – WHO IS THE TARGET AUDIENCE?

There are four critical dimensions in the strategic media planning process – Who (target audience), Where (which markets), When (media scheduling), and How Much (media weight setting). Answers to these four questions form the crux of media strategy. This gives a clear direction for implementation planning. In this chapter, we will discuss the first of these areas – the target audience.

Often known as targeting, this draws heavily from the segmentation techniques used by marketers. It boils down to defining the target audience in simple terms. However, as marketing complexities have grown over a period of time, segmentation techniques have undergone a huge change and are evolving constantly. As per some of the dominant studies on the subject, one could classify the evolution of targeting in four broad ways:

- The first phase was about trying to group people into different demographic segments.
- The second phase moved towards grouping people into various psychographic clusters/segments.
- The third phase, in which a lot of current thinking is taking place, is about mapping consumer relationships with brands and their purchasing behaviours and loyalty levels.
- The fourth phase is the current age, in which addressability and personalization are based on analyses of our digital footprints. At the same time, the rise of digital platforms has accelerated the scale and depth of the first three phases.

DOI: 10.4324/9781032724539-5

However, what we see in practice now, traverses all the four phases. We need to define audiences demographically to understand and address an important element of media strategy, optimize plans, and understand how many people one is reaching at what frequency levels and so on. Most media plan evaluation software needs a demographic descriptor to be able to churn out the reach and frequency delivered by the media plan. The second level is about understanding consumers from a psychographic point of view. These insights help to some extent in fine-tuning media mix and vehicle mix, and help in terms of getting the right brand associations. The third level of understanding of shopping behaviour, loyalty levels – all in a manner help in various elements of defining media strategy for a brand – be it in terms of identifying audiences, or markets or scheduling patterns, or even intensity levels of advertising. The fourth level is about targeting at scale and delivering personalized messaging to consumers.

Reaching out to the right audience is a sure way to begin plan optimization. Should you try to reach everyone, or should you reach the consumers who matter to you? The math is very simple. In a paper written long back by Philip Walker, he suggested a very interesting and simplistic (and a very practical) way of looking at targeting and its effects. According to Walker (1998), good targeting does two things:

- Targeting improves advertising efficiency. When we target the right people based on their demographics, psychographics, and media consumption patterns, it avoids wastage and thereby improves advertising performance.
- Targeting improves advertising effectiveness. When we dig deeper and understand the degree and intensity of consumer engagement with different media, it helps in better selection of media, which eventually makes advertising work harder.

This is the most practical application of targeting in today's media planning context in India. We will focus more on the ways of defining audiences in this chapter, and take the discussion of their media habits, etc., in the chapter on media mix selection.

The Need for Defining an Audience

Why do we need to define an audience for a brand? There are a few reasons:

a. *The use of segmentation in marketing.* Not all products are meant for everyone. A very popular basic tenet of marketing principles was STP (Segmenting – Targeting – Positioning). Marketers have over a period of time adopted this concept, and products have been designed for different kinds of audiences. It's no longer the 'one size fits all' approach to marketing. Today, each brand is targeted at a certain kind of a person, and it is important for the media plan to address the right audience for the brand.

b. *Differences in purchase capacities.* Not all audiences are homogenous sets of people. Even if you look at the NCCS classification system in India, there are various classes, and each class is supposed to exhibit a different kind of purchase behaviour pattern. In the same category, different brands come at different price points, and these price points segment the market on the basis of a price bracket. At each price bracket, there is a type of customer depending upon individual purchase capacity. Take the example of the car category. There are cars ranging from 1 L to you-define-the-limit, and at every Rs 50,000 interval there is a car available. The audience for a Rs 10–12 L car bracket is very different from the audience for a Rs 3–4 L car bracket. Therefore, differences in purchase capacities make it necessary that we identify and address the communication to the right audience.

c. *Differences in purchase behaviour.* Different sets of audiences have different purchase habits. For instance, two people, say a corner Paan shop vendor and a junior executive, might be making the same amount of money per month. Therefore, their purchase capacities are similar, so to say. However, because of their differences in mindsets, their purchase behaviour patterns would differ. This difference in mindsets emanates from their educational background. This is what the earlier SEC system attempted to define – people with a similar occupation/education profiles would tend to behave in a similar manner when it comes to purchase behaviour patterns. The New Consumer Classification System (NCCS) takes it a step forward.

d. *Type of product.* Some products are meant for use by a certain type of audience, and it is important to target the intended audience. For instance, there are a range of men's products, some products meant for women, some for elderly people, some for the youth, and so on. Here, the product itself defines its audience.

e. *Driving marketing efficiency.* A well-defined audience gives you a better leverage to enhance marketing efficiency by delivering the right message to the right consumer, leading to brand growth. In that sense, it would also help reduce waste and eliminate inefficiencies in media spending.

Identifying and Defining an Audience

But how do we go about defining an audience? There are various ways, but no one formula that could help in defining the audience. There are a few methods which I will describe in this section with some illustrations, but they are by no means a complete set. There could be several other ways to define audiences. Let's discuss a few topline methods.

Based on the Experience of the Marketer

Different products are created for different kinds of audiences. Therefore, the first level of information comes from here – what kind of people is this product meant for, and who would be the likely buyer? This information need not necessarily be quantified, it could also be a small qualitative descriptor of the target audience. The media planner's role is to take this information forward, quantify it, and understand the audience's media consumption habits, thereby helping to create the strategic planning framework. As a first step, this input from the marketing team is absolutely critical and a very good starting point. For instance, if the brand is a very expensive watch – therefore, by default some basics like affordability, style consciousness, certain kinds of professions, age, gender – and some other things immediately come to mind. Contrast this with a mass brand of anti-dandruff shampoos – a different imagery starts building in the mind – one is thinking about a whole mass of people with dandruff issues, so on. Or in the Covid era, if it were a premium sanitizer brand, then one would think of an audience who would go the extra length to manage personal hygiene and stay safe. However, this is just the starting point – these definitions need to be further filtered and defined more precisely for media purposes. However we define the audience, we will eventually need to translate it into demographic variables (like age, gender, NCCS, income, etc.) so that one is able to evaluate the reach and frequency of the media plan targeted to reach this audience. Currently, all media plan evaluation software requires a demographic target audience definition against which a plan is evaluated.

Based on Product Usage Norms

You would have heard of the 80:20 norm, where 20% of the consumers account for 80% of the product consumption. In such a scenario, one would like to believe that this is the core audience for the brand, and this is the audience that must be targeted. Or alternatively at times for some kinds of products, marketers look at the potential audience and target them. For instance, for some kinds of durables if the penetration in, say, NCCS A & B is nearly 100%, then one looks at other segments where category penetration still has not reached a saturation level.

Based on Category Penetration Levels

Another simple way is to look at the category penetration across various demographics and try to identify an audience from there. For instance in the case of some durables, the higher the category penetration in a particular demographic group, the less one sees potential available. One might wish to target those segments of audiences where the category penetration is low. On the other hand, for some household-use FMCG products, the higher the category penetration in the audience segment, the better it is for targeting. Take the case of refrigerators, for instance. If it is an entry-level refrigerator brand, one might not want to target NCCS A if the category penetration is very high, say 70%, vs a penetration of, say 30% in NCCS B. Here, it might make sense to consider NCCS B as a more appropriate audience as compared to NCCS A. At the other extreme, say if one is talking about a regular ice cream – a category penetration of 90% amongst kids in the 12- to 15-year bracket vs a category penetration of 20% amongst 40- to 50-year-old adults. One might consider the 12- to 15-year age bracket with a higher category penetration as the one more appropriate. Therefore, the decision at times for audience selection would depend to some extent on category penetration levels depending upon how the brand is seen in the market and what the objectives would be.

In this example depicted in Table 5.1, NCCS A in markets like Delhi, Haryana, Punjab, and Rajasthan is almost saturated. Therefore, one might want to consider targeting NCCS B and C audiences in these markets. However, in UP, given the absolute large size of the market, one might still consider targeting NCCS A here.

Example: Table 5.2 depicts category penetration of an FMCG product category.

Looking at the data in Table 5.2, one could conclude that NCCS A1, A2, A3, B1, and B2 are clear segments that could be targeted. However, if the objective is to drive category adoption, then one would look at targeting segments where the category penetration is low.

Depending Upon the Campaign/Marketing Objectives of the Brand

Most often, this too sets the pace for identifying and defining the audience. For instance, the objective for a TV marketer could be upgrading normal TV

TABLE 5.1 Category penetration (%) of a consumer durable across NCCS

State	A	B	C	D	E	ABC
Delhi	87	76	61	42	28	74
Haryana	91	72	55	33	16	70
HP	13	6	-	-	-	5
Punjab	86	66	46	30	12	61
Rajasthan	85	65	51	26	11	63
UP	72	53	30	14	5	48

Source: Created by the author.

TABLE 5.2 Category penetration of an FMCG product category

NCCS	Category Penetration
NCCS A1	45%
NCCS A2	34%
NCCS A3	29%
NCCS B1	27%
NCCS B2	24%
NCCS C1	21%
NCCS C2	19%
NCCS D1	15%
NCCS D2	13%
NCCS E1	11%
NCCS E2	10%
NCCS E3	10%

Source: Created by the author.

owners to smart TV. While the communication might hinge on an exchange scheme, or may focus on superior TV viewing experience or any other product benefit, from a media point of view, the audience could be defined as normal TV set owners. Within this, one then does a further classification based on price points, etc. Alternately, the objective for this TV marketer could be that we want people to replace their older TV sets with new ones. The audience for media purposes could be defined as people who have purchased their last TV set 10 years ago or even earlier than that. Later, we could fit this into demographic descriptors, understand their media habits, and plan media accordingly. Yet another concept used in several product categories is Heavy-Medium-Light user information. At times the objective could be to convert Light users to Medium users, in which case our audience is all the light users of the product. Or at times, the objective could be to convert non-users into users. Here again, the audience definition is upfront. The important point to understand is that in every marketing objective, there is a hint towards the kind of audience that one needs to target. This could vary from category to category as there are different market dynamics, and at times it could vary for the brand from one campaign to the other depending upon the unique circumstances of the brand. But most times, the marketing objectives help in giving a sense of direction to target audience definition.

Example: Assume Table 5.3 reflects the hypothetical penetration of types of refrigerators by NCCS. If the objective is to target single-door owners to double-door or a higher size, then one would be able to identify the audience as NCCS A1, A2, A3 and B1. These are segments where the penetration of single-door refrigerators is high, and also may have the potential to convert to a higher size.

TABLE 5.3 Penetration of types of refrigerators by NCCS

NCCS	Single Door	Others
Total	26.3%	4.5%
NCCS A1	46.9%	41.0%
NCCS A2	63.6%	19.9%
NCCS A3	63.9%	0.0%
NCCS B1	50.9%	0.0%
NCCS B2	32.2%	0.0%
NCCS C1	20.3%	0.0%
NCCS C2	6.7%	0.0%
NCCS D1	1.5%	0.0%
NCCS D2	0.3%	0.0%
NCCS E1	0.0%	0.0%
NCCS E2	0.0%	0.0%
NCCS E3	0.0%	0.0%

Source: Created by the author.

Buying Decision Process

There are times when there is either a new product concept, or there is no clear direction from the marketing team on the audience; then one looks at the buying process involved. At times this could be aided by research, and at times it could also come through sheer experience in the market by observing everyday situations of consumer buying. For instance, for a high-end refrigerator with huge and tangible benefits over the standard refrigerator, one looked at this process. From here, one could find out that the woman of the house was the one who would realize the need for a better product and would appreciate the product benefits. She would look for confirmation of this through word of mouth and through information available in the public domain, like dealers, advertising, etc. For the actual purchase consideration, the husband too would get involved, as it is a high-end purchase and the evaluation of alternatives would also involve some technical feature comparisons. The purchase is typically done jointly, and the end user is again the woman. To put it into a framework, the proposer is the woman, the recommender is personal, public, and experiential sources, the chooser is the couple, the purchaser is either the couple or the male member of the family, and the user is the woman. To this framework, then, one adds the kind of market the product is going to be made available in, the price points and the kind of families that would see a huge plus in the product benefits offered, and then looks at defining the audience.

Targeting Consumers Who Account for a Large Part of the Consumption

In a few categories, we come across situations where one needs to identify which consumer segments are the ones that contribute to a large part of the consumption and target them as the primary audience. For example, Table 5.4 shows that in the case of the ice cream category, one might come across data which says that the age group 12–19 makes up 20% of the population but accounts for 40% of all the consumption occasions for the category. Based on this, one might want to define 12–19 yrs as the primary audience and then try to filter the definition further. This kind of method might work well typically for categories like colas, biscuits, juices, chips, hair oil, creams, and other categories in the food and personal care segment. A similar view was echoed in 2016, when Marc Pritchard, Procter & Gamble's CMO, declared that the company's approach to targeting on Facebook had been flawed, saying, 'We targeted too much, and we went too narrow. ... The bigger your brand, the more you need broad reach and less targeted media'.

Based on the NCCS-wise pattern of consumption presented in Table 5.5, one could derive the target audience as.

South and East: 12–34 yrs across all NCCS
North and West: 12–34 yrs in NCCS ABC
Apart from this, kids < 12 yrs are another primary audience

Based on Purchase Intentions and Purchase Behaviour

Some large brands to a constant customer conduct tracking research to find out brand/category usage patterns and study purchase behaviour of various consumer segments to find out intentions to purchase. Sometimes, this information is also used to define potential target audiences.

Targeting based on Consumer Responsiveness to Advertising

In current times, there is that much more emphasis on optimizing plans to reach the right audience. A lot of effort is made to minimize spillovers so that the ROI on advertising is better. In the United States, interesting research was done under the code name 'Project Apollo' that attempted to do precisely this – try to understand consumer responsiveness to advertising and use the findings for better media selection, as against targeting by demographics or even by purchase behaviours. As per a paper presented by Joan FitzGerald at the Worldwide Multi Media Measurement (WM3) in Budapest in June 2008, some findings from Project Apollo were presented. The research was based on data captured at a single source level through the use of Arbitron's Personal Portable Meters and a subset of households from Nielsen's Home Scan service which captured purchases of the panel households. While the sample size was small, it was a fairly large-scale experiment involving 5000 households over an 18-month period during 2006 and 2007. The findings demonstrated how consumer responsiveness to advertising could have implications on the media selection and how that has the potential to change

TABLE 5.4 Distribution of consumption occasions of ice cream across zones by age

	East	North	South	West
Occasions/month	112 L	793 L	387 L	666 L
12–14 yrs	23%	21%	22%	15%
15–19 yrs	19%	21%	24%	19%
20–24 yrs	14%	15%	16%	17%
25–34 yrs	24%	21%	20%	23%
35–44 yrs	10%	13%	9%	13%
45-54 yrs	6%	6%	5%	7%
55+yrs	4%	4%	3%	4%

Source: Created by the author.

TABLE 5.5 Distribution of consumption occasions of ice cream across zones by NCCS

	East	North	South	West
Occasions/month	112 L	793 L	387 L	666 L
NCCS A	17%	27%	16%	20%
NCCS B	21%	28%	24%	23%
NCCS C	20%	21%	24%	26%
NCCS D	20%	13%	18%	17%
NCCS E	22%	12%	18%	14%

Source: Created by the author.

optimizations in the future. However, much would depend on industry support to fund such studies at a large scale. In India, I'm not aware whether such a large-scale experiment on single source data has been made yet. IRS does attempt to capture it in a very broad manner through media usage and products/brands bought/used. However, that is not a continuous study of purchase occasions being linked back to media exposure. In the future, the possibilities with this kind of research are endless and can have huge implications on the way media is planned and bought.

Behavioural Targeting

Much has been said and written about this new method. Particularly relevant to the online media where it is possible to study the so called "return path" as termed by Joe Mandese (2008). Behavioural targeting, as the name suggests, is about targeting consumers by studying their behaviour patterns. The most omnipresent example of this is Google serving keyword search ads based on the search behaviour of people. Based on the online behaviour patterns, online planning agencies started targeting people on websites frequented by them. Therefore, for instance, if tech enthusiasts also visit gaming and chat sites, then it might be a good idea to target these people on their usage of such sites other than just the tech sites. However, it has limited usage for traditional media, as it's not possible to track data based on 'return path'; but with more developments, things might change. Behavioural parameters along with demographic and psychographic attributes can lead one to a very sharp definition and understanding of the target audience.

Targeting based on Geodemographics

While the term sounds very fancy, it simply means classifying people by the locality or neighbourhood where they live. While strictly speaking, this is a little bit of a cross between two elements of strategic planning – it involves both whom to target and in which markets. An example of geodemographic targeting is targeting home owners – one does a scan of all the localities/ wards (if you may say), find out in which wards we have a higher percentage of home owners, and target those wards specifically. Therefore, geodemographics involves a demographic filter applied to a geographical region to arrive at the final target. The first demonstration of geodemographics was in 1979 when Baker, Bermingham & McDonald of BMRB presented a paper at the March 1979 MRS Conference, which showed how a neighbourhood classification system could add very useful segmentation to the Target Group Index (TGI). Though not widely used in planning, it is of particular use when looking at planning for local retail establishments. A specific current example is when we were planning for a community newspaper, we used geodemographic targeting as one of the methods to arrive at the final audience and its markets within a city.

> At the same time, as large metros keep growing, we see the emergence of scattered pockets of affluence – be it gated colonies or condominiums. Therefore, one could also assume that these pockets of affluence could have some sort of psychographic homogeneity as well. With the pandemic year of 2020, we saw these gated clusters closing within even further – including even their social life being within the geographical boundaries of these clusters. Since these are high potential consumers, there's a growing need to target these small, homogenous geographical clusters within a city.

The preceding examples show some illustrative broad methods of identifying target audiences, and there could be several other methods depending upon the unique nature of your brand, the marketing situation, and the category. From a media planning perspective, most audiences usually are defined on either or both parameters – demographics and psychographics.

Demographically, audiences tend to get defined on parameters such as gender, age, NCCS, occupation, income, and education. Therefore, you are likely to see audiences being defined as 'NCCS A, Males, 25+ yrs', or 'Females, 25+, NCCS ABC', or 'All Adults 18–35 yrs, SEC NCCS', or 'Males, 35+, NCCS A, MHI 25,000 +', and so on.

These definitions help quantify the size of the audience. They also help in the market identification process and are of great use when it comes to finally evaluating the media plan deliveries in terms of reach and frequency. Since the planning software allows you to evaluate a media plan based on demographic definition of the audience, these definitions are of great help. The plan evaluation tells you what percentage of the audience the plan has reached and at what level of frequency. This is also an essential part of the planning process, and demographic definitions of the target audience help one do this. In practice, most brands have a defined demographic definition.

However, given the nature of demographic descriptors, it does not really give an insight into the mind of the audience we are talking about. Can you try to imagine an 'NCCS ABC, Female, 25+ yrs'? It's a very cold definition of an audience, and it doesn't tell you much about the person. If one looks around today, there are multiple media options that a planner has to choose from. Not all these decisions can be based on numbers alone. There are what we call 'qualitative factors' that also go a long way in defining the final components of a media plan. Apart from other information available about the brand, its history, and critical inputs from the marketing objectives of the brand, psychographic profiling of the audience also lends a huge direction to the so-called 'subjective decisions' in media.

What Are Psychographics?

Psychographics are the quantitative investigation of a consumer's personality, lifestyle, and values.

Personality is a trait – a characteristic in which one person differs from another in a relatively permanent and consistent way. Personality is also a combination of traits, e.g. reserved vs outgoing, conservative vs experimenting, etc.

Lifestyle refers to how people live, how they spend their money, and how they allocate their time (activities, interests, opinions).

Values are enduring beliefs that a given behaviour or outcome is desirable or good. Types of values are materialism, health, hedonism, technology (progress), youth, home, etc. Their usage is for understanding consumption patterns, market segmentation, new product ideas and probably even creative insights. In the United States, audiences are classified into different homogenous psychographic sets, and the system is known as the VALS classification system. In India, however, there is no standard classification system yet, and people use various ways (including custom research) of classifying the Indian population.

The basic utility of psychographic profiling is that it helps us go a step beyond a cold demographic description of the target audience; it helps us uncover what this audience does and buys, it tells us how to best communicate with them, and it helps us gain insight into why the audience behaves the way it does. These insights are of tremendous use to aid decision making in media planning, they could give some real inputs from an account planning perspective, and they can even aid in marketing decisions.

While a lot of brands do their own custom research to get a deeper understanding of the audiences and their purchase behaviour patterns, a syndicated study known as Target Group Index (TGI) helps us do a psychographic analyses of various kinds of audiences.

Target Group Index (TGI)

TGI is a global network of single source data across countries. Used primarily for advertising, marketing and media decision making, TGI is a very useful tool to sharpen planning. TGI India provides information and insights across a huge range of product and service categories that touches upon consumers from different demo-geographic backgrounds. It offers an understanding of their mindsets, special and individual habits, values, and beliefs.

The insights offered by TGI cover:

- Product and brand usage in 18 sectors, typically containing a total of around 400 product groups and 3000 brands
- Leisure activities
- Use of services
- Media exposure and preferences
- Attitudes and motivations
- Demographics
- Sample: around 40,000
- SEC: ABC, Age Group: 15–55 yrs

Information capture is through a face-to-face interview for the readership questionnaire, and a leave-behind questionnaire on product and media. The respondents are given 2 weeks to fill out the questionnaire. This is followed up by telephonic follow-ups and 100% scrutiny.

Kind of Information Available through TGI

While TGI captures data for brands and products and demographics, at the heart of TGI is information on attitudes and values of target consumers.

This it does through measuring responses to around 200-odd attitudinal and behavioural statements to measure the deeper cognitive perception that influences a consumer's attitude and subsequent behaviours.

Specifically, TGI covers the following information:

a. Media consumption habits: Apart from interaction with various kinds of media, TGI also covers time spent with each medium. You could map a day in the life of your target consumer and find out what are the various kinds of media apertures you have to engage with him. The data captured covers traditional media and also extends to include information on direct sales, word of mouth, teleshopping, OOH, mobiles, etc.
b. Changing lifestyle trends: TGI helps map changes in lifestyle through their database captured at various intervals.
c. Segmentation: Advanced users of TGI prefer using cluster and correspondence analysis. Cluster analysis helps in identifying underlying psychographic segments within a TG displaying how far a TG is homogenous or heterogeneous. Correspondence helps to understand graphically the association between brands or products and other variables like attitudes, behaviour, media, etc.
d. Demographic information.
e. Education levels of respondents.
f. Body Mass Index.
g. Languages.
h. Social classifications based on National Social Grade and TGI Socio Economic Levels (SEL).
i. Income and household composition and home ownership.
j. Data on sectors such as food, appliances and household durables, pets and pet food, toiletries and cosmetics, health and pharmaceutical products, shopping, retail and clothing, sports and leisure, sweet and salty snacks, tobacco products, non-alcoholic and alcoholic drinks, motoring, holidays and travel, and financial services.

Applications of TGI Data

TGI data could be used for any or more of the following areas:

a. Creative and communication planning
b. Media planning
c. Media buying/selling
d. New business strategy
e. Sponsorships and sales promotions
f. Market segmentation
g. Market trends
h. Brand management

An Example of Using Psychographics to Segment Audiences: Segmenting the Hair Oil Market

Background

The hair oil market in India is broadly segmented into two types – the Coconut Hair Oil segment (comprising coconut oils, coconut-based, coconut-based light hair oils) and the Perfumed Hair Oil segment (comprising heavy amla based, light hair oils, and cooling hair oils).

Objective of the Exercise

The audience for this particular brand was typically defined in demographic terms such as SEC ABC, Women, 15–34 years. However, this demographic description does not really tell us about the real person behind this definition. The attempt through TGI is to segment the Coconut Hair Oil users into various clusters based on their attitudes and lifestyles and thereby understand the different consumers, their needs, and motivations, and then look at demographic descriptors that fit best.

Methodology

Users of Brand A, B, C, and D (our brand) were mapped against the lifestyle/attitude descriptors to identify statistically significant statements for defining clusters within universe through a correspondence analysis. This analysis helps zero down to the most important set of variables/statements that could be used to create clusters.

While reading Figure 5.1, please read the red graph line as disagreement with the statement given. The greater the degree of disagreement, the bigger the line of deviation. As you can see, in this first cluster, the audience has a negative disposition to any of the Top 10 statements that set this cluster apart. We named the cluster as 'Modernist' given her personality attributes, as shown in Figure 5.2.

The top statements for the second cluster, as seen in Figure 5.3, help classify this cluster as she responds positively to some and negatively to other statements. We named the second cluster as 'Extroverts', as shown in Figure 5.4. The positive statements are depicted in green, and the negatives are depicted in red. The longer the green line, the greater the degree of agreement with the statement. The longer the red line, the greater the degree of disagreement with the statement.

The third cluster again has 10 statements as seen in Figure 5.5, which set the audience apart. Just as with the first cluster, here too we find a huge negative deviation to the statements. However, these statements are different from those that set apart Cluster 1. As shown in Figure 5.6, we've named this

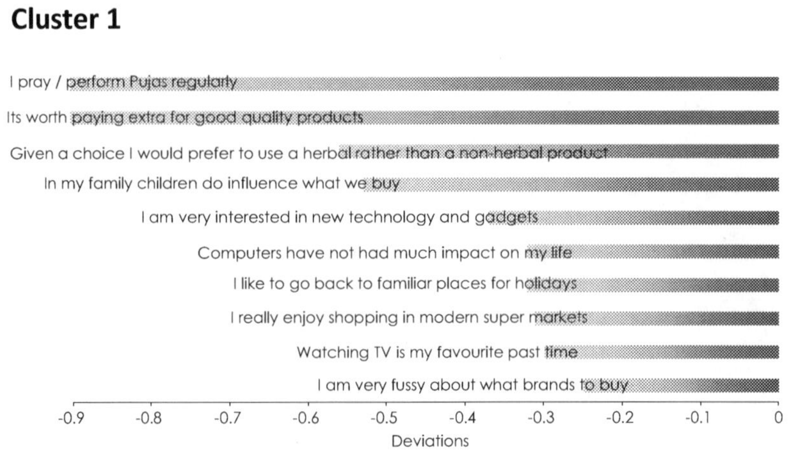

Cluster 1

I pray / perform Pujas regularly

Its worth paying extra for good quality products

Given a choice I would prefer to use a herbal rather than a non-herbal product

In my family children do influence what we buy

I am very interested in new technology and gadgets

Computers have not had much impact on my life

I like to go back to familiar places for holidays

I really enjoy shopping in modern super markets

Watching TV is my favourite past time

I am very fussy about what brands to buy

| -0.9 | -0.8 | -0.7 | -0.6 | -0.5 | -0.4 | -0.3 | -0.2 | -0.1 | 0 |

Deviations

FIGURE 5.1 Responses to statements by Cluster 1.

Source: Created by the author.

Cluster 1

- Most likely
  - Young
  - No regular puja for me
  - Would compromise on quality for price
  - Non-technology person
  - Not fussy about brands
  - Not experimenting with new brands
  - Considers friends above family
  - Money is very important – believes in buying now & paying later
  - Doesn't care too much about a product being herbal
  - Prefers being at home
  - Kids do not influence purchases

Modernist

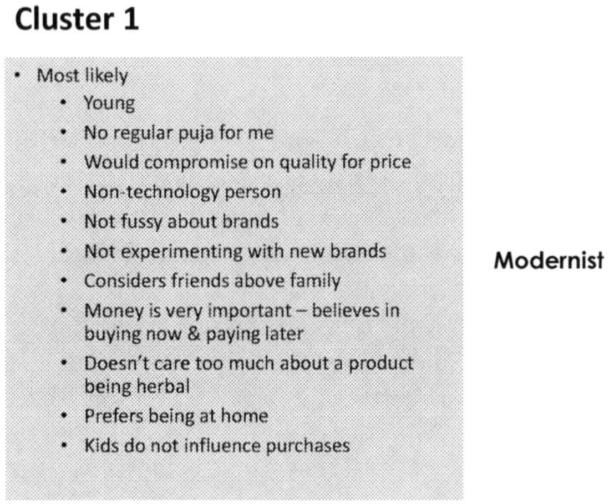

FIGURE 5.2 Personality attributes of Cluster 1.

Source: Created by the author.

cluster as the 'Traditionalist', as she is the 'stereotypical' daughter-in-law that one finds in most conservative Indian families.

In the fourth cluster, as illustrated in Figure 5.7, again we see positive and negative deviations on the top statements for this cluster. As per Figure 5.8, we've named this segment 'Modern Traditionalist'. This is almost like a Modern Traditionalist, a person who has the basic Indian values in place but has shed conservatism and has embraced the modern way of living and thinking. She appeared to be a very balanced person.

Cluster 2

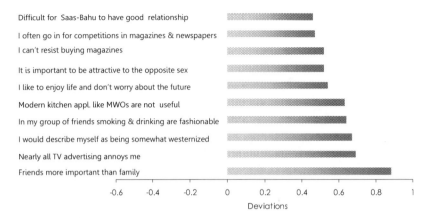

Difficult for Saas-Bahu to have good relationship

I often go in for competitions in magazines & newspapers

I can't resist buying magazines

It is important to be attractive to the opposite sex

I like to enjoy life and don't worry about the future

Modern kitchen appl. like MWOs are not useful

In my group of friends smoking & drinking are fashionable

I would describe myself as being somewhat westernized

Nearly all TV advertising annoys me

Friends more important than family

-0.6   -0.4   -0.2   0   0.2   0.4   0.6   0.8   1

Deviations

FIGURE 5.3   Responses to statements by Cluster 2.

Source: Created by the author.

Cluster 2

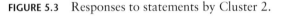

- Most likely
  - Younger age group
  - Places high importance to friends
  - Is westernized
  - Fussy about brands
  - Money very important – finds it difficult to save – buy now, pay later
  - Outspoken
  - Believes Saas-Bahu cannot live peacefully
  - Loves watching TV – though is annoyed by advertising – yet buys advertised brands
  - Enjoys shopping
  - Interested in technology
  - Believes in looking good
  - Believes in Puja
  - Prefers herbal products
  - Kids have a say in purchases
  - Outgoing

Extroverts

FIGURE 5.4   Personality attributes of Cluster 2.

Source: Created by the author.

Figure 5.9 shows how the four clusters looked like in terms of their relative size.

If were to look at our current brand users, as shown in Figure 5.10, and find out what kind of cluster defines each brand, that would give us further

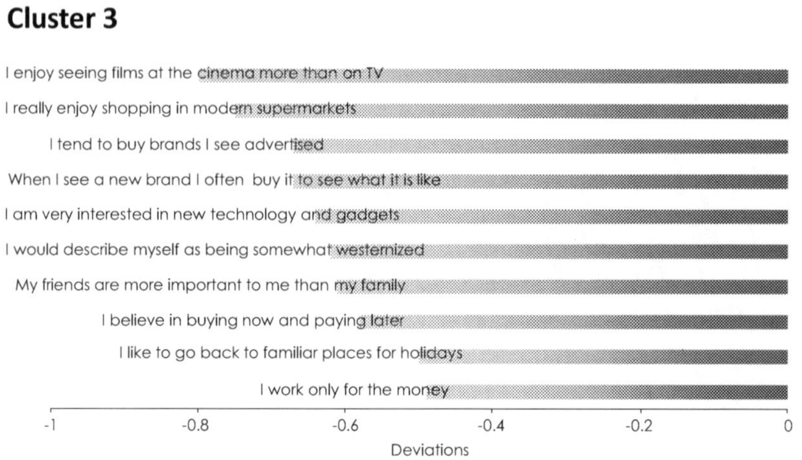

Cluster 3

I enjoy seeing films at the cinema more than on TV
I really enjoy shopping in modern supermarkets
I tend to buy brands I see advertised
When I see a new brand I often buy it to see what it is like
I am very interested in new technology and gadgets
I would describe myself as being somewhat westernized
My friends are more important to me than my family
I believe in buying now and paying later
I like to go back to familiar places for holidays
I work only for the money

-1   -0.8   -0.6   -0.4   -0.2   0

Deviations

FIGURE 5.5 Responses to statements by Cluster 3.

Source: Created by the author.

Cluster 3

- **Most likely**
  - An at-home person
  - Uncomfortable in shopping at supermarkets
  - Would not experiment with new brands
  - Not necessarily buys advertised products
  - Family is all important
  - Doesn't speak her mind if she knows it would upset people
  - Not fussy about brands
  - Shopping for groceries is exciting
  - Knows the importance of money – is not reckless, and saving is not a problem
  - Believes Saas-Bahu can coexist peacefully
  - Is into regular Puja

Traditionalist

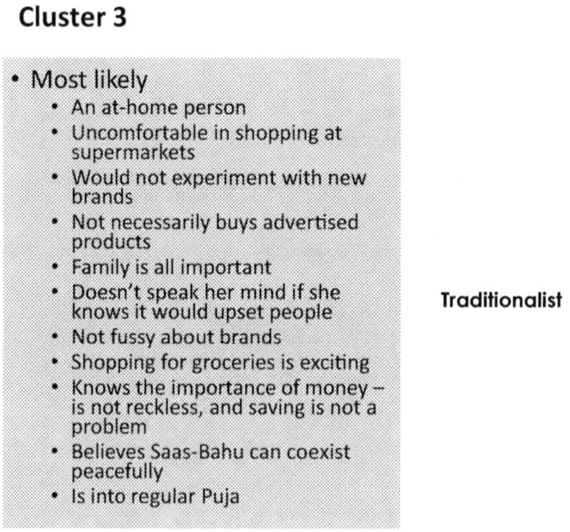

FIGURE 5.6 Personality attributes of Cluster 3.

Source: Created by the author.

insights into our audience and also help us gauge our real competition. Figure 5.10 shows how each brand users were stacked up.

Our brand was typified by the Modern Traditionalist cluster, and 34% of our current users were from this cluster. Contrast this with Competitor 1 which was typified by the Traditionalist cluster, Competitor 2, which came from the Extrovert and Modern Traditionalist clusters, and Competitor 3, which was clearly the Traditionalist cluster.

Cluster 4

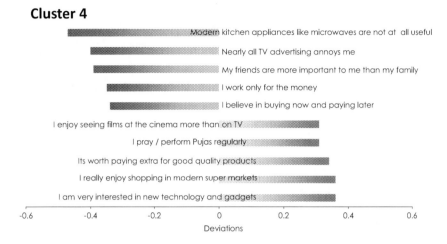

FIGURE 5.7   Responses to statements by Cluster 4.

Source: Created by the author.

Cluster 4

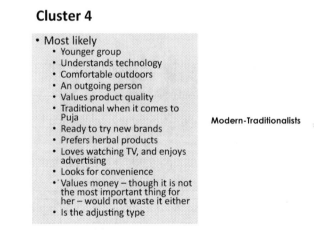

FIGURE 5.8   Personality attributes of Cluster 4.

Source: Created by the author.

We had identified our audience as the Modern Traditionalist (described in Figure 5.11), used this cluster definition as our core audience group, and fine-tuned the media strategy with the plan to take into account the nuances of this group. In real terms, it helped us rationalize the channel mix in TV, the media mix, and we included media other than TV. Doing so helped us rationalize the sponsorship columns and the relevant columns were created to talk to this kind of person. Overall, it helped us put rationale behind the so-called 'subjective' or 'gut feel' decisions.

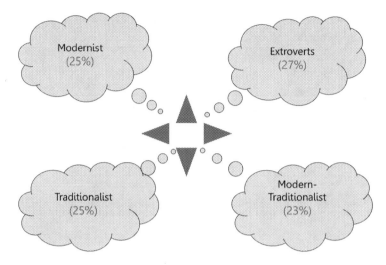

FIGURE 5.9 Distribution of audience across the four clusters.

Source: Created by the author.

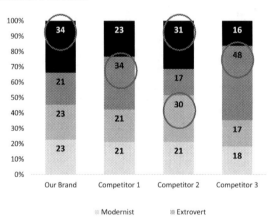

FIGURE 5.10 Brand usage by different customer groups.

Source: Created by the author.

New Thinking on Defining Audiences

The rapid rise of digital platforms that brought in addressability and provided opportunities for personalization at scale has changed the way we started looking at target audiences. Digital media gives out a swathe of behavioural data, which enables us to understand the person we're talking to. As a result, real-time dashboards giving tonnes of information about users

FIGURE 5.11   Description of Cluster 4 audience.

Source: Created by the author.

are in vogue, and the traditional methods of custom qualitative or quantitative research used for segmentation are being increasingly relegated to the background.

Our digital footprints are being used to decode personality types, and relevant ads are being targeted to individuals, giving the advertiser better convertibility or ROI. However, at the same time, the issue around privacy has opened up a plethora of issues. In recent times, the biggest controversy regarding the unethical use of data and breach of privacy was seen when the Cambridge Analytica scandal broke out. Psychological profiles of Facebook users were created, and they were targeted with personalized ads dissuading them from voting for Hillary Clinton in the 2016 US elections.

Digital footprints in the form of cookies enables brands to indulge in dynamic targeting and retargeting. How often would you have seen that your search for cheap tickets to Singapore for a holiday haunts you on the internet wherever you go? To get rid of this, one usually would go to settings and delete cookies and browsing history, and then you start afresh. At the same time, with the imminent cookie-less future, this ability of the digital medium to target and retarget will be under question. The GDPR regulation and other privacy regulators around the world (including the Digital Personal Data Processing Act in India) are putting consumer consent at the heart of digital marketing. Consumer data (even if collected with consent) must be anonymized before being used to target messages. In the near future, we will see Google Chrome doing away with third-party cookies just as Safari, Firefox, and Edge internet browsers have done. This has a direct impact on performance measurement by marketers. If first-party cookies are refreshed, the same user will be counted twice while doing a reach count, thus inflating the reach figures. At the same time, frequency capping would become a problem in a cookie-less digital world. In the absence of these key feedback measures, marketers would end up spending money inefficiently on the digital medium. Retargeting would become almost impossible if one is unable to differentiate between old and new visitors to a website. Also, it would fly in the face of privacy regulations like GDPR. Increasingly, we could possibly see the return of native and contextual advertising on digital platforms. With better consent-management platforms, marketers will need to establish direct connections with their consumers and deliver messages to them after seeking permission from them. Consumers will give permission to use their data, provided the messaging they receive in return is relevant and useful to them. This kind of first-party data might just hold the key to digital marketing in times to come.

Conclusion and the Way Forward

So much for the "Who" part of the media strategy. The objective behind this segment of strategic planning should be to isolate your audience given the overall marketing and brand objective. If one is able to get a peek into the mindset of the audience, then it adds to the finer nuances of your overall strategy, and eventually that will reflect in your plan and its effectiveness in the marketplace. This is one of the most critical starting blocks of strategy planning. Unless one clearly understands who we are talking to, it would be impossible to engage this audience in a dialogue with our brand. Therefore, please go through a rigorous process and understand your audience. There is no formula to do this, and there is no one correct way which can hold true for all types of brands or categories or marketing situations.

In today's day and age, where there is high intensity of competition in the marketplace, it is absolutely critical to understand your audience from every possible view – who they are, how they live, what their attitude is towards living, how they buy, what the key purchase triggers for them are, what their mindset is like, and so on. One might feel that these are the kinds of information area that an account planner would like to look at to help formulate the brand strategy from an advertising point of view. But in the new era of media planning, it is as much about 'media account planning' as much as it is about media planning. The same insights that drive creative development can drive media as well. Therefore, this element of strategic media planning is probably one of the most vital cogs in the overall strategic media planning process.

Chapter Summary

Defining a target audience is often the first strategy variable that is addressed by media planners. It forms the basis for several decisions that are taken down the line while constructing the media plan. Target audience definition draws heavily from the segmentation techniques used in marketing. However, as marketing evolved, techniques for defining audiences also underwent a change. It moved from the earlier methods of defining them in demographic and psychographic terms, to now defining audiences based on consumer relationships with brands and mapping their path to purchase. We are now witnessing a push towards mass personalization and targeting at scale.

Amongst the dominant reasons why one must sharply define an audience is the fact that it leads to plan efficiency and improves campaign effectiveness – when you talk to the right people, in the right context, and through the right kind of media. Besides this overarching need, it is important to define audience due to the following factors:

- Not all products are targeted at all audiences. Marketers often segment consumers based on different factors, and therefore it's important to identify and approach the audience that's most likely to buy into the product.
- There are differences in purchase capacities. This is more so in countries like India, where income inequalities are vast, which results in consumers behaving differently.
- There are differences in consumer mindsets. What is a value purchase for one set of consumers might be a premium for others. Even if income levels of two consumers are equal, their mindset differences will dictate their buying behaviour.
- There are differences in product types. Some products are meant for men, or for women, or for the elderly groups, and so on. In such cases, the first level of segmentation is a demographic one.
- Marketing efficiency needs to be defined. It's important to focus marketing effort on a group of consumers that is most likely to buy into the brand.
- It is important to be able to evaluate the plan reach and frequency. Media plans are optimized and evaluated against a certain defined audience, and hence making it necessary to define the audience.

There are several methods how one could go about defining an audience. Here are a few dominant methods:

a. Based on the experience of the marketer. Different products are created for different kinds of audiences. This often decides the first filter while arriving at a target audience definition.
b. Based on product usage norms. Usually, one would target a group of consumers who account for a majority of the brand purchase.

c. Looking at the category penetration across various demographics and trying to identify an audience. In the case of some durables, the higher the category penetration in a particular demographic group, the less one sees potential available. However, in the case of FMCGs, a higher penetration in a particular audience group is indicative of a higher potential.

d. Depending upon the Campaign/Marketing Objectives of the brand. If the marketing objective for a TV brand is upgrading normal TV owners to smart TV, then current TV owners would be the desired target audience. In another category, the brand might target its heavy user base to retain market shares, or it might want to target its light users to spur market share growth. Therefore, differences in campaign objectives will determine the audience selected.

e. Sometimes, one could use the buying decision process or the path to purchase process to identify audiences for a campaign.

f. Targeting the users who account for a large part of the consumption.

g. Based on purchase intentions and purchase behaviour. Some brands conduct research on intentions and study purchase behaviour to arrive at audience decisions.

h. Targeting based on consumer responsiveness to advertising. With media becoming fragmented and expensive, some brands base their targeting decisions on how consumers respond to their advertising.

i. Behavioural targeting. It is about targeting consumers by studying their behaviour patterns.

j. Targeting based on geodemographics is about targeting people by the locality or neighbourhood where they live.

k. Audience psychographics. Sometimes it becomes important not just to define the audience demographically based on any one or more methods described in this chapter, but also to understand consumer mindset by looking at his/her personality, lifestyle, and values. Using these to understand audiences better is called psychographic profiling of audiences.

With the rapid rise of digital platforms and their ability to identify individual audiences at different stages of their path to purchase, audience targeting is now taking a completely different turn. Behavioural data is being used for targeting at scale, with personalization of messages depending upon the user's behaviour and the stage of his/her buying journey. This has also opened up the privacy issue. In response, brands are now building consent-management platforms in a bid to build their first-party consumer database, which could be used for digital targeting. Consumers could give permission to use their data, provided the messaging they receive in return is relevant and useful to them. This kind of first-party data might just hold the key to digital marketing in times to come.

In today's day and age where there is high intensity of competition in the marketplace, it is absolutely critical to understand your audience from every possible view – who they are, how they live, their attitude towards living, how they buy, the key purchase triggers for them, what their mindset is like, and so on. The decision on whom to target is certainly one of the most vital media strategy decisions.

Further Reading

Barokas, Ben, "Cookies, Consent and User Experience – the Great Disconnect", December 2019, https://www.clickz.com/cookies-consent-and-user-experience-the-great-disconnect/258699/

FitzGerald, Joan, "Measuring Responsiveness from a 360 Degree Angle – Are You Reaching Consumers Who Respond to Advertising for Your Brands?", *ESOMAR*, Issue: Worldwide Multi Media Measurement (WM3), Budapest, June 2008.

Kantar, "About TGI Data", https://www.kantar.com/about-tgi-data

Mandese, Joe, "Life After Demos", *Admap*, January 2008.

Matz, Sandra, Psychological targeting: what your digital footprints reveal about you, Sandra Matz, TEDxChicago, May 2019, https://www.ted.com/talks/sandra_matz_psychological_targeting_what_your_digital_footprints_reveal_about_you/transcript?language=en

"Nudgestock: Patrick Fagan", Cambridge Analytica, June 2020, https://www.redballoonweb.com/nudgestock-patrick-fagan-cambridge-analytica/

Sissors, Jack Z, and Roger B Baron, "Strategy Planning I – Who, Where, When," in *Advertising Media Planning*, 2010.

Sleight, Peter, "Explaining Geodemographics", *Admap*, January 1995.

Straccini, Flavia, "How Do I Deliver Personalisation at Scale?", *Admap Magazine*, 2016.

Terlep, Sharon, and Deepa Seetharaman, "P&G to Scale Back Targeted Facebook Ads, By Sharon Terlep and Deepa Seetharaman" (updated August 17, 2016), *Wall Street Journal*, https://www.wsj.com/articles/p-g-to-scale-back-targeted-facebook-ads-1470760949

US Framework and VALS™ Types, Strategic Business Insights, https://www.strategicbusinessinsights.com/vals/ustypes.shtml

Walker, Philip, "Minimise Waste by Targeting More Efficiently", May 1998

Zohrer, Ruth, "3 Critical Steps in Defining and Reaching an Audience through Advertising", *Admap Magazine*, December 2017.

6

MEDIA STRATEGY PLANNING DECISIONS – WHERE?

Identifying Geographic Markets and Prioritizing Them

The next step in the strategic media planning framework is the decision regarding which markets to advertise in. Once having identified the markets to advertise in, one needs to figure out the prioritization of these markets. Here too, there are various ways of arriving at the decision of market selection, and each method is looked at for a specific marketing situation. I will illustrate a couple of dominant factors that go behind market selection:

a. Distribution: This is a critical factor that decides in which market one should advertise. Logic says that one should advertise in markets where the brand is available. Here too, given the fact that the brand's competitive position in all the markets might not be equally good, there are weak markets and there are strong markets. Advertising in strong markets means one is protecting one's turf and is seen as a low-risk option. Advertising in weak markets might seem a tad risky, but there are marketers who look at identifying some weak markets, putting those markets on higher priority and aiming to develop them. At the same time, there are markets where the brand is not available at all. Here, it is akin to a launch of the product. This is often filled with high risk, but it also gives the brand a chance to capitalize on a new market. Typically, most marketers look towards objectives like protecting sales in key markets, giving additional thrust to growth markets, and developing some long-term potential markets. These are the three key drivers in the market selection and prioritization process.

b. Brand and category sales: These two factors are the most critical when it comes to identifying markets in which to advertise. Information on these

DOI: 10.4324/9781032724539-6

two parameters could be used in multiple ways to arrive at the right markets and prioritization of markets. Markets where the brand sale is high would be automatic choices for a brand which wants to maintain market share. However, when brand sale in a market is low as compared to the category, the brand might want to treat it as an opportunity for growth, and hence might invest. On the contrary, another brand might want to focus on markets that drive higher volumes for them, and might not invest in such markets. Therefore, the brand and category sales data have a large role in influencing market prioritization decisions.

c. Brand objectives: At times, the marketing objectives can determine what kind of markets to get into. For example, an objective could be converting light users of hair oil to medium users. As we discussed in the target audience selection part of the strategy, one would look at the distribution of light users of hair oil and identify the markets where these users reside – this then provides a base for further decisions on markets. Alternately, the objective could be to convert normal TV owners to smart TVs through an attractive exchange offer. Here too, one would identify markets where current owners of normal TV sets live, and then take further decisions.

d. Brand/product usage: Sometimes, one would like to target markets where the product/brand users live in a bid to sell more to existing customers. So, for example, a toothpaste brand might want to advertise in markets where existing toothpaste users live. Clearly, the higher the number of toothpaste users in a market, the higher would be its priority. This would also enable the brand to target existing toothpaste markets if the objective is to sustain sales. Alternately, if the objective is to grow and develop new markets, then the same data could be used to identify markets where toothpaste penetration is low, and one could address these markets with communication that's aimed to convert a non-user or a toothpowder user to use toothpaste.

For every advertiser, there are strong markets, weak markets, and new markets. Advertising in strong markets is the least risky option, while advertising in weak markets is a high-risk option (because sales would be dependent on the kind of advertising intensity, and these are markets where either competition is very strong or the market is relatively underpenetrated). New markets pose an opportunity, but they would also come at a high risk. Therefore, market selection is essentially a call of identifying whether a market is strong, weak, or new.

The market identification and prioritization process involves numerical analysis. In this chapter I will introduce you to two concepts which are fairly popular – the Brand Development Index (BDI) and the Category Development Index (CDI).

Brand Development Index (BDI)

BDI is an indicator of the relative strength or weakness of the brand in individual markets. It works on a simple principle – that every brand has a target audience. This audience is distributed across all the markets in varying proportions depending upon the market. At the same time, the brand also has sales across markets, and this again is distributed in different proportions depending upon the strength and weakness of the brand in different markets. The BDI principle tries to analyse every market from two perspectives – the percentage of the brand's total sales coming from this market vs the percentage of the brand's target audience residing in this market. This is multiplied by 100 to give us an index. An index greater than 100 signifies that in this market a smaller percentage of the audience accounts for a higher percentage of the brand sales, and therefore, the market is strong. For example, as per Table 6.1, if 10% of a brand's audience is in Delhi, but 20% of the brand sales come from Delhi, in this case the BDI is 200 (20/10 x 100). Correspondingly, you could also have another market, say Karnataka as shown in Table 6.2, that accounts for 10% of the brand sales, but 30% of the brand's target audience, and here the BDI is 33 (10/33 x 100). In terms of relative importance, Delhi would be stronger than Karnataka.

Category Development Index (CDI)

CDI is very similar to BDI, explained in the previous section, the only difference being that brand data gets replaced with category data. The CDI principle tries to analyse every market from two perspectives – the percentage of the category's total sales coming from this market vs the percentage of the target audience residing in this market. This too is multiplied by 100 to give us an index. An index greater than 100 signifies that in this market a smaller

TABLE 6.1 BDI for a brand in Delhi

All India Sales of Brand A	1000 units
Brand Sales in Delhi	200 units
% of Brand Sales from Delhi	20%
All India Target Audience for Brand A (000s)	1000
Brand A Target Audience in Delhi (000s)	100
% of Brand A's Target Audience in Delhi	10%

$$BDI = \frac{\% \text{ of Brand Sales in Delhi}}{\% \text{ of Brand's Target Audience in Delhi}} \times 100$$

$$BDI = \frac{20}{10} \times 100 = 200$$

Source: Created by the author.

TABLE 6.2 BDI for a brand in Karnataka

All India Sales of Brand A	1000 units
Brand Sales in Karnataka	100 units
% of Brand Sales from Karnataka	10%
All India Target Audience for Brand A (000s)	1000
Brand A Target Audience in Karnataka (000s)	300
% of Brand A's Target Audience in Karnataka	30%

$$BDI = \frac{\% \text{ of Brand Sales in Karnataka}}{\% \text{ of Brand's Target Audience in Karnataka}} \times 100$$

$$BDI = \frac{10}{30} \times 100 = 33$$

Source: Created by the author.

TABLE 6.3 CDI in Maharashtra

All India Category Sales	1000 units
Category Sales in Maharashtra	300 units
% of Category Sales from Maharashtra	30%
All India Target Audience for Category (000s)	1000
Category Target Audience in Maharashtra (000s)	200
% of Category's Target Audience in Maharashtra	20%

$$CDI = \frac{\% \text{ of Category Sales in Maharashtra}}{\% \text{ of Category's Target Audience in Maharashtra}} \times 100$$

$$CDI = \frac{30}{20} \times 100 = 150$$

Source: Created by the author.

percentage of the audience accounts for a higher percentage of the category sales, and therefore, the market is strong. For an example, refer to Table 6.3, where if 20% of the target audience is in Maharashtra, but 30% of the category sales come from Maharashtra, in this case the CDI is 150 (30/20 x 100). Correspondingly, as shown in Table 6.4, you could also have another market in Gujarat that accounts for 10% of the category sales but 30% of the target audience, and here the CDI is 33 (10/33 x 100). In terms of relative importance, Maharashtra would be stronger than Gujarat.

Together, BDI and CDI, as depicted in Table 6.5, help us understand and prioritize markets.

Classifying markets into High and Low BDI and CDI segments gives a good perspective of the task for the brand in individual markets. For example, a High BDI–High CDI bracket indicates that both the category and the

TABLE 6.4 CDI in Gujarat

All India Category Sales	1000 units
Category Sales in Gujarat	100 units
% of Category Sales from Gujarat	10%
All India Target Audience for Category (000s)	1000
Category Target Audience in Gujarat (000s)	300
% of Category's Target Audience in Gujarat	30%

$$CDI = \frac{\% \text{ of Category Sales in Gujarat}}{\% \text{ of Category's Target Audience in Gujarat}} \times 100$$

$$CDI = \frac{10}{30} \times 100 = 33$$

Source: Created by the author.

TABLE 6.5 BDI-CDI grid

	High BDI	*Low BDI*
High CDI	High Share of Market Good Market Potential	Low Share of Market Good Market Potential
Low CDI	High Share of Market Monitor for Sales Decline	Low Share of Market Poor Market Potential

Source: Created by the author.

brand are doing very well, the market has great potential, and the brand is doing well in this market. The implications for the brand here is that these markets would typically account for a large part of their sales, and these markets would typically be P1 markets for the brand. The second block of High CDI–Low BDI indicates that while the category does well in these markets, the brand has a poor showing here. These are markets where competition for the brand is strong, and the brand should focus on these markets for growth. The third block of High BDI–Low CDI indicates that the brand does exceedingly well in such markets and has a near-monopoly position. Yes, these markets are relatively smaller, but the brand has a dominant position here. It is important for brands in such markets to look at maintaining their market share and sales positions here. If the volume contribution of such markets is high, these markets too at times are higher on priority for the brand concerned, and would typically be either P1 or P2 markets. The fourth segment is the Low BDI–Low CDI segment. Here, both the brand and the category have a limited presence. It could mean that the market potential is very poor in such markets, and the brand is not doing too well here, either. Generally such markets are P3 markets.

TABLE 6.6 BDI-CDI calculation example: Step 1

State	TG (000s)	Category Sales (MT)	Brand Sales (MT)
AP	899	1999	555
Assam	156	760	35
Bihar	334	1303	348
Chhatisgarh	187	504	371
Delhi	425	2650	807
Goa	42	128	32
Gujarat	531	2516	1772
Haryana	245	1078	525
HP	73	139	24
J&K	59	189	41
Jharkhand	287	996	92
Karnataka	473	3345	1897
Kerala	287	1277	126
Maharashtra	1284	6998	5447
MP	623	1997	1525
Orissa	184	972	97
Punjba	373	1572	350
Rajasthan	506	1540	730
TN	634	4513	287
UP	1741	4740	3006
Uttaranchal	175	357	193
West Bengal	569	4591	202
All India	**10087**	**44164**	**18462**

Source: Created by the author.

How does one look at a classifying markets as High or Low on BDI and CDI? While there is no one formula, it could come from individual judgement after taking a look at the numbers. However, a simpler method is to calculate an overall average of BDI and CDI. Markets that score higher than the average could be classified as 'high', and markets that score less than the average could be classified as 'low'. From a hands-on working model, one needs to gather three pieces of information – distribution of category sales across markets, distribution of brand sales across markets, and distribution of target audience for the brand across markets. Once this information is available, BDI and CDI calculations can be done. Here's an example from the biscuits category and a brand named X.

Step 1: *Organizing information by markets*. As shown in Table 6.6, we have the three basic pieces of information required to calculate BDI and CDI – target audience across markets, category sales across markets, and brand sales across markets.

Step 2: *Percentage distribution of TG, brand sales, and category sales across markets.* The same information given in Step 1 is broken up into percentage-wise numbers, as shown in Table 6.7.

Step 3: *Calculation of BDI and CDI.* Table 6.8 lists the formula for calculating BDI. Table 6.9 shows the calculated BDI and CDI numbers. At the bottom of Table 6.9, marked in red, are the average BDI of 77 and the average CDI of 97.

TABLE 6.7 BDI-CDI calculation example: Step 2

State	TG (000s)	Category Sales (MT)	Brand Sales (MT)	TG Distribution	Category Distribution	Brand Distribution
AP	899	1999	555	9%	5%	3%
Assam	156	760	35	2%	2%	0%
Bihar	334	1303	348	3%	3%	2%
Chhatisgarh	187	504	371	2%	1%	2%
Delhi	425	2650	807	4%	6%	4%
Goa	42	128	32	0%	0%	0%
Gujarat	531	2516	1772	5%	6%	10%
Haryana	245	1078	525	2%	2%	3%
HP	73	139	24	1%	0%	0%
J&K	59	189	41	1%	0%	0%
Jharkhand	287	996	92	3%	2%	0%
Karnataka	473	3345	1897	5%	8%	10%
Kerala	287	1277	126	3%	3%	1%
Maharashtra	1284	6998	5447	13%	16%	30%
MP	623	1997	1525	6%	5%	8%
Orissa	184	972	97	2%	2%	1%
Punjba	373	1572	350	4%	4%	2%
Rajasthan	506	1540	730	5%	3%	4%
TN	634	4513	287	6%	10%	2%
UP	1741	4740	3006	17%	11%	16%
Uttaranchal	175	357	193	2%	1%	1%
West Bengal	569	4591	202	6%	10%	1%
All India	**10087**	**44164**	**18462**	**100%**	**100%**	**100%**

Source: Created by the author.

TABLE 6.8 BDI-CDI calculation formula

$$BDI = \frac{\%\,of\,Brand\,Sales\,from\,a\,Market}{\%\,of\,the\,Target\,Audience\,in\,the\,Market} \times 100$$

$$CDI = \frac{\%\,of\,Category\,Sales\,from\,a\,Market}{\%\,of\,the\,Target\,Audience\,in\,the\,Market} \times 100$$

Source: Created by the author.

TABLE 6.9 BDI-CDI calculation example: Step 3

State	TG (000s)	Category Sales (MT)	Brand Sales (MT)	TG Distribution	Category Distribution	Brand Distribution	BDI	CDI
AP	899	1999	555	9%	5%	3%	34	51
Assam	156	760	35	2%	2%	0%	12	111
Bihar	334	1303	348	3%	3%	2%	57	89
Chhatisgarh	187	504	371	2%	1%	2%	108	62
Delhi	425	2650	807	4%	6%	4%	104	142
Goa	42	128	32	0%	0%	0%	42	70
Gujarat	531	2516	1772	5%	6%	10%	182	108
Haryana	245	1078	525	2%	2%	3%	117	100
HP	73	139	24	1%	0%	0%	18	43
J&K	59	189	41	1%	0%	0%	38	73
Jharkhand	287	996	92	3%	2%	0%	18	79
Karnataka	473	3345	1897	5%	8%	10%	219	162
Kerala	287	1277	126	3%	3%	1%	24	102
Maharashtra	1284	6998	5447	13%	16%	30%	232	124
MP	623	1997	1525	6%	5%	8%	134	73
Orissa	184	972	97	2%	2%	1%	29	121
Punjba	373	1572	350	4%	4%	2%	51	96
Rajasthan	506	1540	730	5%	3%	4%	79	70
TN	634	4513	287	6%	10%	2%	25	163
UP	1741	4740	3006	17%	11%	16%	94	62
Uttaranchal	175	357	193	2%	1%	1%	60	47
West Bengal	569	4591	202	6%	10%	1%	19	184
All India	10087	44164	18462	100%	100%	100%	77	97
								Average

Source: Created by the author.

Classifying markets into Low and High BDI blocks could be done in this manner. There are other methods which could be employed, and that would depend upon the individual planner's judgement on the BDI and CDI numbers. In our example, as shown in Table 6.10, we have calculated the average BDI, which comes to 77, and have classified all markets with a BDI score greater than 77 as High BDI markets and below 77 as Low BDI markets. Likewise in the case of CDI, the average CDI is 97, and all markets with a score greater than 97 have been classified as High CDI markets, and markets with a score below 97 have been classified as Low CDI markets. Table 6.10 shows the calculations.

Table 6.11 shows the information in a grid format.

One could also calculate another index known as Market Opportunity Index (MOI), as depicted in Table 6.12. This is nothing but BDI divided by CDI. An MOI that is higher than 100 means that the opportunity for the brand is greater in the market. Table 6.12 indicates how it would look in our example.

This also enables us to take a look at the absolute size of the market. In Table 6.11 UP was in the Low CDI–High BDI bracket vs Assam, which is in the High CDI–Low BDI bracket. The absolute size of the TG, brand, and category sales in UP is far higher than that in Assam, but the relative market priorities are different. However, if you look at the MOI technique, UP shows up far higher than Assam in the order of priority and potential. Therefore, it is important to apply judgement and use BDI and CDI numbers judiciously to take a decision on market identification. It is important to look at the market situations and the brand realities, and also try to address real concerns for the brand when it comes to market prioritization.

Weighted BDI and CDI

Sometimes, some planners apply weightages to BDI and CDI to identify markets. Weight setting is done based on judgement and experience of the planner. Usually, a call on setting weightages is done in consultation with the marketing team just so there is complete alignment with the marketing objective. So for example, you could apply a 0.75 weightage to BDI and 0.25 weightage to CDI, as shown in Table 6.13; it would result in one combined index for a market based on which decisions could be taken.

Identifying Markets Based on Product Usage Data

One can identify markets based on targeting heavy-user HHs or light- or medium-user HHs depending upon the objective in question. For example, an objective could be to convert light users of hair oil to medium users, or single-door refrigerator owners to double-door, etc. Here, the single-door

TABLE 6.10 BDI-CDI calculation example: Step 4

State	TG (000s)	Category Sales (MT)	Brand Sales (MT)	TG Distribution	Category Distribution	Brand Distribution	BDI	CDI	Grid Value BDI	Grid Value CDI
AP	899	1999	555	9%	5%	3%	34	51	Low	Low
Assam	156	760	35	2%	2%	0%	12	111	Low	High
Bihar	334	1303	348	3%	3%	2%	57	89	Low	Low
Chhatisgarh	187	504	371	2%	1%	2%	108	62	High	Low
Delhi	425	2650	807	4%	6%	4%	104	142	High	High
Goa	42	128	32	0%	0%	0%	42	70	Low	Low
Gujarat	531	2516	1772	5%	6%	10%	182	108	High	High
Haryana	245	1078	525	2%	2%	3%	117	100	High	High
HP	73	139	24	1%	0%	0%	18	43	Low	Low
J&K	59	189	41	1%	0%	0%	38	73	Low	Low
Jharkhand	287	996	92	3%	2%	0%	18	79	Low	Low
Karnataka	473	3345	1897	5%	8%	10%	219	162	High	High
Kerala	287	1277	126	3%	3%	1%	24	102	Low	High
Maharashtra	1284	6998	5447	13%	16%	30%	232	124	High	High
MP	623	1997	1525	6%	5%	8%	134	73	High	Low
Orissa	184	972	97	2%	2%	1%	29	121	Low	High
Punjba	373	1572	350	4%	4%	2%	51	96	Low	Low
Rajasthan	506	1540	730	5%	3%	4%	79	70	High	Low
TN	634	4513	287	6%	10%	2%	25	163	Low	High
UP	1741	4740	3006	17%	11%	16%	94	62	High	Low
Uttaranchal	175	357	193	2%	1%	1%	60	47	Low	Low
West Bengal	569	4591	202	6%	10%	1%	19	184	Low	High
All India	10087	44164	18462	100%	100%	100%	77	97	Average	

Source: Created by the author.

TABLE 6.11 BDI-CDI market grid

	High BDI	*Low BDI*
High CDI	Delhi, Gujarat, Haryana, Karnataka, Maharashtra	Assam, Kerala, Orissa, TN, West Bengal
Low CDI	Chhattisgarh, Rajasthan, MP, UP	Punjab, Bihar, Goa, AP, HP, J&K, Jharkhand, Uttarakhand

Source: Created by the author.

refrigerator owners would be the target audience, and we need to find out in which markets they are located. This would help arrive at a decision on which markets to advertise in. Table 6.14 illustrates a hypothetical example of this.

On the basis of the data in Table 6.14, UP, Maharashtra and Tamil Nadu are far bigger target markets as compared to markets like West Bengal, Bihar, and Haryana.

Identifying Markets Based on Sales Contribution

This is again a very simple method to identify markets based on a market's contribution to brand sales. This is useful when the brand is targeting its existing markets either to protect/defend market share or to identify weaker markets which could be prioritized for growth. This method could also be used in combination with other methods (which will be described further ahead in the chapter) to identify markets. Table 6.15 depicts an example from the biscuits category and sales of a Brand A by market.

Based on the data in Table 6.15, one could easily conclude that Tamil Nadu and West Bengal are larger markets than Madhya Pradesh or Rajasthan for Brand A of biscuits.

Identifying Markets Based on Sales Growth

Sometimes brands take on growth objectives and want to strategically focus on growth markets for a brand in order to drive higher sales and market shares. In such cases, relative growth rates of different markets are looked at and then a decision is taken on market identification. Here again, one needs to be careful and not just look at percentage figures. A small market may double its size and show a 100% growth rate, while a large market might just show a growth rate of 10%. In such cases, one should also look at absolute growth figures, and also contribution to growth. These two factors combined could help one to arrive at a more judicious decision. Table 6.16 shows sales growth calculations of the biscuit Brand A.

TABLE 6.12 Calculating Market Opportunity Index from BDI and CDI

State	TG (000s)	Category Sales (MT)	Brand Sales (MT)	TG Distribution	Category Distribution	Brand Distribution	BDI	CDI	Grid Value BDI	MOI CDI	BDI/CDI
AP	899	1999	555	9%	5%	3%	34	51	Low	Low	66
Assam	156	760	35	2%	2%	0%	12	111	Low	High	11
Bihar	334	1303	348	3%	3%	2%	57	89	Low	Low	64
Chhatisgarh	187	504	371	2%	1%	2%	108	62	High	Low	176
Delhi	425	2650	807	4%	6%	4%	104	142	High	High	73
Goa	42	128	32	0%	0%	0%	42	70	Low	Low	60
Gujarat	531	2516	1772	5%	6%	10%	182	108	High	High	168
Haryana	245	1078	525	2%	2%	3%	117	100	High	High	117
HP	73	139	24	1%	0%	0%	18	43	Low	Low	41
J&K	59	189	41	1%	0%	0%	38	73	Low	Low	52
Jharkhand	287	996	92	3%	2%	0%	18	79	Low	Low	22
Karnataka	473	3345	1897	5%	8%	10%	219	162	High	High	136
Kerala	287	1277	126	3%	3%	1%	24	102	Low	Low	24
Maharashtra	1284	6998	5447	13%	16%	30%	232	124	High	High	186
MP	623	1997	1525	6%	5%	8%	134	73	High	Low	183
Orissa	184	972	97	2%	2%	1%	29	121	Low	High	24
Punjab	373	1572	350	4%	4%	2%	51	96	Low	Low	53
Rajasthan	506	1540	730	5%	3%	4%	79	70	High	Low	113
TN	634	4513	287	6%	10%	2%	25	163	Low	High	15
UP	1741	4740	3006	17%	11%	16%	94	62	High	Low	152
Uttaranchal	175	357	193	2%	1%	1%	60	47	Low	Low	129
West Bengal	569	4591	202	6%	10%	1%	19	184	Low	High	11
All India	**10087**	**44164**	**18462**	**100%**	**100%**	**100%**	**77**	**97**			

Average

Source: Created by the author.

TABLE 6.13 Weighted BDI and CDI

State	TG (000s)	Category Sales (MT)	Brand Sales (MT)	TG Distribution	Category Distribution	Brand Distribution	BDI	CDI	Grid Value BDI	Grid Value CDI	Weighted Index BDI 0.75 & CDI 0.25
AP	899	1999	555	9%	5%	3%	34	51	Low	Low	38
Assam	156	760	35	2%	2%	0%	12	111	Low	High	37
Bihar	334	1303	348	3%	3%	2%	57	89	Low	Low	65
Chhatisgarh	187	504	371	2%	1%	2%	108	62	High	Low	97
Delhi	425	2650	807	4%	6%	4%	104	142	High	High	113
Goa	42	128	32	0%	0%	0%	42	70	Low	Low	49
Gujarat	531	2516	1772	5%	6%	10%	182	108	High	High	164
Haryana	245	1078	525	2%	2%	3%	117	100	High	High	113
HP	73	139	24	1%	0%	0%	18	43	Low	Low	24
J&K	59	189	41	1%	0%	0%	38	73	Low	Low	47
Jharkhand	287	996	92	3%	2%	0%	18	79	Low	Low	33
Karnataka	473	3345	1897	5%	8%	10%	219	162	High	High	205
Kerala	287	1277	126	3%	3%	1%	24	102	Low	High	43
Maharashtra	1284	6998	5447	13%	16%	30%	232	124	High	High	205
MP	623	1997	1525	6%	5%	8%	134	73	High	Low	119
Orissa	184	972	97	2%	2%	1%	29	121	Low	High	52
Punjba	373	1572	350	4%	4%	2%	51	96	Low	Low	63
Rajasthan	506	1540	730	5%	3%	4%	79	70	High	Low	76
TN	634	4513	287	6%	10%	2%	25	163	Low	High	59
UP	1741	4740	3006	17%	11%	16%	94	62	High	Low	86
Uttaranchal	175	357	193	2%	1%	1%	60	47	Low	Low	57
West Bengal	569	4591	202	6%	10%	1%	19	184	Low	High	61
All India	10087	44164	18462	100%	100%	100%	77	97	Average		61

Source: Created by the author.

TABLE 6.14 Refrigerator-owning homes across states

State	Total HHs (000S)	Single-Door Refrigerator Owners (000S)
All India	298224	80626
Uttar Pradesh	41812	9389
Maharashtra	27645	9046
Tamil Nadu	21885	8899
Gujarat	15472	5675
Punjab	7136	5113
Kerala	8704	4674
Rajasthan	16216	4610
Andhra Pradesh	15072	4402
Karnataka	16832	3882
West Bengal	24222	3842
Haryana	6207	3429
Telangana	10285	3270
Madhya Pradesh	18605	2703
Odisha	10490	1897
Delhi	3881	1863
Bihar	22518	1243
Uttarakhand	2439	1078
Chhattisgarh	6485	1077
Jharkhand	7868	1070
Himachal Pradesh	1579	994
Assam	8293	838
Jammu & Kashmir	1109	695
Tripura	1109	255
Goa	409	230
Mizoram	263	134
Manipur	453	126
Nagaland	366	107
Meghalaya	699	44
Sikkim	172	40

Source: Created by the author.

In this example, if one were to look at growth rates in isolation, one would incorrectly identify Sikkim and Mizoram as better markets than Tamil Nadu or West Bengal for Brand A. Instead, if you look at absolute growth and contribution to growth markets like Tamil Nadu, Odisha, West Bengal, and Assam would be higher in importance and priority.

Identifying Markets Based on Market Shares

Sometimes, the marketing team might be looking at targeting markets based on their market shares. The objectives could be either maintaining existing

TABLE 6.15 Sales of biscuits across states

State	Biscuit Brand A Sales (MT)	Sales Contribution %
All India	83176	100.0%
Tamil Nadu	14305	17.2%
West Bengal	12042	14.5%
Bihar	8179	9.8%
Maharashtra	6646	8.0%
Assam	6121	7.4%
Odisha	5805	7.0%
Karnataka	4832	5.8%
Uttar Pradesh	4344	5.2%
Kerala	2385	2.9%
Jharkhand	2129	2.6%
Punjab	1986	2.4%
Andhra Pradesh	1948	2.3%
Delhi	1563	1.9%
Telangana	1406	1.7%
Gujarat	1223	1.5%
Haryana	1045	1.3%
Tripura	766	0.9%
Himachal Pradesh	575	0.7%
Madhya Pradesh	539	0.6%
Uttarakhand	490	0.6%
Rajasthan	376	0.5%
Jammu & Kashmir	329	0.4%
Chhattisgarh	316	0.4%
Meghalaya	293	0.4%
Goa	230	0.3%
Manipur	185	0.2%
Nagaland	123	0.1%
Mizoram	88	0.1%
Sikkim	77	0.1%

Source: Created by the author.

market shares or trying to gain market shares in markets with higher competitive intensity. In either case, it's a good starting point to consider in conjunction with sales, growth, contribution to growth, and so on. Table 6.17 illustrates this example from the biscuit category.

Table 6.18 demonstrates how you could also add brand sales contribution and category sales contribution and see how the markets stack up.

Sometimes for competitive reasons, one might want to target markets where category contribution is high but brand market shares are low.

TABLE 6.16 Two-year biscuit sales by state

State	Biscuit Brand A Sales (MT) Year 1	Sales Contri- bution %	Biscuit Brand A Sales (MT) Year 2	Growth %	Absolute Growth	Contri- bution to Growth %
All India	**83176**	100.0%	**92815**	12%	**9640**	100.0%
Tamil Nadu	14305	17.2%	16451	15%	2146	22.3%
West Bengal	12042	14.5%	13246	10%	1204	12.5%
Bihar	8179	9.8%	8587	5%	409	4.2%
Maharashtra	6646	8.0%	7177	8%	532	5.5%
Assam	6121	7.4%	7284	19%	1163	12.1%
Odisha	5805	7.0%	7256	25%	1451	15.1%
Karnataka	4832	5.8%	5943	23%	1111	11.5%
Uttar Pradesh	4344	5.2%	4735	9%	391	4.1%
Kerala	2385	2.9%	2742	15%	358	3.7%
Jharkhand	2129	2.6%	2491	17%	362	3.8%
Punjab	1986	2.4%	2561	29%	576	6.0%
Andhra Pradesh	1948	2.3%	2357	21%	409	4.2%
Delhi	1563	1.9%	1657	6%	94	1.0%
Telangana	1406	1.7%	1603	14%	197	2.0%
Gujarat	1223	1.5%	1479	21%	257	2.7%
Haryana	1045	1.3%	1410	35%	366	3.8%
Tripura	766	0.9%	1149	50%	383	4.0%
Himachal Pradesh	575	0.7%	920	60%	345	3.6%
Madhya Pradesh	539	0.6%	603	12%	65	0.7%
Uttarakhand	490	0.6%	568	16%	78	0.8%
Rajasthan	376	0.5%	447	19%	71	0.7%
Jammu & Kashmir	329	0.4%	398	21%	69	0.7%
Chhattisgarh	316	0.4%	363	15%	47	0.5%
Meghalaya	293	0.4%	346	18%	53	0.5%
Goa	230	0.3%	260	13%	30	0.3%
Manipur	185	0.2%	264	43%	80	0.8%
Nagaland	123	0.1%	192	56%	69	0.7%
Mizoram	88	0.1%	168	90%	79	0.8%
Sikkim	77	0.1%	154	100%	77	0.8%

Source: Created by the author.

Table 6.18 shows that UP is an example of this, where the brand market share is relatively low at 15% while the category contribution is 17.2%, and the sales contribution too is low.

TABLE 6.17 Biscuits sales by brand

State	Category Sales (MT)	Biscuit Brand A Sales (MT)	Biscuit Brand B Sales (MT)	Biscuit Brand C Sales (MT)	Biscuit Brand D Sales (MT)	Biscuit Brand E Sales (MT)	Brand A Market Share
All India	167698	83176	78291	975	2759	2497	50%
Tamil Nadu	14958	14305	259			394	96%
West Bengal	13156	12042	466	94	481	73	92%
Bihar	12702	8179	3641	27	821	34	64%
Maharashtra	19421	6646	12680		29	67	34%
Assam	6252	6121	54		78		98%
Odisha	6741	5805	719		217		86%
Karnataka	10896	4832	5551	64	27	422	44%
Uttar Pradesh	28916	4344	23699	249	434	189	15%
Kerala	3554	2385	964			205	67%
Jharkhand	2927	2129	695		103		73%
Punjab	3338	1986	1133	29	54	136	59%
Andhra Pradesh	2728	1948	301	58	166	255	71%
Delhi	2856	1563	1165	47	30	50	55%
Telangana	2195	1406	701		20	68	64%
Gujarat	5623	1223	4258	34	35	74	22%
Haryana	3193	1045	1960	127		61	33%
Tripura	811	766			45		94%
Himachal Pradesh	849	575	245			29	68%
Madhya Pradesh	9978	539	9388	24		27	5%
Uttarakhand	1430	490	850	32	31	27	34%
Rajasthan	4630	376	3983	73	13	184	8%
Jammu & Kashmir	451	329	76			45	73%
Chhattisgarh	3429	316	3082		31		9%
Meghalaya	293	293					100%
Goa	320	230	90				72%
Manipur	203	185	18				91%
Nagaland	153	123	18			12	80%
Mizoram	88	88					100%
Sikkim	100	77	23				77%

Source: Created by the author.

Identifying Markets Based on Category and Brand Contribution

One could also create a grid of markets based on their percentage contribution to sales for the brand and the category. This would give a good indication of the brand's performance in a particular market vis-à-vis the

TABLE 6.18 Biscuit Brand A sales contribution and category sales contribution

State	Category Sales (MT)	Biscuit Brand A Sales (MT)	Brand A Market Share	Sales Contribution %	Category Contribution %
All India	167698	83176	50%	100.0%	100.0%
Tamil Nadu	14958	14305	96%	17.2%	8.9%
West Bengal	13156	12042	92%	14.5%	7.8%
Bihar	12702	8179	64%	9.8%	7.6%
Maharashtra	19421	6646	34%	8.0%	11.6%
Assam	6252	6121	98%	7.4%	3.7%
Odisha	6741	5805	86%	7.0%	4.0%
Karnataka	10896	4832	44%	5.8%	6.5%
Uttar Pradesh	28916	4344	15%	5.2%	17.2%
Kerala	3554	2385	67%	2.9%	2.1%
Jharkhand	2927	2129	73%	2.6%	1.7%
Punjab	3338	1986	59%	2.4%	2.0%
Andhra Pradesh	2728	1948	71%	2.3%	1.6%
Delhi	2856	1563	55%	1.9%	1.7%
Telangana	2195	1406	64%	1.7%	1.3%
Gujarat	5623	1223	22%	1.5%	3.4%
Haryana	3193	1045	33%	1.3%	1.9%
Tripura	811	766	94%	0.9%	0.5%
Himachal Pradesh	849	575	68%	0.7%	0.5%
Madhya Pradesh	9978	539	5%	0.6%	6.0%
Uttarakhand	1430	490	34%	0.6%	0.9%
Rajasthan	4630	376	8%	0.5%	2.8%
Jammu & Kashmir	451	329	73%	0.4%	0.3%
Chhattisgarh	3429	316	9%	0.4%	2.0%
Meghalaya	293	293	100%	0.4%	0.2%
Goa	320	230	72%	0.3%	0.2%
Manipur	203	185	91%	0.2%	0.1%
Nagaland	153	123	80%	0.1%	0.1%
Mizoram	88	88	100%	0.1%	0.1%
Sikkim	100	77	77%	0.1%	0.1%

Source: Created by the author.

category. It gives planners and marketers a good starting point to start prioritizing markets based on the marketing objectives at hand. Let's understand this through an example of the refrigerator category, as shown in Table 6.19, where we have created a grid of High-Medium-Low category sales vs brand sales. The typical way to look at creating High-Medium-Low intervals is by looking at the lowest and highest values and judgementally creating the appropriate ranges after looking at the data. The data in Table 6.19 could also be interpreted as depicted in Table 6.20.

TABLE 6.19 Market prioritization based on brand and category contribution

Category Contribution	Brand Contribution								
	High State	Cat Contr	Brand Contr	**Medium** State	Cat Contr	Brand Contr	**Low** State	Cat Contr	Brand Contr
High	Maharashtra	10%	9%	Punjab	9%	11%	Karnataka	6%	5%
	Tamil Nadu	13%	11%	Haryana	8%	9%	Kerala	7%	5%
	Uttar Pradesh	12%	14%	NCT of Delhi	7%	8%	Andhra Pradesh	3%	3%
							Assam	0%	1%
							Bihar	1%	1%
							Chhattisgarh	1%	1%
							Himachal Pradesh	2%	2%
							Jammu & Kashmir	1%	1%
							Jharkhand	1%	1%
							Madhya Pradesh	3%	3%
							Manipur	0%	0%
							Meghalaya	0%	0%
							Mizoram	0%	1%
							Nagaland	0%	0%
							Odisha	1%	1%
							Rajasthan	4%	3%
							Sikkim	0%	0%
							Telangana	3%	3%
							Uttarakhand	2%	2%
							West Bengal	2%	1%
Medium				Gujarat	5%	5%			
Low									

Source: Created by the author.

TABLE 6.20 Market prioritization based on brand and category contribution

		Brand Contribution		
		High	Medium	Low
Category Contribution	**High**	P1 Markets	P1 if growth is targeted	P3 Markets
			P2 if there are restrictions	Plan for long-term goals
				These are investment markets
	Medium	P1 Markets	P2 Markets	P3 Markets
		Maintain market share leads and keep investing to maintain	Consolidate brand volumes	
	Low	P2 Markets	P3 Markets	P4 Markets
		Maintain status quo unless category exhibits high growth or new competition enters	Maintain Shares	Ignore

Source: Created by the author.

In this example, we could point out P1 markets as those where both category and brand sales contribution are high. As shown in Table 6.20, these are markets like Maharashtra, Tamil Nadu, and Uttar Pradesh, which account for about 35% of both the brand and category sales. Then there are markets where brand contribution is high while category contribution is medium. These markets could also be considered as P1, as media effort here will help maintain market share leads, and it would be prudent to keep investing in these markets to maintain brand volumes. Then there could be markets where the brand sales contribution is high but the category sales contribution is low. This would imply that these are markets where the brand is particularly strong despite their not contributing hugely to brand sales. We could classify these markets at P2 and maintain status quo unless we see some new competition entering these markets or the category starts gaining ground here.

At the same time, while interpreting the data in this chart, it's important to keep the marketing objectives central in decision making regrading market selections. There could be markets which are medium on brand sales contribution but high on category sales contribution. We could classify these markets as P1 in case the brand is looking for growth here. Alternately, they could be classified as P2 markets.

Markets that have a medium contribution to both brand and category sales could be kept as P2, and the idea would be to just consolidate the brand's existing position in these markets.

There could be markets which are low on brand sales contribution but high on category sales contribution. This means that though the market is good for the category, the brand isn't doing too well here. Depending upon objectives, we could look at these markets where a long-term effort is required to develop them for the brand, and one could identify a few of these markets and start investing in them with a long-term future in mind.

Identifying Markets Based on Brand Market Share and Brand Sales Contribution

Another method is to look only at brand metrics like market share and sales contribution across respective markets and decide on market classification as P1, P2, or P3. Here again, we could create a grid with High-Medium-Low market shares and put it against High-Medium-Low brand sales contribution. Table 6.21 shows the same data set as before, re-casted in this new grid to see the changes.

As is evident from Tables 6.21 and 6.22, the new P1 markets here are UP and Punjab, as compared to Maharashtra, UP, and TN in the previous example. Therefore, markets which have a high contribution to brand sales, and for which the brand's market share is high, would be classified as P1.

Then there are markets which have a high contribution to brand sales but have a medium level of market share in respective markets. These are markets which are important from a brand sales standpoint, but are also extremely competitive markets. These markets could be critical to maintaining brand sales and also to targeting growth and improving market shares.

Likewise, there could be markets which have a high contribution to brand sales, but their market share is low. These markets could also be classified as P1 because the brand is dependent on these markets for volumes, but competitive intensity is high, making the brand vulnerable to risk. Therefore, these could also be treated as P1 markets.

Therefore, if you looked at this grid and the grid in the previous example, in both cases, the marketing objective must provide guidelines in the market selection and prioritization process.

The Need for Market Prioritization

Why does one need to prioritize? Given the fact that there is a finite limit to the budget, one cannot do justice to all the markets; therefore, budgets need

TABLE 6.21 Market prioritization based on brand contribution and brand market share

Brand Market Share	Brand Contribution								
	High			**Medium**			**Low**		
	State	Mkt Share	Brand Contr.	State	Mkt Share	Brand Contr.	State	Mkt Share	Brand Contr.
High	Uttar Pradesh	35%	14%	Haryana	33%	9%	Assam	36%	1%
	Punjab	36%	11%	NCT of Delhi	35%	8%			
Medium	Tamil Nadu	26%	11%	Maharashtra	26%	9%			
Low							Bihar	38%	1%
							Chhattisgarh	31%	1%
							Himachal Pradesh	30%	2%
							Jammu & Kashmir	39%	1%
							Jharkhand	31%	1%
							Mizoram	54%	1%
							Nagaland	35%	0%
							Uttarakhand	35%	2%
							Andhra Pradesh	27%	3%
							Madhya Pradesh	26%	3%
							Odisha	25%	1%
							Rajasthan	26%	3%
							Telangana	27%	3%
							West Bengal	21%	1%
							Gujarat	29%	5%
							Karnataka	23%	5%
							Kerala	23%	5%
							Manipur	17%	0%
							Meghalaya	0%	0%
							Sikkim	0%	0%

Source: Created by the author.

TABLE 6.22 Market prioritization based on brand contribution and brand market share

		Brand Contribution		
		High	Medium	Low
Brand Market Share	High	P1 Markets	P1 Markets	P2 Markets Maintain Mkt Share
	Medium	P1 Markets Maintain Mkt share leads and keep investing to maintain brand volumes and target higher Mkt Shares	P2 Markets Consolidate	P2 Markets
	Low	P1 Markets These are markets to be protected as the brand is vulnerable due to low mkt share and high dependency on these markets for volumes	P3 Markets Consolidate	P4 Markets Ignore

Source: Created by the author.

to be allocated to markets in order of priority. Also, all markets might not be of equal importance. Some markets demand higher investments, while others don't. Sometimes, the marketer might want to focus on some markets for strategic reasons. These are the primary reasons why one needs to look at market prioritization in the strategic planning process. The key questions that the strategic plan should answer are "Which markets should one advertise in?" and "In what order of priority?"

There are various ways to look at market prioritization. Some are very simple, and at times some people have also developed very sophisticated techniques to arrive at this. We will discuss a few key methods through some examples. The starting point, to my mind, is to identify on a blank sheet of paper the key variables that one thinks could have an influence on market prioritization. This would come only after one has gone through the marketing background, competitive situation, brand history, campaign objectives, distribution setup, pricing, and the other parts of the media brief. At this stage, one should not bother about whether information will be available on each of these variables that you think could influence market prioritization. It is important at a first level to identify these factors. Some could be quantified, and some may be purely qualitative factors. Some of the key factors that could possibly influence market prioritization are:

a. *Distribution of brand sales.* This is an important input, and a critical one at that. Where the brand currently sells is a very important factor in deciding market priorities.

b. *Category Sales Distribution.* Where is the category selling? This and the previously mentioned parameter were discussed and used in the concept of BDI and CDI as well. Category sales is an indication of market potential, and most often in market prioritization exercises, this assumes a critical importance.

c. *Distribution of target audience.* Where are the buyers for my brand? This is another factor that could influence market prioritization. In some small markets, one might see a higher TG concentration, and that could swing the market rankings.

d. *Sales growth.* Growth rate of the brand across different markets is another factor that can play a role. Sometimes, there are situations where smaller markets are growing at a very high rate, and at times it might make sense to push them up the ladder of prioritization to drive overall brand growth. At the same time, this needs to be balanced with the absolute size of the market. A market, say Mumbai, that sells 3 million units of the brand might be growing at 10% annually, but another market, say Coimbatore, which sells 300 units might be growing at 100%. The growth rate is higher in Coimbatore, but the absolute size is relatively smaller. These are issues that one needs to balance as we go along the process of prioritization.

e. *Sales targets.* This is another crucial factor for lots of product categories. Internal sales targets could also drive market prioritization. This factor becomes important because it takes care of a lot of things like distribution strength, potentials, internal company expectations, etc.

f. *Market potential indices.* A few studies like RK Swamy Market Planning Guide, NCAER Studies, Market Skyline, etc., rank various markets on different parameters and gives each an Index of Potential. This also at times is an important input in the prioritization process.

g. *Per capita consumption.* Sometimes, per capita consumption (particularly when it comes to personal consumption products) is an important variable.

h. *Distribution strength.*: Relative strength of distribution network across different markets can also play a role in some kinds of categories. It assumes significance typically in mass FMCG products, products like cigarettes, pan masala, confectionaries, ice creams, and so on.

i. *Number of brands available in the market.* There are some markets where there is too much clutter as compared to other markets. This factor is accorded a certain degree of importance in the prioritization process. A higher clutter of brands might mean higher investment required from the brand to maintain or increase market shares.

j. *Media costs.* This too is an important variable in the decision. As we're aware, costs of media vary from market to market, and this could be an important factor in market prioritization, especially when we're dealing with situations where the pressure on the media budgets are very high.

The preceding are just some of the major factors that go behind market prioritization. Several other will come to your mind as you work across a range of product categories and unique marketing situations.

For instance, once we were working on a brand concept for a skin cream which provided multiple benefits to the users. Functionally, it was largely similar to a moisturizing lotion and a cold cream. However, it was an extremely premium-priced cream. The factors that we used for looking at market prioritization were the target audience dispersion, category sales of moisturizing lotion and cold cream, and growth rates of both the moisturizing lotion market and the cold cream market. To this we added an important variable that would indicate the 'premium willingness' of the market. This was calculated using the price realization (value/volume) for both the moisturizing lotion and the Cold Cream categories. The higher the price realization, the relatively more willing the market was to pay a premium.

There was another case of a consumer durable brand where we had used variables like target audience distribution, strength of dealer distribution, level of category saturation (as indicated by category penetration), and the degree of presence of brands from the unorganized sector. These factors helped us arrive at a fairly well-thought-out prioritization matrix – and on the basis of this, sales target allocations were refined.

Basically, the key is to first list out all the factors that could possibly have an influence on market prioritization and then gather information on each of these. Sometimes, you might even need to work with assumptions and use surrogates to reflect the variable. The next step is to find out which of these factors are more critical than the others and allocate weightages to each of the factors identified.

The Use of Index Numbers in Market Prioritization

Since one is working with different kinds of factors in the prioritization process, and each of these factors is different – one number could be a percentage figure, another could be sales volume in MT, the third could be audience size in thousands, a fourth could be an index of media cost, and so on. The challenge is to unite all these different currencies and arrive at a final prioritization. One way that is most popular is the use of index numbers. Information gathered under each variable is converted into an index number, and then it becomes simpler to compare all the variables through one currency and arrive at some answers.

One popular indexing method is relative indexing. I'll illustrate this by working through an example. Assume we identify three factors for prioritization – category sales distribution, brand sales distribution, and an indicator of market potential which was expressed through number of usage occasions in a month for the category. Assume this was for a hair oil brand targeted at women as its primary audience. The factors one could use for prioritization would be as follows.

- *Category Sales Index*: Market-wise contribution to category sales
- *Sales impact*: Contribution to sales used as the Impact Index
- *Usage Occasions*: Used to arrive at Potential Index

Given this information, we created a relative index for each variable. Looking at Table 6.23, Maharashtra accounted for the highest concentration of category sales – 17% of the category sales came from Maharashtra, 15% from Andhra Pradesh, 11% from West Bengal, and so on. In relative indexing, we take the highest value and give it an index of 100. All other values are then relative indexed. In our example here, Maharashtra is given an index of 100. Relative to this, Andhra Pradesh is given an index of 86 (100/17 x 15 = 86). Similarly, West Bengal gets an index of 67 (100/17 x 11 = 67). Likewise, all the other markets are given a Relative Index to Maharashtra, as this is the

TABLE 6.23 Market prioritization inputs for a hair oil brand

Market	Cat Distr.	Brand Distr.	Occasions/ Month (000s)
Maharashtra	17	12	180394
Andhra Pradesh	15	20	62105
West Bengal	11	8	106181
Madhya Pradesh	9	10	43830
Tamil Nadu	10	5	78838
Uttar Pradesh	5	11	23056
Karnataka	7	5	41092
Gujarat	5	5	15904
Bihar	6	4	27212
Delhi	3	5	13294
Orissa	3	4	15499
Rajasthan	2	4	12356
Assam	3	3	11727
Punjab	2	3	4133
Haryana	2	2	3132
Kerala	1	1	1687

Source: Created by the author.

highest value in the column. All the numbers are rounded off, and therefore, you might see a slight variation in the final index.

In just the way we did relative indexing on category sales distribution, we also calculate the Relative Brand Sales Index. The highest value here comes from AP; 20% of the brand sales is accounted for by AP. Here, since AP has the highest value, it gets a Relative Index of 100. All other states are then given a score relative to AP. The calculation is exactly the same as illustrated above. So for Maharashtra, the Relative Index is 60 (100/20 x 12 = 60), for West Bengal the Relative Index is 40 (100/20 x 8 = 40), and so on.

The third variable is indicative of market potential. Here the figures are in thousands. Here again, Maharashtra has the maximum potential as indicated by the numbers in the column. Therefore, Maharashtra is given an index of 100. All other states are then given a Relative Index based on this. So AP gets a Relative Index of 34 (100/180394 x 62105 = 39), West Bengal gets a Relative Index of 59 (100/180394 x 106181 = 59), and so on; the Relative Index is calculated for each market.

Through this, we have now equated all the three variables to one currency. Next, we allocate relative weights to each of the three variables to indicate the degree of importance of each variable. Here, we have given a 25% weightage to category sales, 50% to brand sales, and 25% to market potential. Having allocated these weights, we calculate a combined index and then use the final score to arrive at the final market prioritization. The allocation of these weightages is again a subjective area of decision making. Normally, it is done in consultation with the marketing team, and the decision to allocate a higher weight to some factors and a slightly lower weight to others is made on the basis of the collective experience of the team, the category dynamics, the brand's marketing objectives, and the competitive situation at that time. Table 6.24 shows what the final scores look like.

On the basis of the final scores, one does the final priorities in the form of grading each market into P1, P2, and P3 categories.

How does one look at the cutoffs – which is the last market in P1 category and the 1st market in P2 category? Where does one draw the line? This again comes through judgement, looking at the final numbers and layering it with experience, market situation, brand objectives, and the competitive situation at that point in time. This matrix then becomes the drawing board for all further decisions.

The process of market identification is an extremely critical step in the strategic planning process. It gives a clear direction on which markets to be targeted and in what order of priority. It is advisable to rigorously look at the process, and again, there is no one right formula to arrive at answers here. Each time you look at this for a brand, one must consider all possible factors, identify the key variables, and then proceed further. There would

TABLE 6.24 Market prioritization grid for a hair oil brand

Market	Cat Sales Index (0.25)	Brand Sales Index (0.5)	Potential Index (0.25)	Combined Index	Priority
Maharashtra	100	60	100	80	P1
Andhra Pradesh	86	100	34	80	P1
West Bengal	67	40	59	51	P1
Madhya Pradesh	51	47	24	42	P2
Tamil Nadu	60	24	44	38	P2
Uttar Pradesh	31	53	13	38	P2
Karnataka	41	24	23	28	P3
Gujarat	28	27	9	23	P3
Bihar	35	18	15	21	P3
Delhi	16	24	7	18	P3
Orissa	19	18	9	16	P3
Rajasthan	15	18	7	14	P3
Assam	15	13	7	12	P3
Punjab	13	13	2	10	P3
Haryana	10	9	2	7	P3
Kerala	4	2	1	2	P3

Source: Created by the author.

be times when for the same brand, if the market situation or the campaign objectives change, you might need different factors on which to base your decision each time. Each category has its own dynamics which become crucial for the media planner to understand. Therefore, it is that much more critical for the planner to understand category and brand sales triggers, the effects of pricing, the role of distribution, and so on. Above all, it is critical to align yourself with the marketing objectives of the brand, and to understand the marketing process as much as the media planning process.

Data that Could Be Used for Market Planning and Prioritization

RK Swamy Guide to Market Planning

The RK Swamy Guide to Market Planning covers 541 districts across 32 states. At the heart of the guide is data which is classified into four different types:

a. *Means*: This reflects the prosperity of the town. It covers factors like per capita income, per capita bank deposit, and proportion of households with a monthly household income of Rs 10,000+.

b. *Consumption*: This indicates consumption patterns of the market. This includes factors like ownership of low-, medium- and high-priced consumer durables, car, telephone, and per capita consumption of fast-moving consumer goods.

c. *Consumer awareness*: This indicates exposure to media and includes factors like readership of publications, cinema hall capacity, viewership of TV, Internet access, listenership of radio, and female literacy levels.

d. *Market support*: This indicates the level to which the local market would support marketing activity. It includes factors like employment in trade and transport, bank credit to trade and transport, household electrification, road density, and banked households.

Based on the data points across these four factors, the guide has worked out three kinds of indices for each market.

a. *Market Intensity Index (MII)*: This index gives an indication of purchasing power of the town. It reflects the quality of the market. This index is based on per capita values, and the All India MII has been indexed as 100. All markets with an index of greater than 100 would mean a higher concentration of the affluent population.

b. *Market Potential Value (MPV)*: As the name suggests, this is an indication of the market potential of the town. Greater Mumbai is the city with the maximum potential and has been given an index of 1000. All other towns have been indexed relative to this.

c. *Media Exposure Index (MEI)*: This uses exposure to print, TV, radio, cinema, and Internet. These are measured in per capita terms for each market and are relatively indexed with the All India Index at 100.

The data is used for sales planning, market identification, and market prioritization.

NCAER Reports

The National Council of Applied Economic Research (NCAER) does research work in the area of applied economics with an emphasis on policy analysis and application of quantitative techniques to development issues, regional development and planning, household income, consumption, savings, and energy. The broad areas in which NCAER does research are:

- Growth, trade, and economic management
- Investment climate, physical and economic infrastructure
- Agriculture, rural development, and resource management
- Household behaviour, poverty, human development, informality, and gender

Numerous reports are brought out at periodic intervals by NCAER on these four sets of issues. Some of the reports, particularly the ones pertaining to demographic information, are very relevant while looking at market planning.

Centre for Monitoring Indian Economy (CMIE)

CMIE was established in 1976 by the eminent economist Dr. Narottam Shah. The company is one of India's leading private sector economic research institutions. The information products from CMIE are:

a. *Macroeconomic data*: It is available over a period of time, and it also publishes a monthly review of the Indian economy.
b. *Sectoral data*: CMIE has analysis on 100 sectors including time series data and forecasts.
c. *Firm-level databases*: CMIE has information and analysis on over 10,000 companies. It has a track of all M&A's across India and also a database of over 2.5 L companies in India.
d. *Regional service*: CMIE produces a monthly review on the states of India called the State Analysis Service. Each State Review is replete with data, news, comparisons, and analysis.

Market Skyline Data from Indicus Analytics

Indicus Analytics is an independent research entity engaged primarily in economic research in India. Amongst the series of reports that it brings out, the most relevant ones from a market planning perspective are:

Market Skyline of India: It covers all the 593 districts of India and has information at a district level on consumer expenditures across FMCG products, clothing and footwear, food products, durables, and miscellaneous goods and services. Additionally it has data on asset penetration of key durables, media consumption, income, expenditure and saving patterns, and consumer life stages. This data is of tremendous help in assessing market size and potential.

Metro, Town and Rural Skyline of India: It has data across 7800 cities and all the 5800 rural blocks of India. It is useful for identifying and prioritizing markets based on demographics, affluence, and geo-locations.

District GDP of India: For granular insights on the Indian economy in terms of size of local economy. It covers economic analysis of every district across the three major sectors – agriculture and allied, industry, and services – as well as the 16 sub-sectors.

Neighbourhood Skyline of India: It has micro market level data across 57 cities. It is particularly useful for planning retail locations, and ATM/bank branches. It covers details on affluence levels of neighbourhoods based on income and expenditure patterns of consumers, local connectivity, etc.

Nielsen Retail Measurement

AC Nielsen does a retail audit in India across the food, household, health and beauty, durables, confectionery, and beverage products industries. Done by professional auditors using scanning of product codes and store visits, this very important piece of research helps marketers take decisions on market planning and gives indices on volume and value movements and market share indicators across various zones and types of retail outlets. A monthly study, it gives out key information like market share and trends in offtakes and distribution opportunities, analysing success rates of promotions. It is done based on a sample of retail stores which is projected to the retail universe. The on-field auditors are constantly at stores taking stock reports and keep a track of store purchases.

Information on off take and distribution across a range of categories is available for urban and rural regions across states in India. Importantly, this is available for types of retail outlets such as grocery stores, general stores, chemists, food stores, e-commerce retailers, etc. Micro-level sales and distribution information are now available at state by channel types and by town classes (Metro, Class I, Other, and Rural). This is an extremely important data for marketers to plan their markets.

Apart from the aforementioned sources, the IRS is a very useful tool for macro market planning. The details of IRS have already been discussed in the chapter on media research.

Amongst the four strategy variables, the decision on market planning is an extremely critical piece of information, as markets and their relative priorities will eventually impact the way media budgets are spent. Used as an extremely potent strategic tool, media planners and marketers need to work together on this very critical area of media decision making.

Chapter Summary

Where to advertise is one of the most important media strategy decisions that one needs to make. In order to answer this question, it is important for the media planner to align with the brand marketer, because the answer to this question will determine where the media budgets would be deployed. Should one advertise in markets where the brand is weak vs where it is strong? Should one advertise in new markets vs existing markets? The answers to these questions depend upon several marketing factors like distribution strength of the brand, sales trends over the years, the brand's marketing objective, competitive trends, and brand usage patterns, amongst several others.

To make sense of some of the numbers sometimes planners use indices like the Brand Development Index and Category Development Index to arrive at some answers. Sometimes planners would look at the following methods to identify markets:

- Based on product usage data
- Based on sales contribution by different markets to the brand
- Sales growth levels of different markets
- Market shares in different markets

Sometimes, planners would look at juxtaposing markets on two variables to identify markets. These could be:

- Contribution by different markets to category sales and brand sales
- Brand market share and the market's contribution to brand sales

The idea is to align very closely with the marketing objective and identify the key data sets that would help in sharply identifying markets which would eventually lead to achieving the brand objectives.

Once market identification is done using the method that best suits the brand, then one needs to prioritize markets. Prioritization is critical because all markets are not equally important, and a correct priority will help allocate media targets/budgets depending on the importance of the respective market. Some key factors that could play a role in market prioritization are:

- Dispersion of brand sales
- Dispersion of category sales
- Distribution of target audience
- Sales growth
- Sales target
- Market potential indices
- Per capita consumption
- Distribution strength
- Number of brands available in the market
- Media costs

Planners put together the required data sets and analyse them to prioritize markets using either absolute numbers or relative indexing.

Most of the brand-related data like sales, sales growth, etc., could be available with the marketing team. However, planners also look at several secondary data sources like RK Swamy Guide to Market Planning, NCAER Data, CMIE Data, Market Skyline Data from Indicus analytics, and Nielsen Retail Measurement, as well as several other data sources.

In selecting markets for advertising, it is often difficult to judge at which point to drop markets at the bottom of the list. The place at which the list is divided is called the cutoff point. One way to establish a cutoff point is to select markets on the basis of some arbitrary number, usually in multiples of 10, 25, or 50. This is a widespread practice in the industry. Using this method, whatever markets are listed as number 51 or lower are eliminated. Yet most media planners would agree that there is not always much difference between the 50th market and the 51st market. A more logical way to set the cutoff point is to determine how much weight (in terms of GRPs) should be assigned to the best markets. Weighting systems divide markets into groups titled A, B, C, and so on. An A market might receive a given number of dollars of advertising per thousand population. The B markets receive somewhat less, and C markets receive much less.

Marketing objectives affect the length of a list. For example, if an objective is to protect the brand's share of market from inroads of competitors, then more money might be put into markets where competitors are trying to sell against the brand. Usually a brand has its best markets, so the list has to be reduced somewhat to allocate extra money at the top of the list.

Further Reading

Centre for Monitoring Indian Economy, https://www.cmie.com
Indicus Analytics, Market Skyline of India, www.Indicus.net
Introduction to NielsenIQ Retail Measurement Services, https://nielseniq. com/global/en/client-learning/retail-measurement-services/
NCAER, https://www.ncaer.org
RK Swamy Guide to Planning Market, 2017, https://rkswamybbdo.com/rk-swamy-hansa-guide-to-market-planning.html

7

MEDIA STRATEGY PLANNING DECISIONS – WHEN TO ADVERTISE?

After having arrived at the target group and their psychographic make-up, their media consumption patterns, and market identification and prioritization, the next two steps are to determine the intensity of advertising and take an important decision on the timing of advertising. This is an important decision which requires a detailed analysis of competitive patterns, brand sales patterns, and budget availability and then to arrive at the right time during which to advertise. While there are numerous other ways of getting to the decision, I will illustrate some topline factors that could potentially influence this decision.

a. **When brand sales are the highest**
   This is a fairly simple factor. Let's plot the monthly sales graph over a year and then layer it with monthly sales graphs for the previous couple of years. If one notices a fairly predictable pattern in terms of sales seasonality, then one could base media scheduling patterns based on the sales seasonality.
b. **Dictated by budget constraints**
   Usually such situations arise when budgets are limited and one needs to identify the most crucial period to advertise in. While there are 52 weeks in a year, given the basic minimum intensity required for registering brand presence, we might be able to buy, say, 20 weeks of advertising in the year. Which 20 weeks out of the 52 should we advertise in? This factor is then used in conjunction with the seasonality pattern, and/or the other factors governing the campaign, to arrive at the final scheduling pattern.

DOI: 10.4324/9781032724539-7

c. **Depending upon competitive activity**

There are times when the scheduling pattern and intensity of competitive advertising play a dominant role in influencing our scheduling pattern. Normally, during the course of deciding intensity of media weights, planners do competitive analysis to understand the intensity of category advertising, the scheduling patterns, media mix, and intensity of other brands. This is done to arrive at certain benchmarks given the category competitive considerations. This is then used in conjunction with brand sales patterns and the budgetary constraints one is working under.

d. **Depending upon a specific marketing objective**

Sometimes the scheduling pattern depends upon a specific objective. Take for instance a corporate campaign of a company before going in for an IPO. This is driven purely by the need at that time. A lot of brands try to break the seasonality pattern of sales and bring more normalcy to the sales graph. In such situations too, there are offbeat media scheduling patterns. Or there are times when the brand gets embroiled in some controversy – the foremost marketing task at that time is to reduce damage to brand value and restore credibility. These then determine both the timing and intensity of advertising.

e. **Festive seasons and the Inauspicious season**

In India, there are some periods during the year which are considered inauspicious for buying goods. For example, Shraadh, which that falls somewhere around September, is largely prevalent in the northern part of the country. Or in a market like Gujarat, there is a period known as 'Kamurta', which falls sometime during December end. Now the dominant consumer mindset is to postpone the purchase of goods like consumer durables, cars, etc., and to avoid purchasing during such times. However, there are some marketers who see an opportunity during those times – such times bring less clutter, and it gives them a good chance to ensure good brand saliency and cash in on building awareness during the pre-festival period – and also hopefully convert sales from a certain section of people who do not believe in such rituals. Also, it gives them a chance to break the seasonality pattern of sales. At such times, one might offer a great deal and get customers to at least book their car and take delivery after the inauspicious period is over. Diwali around India is usually a peak festive period, and consumers are out in the market to buy. A lot of brands touch their peak sales during the Diwali festive period which begins from Navratri and ends with Diwali – a period of almost 30 days. Then there are specific days on which buying a certain kind of product is considered auspicious. For instance, a day like Akshay Tritiya is a good day for buying gold and other kinds of jewellery. Likewise, there are several festive days like Gudi Padva, Onam, Baisakhi, Pongal, and Onam, during which people go out for shopping. Then, there are certain days when markets are closed – in some parts of India, it is Monday, while in other places it is Tuesday. There are parts of the country where buying metallic goods on Saturdays is not considered auspicious. These minor nuances also play a role in the micro decisions during the media scheduling decision making. Marketers and media planners do account for this while deciding scheduling patterns.

f. **Product availability**

Advertise when the product is available. This is a fairly simple factor.

g. **Promotional requirements**

There are times when consumer promotions are launched and the need to advertise during a short period of time becomes immediate. It could be during offseason at times. Usually large e-commerce companies launch sale offers during 26 January, 15 August, around Diwali, year-end, etc. Several fashion brands organize 'end-of-season' sales periodically.

Types of Scheduling Patterns

There are three broad strategies associated with media scheduling.

Continuity

As the name implies, this is about consistently advertising with a similar intensity throughout the year. It covers the entire year and all the purchase cycles, works as a reminder, and spreads the budget thinly over the year. This is typically used by FMCG categories that are bought throughout the year. Figure 7.1 shows what the continuity scheduling pattern would look like.

Flighting

Flighting is described as a pattern where there is advertising during a certain time followed by a break, and then followed by another burst of advertising. This is also known as a bursting pattern, where there are small periods of advertising followed by breaks appearing intermittently. This pattern is very typical across many categories. It is not necessary that the intensity of advertising in each burst remains the same – it could be higher or lower depending upon brand objectives, budgetary and other factors. Figure 7.2 depicts the flighting scheduling pattern.

Pulsing

Pulsing is a mix of both continuity and flighting. Here the advertising is continuous, but the intensity keeps changing depending upon various other factors. Here the brand advertises through the year with a pattern like, say,

Continuity

Apr   May   Jun   Jul   Aug   Sep   Oct   Nov   Dec   Jan   Feb   Mar

- Works as a reminder
- Entire purchase cycle covered
- Spreads the budget thinly
- Compromise on Reach & Frequency

FIGURE 7.1   Continuity scheduling pattern.

Source: Created by the author.

Flighting

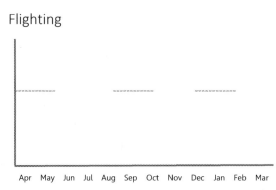

Apr   May   Jun   Jul   Aug   Sep   Oct   Nov   Dec   Jan   Feb   Mar

- Used to take care of sales seasonalities
- Used to cover precise purchase cycles
- Can be used as a competitive ploy

FIGURE 7.2   Flighting scheduling pattern.

Source: Created by the author

1000 GRPs in April, followed by 800 in May, followed by 500 in June, and then again picking up to 1500 GRPs in July, and so on. The variation of this intensity could depend upon various factors like sales seasonality, competitive activity, etc. – all of the factors that we discussed in the initial part of this chapter. This is also a very common scheduling pattern employed by a lot of brands. Figure 7.3 shows the pulsing scheduling pattern.

Pulsing

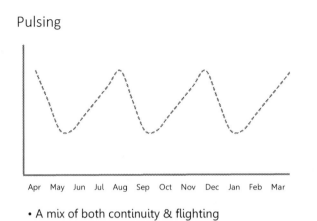

Apr   May   Jun   Jul   Aug   Sep   Oct   Nov   Dec   Jan   Feb   Mar

• A mix of both continuity & flighting

FIGURE 7.3   Pulsing scheduling pattern.

Source: Created by the author.

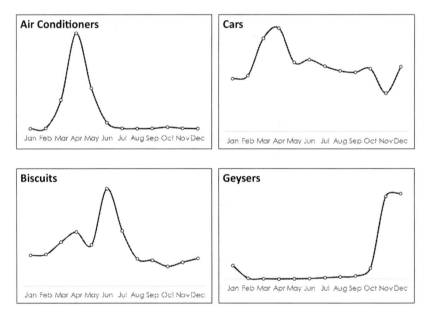

FIGURE 7.4   Scheduling pattern of some categories.

Source: Created by the author.

Scheduling Patterns Followed by Different Categories

Figures 7.4 and 7.5 demonstrate some examples across different categories showcasing how scheduling patterns could vary. One could easily infer category seasonality patterns. So while a categories like geysers and air

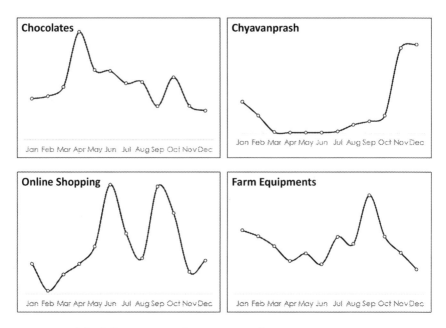

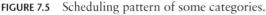

FIGURE 7.5 Scheduling pattern of some categories.

Source: Created by the author.

conditioners are active during their respective seasons, categories like chocolates and biscuits are active through the year.

Some additional factors are involved, and in sophisticated media planning, one sees the use of the following techniques:

a. **Brand awareness mapping with media input**

There are brands which have their own custom research that track brand awareness movements along with other types of information. This information could be used by planners to map brand awareness scores with the GRP input (adjusted for lag effects) and see if there is any pattern that one notices – say, if you able to understand how awareness scores move up or down depending upon the intensity and pattern of media input. This could give very good insights into planning both the intensity and the pattern of scheduling.

b. **Econometric modelling**

CIA Medialab looked at econometric analysis based on historical brand sales, media costs, media coverage curves, advertising memory decay, and sales habit decay, amongst other parameters. The model allowed them to scheduled GRPs across months in a manner such that sales were optimized.

c. **Adstock modelling**

This was covered in detail in the chapter on Effective Frequency and recency. Simon Broadbent introduced this concept of Adstock modelling and just to recap, he believes that advertising effects last longer than just a week and there is a carry-over effect of advertising (Broadbent, 1999). This is at the heart of the Adstock model that he proposes. According to him, Adstock is the net value of current advertising, or the current pressure from past advertising. The theory believes that advertising pressure decays over time at a constant rate depending upon our memories. So for example, if this retention rate is 50%, a 100 GRP advertising pressure in Week 1 will have 50 GRP pressure in Week 2, 25 GRP pressure in Week 3, 12.5 GRP pressure in Week 4, and so on. From a usage point of view, after many experiments, he came up with the idea of using something called the 'half-life' of advertising. This refers to the amount of time it takes for half the advertising effects (as measured by awareness, sales, or any other parameter) to decay. Typically for advertising with longer half-lives would mean that the advertising works well beyond the weeks in which it is aired, and advertising with shorter half-life would mean that the advertising decay rates are far higher. The implications on scheduling/media timing decision are that if the advertising has a short half-life, the brand needs to follow either a pulsing pattern or a pattern of very short flights. If the half-life of advertising is longer, the effects of advertising last longer, therefore brands could follow the burst pattern. The gap between each burst could be higher for brands with longer half-lives and lower for brands with shorter half-lives. While one could redistribute GRPs within a campaign, Adstock's utility as a scheduling tool is not preferred by many.

There is a lot of talk by eminent media researchers on what should be the ideal way to schedule advertising. The dominant thinking currently is about maintaining continuity scheduling – strongly backed by the recency theory. However, most brands do not have enough budgets to sustain continuous advertising throughout the year. Of the 52 weeks, some weeks are of greater sales value than others, and advertisers would like to increase advertising pressures during these times. At the same time, it will be absolutely important for brands to identify the minimum threshold GRPs per week to sustain a continuous presence. In the attempt to be continuously present, there is an inherent risk in spreading the advertising too thin – it would negate all advantages for the brand. Therefore, it is very important to understand the individual brand context before deciding on the scheduling pattern for the brand.

International Research Experiments on Scheduling

Most international studies/research experiments done on scheduling typically point to the usage of continuity rather than bursts. Here are a few key conclusions:

a. An interesting piece of research was done by Erik du Plessis in South Africa based on Adtrack (a system that tracked ad awareness of TV commercials within 3 weeks of their first appearance). Based on this, while there are averages that one could look at, the important point made was that different brands/commercials have different response rates. Brands with stronger impact rates and retention rates should use media differently than brands with lower impact and retention rates. The length of the ad and the likeability of the ad create a differential impact/retention rates for brands. This suggests that different commercials could follow different response curves – and media planners should look at this as a very critical input in the manner in which media is scheduled. There are brands that need continuity scheduling, but there are brands that have done very well in the market with flighting patterns as well (Du Plessis, 1995).

b. Based on analysis of Ipsos ASI's global database, McCrudden (2011) reports that 'Through modeling data collected on thousands of campaigns around the world, with a wide variety of flighting patterns, we have seen that more continuous TV plans tend to maintain advertising presence more efficiently than "burst" plans' (p. 3).

c. Newstead, Taylor, Kennedy, and Sharp (2009, p. 5) of Ehrenberg-Bass Institute suggest that 'continuity schedule is generally the most appropriate advertising strategy'.

d. In the special "What We Know about Advertising" issue of *Journal of Advertising Research* (June 2009), Sawyer, Janiszewski, and Noel report that 'All empirical evidence implies that scheduling repeated exposures more distributed across a time span produce better memory than the same number of exposures massed closer together'.

In the Indian context, not much research has been done at a mass level to understand the link between scheduling and sales. However, there are some large advertisers who do advanced econometric analysis to arrive the optimum GRP levels for various times of the year. But, in practice, a large part of the decision making around scheduling is determined purely through looking at the seasonality of brand sales, competitive situation, available budgets, or specific promotional requirements.

Chapter Summary

Media scheduling is about the 'timing' of advertising. It's an important decision which requires a detailed analysis of competitive patterns, brand sales patterns, and budget availability, and then arriving at the right time during which to advertise. Here are some topline factors that could potentially influence this decision:

a. When brand sales are the highest. Brands could follow their sales seasonality pattern and time their advertising accordingly.

b. Dictated by budget constraints. Most brands will not have budgets to spend round the year. Assume a brand has budgets that could deliver sufficient advertising weight for 30 weeks in a year. In such a situation, one identifies the 30 most important weeks of the year and plans advertising scheduling accordingly.

c. Depends upon competitive activity. In intensely aggressive categories, brands tend to benchmark each other's scheduling patterns. So if Brand A is active during a particular quarter, its competing brands also try to maintain media intensity by advertising around the same time.

d. Depends upon a specific marketing objective. For example, a corporate campaign of a company is released before going in for an IPO. This is driven purely by the need at that time. A lot of brands try to break the seasonality pattern of sales and bring more normalcy to the sales graph.

e. Festive seasons and the inauspicious season. It's a known fact that the Diwali festive time is when a lot of consumer buying takes place. Most brands are active around this time to cash in on the festive mood. Similarly, occasions like Onam, Akshay Tritiya, Navratra, etc., are considered auspicious for buying. Brands try to schedule advertising around these seasons. At the same time, there are some short seasons like Shraadh which are considered inauspicious for buying, and brands too tend to be absent from media in concerned markets.

f. Advertise when the product is available.

g. There are times when consumer promotions are launched and the need to advertise during a short period of time becomes immediate. It could be during offseason at times, or during the flash sales that large e-commerce platforms launch from time to time.

Types of Scheduling Patterns

There are three broad strategies of media scheduling:

Continuity: As the name implies, this is about consistently advertising with a similar intensity throughout the year.

Flighting: It is described as a pattern where there is advertising during a certain time followed by a break, and then followed by another burst of advertising. This is also known as a bursting pattern, where small periods of advertising are followed by intermittent breaks.

Pulsing: This is a mix of both continuity and flighting. Here the advertising is continuous but the intensity keeps changing depending upon various other factors.

Some brands conduct their own custom research that track brand awareness along with other types of information. This information could be used by planners to map brand awareness scores with the GRP input (adjusted for lag effects) and see if there is any pattern. This is used for taking media scheduling decisions. Some brands do sophisticated econometric modelling to schedule GRPs across months in a manner such that sales were optimized. This uses as parameters historical brand sales, media costs, media coverage curves, advertising memory decay, and sales habit decay, amongst others. Another method employed by some brands is that of Adstock modelling, which is based on the premise that advertising has a carry-over effect. When the carry-over effect of previous advertising burst starts to wane, then it's time to advertise again for the brand. Large brands with memorable advertising have stronger carry-over effects, and can afford to stay off-media more often as compared to brands that have a short carry-over effect.

While there's a fair bit of research being done internationally on the scheduling effects, in the Indian context there's not much research done at a mass level to understand the link between scheduling and sales. In practice, a large part of the decision making around scheduling is determined purely through looking at the seasonality of brand sales, competitive situation, available budgets, or specific promotional requirements.

Further Reading

Broadbent, Simon, "How Do Advertising Effects Decay", in his book *When to Advertise*, 1999.

Du Plessis, Erik, "An Advertising Burst Is Just a Lot of Drips", *Admap*, July 1995.

Ephron, Erwin, and Colin McDonald, "Media Scheduling and Carry-over Effects: Is Adstock a Useful TV Planning Tool?", *Journal of Advertising Research*, Vol. 42, No. 4, July/August 2002.

Ephron, Erwin, Papazian & Ephron, and Colin McDonald, "Adstock and Media Planning", *Admap*, September 2002.

McCrudden, Deborah, "Top 10 Advertising Lessons Learned", pp 3, by Ipsos ASI, May 2011.

Newstead, Kate, Jennifer Taylor, Rachel Kennedy, and Byron Sharp, Ehrenberg-Bass Institute, "The Total Long-Term Sales Effect of Advertising: Lessons from Single Source", *Journal of Advertising Research*, Vol. 49, no. 2, June 2009.

Pa, Mi Hui, "Media Scheduling: Continuity vs. Flighting", ARF - Knowledge@Hand, April 2013.

Sawyer, Alan G, C Janiszewski, and H Noel, "The Spacing Effects of Multiple Exposures on Memory: Implications for Advertising Scheduling", *Journal of Advertising Research*, Vol. 49, no. 2, 2009.

Varley, Mel, "Scheduling Media: From Theory to Application", *Admap*, April 1999.

8
DIMENSIONS OF MEDIA STRATEGY – HOW MUCH?

With this topic we come to the fourth and most critical element of the strategic planning process. The question of how much to advertise or the intensity of advertising assumes significance, as this also has a bearing on how much money needs to be spent on media. A lot of rigour is applied in this process, and a lot of optimization techniques are used to get this decision right. However, in spite of all the numerical analysis, there is still an area of individual judgement involved in this decision. Many factors govern/influence this decision. We'll discuss a few prominent factors and then move on to techniques that help us answer this important strategic question:

a. **Competitive environment:** How much is the competition spending? How many brands are active in the market? This is a major factor that is kept in mind while arriving at media target setting for a brand. Eventually, our advertising will be seen in a competitive context, and therefore this has a significant bearing on how much we spends.
b. **Brand/campaign objectives:** What are the strategic marketing objectives of the brand? Sometimes aggressive objectives call for a different level of intensity, and sometimes the objectives are fairly modest.
c. **Audience involvement level:** How much is the audience involved with the category and brand? Higher levels of audience involvement will require a different intensity of advertising versus brands where the audience involvement is very low.
d. **Importance of different markets:** In the "Where to advertise" chapter, we discussed how markets are ranked in order of priority and how tasks for the brand are identified for each market. This also plays a critical role in the intensity of advertising levels across different markets.

DOI: 10.4324/9781032724539-8

e. **Position in the life cycle:** Where is the brand in its lifecycle – is it in the launch, growth, maturity, or decline phase? This also plays a role in determining the intensity of advertising.

f. **Budgetary constraints:** How much can the brand eventually afford and spend also determines the level of intensity and even the overall media approach at times. All brands have targets on sales and profitability – this eventually boils down to a certain finite amount that the brand can afford to spend.

g. **ROI on advertising:** This is something that is acquired after years of experience and through research. What would be the advertising ROI is an important factor in determining the intensity. If the advertising ROI for the brand is high, then advertising intensity could be lowered, and vice versa.

h. **Media objectives:** What are the key media objectives? Are we trying to maximize reach or frequency, or are we looking at maintaining a continuity? This has a huge bearing on the composition of the final media plan itself, and it also has a huge influence on the level of advertising intensity.

i. **Media consumption habits of audience:** This has an important influence on the intensity of media weights. If the audience is scattered across multiple types of media and is a light consumer of media, then the advertising intensity levels will vary drastically, from a situation where the audience is not too thinly spread out. Also, the level of fragmentation in each media will determine the intensity levels. For instance, in a highly fragmented market, the intensity of media would have to pitched at a higher level to register any degree of impact versus a market where fragmentation is not an issue.

j. **Strength of communication:** The strength of the final creative product will also determine the intensity of media weight put behind it. A very strong and powerful brand message might require a slightly lower intensity of advertising as compared to that required for a complex and average piece of communication.

k. **Market position of the brand:** How strong the brand is in the market in terms of its market share also helps determine intensity levels of media weight. Typically one has seen that growth/launch brands with slightly lower market shares are that much more aggressive in media and have a much higher intensity of advertising as compared to dominant brands with very high market shares. Though this is not true in all situations, generally this is an observed pattern.

There could be many other factors that one could have in addition to these while considering each unique marketing situation.

There are a few techniques of setting media weights, like geographic weighting, competitive benchmarking, Effective Frequency, and recency. Let's discuss these in slightly greater detail.

Geographic Weighting

This is about setting individual media weights basis the market priorities. There are two methods used here:

Allocating Budgets for Different Markets

In this method, each market is allocated a fixed budget depending upon its relative importance for the brand. However, given the fact that media costs vary from market to market, in this method the GRP levels for different markets can get lopsided – one would buy more GRPs in relatively cost-efficient markets, and lower GRPs would be bought in expensive media markets. Consider, for instance, the cost of achieving 80% reach in a market like Guwahati versus that in Mumbai. The cost of reaching 80% of the audience in Guwahati is far lower than the cost of reaching the same percentage in Mumbai given the huge differences in media costs. Assuming the same budget amount is allocated for Guwahati and Mumbai, the plan would buy more GRPs in Guwahati and relatively fewer GRPs in Mumbai. This might not be a good method to follow, and one must factor the relative cost of media while allocating budgets. However, the advantage of this method is that from a marketing point of view, the A:S ratios (advertising to sales ratios) are balanced for each market. This is an important element of control from a marketing standpoint.

Allocating GRPs for Different Markets

In this method, each market is allocated a certain level of GRP depending upon its relative importance. This method allows for proportional communication across different market priorities; however, at the same time, the A:S ratios are slightly unbalanced. In the same Guwahati–Mumbai example, if the same GRPs targets are set for the two markets, the budget required for Guwahati will be far lower than the budget required in Mumbai. While A:S ratios do get distorted, this does seem to be the more logically correct method in most situations.

Example: Mapping sales and media budgets for individual markets for market prioritization. Consider for example there is a durable brand (which wants to use only print media, as it has a highly seasonal and localized communication). Based on the marketing team's historical experience, they have the following data available, as shown in Table 8.1, on percentage of sales from each market vs the percentage of media budget spent in each market:

From the information in Table 8.1, one can calculate an index of returns for each market which is calculated as percentage of sales divided by percentage of budget. If this is greater than 1, it means that the relative returns from

TABLE 8.1 Last year sales vs media budget spent across states

State	% of Total		State	% of Total	
	Budget	Sales		Budget	Sales
Andhra Pradesh	11.1	27.2	Punjab/Haryana	5	5.95
Tamil Nadu	10	6.8	Delhi	8	3.9
Karnataka	5.04	4.9	Bihar	8	8.9
Maharashtra	14.1	12.9	Uttar Pradesh	9	-
Goa	0.5	0.45	Orissa	2.9	4.9
Gujarat	9	8.9	West Bengal	3	-
Madhya Pradesh	10	14.8	Kerala	0.36	0.36
Rajasthan	4	0.04			

Source: Created by the author.

TABLE 8.2 Index of returns on media spend across states

Returns on Money Spent				
More than Proportionate		Less than Proportionate		At Par
Market	**Index**	**Market**	**Index**	**Market**
Andhra Pradesh	2.5	Tamil Nadu	0.7	Karnataka
Orissa	1.7	Rajasthan	0.01	Maharashtra
Madhya Pradesh	1.5	Delhi	0.5	Goa
Punjab/Haryana	1.2			Gujarat
Bihar	1.1			Kerala

Source: Created by the author.

this market are higher. If the score is below 1, it signifies that one gets less than proportionate returns, and if the index is 1, then it means proportionate returns. Table 8.2 shows how the various markets stacked up in terms of their sales return vs the budgets spent in the market:

Going by experience, the team thought that it is important to consolidate our position in markets which contribute a major part of the sales and also offer a higher or equal return in value for money spent. Tables 8.3 through 8.5 show how the markets were prioritized into three different priority blocks.

Market Analysis – Category A: These are markets that account for a bulk of the sales and also offer a good return on money spent.

Market Analysis – Category B: These are markets which, though second on priority, have a significant share of total sales. Together these markets account for 12% of sales.

Market Analysis – Category C: These are the balance markets which add up to 10% of total sales and offer less than proportionate returns.

TABLE 8.3 Category A markets

Market	% of Total Sales	Return on Money Spent
Andhra Pradesh	27	2.5
Madhya Pradesh	15	1.5
Maharshtra	13	0.9
Gujarat	9	1.00
Bihar	9	1.1
Orissa	5	1.7
Total	78%	

Source: Created by the author.

TABLE 8.4 Category B markets

Market	% of Total Sales	Return on Money Spent
Tamil Nadu	7	0.7
Karnataka	5	1.0
Total	12%	

Source: Created by the author.

TABLE 8.5 Category C markets

Market	% of Total Sales
Punjab/Haryana	5.95
Delhi	3.9
Goa	0.45
Kerala	0.36
Rajasthan	0.04
Total	11%

Source: Created by the author.

Media weights were set according to this overall direction, and Category A markets were given a higher intensity of media weights vs Category B and Category C markets, as shown in Table 8.6. This factored two realities in the weight setting process – relative importance of the market, and the absolute proportion of sales that the brand garnered from each market. This is what the final plan delivered – it ensured that current important markets are secured and the A:S ratios don't get too lopsided. The only major problem with this method is that it could work for brands which use media where the media spend could be clearly allocated to a market. For example, when TV is used, particularly Hindi GEC, how does one allocate media budget across each market accurately? While there are crude formulas that people employ at times to do this, in practice they are seldom used.

TABLE 8.6 Plan performance across markets

Market	Plan Reach %	Avg OTS	Market Category
Andhra Pradesh	85	18.1	A
Madhya Pradesh	89	17.8	A
Maharshtra	85	17.9	A
Gujarat	88	18.2	A
Bihar	84	17.3	A
Orissa	83	18.4	A
Tamil Nadu	75	12.2	B
Karnataka	74	12.6	B
Goa	70	6.2	C
Punjab/Haryana	72	5.7	C
Delhi	69	5.6	C
Kerala	68	5.7	C
Rajasthan	65	5.5	C

Source: Created by the author.

Competitive Benchmarking

As the name suggests, competitive benchmarking is about benchmarking the intensity of our advertising versus the competition. It is all about trying to match up to or outdo competition in terms of media weights. This is a very common method of benchmarking and used widely across a range of product categories, particularly in highly competitive categories which are of an impulse-buy nature. Categories like soft drinks, chocolates, wafers, and chewing gums typically use this method frequently. This method is appropriate for categories which rely heavily on 'promotions', where share of voice (SOV) in the market translates at some level into share of market (SOM). There are times during a brand launch when planners study the intensity levels maintained by other successful launches across categories, and factor this while working out their plans.

Since it is based on analysis of historical data, one needs to study competitive trends very carefully to arrive at the right benchmarks. There are times when people correlate SOM with SOV, and then try to arrive at some sort of a pattern – and evolve a benchmark that, given this market share and competitive position, can be used to determine what kind of SOV to target. The overriding caution here is that one needs to be very careful in predicting trends. While there is no fixed formula to arrive at the link between SOV and SOM, Prof John Philip Jones conducted extensive research across multiple brands across countries and created some broad benchmarks (Jones, 1990).

Jones essentially is saying that for brands with lower market share, one needs to plan a higher SOV to steadily gain market share over a period of time. Then there are brands that operate in the 19–21% market share region which should ideally maintain a similar SOV. Then there are market leaders who have market share in excess of 22%. These brands, given their market leadership status, could afford to have a comparatively lesser SOV. This method suggests what the SOV should be for a given SOM, and it doesn't work the other way round, where one could pitch SOV at a high level hoping that the corresponding market share would be achieved. Also, these are broad thumb rules that have been arrived at after studying many brand patterns across categories and countries. However, given the fact that every brand has its own unique marketing and competitive situation, it does become very difficult to generalize and apply a formula for all – this is precisely where one should look at the aforementioned numbers more from a rationale/logic point of view rather than read them as cast in stone. Brands with a lower market share are typically new or in their growth stage, and in order to increase market share and compete with the market leaders, one might need to maintain more than proportionate SOV as compared to market share. At the other end of the continuum, brands which have reached a market share peak in their respective categories and are in the mature stage, which typically have the objective of maintaining market share, could possibly look at a slightly lower SOV given their dominant status in the category. How high or low the SOV: Market Share Ratios are should again depend from brand to brand given the marketing and the competitive situation.

So how does one approach competitive benchmarking, and what the critical data points that one should analyse before arriving at brand benchmarks? There are a whole lot of analysis areas that one could get into, but I will explain a few topline analysis which could come in handy.

Category Spending Trends

It is important to map category spending trends and understand at a macro level which kind of media the category spends in – whether it is TV or print or other media. It is important also to break up the category spends across different category segments. Take for example the shampoo category, which is segmented broadly into two segments – cosmetic and natural. It is important to understand directions in which each of these segments are going. Figure 8.1 showcases an illustrative example of this:

The category is usually segmented along the following sub-segments – Anti-Dandruff, Economy, Popular, and Premium. Figure 8.2 shows the mapping of spending patterns across each of these segments.

This gives a broad sense of direction in which the category is headed, and tells us spending growth patterns and skews across various sub-segments within the category.

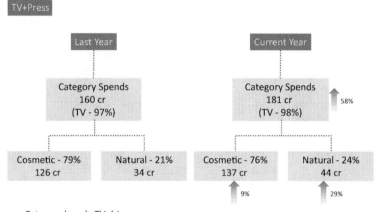

•Category largely TV driven

•Cosmetic is the dominant category ; spends skew towards the cosmetic category in both years – similar to the market shares skew

FIGURE 8.1   Category spends on media.

Source: Created by the author.

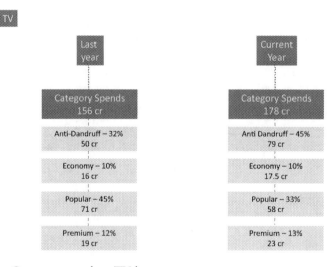

FIGURE 8.2   Category spend on TV by segments.

Source: Created by the author.

Category Scheduling Pattern

It is important to understand the scheduling pattern of the category. It tells us the degree of competitive pressure at various times of the year. Also, if done over a couple of years, it gives a fair trend of the direction the category is taking and what one could expect in the coming year. Figures 8.3 and 8.4 demonstrate how the shampoo category could be mapped.

Market-wise Spending Skews of the Category

This again is a useful input in the competitive analysis segment. It tells us the category spending skews across markets. It is indicative of the degree of

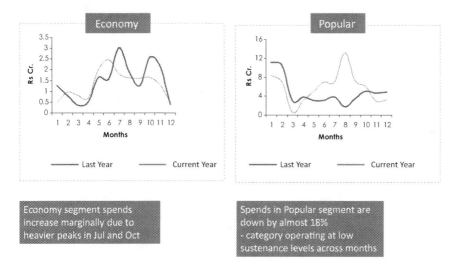

FIGURE 8.3   Economy and Popular segment scheduling pattern.

Source: Created by the author.

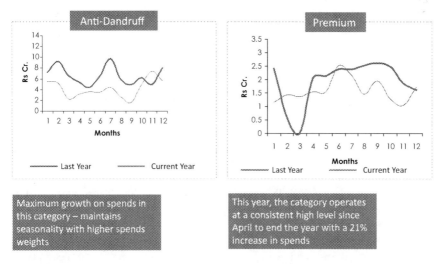

FIGURE 8.4   Premium and Anti-Dandruff segment scheduling pattern.

Source: Created by the author.

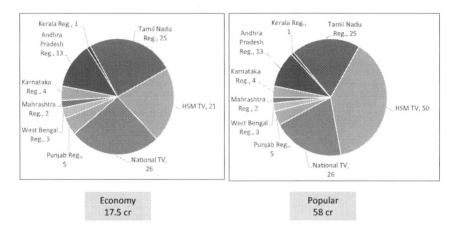

Category Spend Skews
Jan-Dec Current Year

FIGURE 8.5 Economy and popular segment TV spending pattern.

Source: Created by the author.

competitive pressure in different markets, and this has a direct bearing to the eventual benchmarks that we set for the brand. Figure 8.5 shows how the shampoo category spends are distributed across markets.

Portfolio Skew

In many categories there are one or two dominant players, who have a portfolio of brands spread across various segments of the market. At times, it might become important to understand, where are the big competing brands focusing? It has both media as well as strategic implications.

As shown in Figure 8.6, Company A is focused on Anti-Dandruff and Popular segments and is decreasing spends in the Popular segment and has increased its focus on the Anti Dandruff segment. By contrast, Company B has not changed much over the last 2 years in terms of its core focus segments.

Absolute Spend, Share of Spends, and Growth Pattern

Brand-level detailed analysis is typically done for the directly competing brands and the brands one thinks from where one could look at deriving some learnings. Just on the lines of category spending patterns, it is important to analyse spending patterns by brand and find out which media are the spends skewed to and what are the growth rates of spending across each type of media, as well as what kind of money the other brands are spending, their

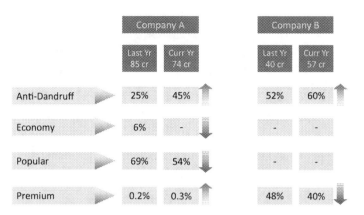

FIGURE 8.6   Spend distribution across brand portfolio.

Source: Created by the author.

relative share of spend in the category, and the growth rate of spends across media.

This has a direct bearing on the final benchmarks that we arrive at for our brand.

Brandwise Scheduling Pattern

Individual brands' scheduling patterns gives us a broad sense of their scheduling strategy and also an indication of the intensity at various times of the year. We must take this into account while arriving at our scheduling and media intensity decisions.

Brand Spend Skews across Markets

This again tells us where specific brands are focusing their media efforts – whether it is a more national media-led plan, or whether their increasing focus is on regional markets, and so on. Figures 8.7 through 8.9 show how brands A, B, and C have spent their budgets across markets.

In the previous example, it is clear that Brand C has shifted focus from regional to national, while Brand B remains largely focused on TN and AP, and elsewhere too is largely regional in focus, and Brand A has increased its focus on the Hindi markets.

Genre Mix

If in TV, what kind of genres are the competing brands using, what kind of genres within print, and other media? This tells us a little bit about the kind of audiences individual brands seem to be targeting. At a later stage, this

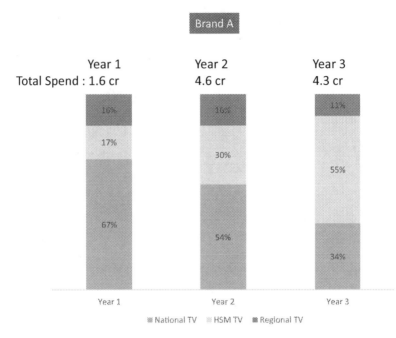

FIGURE 8.7 Brand A TV spend skews.

Source: Created by the author.

information could also come handy when one gets into media buying. More of that later.

Daypart Usage

This is normally done for categories and brands that are primarily using TV – which dayparts are the competing brands being advertised on across which genre. In conjunction with the previous point on genre mix, it tells us about the audience being targeted and gives us a broad sense of the kind of clutter and competitive intensity that one is likely to face. Figure 8.10 shows how the budgets have been split daypart-wise for different brands.

Size/Duration Analysis

Sometimes, planners also analyse data on the commercial duration in TV and the size of ads in print to get a sense of impact of competitive activity. Some brands might show a fewer number of exposures across media but have been using large-format ads that have a different impact in the market versus

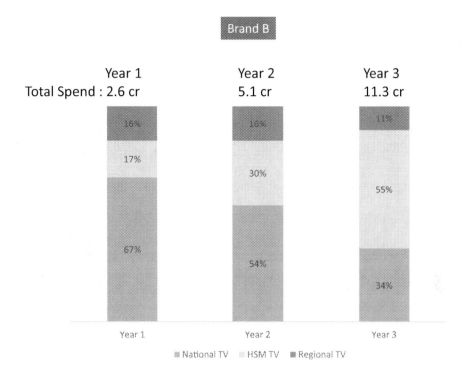

FIGURE 8.8   Brand B TV spend skews.

Source: Created by the author.

brands which are very high frequency, but use very small formats of advertising.

Share of Voice

Apart from share of spend, it is also important to measure share of voice trends for various brands. This gives us an indication of the relative media weights used by various brands. This is normally done on the basis of GRPs. A brand's GRPs expressed as a percentage of the category GRPs is called share of voice (SOV). This gives a more accurate indication of relative brand media weight as compared to a share of spend. This helps in setting up benchmarks for a brand. Also, at times, one could compare it with the market shares of individual brands and arrive at some sort of a thumb rule for the category.

A little bit of explanation is required here when one is looking at GRPs. A 30-second commercial aired across 100 different programmes gives us a GRP of, say, 300. Assume the cost of the plan is 3 cr. If the same programmes are used by another brand, but the commercial duration is 15 seconds, it would

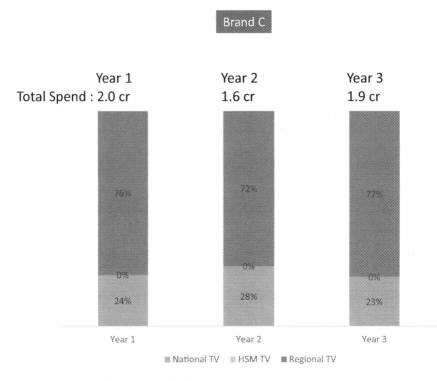

FIGURE 8.9 Brand C TV spend skews.

Source: Created by the author.

	Morning	Afternoon	Evening	PT
Brand A				
Yr 1	16%	19%	41%	23%
Yr 2	12%	39%	19%	30%
Yr 3	24%	26%	12%	39%
Brand B				
Yr 1	9%	26%	14%	51%
Yr 2	9%	25%	8%	58%
Yr 3	7%	37%	10%	45%

FIGURE 8.10 Brandwise spend across dayparts.

Source: Created by the author.

still give 300 GRPs for the brand, and the cost would be say 1.5 cr. In this case, while the SOV for both the brands will be exactly the same, the share of spends will differ drastically. Therefore, SOV measured this way might give misleading results at times. To avoid this, sometimes planners use something known as 'normalized GRPs' for SOV calculations. In this process, GRPs are 'normalized' to a fixed duration, like 10 or 30 seconds. In our example, if the GRPs are normalized to, say, 30 seconds, Brand A will still have 300 normalized GRPs, as the average commercial duration is 30; while Brand B will have 150 normalized GRPs (300/30*15).

Effective Frequency Approach

The third approach worldwide has been the Effective Frequency–led approach. We've already discussed Effective Frequency and its related issues in the earlier chapter on the subject. Just to recap, Effective Frequency is the frequency at which communication takes place, and Effective Reach is the level of reach at the Effective Frequency level. As we discussed, Effective Frequency levels for a campaign are influenced by a lot of factors, and a bit of subjective judgment is involved. However, different agencies have different models on Effective Frequency – the objective of all, though, is the same – all striving to help arrive at the Effective Frequency level.

Stage 1: Marketing and Campaign Context

Before beginning work on this approach, we must have a thorough understanding of the brand objectives. Is it a launch? Is it the launch of a variant? Is the campaign about maintaining Brand TOMs, or is it about maintaining market shares, or is it a campaign to counter a competing brand launch? And so on. This largely sets the campaign context. Having established the context, one goes further to define some more conditions like whether the brand is new or an established brand, whether the benefit is new or we are offering more of the same, the business potential of the brand, the kind of investment that has gone behind it, and so on. All of these serve to give us a good marketing background to understand how to arrive at a decision on the media intensity for the campaign. Of course, there is subjectivity involved, but as I had mentioned while discussing Effective Frequency, it is about a team's collective judgement of the situation – the media planners, the account planning team, and the marketing team together bring their collective experience to the table and discuss each of these issues. The second stage is about arriving at an Effective Frequency level for the campaign. I will revisit what we discussed in the chapter on Effective Frequency and will reiterate the point made about the Effective Frequency reckoner.

Stage 2: Estimating Effective Frequency

Let us revisit some references from the chapter on Effective Frequency, where we discussed different ways of arriving at the Effective Frequency for a campaign. You will recall that there is no one universally right way to arrive at the level of Effective Frequency. At the Effective Frequency Conference organized in 1982 by the Advertising Research Foundation, Joseph Ostrow of the FCB agency presented a reckoner. There are numerous models used by different agencies across the world that help them arrive at a certain number. Each model is slightly different from the other. However, the operating logic behind each model is similar – it is largely based on the factors that influence the levels of Effective Frequency.

Ostrow's Model

Ostrow's model assumed a base Effective Frequency of 3, and then up-weighted or down-weighted it based on marketing, creative, and media factors. The model works on the following three factors:

1. Marketing Factors

    a. Established brands vs new brands
    b. High market share vs low market share
    c. Well-known brand vs less well-known brand
    d. High brand loyalty vs low brand loyalty
    e. Long purchase cycle vs short purchase cycle
    f. Infrequent use of product vs frequent use of product

2. Copy Factors

    a. Simple copy vs complex copy
    b. Uniquely differentiated copy vs ordinary copy
    c. Continuing campaign vs new campaign
    d. Product sell copy vs image sell copy
    e. Single-copy campaign vs multiple-copy campaign
    f. New message vs older message
    g. Large ad units vs smaller ad units

3. Media Factors
    a. Low advertising clutter vs high advertising clutter
    b. Compatible editorial environment vs non-compatible editorial environment
    c. High attentiveness vs low attentiveness
    d. Continuous advertising vs flighted advertising
    e. Few media used vs many media used
    f. Opportunities for media repetitions vs few opportunities for repetition

From the assumed base frequency of 3, for each parameter if we need a lower frequency, we subtract 0.2 or 0.1 from the base frequency of 3. For example if the brand is established, then we need lower frequency, so we subtract either 0.2 or 0.1 from base frequency of 3 depending on how established the brand is. Similarly, as we move to.wards factors where we need a higher frequency, we add either 0.1 or 0.2 to the base frequency of 3 depending upon how strong the factor is.

So in this case, a brand was new, had a low market share, was less well known, had a low loyalty, had a short purchase cycle, and was a daily use product. In this case, the marketing factors would add a value of 1.2 to the Effective Frequency (0.2 for each factor). Similarly, we evaluate the creative factors, and assign scores. Assume those factors add up to a value of 0.8. Similarly, evaluate the media factors and say, these factors add a value of 1.0 to the Effective Frequency.

Combining the values of the three factors, we get an Effective Frequency of 5 (base frequency of 3 + 1.2 from marketing factors + 0.8 from creative factors + 1.0 from media factors).

Now one might say that some of these variables are subjective in nature. And how does one evaluate what rating to give such variables? Yes, an element of subjectivity and individual judgement is involved, but the correct way to arrive at this is to have a joint discussion with the Account Planning team and the advertiser to arrive at some sort of consensus on the scale. This would still be largely based on judgement and would still be subjective, but at least it would have all the decision-making constituents on the same page as far as objective setting is concerned.

Usually, Effective Frequency levels are set for a 4-week period. This is primarily because that's taken as a planning cycle. Therefore, if someone has a 3-month campaign, the levels of Effective Frequency could be moderated in month 2 and further down in month 3.

Stage 3: Estimate Optimum Reach at the EF Level

Having identified the campaign's Effective Frequency at 5+, the next step is to arrive at the level of reach required at this Effective Frequency level. In an ideal situation, the advertiser would like to reach 100% of the target audience at the Effective Frequency level. But given the media consumption habits of the target audience, and given the reality of 'diminishing returns', one has to climb down from the ideal situation and arrive at an 'Optimized level of reach'.

The process is fairly straightforward. Given the fact that Effective Frequency for the campaign has been identified (in our example, say the EF is 5+), the planner then needs to find out the optimum level of reach possible at 5+. For this, one has to make multiple media plans (since Effective Frequency is set for a particular medium, let's assume we're planning for TV right now) at various levels of GRPs. Each of these plans is optimized and evaluated to deliver maximum possible reach at 5+. The process is that one makes a base plan, say of 100 GRPs, and then keeps making plans with a 100 or 200 GRP increment and monitors Reach at 5+ for each plan. At every stage, it would also be possible to calculate Incremental GRPs percentage, and Incremental Reach percentage. The idea is to understand that x% of incremental GRPs brings about a y% increment in Reach. Given the law of diminishing returns, it would be observed that at the initial level of this exercise, a smaller percentage increase in GRPs will result in a higher percentage increase in reach. As we keep going along, the reach curve will start to flatten with every percentage increase in GRPs will result in a relatively lower percentage increase in Effective Reach (given the law of diminishing returns). There will come a stage at a certain GRP level where percentage increase in GRP will bring about an equal percentage increase in reach. Beyond this point, any percentage increase in GRPs will bring about a slightly lower-than-proportionate increase in reach. It is at this point that diminishing returns start to set in. This has been illustrated through Table 8.7 using hypothetical numbers.

Looking at the example in Table 8.7, there are 10 optimized plans that one has made – each plan adds an incremental 100 GRPs, and we correspondingly note the percentage reach at the Effective Frequency (5+) level. In practice however, TV planning softwares have built-in optimizers which will create optimized plans. The aforementioned example is to illustrate the concept.

Percentage incremental GRPs and percentage incremental reach have been calculated. The last column indicates what percentage change in reach occurs

TABLE 8.7 Estimating optimum reach at effective frequency 5+

Plan	Plan GRPs	Reach at at 5+	% Incremental Reach (a)	% Incremental GRPs (b)	Incremental Reach/Incremental GRPs (a/b)
1	100	5			
2	200	20	300	100	3.0
3	300	40	100	50	2.0
4	400	60	50	33	1.5
5	500	75	25	25	1.0
6	600	85	13	20	0.7
7	700	90	6	17	0.4
8	800	91	1	14	0.1
9	900	92	1	13	0.1
10	1000	93	1	11	0.1

Source: Created by the author.

over a % increase in GRPs. Notice that as we move from Plan 1 to Plan 4, a certain percentage increase in GRPs brings about a more-than-proportionate increase in reach – this indicates that reach is increasing at a faster rate than GRPs, and every incremental GRP brings about a more than proportionate increase in reach. By the time we reach Plan 5, you would see that a 25% increase in GRPs brings about an equal 25% increase in reach at 5+, which is absolutely in proportion. Beyond this, from Plan 6 onwards, at every level, the percentage increase in reach is less than proportionate to the percentage increase in GRPs. Therefore, from Plan 6 onwards, diminishing returns start to set in. This is what one would call the optimum reach possible at an Effective Frequency of 5+. Therefore, a plan of 500 GRPs which delivers 75% reach at 5+ is the optimum level that can be delivered in the market.

One could plot this table on a graph, and this is how it would look with realistic numbers for a hypothetical TV plan aimed at a certain defined target group. Figure 8.11 shows GRPs plotted on the X axis against reach at 5+.

Figure 8.12 shows GRPs plotted on the X axis against the proportionate increase in reach at 5+ on the Z axis.

Figure 8.13 shows the Optimum Reach at 5+. That's the point at which the Incremental Reach/Incremental GRP curve reaches 1 on the Z axis. Connecting it down to required GRPs, it gives 396 GRPs.

On the X axis are GRPs. On the Y axis is reach at 5+. The third value axis to the right is the percentage change in reach over the percentage

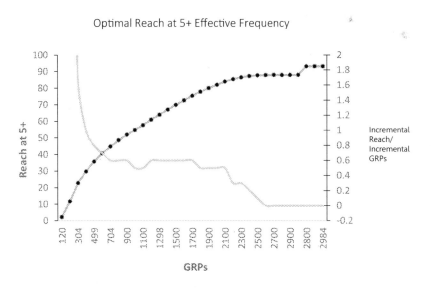

FIGURE 8.11   Optimum reach at 5+ effective frequency vs GRPS.

Source: Created by the author.

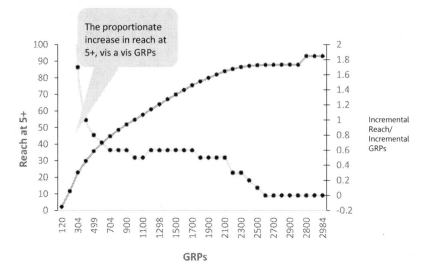

FIGURE 8.12 Proportionate increase in reach at 5+ vs GRPs.

Source: Created by the author.

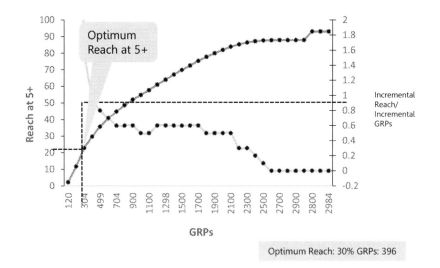

FIGURE 8.13 Finding the optimum reach at 5+.

Source: Created by the author.

change in GRPs (the calculation as indicated in the last column of the example cited earlier).

So in this realistic case, we see that the Optimum Reach possible at 5+ EF for this brand in this market is 30%, and at that level, 396 GRPs would be required. Beyond this point, diminishing returns would set in. Likewise, optimum levels are arrived at for each market.

It is here that the trade-offs begin. In an ideal situation one would like to reach 100% of the audience at 5+, but that is not possible because of diminishing returns. However, at the same point in time, one might feel that while 30% is the optimum reach possible, it might be too low and will not be enough for the brand. What does one do here? From here on, it becomes a trade-off between getting the highest possible level of reach and not travelling too far down on the diminishing returns curve. In our situation, it is possible to achieve 40% reach in this market, but the reality is that after 30% reach, every incremental GRP will bring you less than proportionate increase in reach. What it also means is that it would take more GRPs (and therefore cost more money) to reach every additional person. As shown in Figure 8.14, to get a reach of 40% at an Effective Frequency of 5+, we will need about 598 GRPs. At the same time, since after 30% (the optimum level), diminishing returns sets in, the plan will operate inefficiently. This in effect means that for

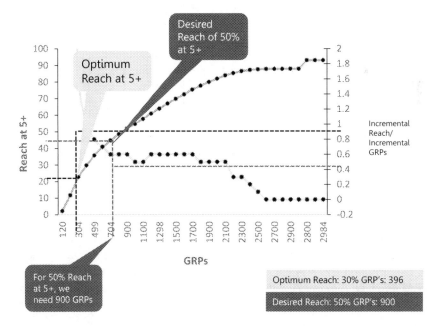

FIGURE 8.14 Plotting GRPs required for 50% reach at effective frequency of 5+.

Source: Created by the author.

TABLE 8.8 Optimum benchmarks across markets

Market	Optimum at 5+		GRPs Required
	Reach %	GRPs	for 50% at 5+
A	30%	400	900
B	39%	550	737
C	44%	500	600
D	28%	400	800
E	26%	300	700

Campaign Benchmark: Reach 50% at Frequency of 5+

Source: Created by the author.

every incremental reach percentage point beyond 30%, we will need to proportionally buy more GRPs.

At this stage, one could also bring in the competitive perspective and analyse what other competing brands deliver at 5+. This would take into account competitive realities and will help take a better decision. Assuming that analysis is done, one finally arrives at the conclusion that the campaign would require a minimum of 50% Effective Reach at 5+. This would certainly mean travelling down the diminishing returns curve, and we would be spending more money to reach every incremental person at this level of EF, but this is a demand of the competitive scenario.

Table 8.8 shows the final benchmarks across markets.

While for Market A, the optimum level is 30% and the GRPs required at this level are 400, for a 50% reach at 6+, the campaign would require 900 GRPs. Likewise, the levels could be set for all the markets.

Therefore, in the Effective Reach setting process, there are a couple of dominant practices. One is a thumb rule that says let's at least aim for a minimum of 50% Effective Reach at the EF level. Others look at matching competition at the given EF level, and the third is the trade-off between the desire to reach 100% and not travelling too far down the diminishing returns curve.

The second and more practical method used by some is to find out the Effective Frequency required for the brand, and then benchmark the Effective Reach to competitive levels. Therefore, if a brand if sets its EF benchmark at, say, 5+, it would be prudent to see how much Effective Reach a competing brand delivers at 5+, and then take a view. In a sense, the planner has three broad options to choose from:

a. Settle for the Optimum Effective Reach in the market. This is seldom done, however, as given the degree of fragmentation in the media space, the optimum levels are fairly low in a given market.

b. Take a thumb rule of 50% Effective Reach at the desired EF level.

c. Look at the Effective Reach delivered by competition at the EF levels desired, and do a benchmarking of sorts. This approach also helps taking the competitive environment into consideration.

The Effective Frequency approach as discussed earlier is fine for say products with defined purchase cycles. What about products like automobiles, two-wheelers, chocolates, OTC drugs, cigarettes, soft drinks etc.? There are no ready-made answers. Generally for impulse-buy kind of products, the goal is to build high recall in a short period of time, track response, and then work towards boosting recall levels.

Recency Approach

Before we get into looking at recency from a media weight setting point of view, it is important to understand the concept behind recency and how it came about. In the Effective Frequency chapter, we discussed how there was a huge debate around the concept and the use of a magic number. Here's a quick recap of the recency concept discussed in that chapter.

Erwin Ephron has been at the forefront of research on the recency concept, and according to him, recency is based on a couple of very simple premises (Ephron, 1995):

- Consumers buy products because of an inherent need, not because of advertising. If the toothpaste tube has got over or is just about to, that's when the consumer starts thinking about buying toothpaste, and likewise for most other products. There are certain things that happen in everyday life that trigger the need to buy. And advertising works best when there are people ready to buy. Therefore, targeting the message becomes important. Which consumers are ready to buy, and when are they in the market, are the most important considerations in the recency approach. If we get this right, then a single exposure to the consumers will work.
- The closer the message to the moment of purchase, the higher the chances of it influencing brand sales. Therefore, timing of advertising becomes critical.

Therefore, *when* a person gets a message is more important than *how many* messages he gets. This is because advertising just before the purchase brings about a higher brand share, and because purchases are happening every day, it is important that media focuses on continuity of advertising. And it makes better sense to reach three people rather than one person three times, and recency approach favours reach maximization. Therefore, the three key recency arguments are:

1. Timing of the message is critical.
2. Continuity of advertising presence. More weeks make better sense than more media weight.
3. Reach over frequency. Because one exposure before purchase is enough, it is important to reach out to many more people and influence that many more brand choices. It is important, however, to get the timing right.

Implications on Planning

Recency impacted the traditional way of planning and thinking about media. The key areas of change are:

1. *Shorter planning interval.* The planning cycle was generally taken as 4–6 weeks. Most media plans were optimized to deliver a certain level of reach and frequency during this period. Recency changes this thought a little bit. As per this, weekly planning should be the unit of planning. A 4 week planning cycle worked towards accumulating reach and had a variable pattern of delivery during each week. A weekly planning schedule would help minimize weekly fluctuations in media deliveries.
2. *Reach Maximization.* While traditional thinking was to understand Effective Frequency for a brand, and then optimize reach at the level of Effective Frequency, recency favours reach over frequency. As per the theory, since one exposure is enough, it is important to reach out to as many different people as possible. While earlier planning media weights was reflected in terms of 4+/50 (Optimize plan to deliver a 50% Effective Reach at a 4+ Effective Frequency), the recency theory could well say 1+/90 (Optimize plan to deliver a 90% Effective Reach at a 1+ Effective Frequency). This, coupled with weekly planning, marked a major change. One needs to maximize reach every week versus reaching people at a certain EF level over a 4-week period.
3. *Message dispersion.* How does one maximize or accumulate reach? By reducing duplication in the media plan. The less duplication the vehicles in the plan have, the higher the reach build. This was something that we discussed in the earlier chapters on basic concepts when we discussed the topic of duplication. By scattering the brand message across various types of media, and by scattering the message across different vehicles within the selected media, reach maximization could be achieved. So for instance, in TV planning, one would look at spreading the message throughout the day across different dayparts, and try to maximize reach. In Print, one would try to cycle though the various sections of the newspaper, or in

magazines, one would try to cycle through various genres, in radio through various dayparts, and so on. The underlying thought is to minimize duplication within the media plan, and to maximize reach. All media selection no doubt will continue to be based on the target audience's media consumption habits and intensity. This thought was a major departure from the Effective Frequency approach, where a certain degree of duplication was necessary – after all you had to reach one person, say, three or four times for that person to understand the message.

4. *Continuity*. Since consumers are there in the market every day, it is important that advertising focus on continuity. More weeks of advertising should be favoured over fewer weeks of higher intensity. How this works is that one needs to find out weekly brand purchases, identify the most important weeks which account for a significantly large portion of the sales, and try to cover those weeks with the objective of maximizing reach. However, it is important to arrive at a certain minimum weekly weight. Therefore, maximizing reach and continuity are the two important tenets from a media weight setting point of view.

According to recency theorists, this theory applies across most products. There are a lot of arguments doing the rounds in terms of whether one exposure will be enough, whether continuity pattern of ours might get marginalized with concentrated bursts of competitive advertising, what the impact of the purchase cycle will be, whether this approach can work with premium brands targeting a niche audience, how to manage one's SOV goals, what if one is into brand building, what about a brand launch situation, and so on. But the most effective approach, as outlined by John Philip Jones, is as follows (Jones, 1990):

- Aim to cover a substantial proportion of the brand's target group once every week with as little duplication as possible. 'Substantial proportion' is a judgement call.
- To achieve this, determine the optimum number of weekly GRPs and establish the best media and dayparts to use in order to minimize audience duplication. These procedures require expert knowledge of the media consumption of audiences.
- Run your weekly advertising pattern for as many weeks as the budget permits. If there are any gaps, try scheduling in such a manner that the gaps in advertising are taken during off-seasons, or months will lower sales.

However, there is no real substitute for studying the circumstances of each brand one is interested in – it is unwise to rely on any generalization. We should beware of assuming that any one rule is right.

The moot point is that one should not generalize things; look at a specific brand and competitive situation and then work on delivering the objective at hand. At times, it could be a mix of competitive benchmarking initially, probably even the Effective Frequency approach in the initial stages, and then follow through the recency approach.

Most importantly, while framing our media strategy, we must know how the brand behaves in relation to its advertising, promotions, and price, and in relation to the target consumers and the competition before we decide on the right balance between reach, frequency, and continuity.

Eventually, the decision hinges around this balance of reach, frequency, and continuity. Imagine these three like the three sides of a triangle, with the budget defining the area of the triangle. Within the area, remaining the same, one could stress on reach, or continuity, or frequency – whatever might be best suited to the brand's objective, and what might be most appropriate given the competitive environment.

When to Emphasize Reach?

Typically, reach is emphasized when there's something 'new' being introduced in the market:

- New distribution
- New features
- New message
- New sales promotion
- New packaging
- New variants

How Does One Set the Reach Levels?

Again, there is no one right method. Most times it is based on individual experience; sometimes it is through research done for specific brand situations, benchmarking with previous year's levels for the brand, most often on the basis of competitive benchmarking; and at times people work backwards using the AIDA model.

When to Emphasize Frequency?

When message repetition is necessary either for comprehension or for reminding consumers. Along with this, the dominant logic behind frequency was that advertising effectiveness is built through repetition, and therefore it is important to find out the basic threshold level of frequency required.

TABLE 8.9 Thumb rules for prioritizing reach or frequency

		Frequency	*Reach*
Consumer Purchase	Purchase Cycle	Short	Long
	Purchase Decision	Unplanned	Planned
	Interest	Low	High
	Loyalty	Low	High
Competitive Situation	Point of Purchase	Many Brands	Few Brands
	Quality	Parity	Superior
Creative	Complexity	Complex	Simple
	Campaign Maturity	New	Old
Media	Environment	Cluttered	Uncluttered

Source: Created by the author.

How Does One Set Frequency Levels?

Once again, there is no one right method. There are numerous EF models, such as Ostrow's model, and most media agencies have developed their own internal model to set EF levels. An important method, of course, is benchmarking with competition; people also sometimes do custom research to arrive at the right level of frequency. At times, previous experience comes into play.

Some Thumb Rules for Focusing on Frequency and Reach

Table 8.9 lists some generic thumb rules to follow when deciding between reach and frequency optimizations.

Chapter Summary

This is the fourth area, and one of the most critical areas, of planning media strategy. The question of how much to advertise or the intensity of advertising assumes significance as this also has a bearing on how much money needs to be spent on media.

Here are some of the key factors that influence the decision on how much to advertise:

a. *Competitive environment.* Often brands tend to benchmark their media weight with competing brands. Therefore, we usually see high media weights in intensely competitive categories.
b. *Brand/campaign objectives.* The campaign's marketing objectives usually set the pace for media weights. Aggressive objectives usually call for higher weights.

c. *Audience involvement level.* When audience involvement with the brand/category are high, it has a bearing on the kind of media weight one puts behind the campaign.

d. *Importance of different markets.* Markets that are higher on priority usually get a media weight than the markets lower in the order of priority.

e. *Position in the life cycle.* New/young brands typically have higher media weights, while mature brands can afford to go with lower media weights.

f. *Budgetary constraints.* Budgets define the intensity of media weights, and brand spends on media are a function of their sales and profitability.

g. *ROI on advertising.* Brands that have a high ROI (due to superior and highly optimized planning) can lower their advertising intensity, and vice versa.

h. *Media objectives.* Aggressive objectives would determine the intensity of media presence.

i. *Media consumption habits of audience.* In a fragmented media market, brands need to maintain a higher presence in media to generate ideal reach and frequency levels.

j. *Strength of communication.* Brands with superior communication can lower their advertising intensity compared to brands with very average communication.

k. *Market position of the brand.* Usually, growth/launch brands have a higher share of voice as compared to share of market. For large/mature brands, advertising intensities could be lower.

Key Techniques of Media Weight Setting

a. *Geographic weight setting*

  i. *Allocating budgets for different markets.* In this method, each market is allocated a fixed budget depending upon its relative importance for the brand. However, given the fact that media costs vary from market to market, in this method the GRP levels for different markets can get lopsided – one would buy more GRPs in relatively cost-efficient markets, and lower GRPs would be bought in expensive media markets.

  ii. *Allocating GRPs for different markets.* In this method, each market is allocated a certain level of GRP depending upon its relative importance. This method allows for proportional communication across different market priorities, however, at the same time the A:S ratios are slightly unbalanced.

b. *Competitive benchmarking.* This method is about benchmarking the intensity of our advertising versus the completion. This is a very common method of benchmarking and used widely across a range of product categories. Planners look at historical data of category spending and try to arrive at benchmarks. Sometimes share of market is correlated with share of voice to identify a pattern and take media weight decisions based on these ratios. When looking at competitive benchmarking, media planners consider category spending trends, scheduling patterns, market-wise skews of advertising spends, portfolio spend skews for key competing brands, absolute spends, growth rate of spends, genre mix, media mix, daypart-wise spread of advertising, and share of voice trends across different markets.

c. *Effective Frequency approach*. In this method, using one of the frequency estimator models, one arrives at the Effective Frequency for brand based on the campaign and market conditions. Based on this Effective Frequency, one arrives at the optimum reach in different markets. However, the desired reach in some markets may be more than the optimum reach. In such cases, one travels down the diminishing returns curve to settle at the right "trade-off" between optimum reach and desired reach.

d. *Recency approach*. This method advocates maximizing reach over a continuous period. Plans that follow this approach have shorter planning intervals, maximize reach, disperse the message across media and across dayparts, and try to maintain a continuous presence in media.

Setting Reach Thresholds

Typically, reach is emphasized when there's something 'new' being introduced in the market. It could be a new message, new promotion, new variant, new feature, etc.

Usually reach for a campaign is arrived at based on competitive benchmarking, or through research done on specific brand situations, or benchmarking based on previous experiences of the brand, and so on.

Setting Frequency Thresholds

Frequency is emphasized when message repetition is necessary either for comprehension or for reminding consumers. Along with this, the dominant logic behind frequency was that advertising effectiveness is built through repetition. Therefore, it is important to find out the basic threshold level of frequency required. There are many frequency estimator models that agencies use to arrive at the frequency number for a campaign, or it could be benchmarked with competition.

Further Reading

Ephron, Erwin, "More Weeks, Less Weight: The Shelf-Space Model of Advertising", *Journal of Advertising Research*, Vol. 35, No. 3, 1995.

Jones, John Philip, "Ad Spending: Maintaining Market Share", *Harvard Business Review*, January–February 1990, https://hbr.org/1990/01/ad-spending-maintaining-market-share

Ostrow, Joseph W, "Setting Effective Frequency Levels," in *Effective Frequency*, Advertising Research Foundation, 1982.

Sissors, Jack Z, and Roger B Brown, *Advertising Media Planning*.

9

PRINCIPLES OF STRATEGY PLANNING

Media strategy is a series of actions planned to achieve the media objectives, which in turn are based on the advertising/communications objectives and marketing objectives. Is it just about identifying a demographic target and hurling packets of GRPs across the most critical markets at the most important times of the year? While these used to be an important part of the process, they are no longer integral to the entire process.

However, over the last decade or so, the face of media, as we've known it, has changed drastically. Some of the key changes that we've seen are:

- The rise of the digital medium. Digital will account for 40% of the total advertising in India in 2023 and is projected to go up to 45% by 2024, making it the largest advertising medium in India (Dentsu's digital advertising report; Dentsu Aegis, 2023).
- With over 900+ TV channels accounting for 1.6 billion impressions/year, 400 million print readers, 600 million Internet subscribers, about 1800 film releases clocking 1.5 billion footfalls a year, along with 1100 operational radio stations, India's media footprint is huge. With so many options, media fragmentation is at an all-time high.
- The media landscape is changing from the erstwhile horizontal segmental division of media in buckets like TV, print, digital, radio, cinema, and OOH to a more segment-agnostic direct-to-consumer model characterized by content flowing from content producers to consumers via aggregators, distributors, and platforms. In this new world, the ability to forge direct-to-consumer relationships at scale, combined with the ability to analyse media consumption data, will hold the key to success.

DOI: 10.4324/9781032724539-9

- The resultant transformation of traditional media is likely to have a huge bearing on how content is produced, distributed, and monetized in India.
- In an attention-deficit era, the traditional boundaries of competition are being pushed further. Media, on the content creation front, compete with numerous content creators ranging from blogs to influencer channels, on the distribution front one competes with aggregators and platforms. With the balance of power shifting to the consumers, brands to now have to compete for attention.

As a result of these factors, traditional media planning has evolved over a period of time. These forces of change are pushing media planners to think differently, so that one is completely aligned with delivering business results. A better consumer understanding both demographically, and psychographically, helps better decision making. There are times when quantitative data is either just not enough, or just not there to help decision making. In such situations, understanding of consumer behaviour, communication, impact of media, and the competitive market forces help take better decisions. Today, media is increasingly becoming part of the idea rather than just be involved with the placement of the final creative product. There was a time when buying efficiencies were important, and there was a time when sophisticated media models were part of agency credentials. Now, consumer understanding, market understanding, understanding the way communication works, and demonstrating the ability to magnify media impact are the cutting-edge differentiators – the focus is back on media thinking.

So what are some of the key issues that one should consider in the strategic decision making process? Let's take this discussion via tackling some key questions that face media planners and brand marketers.

Whom to Target?

It begins with the consumer. One of the starting points could be, how does a consumer respond to advertising and brand communication? What is the role of communications in altering his/her buying behaviour? How does he/she consume media? How does he/she decide to buy in the given category? Increasingly, we have begun making attempts to understand the human being behind the demographic definitions of SEC/Age/Gender – we have begun to define him/her more in terms of their attitudes, behaviour, value systems and lifestyles. These were domains that the typical Account Planner dealt with – these are the new descriptors that media agencies have started talking about.

However, targeting principles in the current era have undergone quite a change. With the always-on digital tracking systems, some people believe that the targeting part of the process is out of the equation because the digital medium allows us to precisely understand behaviour of consumers. However, as we're now well aware, in a 'cookie-less' era, targeting and retargeting (which were the easiest ways to reach consumers) is going to be challenged. At the same time, there are advertisers who believe that mass targeting is the way forward, because there are the obvious perils of 'over-targeting'. Marc Pritchard of Procter & Gamble (quoted in Terlap and Seetharaman, 2016) had gone to the extent of saying that they targeted too much and went too narrow, which was an incorrect strategy to pursue. He sees great benefit in mass-targeting, particularly for mass consumer FMCG brands.

At the same time, on the issue of targeting, there is often the debate of targeting the existing loyal customers vs targeting new customers. In their book, *The Long and the Short of It: Balancing Short and Long-Term Marketing Strategies*, Les Binet and Peter Field spoke about two ways in which marketing communication works – for brand building (usually longer term), and for sales activation (in the short term). For brand building, they propose broad reach and suggest reaching out to many consumers irrespective of whether they are in the market to buy the product or not. They believe that the cumulative impact of repeated exposures will lay down deeper memory tracks for the brand and will favourably predispose such consumers to pick up the brand whenever they are out in the market. On the other hand, short-term sales activation is important to keep the brand in business on a daily basis. For this, they've suggested applying sharp targeting and using media that allows them to achieve the desired results. Therefore, for long-term brand building, one should look at mass targeting and use media that gives them this scale; while for short-term sales activation, one should look at sharper targeting and gravitate towards media that helps them deliver this (Binet and Field, 2013).

Proponents of targeting loyal customers believe that these customers are easy to define and track in a digital era; hence, using data analytics, one could influence their behaviour when it comes to buying a brand. Strengthening this argument is also the fact that digital media has lowered the cost of talking to such customers. Brands naturally tend to gravitate towards social media to establish direct contact with such customers, and sometimes the data is so compelling that one is often found shifting budgets from traditional media into digital and social media. But would that always be the right approach and hold the brand firm in the long run? Professor Byron Sharp of the Ehrenberg-Bass Institute, University of Southern Australia (Ehrenberg-Bass, 2017), suggests that 'Sales growth won't come from relentlessly targeting a particular segment of a brand's buyers'. Echoing a similar view is Unilever Chief Marketing and Communications Officer Keith Weed (2017), who put it succinctly: 'If you get too targeted, you reinforce people who love your brands to use more … [but] there are only so many cups of tea you can drink in a day' (quoted in Bouvard, 2017). Both of them are clearly stating the case for mass targeting and mass marketing. Sharp believes that sharp targeting produces short-term effects, but for the long-term brand health, it's important to look at mass targeting. Concluding this thought, Binet and Field suggest that it's important for marketers to consider both brand building and sales activation, but must get the ratio right. They've suggested a ratio of 60% effort directed towards long-term brand building (read mass targeting) and 40% effort towards short-term sales activation (read tight targeting to loyal customers) (Binet and Field, 2013).

What about Reach and Frequency?

Taking the previous section's discussion forward, a clear case is emerging to balance the long term and the short term. Going by the arguments put up by Sharp, there are very compelling reasons why reach matters more than ever before. Binet and Field too have also spoken about mass reach and the long term. This is also supported by the 'Profit Ability' study by Ebiquity, Gain Theory, and Thinkbox (2018). A key conclusion of this report is that TV drives business profitability primarily because of the mass reach it provides. Therefore, media which deliver scale should matter most to brand marketers. In an increasingly fragmented media space, Reach would matter more than ever before and media that have scale, would drive business results better (Ebiquity, Gain Theory, and Thinkbox, 2018).

The frequency issue has already been discussed in the earlier chapter on Effective Frequency. We've moved from the 3+ theory to 1+ (proposed by recency theorists). The new thinking on frequency suggests numbers between 3 and 10 exposures, after which more exposures have a negative effect. On digital media (with retargeting capabilities), frequency capping is increasingly finding favour. However, going forward, in a cookie-less world, planners would once again be searching for new answers as the existing frequency capping mechanisms might not be able to cope. We would end up with wasteful frequencies as the distinction between existing and returning users would blur. Therefore, it would be important for brands to consider looking at correlating media exposure with business results, and also to look at competitive considerations to arrive at the optimum frequency levels for their brand.

How Should One Look at Budget Allocations, and What Kind of Media Will Deliver Results?

Just a decade ago, we had the concept of paid media. Here, one bought media and reached a certain number of people with some frequency. However, with the scaling up of digital media and its several platforms, we now talk of three kinds of media – paid media, owned media, and earned media.

Paid media: This media is bought upfront. Examples are paid advertising in TV, print, digital, cinema, OOH, radio, and so on.

Owned media: This media is created and controlled by the brand. Examples could be the brand's website, app, official Facebook page, Twitter handle, etc.

Earned media: This media is generated by consumers and users of social media. This could include product reviews, unboxing videos on YouTube, third-party news articles in newspapers and magazines, news bytes on TV, and so on.

Brands usually have been so far working only on paid media and it's allocation across mediums. However, in today's scenario, owned and earned media also pay a big role in driving brand business. In fact, the impact of earned media is huge because that's a neutral endorsement of one's brand by a third-party consumer or media outlet. You would have often noticed how brands in their advertising directly cue their brand's website or Facebook page to direct the consumer to owned media.

Peter Field and Les Binet in their paper "Marketing Effectiveness in the Digital Era" posit that paid media is a pre-condition to drive owned and earned media (Binet and Field, 2017). Therefore, brands in contemporary times typically tend to create a huge mass market pull through paid media and, with the right creative quality and product experience, seek to drive both owned and earned media to achieve the maximum impact on brand salience, and brand business.

Within paid media, budget allocations take place primarily based on the width/scale of reach offered by media (in case mass reach is a brand objective), or depth of profile offered by media (in case the brand objective is to engage with sharply targeted audiences). Add to this the characteristics of different media that play a role – for instance, usually video is used to communicate emotion, print is used to communicate detail, and so on. It's important to understand that media too is quickly adapting and changing based on the requirements of brands. Let's quickly take a view across media and see how it works today:

Print: The same newspaper brand now sees itself as a content creator with its content being distributed across multiple channels like the newspaper, website, app, emails, WhatsApp editions, Facebook pages, Twitter handles, digital newspapers, e-papers, etc. Similarly, it offers the ability to establish mass on-ground events leveraging its physical infrastructure and its local community connect. They leverage their environment to set the agenda for brands and create context. They have the ability to create both text and video content, and to offer bouquets of solutions to brands. In India, with about 400 million readers, print media provides scale, localization, and the ability to customize commercial content based on geo-locations.

TV: It is by far the largest medium in India, with 840 million viewers and 1.6 billion impressions/year. It provides the ability to repeat communication at scale, and is therefore preferred by a vast majority of advertisers to play a major role in the media plan. Typically, FMCG brands (that require mass reach) are the major advertisers on TV. The other big reason supporting the cause of TV is because of empirical evidence by the 'Profit Ability' study by Ebiquity, Gain Theory, and Thinkbox. A key conclusion of this report is that TV drives business profitability primarily because of the mass reach it provides. However, with the OTT services growing in scale at a rapid pace, TV's ability to provide mass reach could be challenged in time to come. However, large TV networks in India have launched their own OTT services to reach out directly to viewers. So the Star Network has Hotstar, Zee has Zee5, Sony has SonyLIV, and Colors has Voot. Several regional channels too have their own OTT service catering to respective language geographies. Connected/smart TVs are making a gradual entry into India, but conventional TV would far outstrip connected TVs in the near foreseeable future.

Radio: Radio has about 225+ million listeners in India and has the ability to relay localized messages. While usually it is used as a support medium to amplify the main campaign on TV and print, FM radio stations have gone beyond and offer integrated solution to brands. These solutions range from creating local hype, contests, integrated RJ talk, activations, integrations with web radio, sponsorships of IP properties, etc. As a medium, it's perfectly suited for localised SME and retail advertisers, yet at the same time large radio networks in India also provide reach across over 100 major towns. Competition is slowly emerging in the form of streaming services, but increasingly most large private FM networks have set up their own web radio stations. At the same time, the unique entertainment content generation capabilities of radio, and the local community connect strength of radio, will come in handy over the next few years as they go about reinventing business models. Already, we've seen a large radio network, 'Radio Mirchi', which went into a rebranding exercise and have rebranded themselves as just 'Mirchi', in a bid to suggest that they are ready for the new media landscape.

Digital: This includes advertising like banner ads and popups on websites, OTT services, and videos accessed on online platforms like YouTube, search, and social media. There are third-party video ads inserted in online channels, and sometimes brands too create their own video content to be put up online. With 881 million Internet subscribers in India as per *TRAI Report* (January–March 2023), a smartphone subscriber base of almost 400 million, and 15 million Smart TVs, Indians are spending about 3.5 hours daily on their phones and have downloaded

28.9 billion apps in 2022 alone (Windows of Opportunity, FICCI-EY Report, 2023). As a result, OTT and other Internet services have noticed a huge growth uptick. Advertising continues to rise on digital, and the media now provides engagement at scale and brands are warming up to the medium. Brands are looking at using digital along with conventional media like print and TV to drive synergistic efforts that lead to extending campaign reach and engagement. Digital is a good way to reach out to light TV viewers or non-print readers. In an era of media fragmentation, brands that need mass reach are increasingly turning to use digital in conjunction with conventional media.

Out-of-home (OOH) advertising: This includes traditional OOH, transit media, digital OOH, wall paintings, and ambient media, amongst other formats. A highly localized medium, OOH is usually used by real estate, local retail, media, FMCG, and financial services. Currently digital OOH and transit media are growing rapidly. Brands usually are present on OOH for salience, immediacy, quick local reach build-up, and its ability to localize messaging.

Does SOV Matter in a New Era?

The conventional thinking on media was always around the equation between share of market and share of voice (SOV). Typically, new brands, and those on the growth path, were advised to maintain a higher SOV as compared to market share. At the same time, legacy brands with large market shares could afford a lower SOV. This was well explained by John Philip Jones as well in his book *When Ads Work*. For a long time, this remained the template for a lot of brands across categories. This was endorsed by Binet and Field as well when they said that brands that keep their SOV lower than market share, tended to fail (Binet and Field, 2017). SOV, however, is share of paid advertising. The rule of thumb was to generate excess SOV (ESOV) to the brand's market share. Till date, this is a practice with a lot of brands across categories. However, with the mainstreaming of digital media, we've also seen the rise of owned media and earned media. Leading experts around the world are now talking about share of experience (SOE), which is about collectively looking at paid-owned-earned media and a brand's relative share of these customer experience touchpoints. In a fragmented media space, this thinking is gaining a lot of traction amongst advertisers. Just like one looked at excess SOV (ESOV), brands would now increasingly start looking at excess SOE (ESOE).

What's the Importance of Context?

While we talk of share of experience, brands are also now increasingly conscious about the context or environment in which their ads are placed.

Recently there was some controversy when some brand's ads were placed on a video platform on which some objectionable/extremist videos were played. This was part of a programmatic buy where the brand had no control of where the ads were placed. Following a huge backlash, brands are increasingly wanting to take back this control and stop blindly chasing cheap CPMs to deliver campaign targets. As Faris Yakub, Founder of Genius Steals, says, 'Since we process information differently depending on context, it follows that medium has an impact on the efficacy of brand communication' (Yakub, 2018). Accordingly, all impressions aren't equal. The effect of watching a TV commercial vs reading a press ad or a banner popup on the screen, are all different. They talk to people in different contexts and in different states of mind, and thereby have a different impact. Yakub posits that one shouldn't just be guided by reach, frequency, and cost, and instead look at context and the impact of impressions on the brand. Professor Byron Sharp, the author of *How Brands Grow*, said it directly that context comes first before the CPT while offering the advice, 'buy the largest number of the highest quality impressions against the entire buying market for the category for the lowest price' (Yakub, 2018).

So when planning for context, it is advisable to consider the impact of the timing of your advertising. When the person gets the message is more important than how many messages he/she gets. The location is the second important factor – where the person gets your message is equally as important. One might reach the person alright, but is he/she in a state of mind to even think about your product at that point in time? The third important aspect is the device on which he gets the message. Trying to advertise for a country's tourism industry might need a better landscape visual space in media – maybe the laptop screen would work better than a mobile screen. The fourth factor, and arguably one of the most critical aspects that drives context, is the content of media which carries the advertising. If the media title is trusted and credible, these would have a definite carry-over effect to the advertising carried in the vehicle.

There are a lot more sophisticated models that help us fine-tune or optimize scheduling decisions. However, there's also a parallel migration to understanding consumer buying and decision-making cycles and trying to get a sense on how and when brands are bought. There are optimizers that will help you maximize reach or frequency levels, but there is also a parallel talk of how to get the central communication idea 'live' in an environment beyond GRPs.

The important thing is to *ask questions* at every stage of the process:

- Who is the audience, and what do we want them to do after seeing our communication?
- In what context will they best accept our messaging? This requires a study of patterns of media use, intensity, time of media consumption, etc.

- How do people buy in the category, and what role does the category play in their lives?
- What is the relationship the audience has with the brand? How could you tap into this relationship and make it stronger? What kind of media will help you perform this task better? Is there any media equity/property that the brand owns, and how could you leverage that to drive the brand's business?
- What are the apertures or windows that the audience offers to you during the course of his/her day, and how can you influence their brand choice when they are in the market to buy?
- How can you dip into the cultural context of your audience and leverage them for the brand?
- What can you offer the target audience in exchange for their attention?
- Which markets are of utmost importance – from strategic, distribution, target, and competitive points of view?
- What should be the right balance of reach/frequency/continuity in planning terms?
- How does one find the right balance between the long-term and short-term brand needs?

Answers to some or most of these questions give a lot of pointers to various steps in the strategic planning process. They open up what are known as 'media apertures' to address the audience. The fundamental task is to get the consumer to take the desired action. A thorough understanding of consumer behaviour, market forces, and the media environment will help take the right decision and help deliver brand objectives. It might not necessarily be a fancy-looking document with lots of charts and graphs and a whole lot of jargon thrown in. The simpler the thought, the better the chances of its eventual success. The fundamentals remain the same – *connect* with consumers and make the advertising work harder to achieve the objectives spelt out within all the constraints.

The Rise of Content Marketing

In a cluttered and fragmented media space, getting audience attention and being able to engage meaningfully with them is a key goal of media planning. However, despite the hyper-connected world we live in, more and more people are tuning out of advertising. The use of ad blockers is at an all-time high, with 47% of Internet users globally using an ad blocker. With TV viewership fragmenting across different screens, there's a switch-out happening during ad breaks, and there's multitasking happening while watching TV. Newspaper pages are being flipped over when it takes six pages to get to the front page for news. With FM radio stations playing out similar kind of music to appeal to a mass taste, station loyalties are low, and switching behaviour is rampant on FM radio stations during the ad breaks. And all of us know that popcorn is being bought when the ads are playing in the theatre. With mobile phones becoming ubiquitous, I wonder how many people even notice the big billboard during their commute. Consumers find advertising intrusive, and sometimes even annoying and irrelevant. In such times, how do brands communicate with consumers and show their relevance in peoples' lives? If people are avoiding advertising, then they must surely be going to content. And brands are now increasingly starting to leverage content to engage with their audiences.

Content marketing is awash with several jargonized names. So often we find jargon like branded content, promoted content, sponsored content, specialist content, curated content, ad-funded content, influencer content, native advertising, and so on. According to the American Marketing Association, 'Content marketing is a technique of creating and distributing valuable, relevant and consistent content to attract and acquire a clearly defined audience – with the objective of driving profitable customer action' (American Marketing Association, n.d.). In short, brands are interweaving their brand stories with the content narrative. In that sense it is brand story-telling. As described by Bryan Eisenberg (2017), author and customer experience expert, "Effective content marketing is about mastering the art of storytelling. Facts tell, but stories sell".

So How Does One Go about Content Marketing?

The first and most obvious step is to understand your consumers. In the content marketing lexicon, it's called understanding user personas. This is nothing but a thorough demographic, psychographic, and behavioural analysis of your consumers. It's important to understand what media they consume, when they consume media, what topics interests them, and what they give their attention to. If you are able to decipher this, this would help you from the base of your content creation strategy.

The next step is to align this audience persona understanding with the brand theme. If your audience is, say, extremely health conscious, then it would be important to assess whether your product is the right fit, and whether the brand theme and tonality are in alignment with the kind of messaging this audience wants to receive.

While studying the audience's media behaviour, it is pertinent to understand their media consumption behaviour and assess which platforms they are on, and what format of content they are giving attention to. This will help decide whether you need to create a text article, or an infographic, or a long-form or short-form video. At the same time, each of the content pieces that we create must be customized for individual platforms.

The content pieces that one creates must tell your brand story subtly. Make the sales pitch too obvious, and you lose audience attention. So the right balance must be created. In fact, at the heart of content creation lies intent. You must create content that adds value to the life of your consumer. Only if the content piece passes this test will the consumer give his/her attention. The content should be useful and informative to the consumer. If it is useful, he/she is likely to engage with it and also possibly share it with his/her group of contacts.

In a BBC Science of Engagement study (2017), a key conclusion was that content will get better attention from consumers if the brand involved is completely transparent. Another key conclusion underlined the critical importance of the publisher's editorial environment and how it enhances the value of branded content carried within this. The study also emphasized the importance of quality of content. Consumers expect good-quality content, and brands must invest enough to match the editorial quality of the environment in which the content would be placed.

Types of Content

Licensed content: This content is created by the publishers and is therefore completely customized to the editorial environment of the platform. Several large media houses have set up content studios to create content for brands based on a brief.

Original content: This is content created by the brand. It could be text, video, audio, an infographic, or even a creation. An example of this is the creation of the 'Fearless Girl' statue, which went viral with billions of Twitter impressions and Instagram posts.

User-generated content: This is content created by users and used by brands.

And What about a Cookie-less World?

A big advantage that digital media brought to the table was addressability – the ability to address different audiences across different stages of the purchase funnel, and the ability to target them precisely and retarget them. All of this was largely based on cookies which enabled to identify and track a web user's digital footprints and follow him/her. Privacy concerns and regulations first led to Safari and Firefox disabling cookies. Now with Google Chrome also joining the chorus and disabling cookies, the entire ad-tech industry is debating ways and means to target and retarget audiences. Cookies were essentially a crude form of a user ID which was used to find out location, devices, sites accessed, browser used, and web surfing patterns of the ID. With this ID now becoming defunct, the digital planning world is in a bit of a disarray for want of options. Clearly, the ability to target and retarget using programmatic engines will be severely restricted. At the same time, the ability to measure campaign reach and frequency will be impacted. One could still measure it for individual publishers, but measuring the campaign across thousands of sites will be under stress. Search and social don't seem to be affected as much, as they had their own reach-frequency evaluations which were very specific to their individual platforms. But the ability of programmatic engines to trade and track and deliver campaigns comes under question. The only way out as of the present is to harness first-party data and utilize it to the best of your ability.

However, cookies were a weak identifier to begin with. They expired and took the user data with them. They weren't working on mobiles as effectively they were with desktops. With no immediate replacement, Google, in their blog post, said:

> We will continue to support first-party relationships on our ad platforms for partners, in which they have direct connections with their own customers. And we'll deepen our support for solutions that build on these direct relationships between consumers and the brands and publishers they engage with.
>
> *(Temkin, 2021)*

Essentially, they have suggested that going forward, first-party data, which has been collected with consent from users, is the only data that could be used for targeting. Several ad-tech firms have created ID solutions, but at the moment, it is ambiguous whether these solutions can be integrated and used with the Google Ads system. Instead, Google has created a system called FloC (Federated Learning of Cohorts). Put simply, FloC would track a user's browsing habits and group him into a cohort based on his/her behaviour. So there would be many cohorts which could then be used for targeting as compared to individual targeting during a cookie era.

The key impacts of this are:

- The importance of first-party data becomes critical. Brands that have harnessed this data well and have accounted for de-duplication will have an advantage in the new digital advertising ecosystem.
- Use Google fLoC to target cohorts. This will account for a large chunk of the internet users. For IOS users, there are no alternatives.
- Brands would now need to create individual strategies for each of the walled gardens. They would need to match user data on their servers with the data on the platforms of different walled gardens, and try to mount digital retargeting and remarketing campaigns.

So as the cookie crumbles, it is back to the basics. The importance of right people, right place, right timing, and right context was probably getting lost somewhere in the digital jungle. It's just got dark in there, and what would pull you out is a map that leads you on with the basics. And at the heart of this is knowing about your customers without pushing the privacy wall too far back.

Planning in an Altered Digital Landscape: An Alternate Point of View

Over the last few years, we've seen several 'rules' of media planning being fundamentally altered. Reach and frequency have newer dimensions around them. Debates on media and marketing effectiveness have multiplied, and a never-before-seen focus on performance marketing takes centre stage. With the balance of power shifting to the consumers, brands now have to compete for attention. How precisely should they do that? There are several new models of thinking, and one that really put it up front precisely has been done by Sandeep Menon. He writes about leveraging the four levers of data, tech, money and content (Menon, 2021):

> I keep hearing from traditional marketing folks, that something very strange is happening to marketing. And not in a good way. "All marketing just can't be performance marketing", "the art of marketing is disappearing under the weight of the tech", "when did marketing become statistics", "doesn't anyone care about brand anymore", "attribution measurement is just smoke and mirrors" etc. You get the picture.

Now, it is true that the ability to measure ROI in the digital world has led to a surge of interest in "measurable marketing". Most marketing teams are starting to track and measure leads to sales performance almost like sales teams. And businesses obviously love this. But beyond all that, there seems to be something else at play here. It appears that "digital" has fundamentally altered the landscape and hence the models based on which the practice of traditional marketing was carried on.

It has reset our definition of "consumer", improved our ability to personalize messaging while simultaneously reducing our control over brand conversations, mainstreamed the focus on corporate behavior behind the brand, flattened the purchase funnel, scattered the purchase journey and so on. So if one came from a world of neat models like 4Ps, Porters forces etc., it may be time to view marketing from a somewhat different lens.

This discussion can obviously get very complicated, especially if we dive into the deep end of mar/ad-tech, personalization, attribution and AI etc. It's easy to get lost in that maze. People tend to get all wound up in the nuts and bolts, without factoring in the fundamental changes to the building blocks.

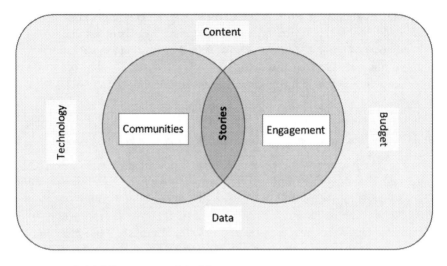

FIGURE 9.1   Initial Engagement Model.

Source: Marketing: Reboot for the digital age, Sandeep Menon

One can start believing that all marketing has become "performance marketing", while in reality the role of marketing in curating relationships is becoming even more critical by the day.

In this regard, it may be useful to just start with a very simple, new model of looking at the marketing and consumer landscape. Figure 9.1 illustrates the initial model that I now personally start with, is as follows:

Let's look at each of these components, in order to understand the model better.

The underlying assumption is that marketing is now all about creating vibrant communities around your brand or product premise and engaging effectively and deeply with these communities. And in the process of doing that, one ends up impacting a broad swathe of individuals within those communities.

So how does one do that? The bridge to reach communities appears to be good old "stories". The better the stories we craft, the deeper the engagement with our desired communities.

HYPOTHESIS 1

– Think "communities" rather than "consumer": An era of hyper personalization and almost intrusive targeting may lead us to believe that we are now ready to focus even more sharply on who our consumer is and talk only to that person. But the reality in the digital world is that it is actually harder to define who exactly needs to be spoken to, in order to close a sale! Counter intuitive, isn't it? The reason is that when a potential sale goes through its interest-consideration to purchase cycle, it is now dependent on not just a consumer making up her mind, but many other factors such as influencers, opinion leaders, peers, experts, rating engines, reviewers and critics, YouTube unboxers and so on.

It gets really complicated because there is no longer a clean "funnel" that the consumer passes through, while receiving conveniently phased marketing messages at every stage. Instead, the potential buyer moves back and forth, while being buffeted by varying voices from the ecosystem of interested parties around the brand or product.

One might argue that some version of these forces always existed in a marketing ecosystem, but their influence is greatly magnified in a social media led digital ecosystem.

So how does one handle this complex ecosystem of people that need to be spoken with? It's very hard to segment and target all of them separately & effectively. An easier alternative is to actually think of them as "one community" and target all marketing to that community.

HYPOTHESIS 2

– Engagement rather than outcomes: It's much harder to engage with the community, because the community doesn't care that you want to sell a new rat trap to the kid down the road. They are instead interested in how the brand or product relates with each of them in their individual lives, hopes and dreams.

It wants you to respect its independence of opinion, while making each individual feel special at the same time. Many of these expectations are contradictory in nature and hard to craft into one common communications strategy. So rather than trying to blend multiple outcomes, it becomes more practical to simply strive for (and measure) greater engagement, which then hopefully flows organically to desired outcomes.

HYPOTHESIS 3

– Stories form the bridge: The gap between complex communities with varying expectations/needs and a marketer who wants to drive deep engagement with them is a tenuous chasm. The very traditional medium of stories has emerged as an effective bridge. Why? Because communication connects with the human element, which forms the basis of all relationships and it allows us to impact individuals deeply, while still speaking to the community.

Here is where the good old facets of brand values, creativity, art etc. come in, because your messaging has to be sufficiently broad to cover everyone, while driving very specific business results. That can't be done by blasting out product/feature & benefits driven communication like the good old days. It has to far cleverer and more subliminal communication. And that is what we are seeing from many brands today that don't seem to say anything about the product. Instead they take you on a journey, that somehow feels good. Think Gillette's "the best that men can be" campaign, Facebook's "Pooja Didi" campaign, Tinder's "in our own way" campaign and so on...

Great! But how does one actually execute all of this?

Again, a simple high level method is to look at 4 fundamental drivers that help drive engagement in the digital world. How good is the content, how well has data been leveraged, how effectively has technology been used... and of course, how much spending power do you have ù. An optimum balance of these 4 levers can help us craft deeper engagement with our communities, through stories.

a) **Content: Hallelujah! Creativity lives. What's more, it's critical.**

When brand managers whine at their agencies, saying "can you make it viral?" ... this is what they are actually asking for. Intelligent, engaging, emotionally aware "content" that grabs peoples attention.

This can be a whole plethora of vehicles such as video, gaming, polls, advertising, blogs, hybrid models and so on. But the underlying theme is the ability to interact in a meaningful and entertaining manner with an audience. One that will click away in a second, if you are even a tiny bit banal in your approach. So for those who say "the art of marketing is dead", I would counter that it is even more critical now. Because we are dealing with a broader and more fickle audience.

Gone are the captive hostages who would blindly sit through a repetitive, nauseating ad, 12 times in a day. Just because it was coming in between a live match that one could only watch on that one medium, at that very time. The new age marketer literally needs an entire universe of "creators" by her side.

Authors, domain specialists, scriptwriters, visualizers, singers, film makers, photographers, comedians, movie directors, gamers, video editors, artists and so on. Plus someone who can make it all stick together. The breadth of creativity needed is much, much more.

b) **Data: Needs no introduction. It's available in buckets. It needs very smart people, technology and tools to leverage it.**

If you do not have a formal data strategy and the right AI and analytics tools that are mining insights, which are then tailored into your content strategy, you are pretty much toast. Might as well pack up and go home. Enough said.

Everyone's heard the "data is the new oil" spiel already. Research tells us that data driven orgs are 23 times more likely to acquire customers and 6 times more likely to retain them! Get yourself either a really good analytics partner or a dedicated team.

c) **Technology: It's a tool. And a damn effective one. You're being offered a Ferrari. Don't insist on driving your old Ford Escort ☺.**

While saying this, I must acknowledge that the plethora of marketing tools and aids available out there now can be potentially blinding. Right from campaign planning and automation, to targeting, personalization, tracking, geotagging, attribution etc. There are multiple options that can be used at every stage.

Tech is very much of a double edged sword. When implemented badly, it can exist just for itself, with marketing teams groaning and using tools that they don't really believe in. But when intelligently architected and held together, they can multiply marketing efficiency multifold.

A common mistake made is that marketing (or even worse, sales or finance) defines their requirements piecemeal and IT procurement goes out and buys/implements the tools. The role of a highly skilled solution architect or consultant who looks at the entire marketing business process holistically and then defines the full solution stack is still evolving. But it is certainly worth investing into.

d) **Budgets: Self-explanatory and the one thing that always remains constant. The more money you have, and the smarter you can spend it, the more successful your digital campaign is likely to be.**

The catch is that you can have a lot of money and end up spending it very unwisely in the digital world. And this circles back to tech and data once again. For e.g. If you don't really understand ad-tech, marketing to communities can turn into a fancy version of "spray and pray". If your analytics team isn't tracking ROI closely, it can hark back to the old days of "just account it against brand equity" and so on.

No matter how much you love the good old days of not being answerable on budgets, it's time for marketing leaders to get hard-nosed about spends. Because the environment now allows us to be. And if we don't, then someone else will take a long, hard look at how the money is being spent.

I'd like to conclude by citing the example of a brand that is pretty close to my heart. a.k.a Royal Enfield, the iconic biking brand that seems to have been unstoppable in the last decade. If you examine their marketing (across channels) closely, you would notice that they really don't focus on saying that their motorcycle is better in any way. Instead, they pour all their efforts into building the travel biking community. And into capturing what is euphemistically called "the spirit of biking". They talk to influencers as well as buyers. Adventure riding and human interest stories form the bedrock of their communication. The net result is a die hard, aspirational community that simply pays no heed to any logical arguments about speed, reliability, handling etc. They would much rather just "belong". That is a very powerful brand position to be in. They could certainly do much better on leveraging data and technology. But they seem to have pinned community engagement down pretty well.

So finally, the aim of a digital campaign can be pretty simple actually. Just focus on increasing the size and strength of the engagement-intersection area as depicted in Figure 9.2. And the way to do it, is by leveraging the 4 levers of data, tech, money and content. Pretty simple, isn't it? 😊

Chapter Summary

Media has come a long way from being a one-way street. India is right now one of the most complex media markets in the world, with 900+ TV channels accounting for 1.6 billion impressions/year, 400 million print readers, 600

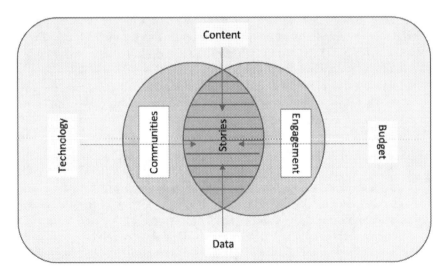

FIGURE 9.2 Model of engagement in contemporary times.

Source: Marketing: Reboot for the digital age, Sandeep Menon

mn Internet subscribers, and about 1800 film releases clocking 1.5 billion footfalls a year, along with 1100 operational radio stations. In an attention-deficit era, the traditional boundaries of competition are being pushed further. Media now competes with numerous content creators ranging from blogs to influencer channels, and with aggregators and platforms regarding distribution. With the balance of power shifting to the consumers, brands now have to compete for attention.

Media planners today strive to ensure that media is increasingly becoming part of the idea rather than just involvement with placement of the final creative product. There was a time when buying efficiencies were important, and there was a time when sophisticated media models were part of agency credentials. Now, the focus has returned to media thinking, as consumer understanding, market understanding, understanding the way communication works, and demonstrating the ability to magnify media impact are the cutting-edge differentiators.

The following are the core issues that issues that one should consider in the strategic decision-making process:

1. *Whom to Target?* There are three basic issues under this:
   - Increasingly we have begun to make attempts to understand the human being behind the demographic definitions of SEC/age/gender – we have begun to define him/her more in terms of their attitudes, behaviour, value systems, and lifestyles.
   - There's a belief amongst some digital thinkers that the targeting part of the process is out of the equation because the digital medium allows us to precisely understand behaviour of consumers. However, extreme targeting too is a problem. There are advertisers who believe that mass targeting is the way forward, because there are the obvious perils of 'over-targeting'
   - There is often the debate of targeting the existing loyal customers vs targeting new customers. Les Binet and Peter Field suggest that marketers must consider both brand building and sales activation, but must get the ratio right. They've suggested a ratio of 60% effort directed towards long-term brand building (mass targeting) and 40% effort towards short-term sales activation (tight targeting to loyal customers).

2. *What about Reach and Frequency?* The new thinking suggests that in an increasingly fragmented media space, reach would matter more than ever before, and media with scale, would drive business results better. The new thinking on Frequency suggests numbers between 3 and 10 exposures, after which more exposures have a negative effect. And we're still searching for possible answers for a cookie-less future that will be inherited by

digital media. Therefore, it would be important for brands to consider looking at correlating media exposure with business results, and also to look at competitive considerations to arrive at the optimum frequency levels for their brand.

3. *How should one look at Budget Allocations & What kind of media will deliver results?* With the rise of the concept of paid-owned-earned media, brands need to increasingly take cognizance of the role of each of these. Brands in contemporary times typically tend to create a huge mass market pull through paid media, and, with the right creative quality and product experience, seek to drive both owned and earned media to achieve the maximum impact on brand salience and brand business.

   Within paid media, budget allocation methods to different media are changing with the constant evolution of media. Traditional media has reinvented themselves and now leverages its environment to set the agenda for brands and create context. Traditional media has the ability to create both text and video content, and offer bouquets of solutions to brands. Rather than relying solely on digital, brands are looking at using digital along with conventional media like print and TV to drive synergistic efforts that lead to extending campaign reach and engagement.

4. *Does SOV matter in a new era?* The earlier rule of thumb was to generate Excess SOV (ESOV) wrt to the brand's market share. However, with the rise of Owned Media and Earned Media, experts around the world are now talking about Share of Experience (SOE) which is about collectively looking at Paid-Owned-Earned media and a brand's relative share of these customer experience touchpoints.

5. *What is the importance of context?* The dominant thinking today is that all impressions aren't equal. Different media talk to people in different contexts and in different states of mind, and thereby have a different impact. Therefore, beyond just reach, frequency, and cost, it becomes important to consider the context and the impact each impression creates for the brand. While planning for context, it is advisable to consider the impact of timing of your advertising, the location where the person gets your message, the device on which he/she gets the message, and the credibility of the media brand which carries the advertising.

6. *Content marketing.* Despite the hyper-connected world we live in, more and more people are tuning out of advertising with consumers due to excessive intrusion and irrelevance. Given this situation, brands are trying to interweave their brand stories with the content narrative. This calls for brand custodians to understand consumers, aligning this understanding with the brand theme, and customizing content so that it finds relevance with customers.

7. *A cookie-less world.* Riding on cookies, a big advantage that digital media brought to the table was addressability – the ability to address different

audiences across different stages of the purchase funnel, and the ability to target them precisely, and retarget them. This is going to be challenged in the near future with the phasing out of cookies. In such a scenario, the importance of first-party data becomes critical for brands. This brings us back to the basics – the importance of right people, right place, right timing, and right context that was probably getting lost somewhere in the digital jungle. And at the heart of this is knowing about your customers without pushing the privacy wall too far back.

Further Reading

American Marketing Association, "Content Marketing," n.d., https://www.ama.org/topics/content-marketing/

AppAnnie, *State of Mobile 2020*, n.d., https://www.ficci-frames.com/assets/images/reports/reports-2020.pdf

BBC Science of Engagement Study, March 2017, https://www.bbcglobalnews.com/insights/science-of-engagement/

Binet, Les, and Peter Field, *The Long and the Short of It: Balancing Short and Long-Term Marketing Strategies*, June 2013. Institute of Practitioners in Advertising.

Binet, Les, and Peter Field, "Marketing Effectiveness in the Digital Era", IPA, June 2017, https://ipa.co.uk/knowledge/publications-reports/media-in-focus-marketing-effectiveness-in-the-digital-era

Bouvard, Pierre, "AM/FM Radio Is America's #1 Mass Reach Media: Here's Why It Matters", July 19, 2017 https://www.westwoodone.com/2017/07/19/amfm-radio-is-americas-1-mass-reach-media-heres-why-it-matters/

Dentsu Aegis, 2023, *Digital Advertising in India 2023*.

Ebiquity, Gain Theory, and Thinkbox, "Profit Ability, The Business Case for Advertising", 2018. https://www.thinkbox.tv/research/thinkbox-research/profit-ability-the-business-case-for-advertising

Ehrenberg-Bass, 2017, https://marketingscience.info/losing-loyalty-the-world-according-to-byron-sharp/

Eisenberg, Bryan, "Content Marketing: Superheroes Teach the Art of Storytelling", 2017, https://www.bryaneisenberg.com/contentmarketingsuperheroes/

Gowthaman, R., "Future of Data Driven Marketing", LinkedIn, 2021, https://www.linkedin.com/pulse/future-data-driven-marketing-gowthaman-ragothaman/

"Losing Loyalty: The World According to Byron Sharp", published by Ad Age, June 2017, https://www.marketingscience.info/ (https://www.marketingscience.info/losing-loyalty-the-world-according-to-byron-sharp/#:~:text=Byron%20Sharp%20would%20like%20you,learned%20about%20marketing%20is%20wrong.&text=%E2%80%9CSales%20growth%20won't%20come,fantasy%20is%20harming%20marketing%20effectiveness.%E2%80%9D

Menon, Sandeep, "Marketing: Reboot for the Digital Age", LinkedIn, 20 September 2021, https://www.linkedin.com/pulse/marketing-reboot-digital-age-sandeep-menon/

Pritchard, Marc, "P&G to Scale Back Targeted Facebook Ads", Wall Street Journal, https://www.wsj.com/articles/p-g-to-scale-back-targeted-facebook-ads-1470760949

Temkin, David, Director of Product Management, "Charting a Course towards a More Privacy-First Web", David Temkin, Director of Product Management, Ads Privacy and Trust, published 3 March 2021, https://blog.google/products/ads-commerce/a-more-privacy-first-web

Terlap, Sharon, and Deepa Seetharaman, "P&G to Scale Back Targeted Facebook Ads", *Wall Street Journal*, updated August 17, 2016, https://www.wsj.com/articles/p-g-to-scale-back-targeted-facebook-ads-1470760949

Windows of Opportunity: India's Media & Entertainment Sector, March 2023, Ernst & Young & FICCI Report, https://assets.ey.com/content/dam/ey-sites/ey-com/en_in/topics/media-and-entertainment/2023/05/ey-me-report.pdf

Yakub, Faris, 'How to Balance Your Media Plans', Medium.com, August 2018, https://medium.com/@faris/how-to-balance-your-media-plans-8f2485898595

10

MEDIA MIX SELECTIONS

This is a very important part of the media planning process, though sometimes planners would merge this area under the 'Who' (target audience selection) part of the strategic planning process. This is however, an important step towards the final construction of the media plan. It is important to arrive at a decision on the media mix to be used, in what intensity, and what should be the role of each element in the media mix. Given the huge complexity of research, the definition of a viewer is different from that of a reader, from that of a listener, etc. Different media have different types of currencies, and that brings in another set of complexity in media – that of comparability of different media on a uniform parameter. However, there is a unique value that each media brings to the table, and it is therefore critical from a strategic planning point of view to find out for the brand, which values of media could be best harnessed to achieve brand objectives.

What Is a Media Mix?

A media mix is a combination of media selected and used in a media plan. A simple example of media mix could be the combined use of TV and print for a campaign. Another campaign could use a media mix of TV, print, and digital for a campaign and so on.

The selection of media mix also happens to one of the most complex decisions in media given the huge number of options one has to choose from. There are diverse forces at play trying to influence this decision – cost efficiency vs impact, budget limitations, cost of media, fragmentation of media, measured media vs non-measured media, competitive forces, and so on.

DOI: 10.4324/9781032724539-10

Historically, the two biggest media options used in India have been TV and print, which accounted for roughly 65% of the total ad spends in the country. However, in the last few years, Internet has gained rapidly and now is the largest medium, accounting for 48% of the ad spends in India. This is followed by TV at 30% and print with 16%. The balance of 6% is accounted by outdoor, cinema, and radio (Windows of Opportunity, EY & FICCI, 2023).

Why Do We Need a Media Mix?

The big reason for a media mix is that people are living increasingly complex media lives. The average Indian today spends on an average of about 10–11 hours on media. For an average working person, the day could begin with the newspaper while the TV news is on; during the commute, one could be listening to FM and be exposed to OOH/ambient media outside, while in the workplace, the Internet could be on; evenings could again wind down by listening to the radio while travelling, while the mobile is on; and the day ends with TV and mobile being used simultaneously. For students, they would index higher on digital, while housewives would index higher on TV consumption.

In India, we have over 900 TV channels, over 400 large/medium newspapers, hundreds of magazines, over 300 radio stations, thousands of outdoor/ambient media sites, and millions of websites – all beaming content and ads incessantly. In an era defined by audience fragmentation, low attention spans, and high ad avoidance, it is challenging to create a media plan that seamlessly carries the brand idea across media options that achieves the desired reach and frequency targets, and one that gives a good ROI on the media spend. I had always likened the task of a media planner to that of a fund manager, who allocates a client's money across a range of stocks and tries to achieve the best return while at the same time balancing risk and stability in creating the portfolio. A media planner too has to navigate and fully understand how audiences consume media, what time and attention they give to media, what opportunities are available in media which could be leveraged for the brand's benefit, how best to optimize reach and frequency for the campaign, and also ensure that he/she achieves efficiency in media buying. The media plan too is similar to a portfolio of choices that will work together to communicate the brand's message to a sizeable number of people with a desired frequency, and done cost efficiently, to eventually ensure that the brand's marketing objectives are met and the plan generates a good ROI.

We need a media mix because more people are consuming more media than ever, and are increasingly being fragmented. Reaching the same number of people with desired frequency is getting more difficult by the year precisely because of this. With fragmentation leading to compromising reach, no one medium is now sufficient enough to do justice to a brand, and hence one needs a mix of media to augment plan reach and frequency. We also need a media mix to reinforce the brand's message in different ways during the consumer's path to purchase. And due to diminishing returns setting in quickly for every media, the only way to shift the curve upwards, and get a better ROI, is by using a media mix.

At the heart of selecting a media mix lies the larger challenge of fragmentation vs integration, as Keith Weed, chief marketing and communications officer at Unilever (2013), summarized, saying 'The thing that keeps me awake at night is integration versus fragmentation'. He outlined the need 'to hold our brands together' and make them consistent and relevant 'in a market and media that's fragmenting'.

Maximizing media effectiveness also boils down to the context in which the message is delivered. We've already discussed earlier how context is impacted by the device on which the message is delivered, the time when it is delivered, and the content environment in which the message is served.

There are several layers of decision making while arriving at a media mix:

- *Media consumption patterns of the target audience*: In practice, the most important analysis one does while selecting a media mix is to study and analyse the patterns of media use by the target audience. Depending on what media the audience consumes, one is able to put together a basic media mix.
- *Understanding communication requirement of the brand*: This is then layered with an understanding of the brand's message and trying to identify media that would best convey the message. For example, if the brand has to convey emotion, then video makes itself a natural selection. However, within video, one has to consider the options of linear TV, OTT channels, online video platforms, social media, and influencer networks amongst other options. However, if the brand has to convey a lot of detail, then text and long-form video make better sense.
- *Media opportunities*: Another aspect that one looks at while deciding a media mix is to see what kind of opportunities there are in the media environment. Is there a big sporting tournament or a reality show that could be used to launch the campaign for a quick reach build-up?
- *Media suitability*: Are there attributes in specific media which make them better suited to deliver the brand message?
- *Innovation opportunities*: Are there any specific innovative opportunities that media offers that could help create a brand property?
- *Competitive analysis*: An analysis of the competition also gives some pointers on how other brands in the category are allocating their money across media.
- *Cost efficiency*: Important input in taking media mix decisions are absolute cost and the cost efficiency of different media.

Depending upon a mix of these factors, a media mix is created for a brand. Different categories and brands make their own choices based on availability of budgets, cost efficiency criteria, brand requirements, role of each media in the mix, and so on. As you can see in Table 10.1, there are categories in the FMCG sector like food and beverages, personal care, hair care, etc., where

TABLE 10.1 Spending skews across categories

Category	Skew	Relative Index		
		Digital	Print	TV
Food & Beverages	High TV Skew	14	36	193
Personal Care/Personal Hygiene	High TV Skew	12	34	195
Durables	High TV Skew	28	104	141
Building, Industrial, & Land Materials/Equipment	High TV Skew	99	48	134
Telecom Products	High TV Skew	51	26	177
Hair Care	High TV Skew	7	60	181
Household Products	High TV Skew	18	49	182
Laundry	High TV Skew	1	46	194
Telecom/Internet Service Providers	High TV Skew	44	23	183
Alcoholic Drinks	High TV Skew	7	10	214
Babycare	High TV Skew	19	26	196
Cosmetics	High TV Skew	78	21	164
Agriculture	High TV Skew	16	79	163
Personal Healthcare	High Print Skew	11	156	117
Textiles/Clothing	High Print Skew	62	130	104
Auto	High Print Skew	42	181	83
Retail	High Print Skew	107	191	37
Personal Accessories	High Print Skew	64	176	73
Tobacco & Related Products	High Print Skew	0	349	0
Miscellaneous	High Print Skew	71	248	22
Education	High Digital & Print Skew	166	150	29
Banking/Finance/Investment	High Digital & Print Skew	173	109	50
Media	High Digital & Print Skew	167	139	35
Office Automation	High Digital & Print Skew	145	212	1
Corporate/Brand Image	High Digital Skew	152	77	84
Fuel/Petroleum Products	High Digital Skew	167	37	101
Services	High Digital Skew	196	57	70
Computers	High Digital Skew	292	61	10
Total		100	100	100

Source: Created by the author.

the skew is very high towards TV. Similarly, there are categories like auto, textiles, and retail, which are skewed towards Print for its advantages of localization, giving out greater detail, etc. Likewise, there are categories like computers, corporate image, etc., which have a digital skew. Then there are categories like education, banking, and media, which are low on TV and have a relatively higher skew towards print and digital. Table 10.1 showcases a broad analysis of media skews across different product categories. An index above 100 indicates the relative higher skew/bias towards the particular form of media.

Major Types of Media

Television

Television remains the dominant media in India, accounting for well over 40% of the total advertising spends. As seen in Table 10.1, there are several categories for which TV remains the lead medium, because of:

- *Ability to deliver mass reach*: TV has a reach of more than 800 million. Several marquee sporting properties, like the IPL, the Olympics, other cricket tournaments, and reality shows, are instant attractions for brands given the reach potential these properties offer.
- *Ability to demonstrate product usage/benefits*: Most FMCG products tend to either do a problem-solve creative approach which needs before-after demonstration, or slice-of-life advertising, or brand ambassadors, etc. – all of which lend themselves easily to the TV environment.
- *Ability to communicate emotion*: This is required for brand saliency and long-term brand building. Binet and Field have suggested a ratio of 60% effort directed towards long-term brand building (read, mass targeting) and 40% effort towards short-term sales activation (read, tight targeting to loyal customers)
- *Ability to target a wider variety of audience*: It can target different audiences through different genres. We have in India about 900+ channels that deliver about 1.6 billion impressions/year. Alongside a host of national channels, there are numerous regional channels catering to specific geographies and linguistic groups. In fact, regional channels account for a little over 50% of the total viewership – suggesting how important the regional channels are.
- *Ability to build frequency*: It helps build up quick reach, and does so cost-efficiently. This makes TV a natural go-to option for several brands. Over 10,000 advertisers use TV every year to advertise.

Leading TV networks in India have now aggressively started investing in OTT services, by creating new IPs, repurposing existing content, and acquiring new content. This makes TV far more flexible and straddles both the conventional TV space and the digital space, giving more options to brands. Connected TVs or smart TVs, though at a nascent stage currently, are expected to grow in years to come. Over the last few years, time spent watching TV has only gone up, and with existing networks launching their OTT services, TV is poised to continue to be a big favourite amongst brands.

Print

Print accounts for 26% of the advertising spend in India, and is amongst the leading mediums alongside TV and Digital. Print offers several advantages to brands:

- *Mass reach*: Several large newspapers in India offer mass reach. Often a favoured medium for brand launches, print lends a sense of scale and immediacy to the campaign. Newspapers are read by over 400 million people in India, and are amongst the big reach providers in the country.
- *Localization*: Print has this unique ability to localize content and creative messaging. Almost all newspapers across India have multiple editions – each catering to a district or even a sub-district at times. Each of these editions has content that is relevant to that particular micro-geographical unit, and the content is customized (even accounting for the local dialect) – the locals are the newsmakers and the news consumers. This provides a platform for local advertisers to use local pages to cater to the local market. For large national brands wanting to customize a brand message to a specific city/state, it is eminently possible through print.
- *Immediacy*: Newspapers provide a live environment in the sense that they reflect the daily topicality and news of the world around communities. This creates a perfect environment for many brands who use topicality in their communication. For example, when India beat Australia in the 2021 Test Series, Byju's had an ad the next day which was based on India's victory. Take a brand like Amul Butter, which has been doing topical advertising for decades now. The newspaper provides a perfect live environment to place such advertising.
- *Ability to communicate detail*: Newspapers have the ability to communicate long-form advertising, to carry product detail, explain features, etc.
- *Ability to sharply target*: Magazines have the special ability for sharp targeting. One could talk to different kinds of audiences through magazines across different genres.

Additionally, print provides a context for brands through its content. As a medium, it gives a lot more control to the reader. The advertising doesn't intrude – rather, the reader selects what he/she wants to give attention to. The editorial environment lends a context which is very useful in determining the extent of the reader's engagement with the newspaper/magazine. At the same time, print in India (largely newspapers) is consumed largely in the mornings – at a time when our cognitive ability isn't fatigued. The reader is giving 100% attention to the medium, as there's little multitasking possible while reading. The relevance and role of newspapers in the digital era stems from the fact that they stand as the last bastions of credibility. With both digital and TV news creating multiple opinions, and with fake news abounding, newspapers provide the balanced opinion that one needs to have a point of view and make conversation. Therefore, the environment, the context, the degree of engagement, credibility of the medium, mass reach, ability to customize, localize, and sharply target – all of them make print an important influencing force in the path to purchase.

The other big advantage that print companies offer in India is the leverage of its physical infrastructure. Print offers advertisers in-print and on-ground customized branding solutions. So for example, a Masala brand could engage the services of a newspaper brand, where an on-ground cookery event is created and promoted, and is then covered in the pages of the newspaper. The Masala brand gets context, brand saliency, ability to sample, and localized reach and is able to gradually create a market for itself. Similarly, a mutual fund brand could tie up with a local newspaper to organize investor camps, create a context for financial literacy, generate a database of local investors, and create traction for the brand in local markets. Several success stories of this kind are seen around the country. Most newspaper brands in India have deep connections with local communities and often have women's clubs, youth clubs, children's clubs, etc. – all of which could be leveraged by brands. Some newspaper brands even leverage their distribution wings to generate highly targeted door-to-door promotion and sampling campaigns. Print brands have this unique ability to create branded content which is placed in contextual locations within the newspaper. They have the power to create an agenda for brands. Most print brands also have presence in digital through websites, apps, e-papers – and brands could use both online and offline channels for communicating.

Radio

Radio accounts for about 4% of the advertising spends in India. There are about 1100 odd operational radio stations in India, of which there are about 360+ private FM stations covering about 100 cities. There are over 220 million radio listeners in India, making it a fairly large medium. There are some distinct advantages of using radio in India:

- *Local reach*: It's a medium that's highly suited for localized campaigns. Local radio stations provide reach within and around the city. It's ideal for a lot of retail brands who wish to tap into the local demand.

- *Low cost*: Radio is a relatively low-cost medium, and hence several brands use radio as a support medium in their campaigns. It serves as a good medium to generate localized low cost frequency.
- *Ability to provide integrated solutions*: Private FM radio stations offer integrated and interactive solutions to advertisers through contests, dial-ins, and on-ground events, and help create context for brands by leveraging the RJs to help create local hype.

Most large private FM networks have set up their own web radio stations. The mobility of radio, along with its advantages of being low cost, make it a good support medium which could be used for sharp geographical targeting.

Digital

Digital accounts for about 24% of the advertising spends in India. With 776 million Internet subscribers in India as per TRAI Report July–September 2020, almost 400 million smartphone subscribers, and 15 million smart TVs, Indians are spending about 3.5 hours daily on their phones and have downloaded 20 billion apps in 2019 alone. As a result, a lot of brands are now making digital an integral part of the media mix. It's a huge medium, and it offers a lot of unique advantages to brands:

- *Sharp targeting*: One of the biggest advantages of digital is sharp targeting. Based on audience behaviour patterns, it is possible to target a very specific audience. Most brands have leveraged this ability of the digital media to generate short-term sales spikes.
- *Digital expands campaign reach*: With rising digital penetration, and the huge base of Internet and mobile subscribers in India, the medium also now has a huge scale, and is capable of providing mass reach. Though few brands use digital for mass reach, they often pair it with another medium like TV or print to help extend the reach curve. Adding digital to a TV plan could mean reaching out to lighter viewers of TV or lighter readers/non-readers or print. The other way to look at this is when the TV or print reach curve starts flattening (when it hits diminishing returns), add digital, and boost campaign reach. So when traditional media reach a saturation point, adding digital would be a good idea.
- *Multiple creative formats*: Digital offers multiple creative formats – audio, video, influencer marketing, social conversations, native content, contesting, conventional banners, etc.
- *Low cost*: Digital is usually more cost-effective than the conventional large media like TV or print. This provides an opportunity for several small brands to use the medium

- *Ease of measurement*: The big promise that comes with digital is its measurability. That gives a sense of comfort to advertisers in terms of number of clicks, site visits, sales leads, or other campaign performance measures. It makes establishing campaign ROI easy.
- *Greater campaign control*: Digital gives brands a greater control over the campaign. If the campaign is generating results, then one could extend it, and if the desired results are not happening, one could modify the plan very quickly. This is an advantage that digital offers over conventional media.

Advertising continues to rise on digital, and the media now provides engagement at scale and brands are warming up to the medium. Brands are looking at using digital along with conventional media like print and TV to drive synergistic efforts that lead to extending campaign reach and engagement. In an era of media fragmentation, brands that need mass reach are increasingly turning to use digital in conjunction with conventional media.

Out of Home (OOH)

Just like radio, OOH also accounts for just about 5% of the advertising spends in India. The medium is highly fragmented, with both organized and unorganized players running the industry. This includes traditional OOH, transit media, digital OOH, wall paintings, and ambient media amongst other formats. A highly localized medium, OOH is usually used by real estate, local retail, media, FMCG, and financial services. Currently digital OOH and transit media are growing rapidly. Brands usually are present on OOH for salience, immediacy, quick local reach build-up, and its ability to localize messaging. The medium suffers due to lack of measurement, yet it offers several advantages:

- Geo-targeting can be best attained through OOH.
- OOH is a great medium to build local reach and immediacy. It's great for building local brand saliency.
- It's a great medium to create local impact. Large format outdoor advertising is a sure-shot route to this. Add to this several innovative ideas, and OOH can catch attention like no other medium does.

Digital OOH (DOOH) formats are evolving at a rapid pace and will drive the industry forward and offer far more flexibility and options to brands. However, for the most part, OOH would be used to drive brand saliency, large-scale local impact, and as a support medium to other media like print, TV, and digital.

Cinema

While in-cinema advertising is a very small part of the advertising ecosystem in India accounting for just about 1% of the total advertising spends. About 100 million people visit cinema in a year in India. Other than advertising before the film, and during the interval, there are other formats like subtle brand placements within the film, and branding at the cinema theatre. Cinema remains a low-cost medium, preferred largely by local advertisers.

Key Factors Kept in Mind while Selecting a Media Mix

a. *Focus*: Some media might just work better than other media. *Reading people* versus *viewing people*.

b. *Synergy*: Mixed exposures may magnify the impact of the communication and make it work harder. Sell the car on TV, and the deal in print. Some combinations of media bring with them a certain synergy which truly add to the communication impact. This factor plays an important role in the media mix selection decisions. In fact, the attempt in most media planning exercises is to arrive at a mix of media that have the best synergy with each other to make the advertising work harder. Each medium has a certain role to play in the campaign – sometimes outdoor and newspapers are used to announce launch and create instant awareness, while radio and TV play the role of high-frequency reminders. At times, this role may be reversed, and a high-impact campaign could be launched on TV to announce the brand name and build brand saliency over a very short period of time, and print is used tactically to explain the product details and tell people where the brand is available, etc. In every media plan, the role for each medium must be defined.

c. *Absolute cost*: Different media come at different costs, and some media cost a huge amount of money vs some that come at a low cost. Depending on budget restrictions, the choice of media can vary. There are times when the budgets are very limited, and at times advertisers tend to opt for one medium rather than using multiple media to avoid the danger of being too thinly spread to register impact or presence. The dominant thinking here is, let me take the medium which would work best for my campaign, and ensure a decent presence out there rather than scatter messages across different types of media.

d. *Reach of media*: For a given definition of an audience, different media have different reach levels. For instance, for a very premium audience, say, for a very fancy car, the Internet might show up dramatically higher on reach as compared to, say, the Internet reach amongst mass audiences for something like, say, a toilet soap. The general pattern is that as we move across different types of audiences, different media show up on reach.

Depending upon the brand and its TG, one of the key factors used in selecting media mix is dependent on the kind of reach each media has.

e. *Cost efficiency*: What the relative cost efficiency of each medium is vs the others is also an important determining factor. However, this is also a very complex argument to build because different media types have different currencies to define their respective audience size. As stated earlier, the definition of a viewer is very different from that of a listener or a reader, and so on. To add to it, there are different researches that bring these numbers to you, each with a different methodology, market coverage, etc., thereby making the task of inter-media comparisons very difficult. To add to this, the creative units used across different types of media vary – what would you equate a 400-sq-cm ad to in TV – will it be a 30-second spot, or a 40-second spot, or a 10-second spot, or what banner size will compared to the 400-sq-cm print ad. There is an element of subjectivity involved here, because while one might equate a 30-second spot on TV with a 240-sq-cm ad in newspapers, does this equation change with the positioning of the ad? What if the 240-sq-cm ad is placed on the Front Page rather than on page 17 – does this change the relative equation? There are no ready-made answers here, because intermedia comparisons are like comparing apples with oranges. Yet, these comparisons are done at a macro level, some basic equations are assumed in terms of equating creative units across media, and people generally do a comparison at a medium level to, say, what it would cost to reach 70% of this TG through print vs that in TV? This at times helps in taking a macro call on the media mix, and the relative weight of importance to each element of the media mix.

f. *Advertising exposure weights*: As we discussed in the initial parts while discussing basic concepts – exposure in normal terms means exposure to the vehicle and not to the advertising, if one compares the two dominant media – print and TV. For TV, it is now possible to get advertising viewership as well as the programme viewership, and one can work out a broad index to say what percentage of the average programme viewer watches the commercial break. But in print, there are no such metrics – what percentage of a newspaper reader reads the average ad – because unlike TV, where ads are placed in commercial breaks most often, ads in print are part of the reading environment. One may have read the page on which the ad is, but has not seen the ad. One may have read the paper on the day you released the ad but did not turn to the page on which your ad is. As you can see, there are no ready-made answers to different situations that crop up. However, there are some publishers and some agencies that have done what are known as reading and noting studies, which tell the relative conversion percentage of readers who read ads, and further than classifies the impact differentials following different positions of the ad, and different sizes. Answers to things like, will a Top of Column 240-sq-cm ad on page 3 work better than a 240-sq-cm ad on the Front Page, or will a half-page colour ad on the back page work better than a 240-sq-cm front-page BW ad – have been possible, but these studies are custom studies done once in a while, and they generally cover some indicative markets. The point is, while comparing media, this factor of relative advertising exposure also plays a role in the final decision.

g. *Frequency weights*: How do the second exposure and successive exposures work in newspapers as compared to that in TV? If you take a view of the Millward Brown study, successive exposures in TV works as a reminder, while in print it might fall on a blind spot. Therefore, it is important to rotate positioning, sizes, and communication messages in print to register greater impact. Alternately, use devices like fixed position, or column branding to work as a reminder. Likewise, for other media. At times, it is important to take this factor into account to get the right results.

h. *Media habits of audiences*: Different audience groups consume different types of media, at different times of the day, and with varying intensity levels. There are light viewers of TV who might be heavy consumers of print or Internet, and there could be medium consumers of TV, who might be light on print and heavy users of the Internet. These differences play a huge role in identifying the media mix, and the role of each element in the media mix, and the relative weight if importance in terms of budget allocations.

i. *Media neutral planning*: This is something that often gets discussed about in planning circles across the world. Planners have always looked just beyond the demographic and reach numbers of the available media platforms. Insights from TGI or other secondary research and emerging trends in the market are now increasingly playing a much more decisive role in taking decisions on the media mix. It's eventually about understanding the consumer in the overall communications framework and using the multiple windows of opportunities emerging from this.

The aforementioned were some of the topline factors which could play a role in media mix selections, but they are not conclusive and do not suggest the best fit formula to arrive at a mix. Each campaign comes with its own set of issues, and that should largely govern media selections – and sometimes the best fit solution might not have traditional mass media at all. Some leading advertisers have started thinking differently and have taken cognizance of the new realities of media. Some important things have changed in the decision-making sequence at the advertiser end – some of them have said that a broad media strategy will precede the advertising development process. This is a huge change from the earlier period where creative formats largely dictated eventually what media must be used. Some advertisers have based agency compensation on brand performance and have made it media neutral. Most marketers have accepted that media has changed over a very short period of time, and they need to modulate their thinking about media mix, and basing the plan on one media is now slowly being phased out. This is evident from the growth rates one notices in different media types – both in absolute spends and in percentage growth terms.

An interesting study done by Ebiquity attempted to find out what are the key attributes that an advertiser looks for in media, and against each of these attributes, how different media stack up. According to the study, targeting right people at the right time was the top most desired attribute. This was followed by campaign ROI, ability of the medium to trigger an emotional response, increasing brand salience and maximizing reach. At the far end of the list were factors like transparent third-party measurement and production costs.

Clearly, the most important attribute advertisers look for is the targeting ability of the medium. On this index, clearly online media works best.

On all the other major parameters – campaign ROI, triggering a positive emotional response, increasing brand salience and maximizing campaign reach – TV is amongst the most preferred. Though this study wasn't done in India, the media attributes cited by advertisers seem universal, and that also explains why TV is so popular as an advertising medium here.

Having identified a media mix, and the role in the plan, the next big question is that of allocating budgets across media. Usually, this flows from the role one has assigned to different media, which defines how much to put on which media. From a practical standpoint, while there is no standard formula, most brands go either by their previous experience on media mix usage, or look at competition to understand relative intensity of media budgets. However, there is an interesting study "Demand Generation" done by Gain Theory on budget allocation. The study was based on an econometric modelling of 50 advertisers across 14 categories, and finally zeroed down to 6 categories – FMCG, finance, retail, online retail, automotive, and travel. This study also concluded that mixed media used in combination works better than overdependence on any one single media. This study identified the key variables of advertising effectiveness, and used these to create a Demand Generator – a free tool to determine the optimal budget allocation across media based on specific brand objectives. In the free tool available online, one had to choose a category from the six aforementioned categories, Appeal (Mass Market or Niche), Percentage of online sales (from a predefined set of ranges), a brand size (in monetary terms), annual spend, output (revenue or profit), and whether one wanted to minimize risk (yes or no). Based on these inputs, the tool would generate an optimal budget mix across a range of media. Though done from a UK perspective, it demonstrates that with adequate data points, one could possibly look at creating future models of budget allocation across media – an area that is otherwise grey.

How Does One Look at Media Integration?

With fragmented media comes fragmented attention, and this poses the biggest challenge in selecting a media mix and creating a seamless brand presence across media.

Integration essentially is about how we create synergies between the different media that we choose. These synergies could be about creating a brand idea that is seamlessly played out across different media. On each media, the idea (rather than being replicated), is adapted to the particular medium based on the environment of the medium and the way it is consumed by its audience.

Interesting research was done by the Advertising Research Foundation based on a wide scale study of 5000 global campaigns (representing $375 billion of advertising across 41 countries) to understand what combination of media gave the best ROI. Five key highlights as per Jasper Snyder – EVP, Research and Innovation, Cross-Platform, The ARF:

- Campaigns that used more media proved to be more effective from an ROI perspective
- When platforms are combined, it results in incremental ROI for the campaign. In their study, when print was added to TV, the incremental ROI was 19%. When radio was added to TV, it created an incremental ROI of 20%. But when digital was added to TV, it resulted in an incremental ROI of 60%, suggesting that adding digital to TV plans created a "kicker" effect on campaign ROI.
- A balanced mix of traditional and digital media works for both younger and older audiences.
- The study flagged an important issue regarding consumer irritation from frequent targeting. Serving more than required frequency would work negatively for the brand.
- A significant portion of the campaign impact is derived from creative. The study also suggested that integrated campaigns using the same creative thought across different platforms get better results.

Clearly, the ARF makes the case for combining digital to TV to get a reach spike and get the best ROI for the money spent. Taking this thought forward, Facebook had done a study of several campaigns in an attempt to find out how best it complements TV. As per their study, a majority of TV viewers used their phone while watching TV. They noticed spikes in Facebook usage whenever there were ad breaks on TV. Facebook asked Kantar Millward Brown and GfK to study the impact of TV and Facebook on consumer packaged goods in Europe. These studies proved that exposure on both Facebook and TV lifted ad recall by 18.9% as compared to a 14.8% ad recall for TV only, and 8.4% for Facebook only. This study established the complementary role that Facebook could play with TV campaigns. In addition to generating additional reach and frequency for the campaign, combining Facebook with TV also gave a boost to ad recall.

Similarly, Twitter also commissioned Nielsen to analyse the synergistic effect of Twitter and TV. Nielsen used data from Nielsen Digital Ad Ratings and the Nielsen People Meter panel for this purpose. The study was done for two TV marketers for their programmes. The study concluded that audiences are more likely to tune-in to linear TV after being exposed to Twitter media, thus demonstrating the synergistic effect of Twitter and TV.

Looking at the recency theory propounded by Erwin Ephron, he says that diminishing returns is a reality of life in media. Every medium will reach its level of diminishing returns. And if the goal of planning is to maximize reach, then the moment reach starts peaking with, say TV, it's time to add the next medium, say print, because print will duplicate less with TV, as compared to TV's duplication with TV. Advertising, more and more in one medium, will buy you lesser incremental reach as we go along, and your chances of reaching out more often to heavy watchers of TV is much higher resulting in lopsided plan deliveries. However, Ephron points out that multimedia planning is clearly the future (Ephron, 1995).

The only Indian experiment on media multiplier (largely done for TV and print, which then accounted for over 80% of the advertising spends) was conducted long ago – but the conclusion was still the same: sufficient TV and sufficient press is better than sufficient TV alone, which is better than sufficient press alone. The point is that mixed media schedules work better than single media schedules. This belief has been validated both through research and through personal experiences of a lot of brands that have employed this strategy.

There is an increased interest in multimedia planning, but the biggest issue facing multimedia planning is the absence of a single currency for audience and the lack of single source data. A lot of agencies are using a lot of models to arrive at a unified plan reach and frequency levels, but it still stops at just that. Multimedia planning is taking place, but the research that supports these decisions does not exist. While marketers have moved upstream and are looking at moving beyond just reach and frequency, and are looking at product placements, sponsorships, PR, events, and other forms of promotion, the research industry has remained confined to various silos of individual media. Media owners have moved their media brands across platforms and devices, but they know very little about cross-media behaviour patterns.

Any investment in this direction will help optimize budgets. With more digital platforms and devices opening up the lines between individual media themselves have begun to blur. Today it's possible to watch TV in multiple ways – watch Live TV, record a programme and watch later, watch TV on a PC or a handheld device elsewhere – the places of access, the times of access, and the degree of involvement with the content are constantly changing. Similarly, when it comes to newspapers, you can read a physical printed copy, go to the newspaper's online site, read the e-paper, read the content on mobile and other handheld devices, subscribe to RSS feeds, interact with the content on social media, and so on. Suddenly, the decision-making dynamics change in these environments, and therefore, we need to necessarily begin with the customer rather than the platform. And because your audiences are using a media mix – that's the big argument for brands also to use a media mix.

Chapter Summary

This is a very important part of the media planning process. Though sometimes planners would merge this area under the "Who" (target audience selection) part of the strategic planning process. This is however, an important step towards the final construction of the media plan. It is important to arrive at a decision on the media mix to be used, in what intensity, and what the role should be of each element in the media mix. Given the huge complexity of research where the definition of a viewer is different from that of a reader, from that of a listener, etc., different media have different types of currencies, and that brings in another set of complexity in media. However, there is a unique value that each media brings to the table, and it is therefore critical from a strategic planning point of view to find out for the brand, which values of media could be best harnessed to achieve brand objectives.

Most media plans use a media mix. When more than one media is used in a media plan, it's called a media mix. Using a media mix has become necessary because more people are consuming more media than ever before. With hundreds of options for the consumer across every type of media, we're witnessing a huge fragmentation of audiences. In an environment defined by audience fragmentation, low attention spans, and high ad avoidance, it's quite challenging for media planners to take the brand message seamlessly across media, achieve the optimum reach and frequency, and get the best ROI on the budget invested. While making a decision on media mix, the media planner must consider several things:

- An analysis of the patterns of media use by the target audience
- Understanding of the brand's message and aligning it with media that could best convey the message.

- Looking for opportunities available in media
  - Is there a big sporting tournament or a reality show that could be used to launch the campaign for a quick reach buildup?
  - Are there attributes in specific media which make them better suited to deliver the brand message?
  - Are there any specific innovative opportunities that media offers that could help create a brand property?

- An analysis of the media being used by competing brands

The major types of media available in India are TV, print, radio, cinema, out-of-home, and digital. Each of these media have their strengths and weaknesses, and brands choose to use different media depending upon the analysis of the aforementioned factors along with reach, cost, and cost efficiency parameters.

With fragmented media comes fragmented attention, and this poses the biggest challenge in selecting a media mix and creating a seamless brand presence across media.

Integration essentially is about how we create synergies between the different media that we choose. These synergies could be about creating a brand idea that is seamlessly played out across different media. On each media, the idea (rather than being replicated), is adapted to the particular medium based on the environment of the medium and the way it is consumed by its audience. Several studies are being conducted to find out the efficiency and response of different media. However, all studies point to the fact that using combinations of media works better than using only a single media for a media plan.

While the interest in multimedia planning is high, the biggest issue facing multimedia planning is the absence of a single currency for audience and the lack of single source data. Marketers are looking at product placements, sponsorships, PR, events, and other forms of promotion, beyond the rudimentary variables of reach and frequency. However, the research industry has remained confined to various silos of individual media. Media owners have moved their media brands across platforms and devices but know very little about cross-media behaviour patterns. Going forward, however, we see a concerted effort being put in by media and research agencies to create better metrics for multimedia planning. Till then, brands continue to mix and match different types of media and gauge response levels to sharpen their plans.

Further Reading

"Big-Picture Planning: Understanding Value in a Multi-Screen World", Facebook IQ, Facebook, April 2018.

Capoblanco, D J, "Advertising on Twitter Drives Audiences to Watch TV", Twitter, April 2018, https://marketing.twitter.com/en/insights/advertising-on-twitter-drives-audiences-to-watch-tv

Demand Generator, Thinkbox, https://www.thinkbox.tv/demandgenerator/

Ephron, Erwin, "More Weeks, Less Weight: The Shelf-Space Model of Advertising", *Journal of Advertising Research*, Vol. 35, No. 3, 1995.

"How Advertising Works", New York Advertising Week Conference, https://thearf.org/category/tag/how-advertising-works/

Levine, Barry, "Two New Studies Look at What Kinds of Campaigns, Mobile Ad Formats Work Best", September 2016, https://marketingland.com/two-new-studies-look-kinds-campaigns-mobile-ad-formats-work-best-193201

"Re-evaluating Media: What the Evidence Reveals about the True Worth of Media for Brand Advertisers", Ebiquity, March 2018.

Windows of Opportunity, India's Media & Entertainment sector, March 2023, Ernst & Young & FICCI Report

11

VEHICLE SELECTION I – TRADITIONAL MEDIA

Once the media mix has been decided, the next stage is making the actual media plan. This involves translating the strategy into an actionable plan. It should be directed to the right audience in the right markets at the right time with the right intensity of media weight with the right media mix in the most effective possible manner and with the optimum use of budgets. This is a huge task in itself given the huge number of media options one has to choose from – ranging from 900+ TV channels, to 600 publication titles, to 1100+ radio stations, to thousands of OOH sites, to thousands of cinema halls, and the millions of websites. How does one ensure that the best mix of vehicles is chosen to deliver as per the brand's media strategy? Each vehicle comes with its own unique environment, its own currency, its own decision variables and complexities. Let's go through this by medium and try to explore each area separately.

Television Planning

There are four broad areas of decision making in TV planning:

- Genre/channel selection
- Programme/daypart selection within the selected channels
- Plan optimization techniques
- Dealing with sponsorships

Let's discuss each of these separately.

DOI: 10.4324/9781032724539-11

Genre/Channel Selection

There are numerous genres and channels available in India. At last count there were over 900 channels distributed across various genres. Channel selection is influenced by the following factors:

1. *Audience fit*: At a macro level, the decision is to look at genres which will be in sync with the audience and markets spelt out in the strategic planning document. Some genres will immediately start making sense when one looks at the audience. For example, if the audience is kids, then very clearly the kids genre and the kids channels make a case for themselves, and then one gets down to detailed analysis within the genre. If the audience is women, then one immediately starts looking at the general entertainment genre; if it is youth, then one looks at a different mix, vs when the audience is men, where news and sports genres get priority. Therefore, the audience largely dictates at a very broad level the genre mix that the plan would eventually comprise. This at times would require analysis to decide the importance of each genre or each channel. The analysis that one does here would be largely to study the profiles of various channels and see which profile would suit the audience the best. However, in the BARC system, one can define audience only on the basis of demographics – age, gender, and NCCS. For all other qualitative filters like psychographics, etc., one could do an analysis to find out the channel affinity of the defined audience to arrive at a broad genre/channel mix. Table 11.1 shows the affinity index calculation.

TABLE 11.1 Affinity index by channel

Channel	Reach		TG
	Amongst 2+yrs (Universe)	NCCS AB, Women, 25+ yrs (Defined TG)	Affinity Index
A	23%	25%	108
B	18%	35%	199
C	17%	25%	146
D	14%	10%	69
E	13%	5%	37
F	12%	15%	128
G	12%	20%	171
H	11%	6%	53
I	11%	8%	71
J	11%	24%	214

Source: Created by the author.

As demonstrated in Table 11.1, one could calculate an affinity index to find out the audience affinity to channels. Channel A has a reach of 23% amongst the overall universe of TV viewers, but a 25% reach amongst the defined TG of women, NCCS AB, 25+ years. The affinity index would be 108 (25/23*100). As you can see, the audience shows a relatively higher affinity to channels B, J, G, and C. One could do a similar analysis at a genre level and identify broad genres for the TV plan. The affinity index would help identify channels/genres towards which the defined audience shows a definite skew. Table 11.2 illustrates an example of calculating affinity index at a genre level.

For an upmarket NCCS A audience, there is a clear affinity towards English channels. Among the regional channels, they display a higher affinity for regional-language G channels. However, language channels are chosen more from a market perspective versus an audience perspective. They would be chosen if they are relevant to the market selected.

2. *The audience's viewing intensity*: At times channel mix or genre selections are also done on the basis of what genre and with what intensity the audience is watching. While best fit matches the audience profile with the genre or channel profile, the viewership intensity also has a major role to play in the final selection of genres. There are times when the genre fit is great with the audience, but the absolute viewership share of the genre is so miniscule that it might not eventually deliver the minimum basic reach required for the campaign. Therefore, it is important to also see apart from the best fit, what the genre delivers in terms of viewership numbers. The analysis that one does here is to look at genre audience size of viewing for

TABLE 11.2 Genre-wise affinity index

Genre	Affinity Index for NCCS A	Genre	Affinity Index for NCCS A
Hindi Genre A	105	English Genre C	150
Hindi Genre B	104	Other Genre C	120
Other Genre A	90	English Genre D	125
Other Genre B	86	Other Genre D	120
Hindi Genre C	120	Regional Language A	90
Hindi Genre D	180	Regional Language B	55
English Genre A	145	Regional Language C	65
English Genre B	140	Regional Language D	80
		Regional Language E	75
		Regional Language F	65
		Regional Language G	116

Source: Created by the author.

the defined audience. Carrying forward the same example in Table 11.3 for the NCCS A audience, we can see that while the Hindi Genre A and B channels show a mild affinity in terms of the absolute audience size, they rank the highest. Similarly, for genres like English Genre C and Other Genre C, where the audience affinity is high, the absolute viewership base is low. Therefore, one must look at both affinity and the absolute audience size in tandem to arrive at decisions on channel/genre. This, coupled with some other analysis, would help zero down on the final channel selections.

3. *Channel shares*: Once a broad genre-level decision is taken, percentage share of viewing of each channel plays an important part of the decision-making process. How does one look at channel shares? To begin with, one looks at overall channel shares within the genre, and then breaks up the day into broad dayparts and try to study the strength of various channels during various dayparts. Some channels might have a higher channel share during the morning time band, while some others might be doing very well in evening or prime time bands. This information is generally layered with the TV viewing patterns of the audience, and based on this, decisions are taken.

So one would begin the analysis by looking at the share of the genre. For instance, if news shows a high affinity for the selected audience, then one could do a further analysis to see how much viewership share is garnered by the news genre. In the hypothetical example explained in Figure 11.1,

TABLE 11.3 Viewing intensity along with affinity index

Genre	for NCCS A	TVTs/ AMAs (000s)	Genre	for NCCS A	TVTs/ AMAs (000s)
Hindi Genre A	105	116210	English Genre C	150	41004
Hindi Genre B	104	87394	Other Genre C	120	56258
Other Genre A	90	15387	English Genre D	125	24789
Other Genre B	86	19873	Other Genre D	120	15467
Hindi Genre C	120	58615	Regional Language A	90	72188
Hindi Genre D	180	25678	Regional Language B	55	19356
English Genre A	145	36486	Regional Language C	65	15286
English Genre B	140	31254	Regional Language D	80	27965
			Regional Language E	75	22589
			Regional Language F	65	31678
			Regional Language G	116	43673

Source: Created by the author.

Channel Share

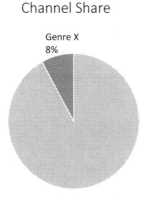

Genre X
8%

% Share of Impressions

FIGURE 11.1   Genre shares.

Source: Created by the author.

assume Genre X accounts for 8% of the total TV viewing impressions. This analysis should ideally be done over a six- to eight-week period so that any incidental fluctuations are averaged out and the data are stable enough for future decision-making.

Having established the genre share, one could look at sub-genres within the genre to get closer to a decision. Here one could divide the sub-genres into the five as depicted in Table 11.4. So, for instance, Language A Channels account for 50% of the viewership share within the genre, and Language C Channels account for 39% of the viewership share.

However, one needs to go a step ahead and assess the reasons for skews to any particular sub-genre. Language A also has a higher number of channels as compared to any other sub-genres, and hence, it reflects in a higher cumulative viewership share. There would be some genres that cannot be divided into sub-genres, and hence, the next step in the analysis would move towards channel shares. In the case of Genre X, the analysis could take the shape as shown in Table 11.5:

From here, it could be observed that the top three channels are Language A channels followed by Language C channels.

4. *Market-level skews for channels*: India is a diverse country with different regional languages. Over the last decade or so, we've seen regional channels acquiring greater importance in terms of absolute viewership. A lot of brands have necessarily used regional channels to either target a specific geography, or to add to media intensity in a particular region, or maybe cover up the shortfall wherever large national channels fall short in terms of GRPs. Also, as we've discussed in earlier chapters, market

TABLE 11.4 Channel share by language within the genre

Channel	Impressions (000s)	Share within Genre
Language A	45	50%
Language B	5	6%
Language C	35	39%
Language D	2	2%
Language E	3	3%
Total	90	100%

Source: Created by the author.

TABLE 11.5 Channel shares within the genre

Channel	Sub-Genre	Impressions (000s)	Share within Genre X
A	Language A	16	18%
B	Language A	12	13%
C	Language A	10	11%
D	Language C	8	9%
E	Language C	7	8%
F	Language B	7	8%
G	Language B	6	7%
H	Language A	6	7%
I	Language C	5	6%
J	Other Languages	13	14%
Total		90	100%

Source: Created by the author.

selection and prioritization of markets is an important aspect of strategic planning. Taking the market priorities from there, one needs to analyse how the viewership pattern varies by geographic markets. At the same time, some genres of viewing are favoured by some regions, and it's important to consider these while planning the channel mix. In the case of the Genre X example, as depicted in Table 11.6, it might be prudent to identify which markets show a higher skew towards the genre, and base the plan accordingly. In this analysis, one looks at the distribution of viewers across different markets for overall TV viewing vs that of Genre X. This would tell us which markets are over-indexed or show a higher skew towards Genre X.

In Table 11.6, we've looked at impressions and their distribution by markets for Total TV and for Genre X. The data points to a skew for Genre X towards UP/Uttarakhand, Rajasthan Delhi, Bihar/Jharkhand, MP/Chhattisgarh, and Kerala – these are markets that show a high affinity

TABLE 11.6 Market-wise skews for channels

Zone	Market	Impressions (000s)		Distribution of Impressions		Index
		Total TV	Genre X	Total TV	Genre X	
North	Pun/Har/Ch/HP/J&K	69	5	6.3%	5.6%	88
	UP/Uttarakhand	87	12	7.9%	13.3%	168
	Rajasthan	31	6	2.8%	6.7%	236
	Delhi	29	6	2.6%	6.7%	253
North Total		**216**	**29**	**19.7%**	**32.2%**	**164**
East	Assam/NE/Sikkim	17	1	1.5%	1.1%	72
	Odisha	38	2	3.5%	2.2%	64
	West Bengal	63	5	5.7%	5.6%	97
	Bihar/Jharkhand	31	10	2.8%	11.1%	394
East Total		**149**	**18**	**13.6%**	**20.0%**	**148**
West	Guj/D&D/DNH	69	2	6.3%	2.2%	37
	Mah/Goa	162	8	14.7%	8.9%	35
	MP/Chhattisgarh	70	8	6.4%	8.9%	60
West Total		**301**	**18**	**27.0%**	**20.0%**	**140**
South	Karnataka	97	7	8.8%	7.8%	88
	AP/Telengana	150	8	13.6%	8.9%	65
	Kerala	48	5	4.4%	5.6%	127
	TN/Pondicherry	138	5	12.6%	5.6%	44
South Total		**433**	**25**	**39.4%**	**27.8%**	**71**
All India		**1099**	**90**	**100.0%**	**100.0%**	**100**

Source: Created by the author.

to the genre and account for a large percentage of the genre's viewers. One could take a look at these markets, and adjust the channel mix accordingly to take care of variations in plan deliveries. Such analysis could be done for other genres, and it gives a clearer picture on which market is under-served/over-served for particular genres.

5. *Cumulative reach and reach build-up*: Another major variable that has an influence on the decision on final channel mix selection is that of reach build-up. How quickly a channel accumulates reach and what the cumulative reach is for the channel also impact the selection parameters. Generally, some channels deliver quick reach, while others take time to

build reach. At times the campaign requirement is to build quick reach in a very short period of time. Here, one looks at channels which will help achieve this task. Generally, for channels that have some high-rated programmes, the reach build-up is quicker. Also, channels that have variations in their programming are able to generate quicker reach because they are able to get different people to view different kinds of programming on the channel. The lower the duplication between programmes within the channel, the better the ability of the channel to deliver reach. The higher the duplication between the different programmes within the channel, the better the channel's ability to deliver higher frequency. Then there is this concept of cumulative reach, often also known as 'cume reach' or simple cumes. When a channel says that its cume reach is 65%, it generally means that 65% of the defined audience in the defined markets have tuned into the channel for at least a minute during the last 4 weeks. One could change basic definitions around this and look at cume reach for a week, and the base filter definition of viewing could be defined as 5 minutes or more instead of 1 minute, and so on. However, generally most channel marketers use cume reach as people tuning into the channel for 1 minute or longer during the last 4 weeks. Figure 11.2 illustrates how the cumulative reach charts could be seen. Channel C begins with a higher reach, and the reach build too is the fastest amongst the three channels. Typically, new campaign launches target quick reach build-up, and an analysis of this kind helps figure out reach builders. Sometimes a single property like an IPL could be plotted against other similar properties to see which one would generate the quickest reach build-up.

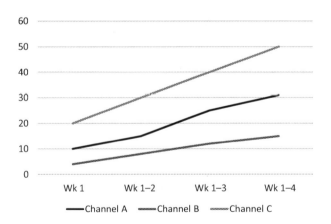

Cumulative Reach & Reach Build-Up

FIGURE 11.2 Cumulative reach and reach build-up.

Source: Created by the author.

6. *Channel stickiness*: This is another related concept to the cumulative reach concept just discussed. How loyal are the viewers to the channel, or what is the stickiness level of the channel? This is important for a planner to see, as this has a bearing on the impact of the channel. For example, a channel A might have a very high cumulative reach of, say, 90% within the defined audience and defined markets. However, the moment one changes the definition of viewing from 1 minute+ to 5 minutes+, the cumulative reach drops down to, say, 50%. Compare this to another channel, say Channel B, which has a cumulative reach of 75%, but when we change the definition of viewing from 1 minute+ to 5 minutes+, the cumulative reach drops to 60%. These numbers clearly indicate that probably Channel B has a better capacity to hold on to its viewers, and that the stickiness of Channel B is higher than Channel A. If you were to look at it as a formula, stickiness could be calculated as:

$$\frac{\text{Cume Reach of a Channel @ 5 min+}}{\text{Cume Reach of a Channel @ 1 min+}} \times 100$$

This is one of the formulas that is generally used. At times, one could look at cumulative reach for just a week instead of 4 weeks, and one could look derive stickiness index based on 5 minutes+ viewing and 10 minutes+ viewing, depending upon the situation and assumptions one has made.

In our example, Channel A has a stickiness index of 56, while Channel B has a stickiness index of 80. In the final mix, probably Channel B stands a better chance to be part of the plan. A higher stickiness means the channel has a better ability to hold on to its audience, while a lower stickiness means that there are a lot of floating viewers who make up the audience of the channel. Therefore, taking this forward, communication placed in channels with higher stickiness stands a better chance of noticeability. Basically, stickiness lets you also involve the channel viewing intensity along with the reach-delivering ability of the channel into the decision-making grid while selecting the channel mix.

7. *Audience fragmentation*: There was a point in time in India when there was just Doordarshan ad programmes like *Ramayan* and *Mahabharat*, which were the ultimate in delivering mass audiences. On Sundays, when the programmes were aired, streets would be deserted and the audience (bereft of any big TV entertainment) sat glued to their TV screens. Those were simple days for media. Then the entire cable-and-satellite revolution swept the country sometime from the early 90s, and since then, we've come a long way. Yes, the number of people viewing TV have increased since then, and so have the viewing options and the time spent watching TV. But this audience is now fragmented across a large number of channels. The higher the degree of fragmentation in the market, the more the

number of channels required to achieve plan reach and frequency numbers. Think back to the media weight setting process, where we were discussing how to arrive at the effective reach level and were discussing how diminishing returns play a role in media. In that context, the higher the level of fragmentation in the market, the earlier the start of the diminishing returns curve. Analysing the extent of fragmentation has an important role to play in the channel mix decision.

Programme/Daypart Selection

Once the genre selection and the channel mix are done, the next step involves programme/daypart selection. Normally, programme selection is looked at for key GEC channels, while for niche channels like news, music, etc, people look at daypart selections. There are times when even for niche channels, programme selections are looked at especially when some big-ticket sponsorships are involved, but by and large for niche channels, daypart selections are done. Most of the time, the analysis for both channel selection and programme/daypart selection takes place simultaneously, and one does not necessarily break it down into two sequential steps of first channel selection followed by programme selection. However, for the purposes of our discussion, we've kept them separate. There are a lot of ways in which planners look at this area of analysis. We will discuss a few most prominent ways of looking at this:

1. *Absolute viewership*: The absolute rating of a programme, or the number of viewers, or a drop-down list of the Top programmes within the selected genre is a good starting point. Similarly for daypart selections, where this analysis could be done with predefined dayparts. Table 11.7 gives an example of the GEC genre, where we take a look at the Top programmes across different audiences in the Hindi-speaking markets (HSM).
2. *Audience profile of the programme*: Given the definition of the target audience, one tries to look at an overall profile fit with the programme. One might want to do a small check on the SEC-wise or age-wise distribution of the programme's audience and see whether it sits well with the audience definition. Or at times, even without the numbers, one can do a broad qualitative check when it comes to programme selection and audience fit issues.
3. *Programme viewership vs commercial break viewership*: When peoplemeter data for TV viewership started, it added another area of fine-tuning the plan. There is a general belief that when the commercial break happens, viewers lose interest and move out of the room either to finish some small household chores, or talk on the phone, or put the TV on mute, or read something, and so on. While peoplemeters cannot capture all that people

TABLE 11.7 Programme viewership

Channel	Programme	Time	Ratings %			
			2+ Yrs	Males	Youth	Females
A	E	22:00	3.3	3.0	3.1	4.1
B	F	21:30	2.9	2.6	3.0	3.4
D	G	21:00	2.3	2.0	2.3	2.6
C	H	20:00	2.2	2.0	2.0	2.4
A	I	20:30	2.0	1.6	2.0	2.5
A	J	19:30	1.9	1.5	2.1	2.4
B	K	20:00	1.9	1.6	1.9	2.4
C	L	22:30	1.9	1.7	1.8	2.3
C	M	21:30	1.8	1.6	1.7	2.2
B	N	20:00	1.7	1.4	1.8	2.2
B	O	20:30	1.6	1.5	1.5	1.7
A	P	21:00	1.6	1.4	1.5	1.9
A	Q	20:00	1.6	1.2	1.8	1.8
C	R	16:00	1.6	1.2	1.4	1.7
C	S	19:00	1.5	1.1	1.7	1.8

Source: Created by the author.

do when there's a commercial break, they do give us an indication of the number of people in the room with their viewership status as 'on'. Along with programme ratings, it is also possible to get the viewership rating of commercial breaks within the programme. This data too is of immense use when judging the value of that programme to the media plan. A very basic analysis here could be a small index of sorts which indicates commercial break viewership as a percentages of programme viewership. Also, normally, most plan evaluations are done on the basis of commercial break ratings.

4. *Clutter levels*: As all of us know, clutter levels on TV have increased dramatically over a period of time with the mushrooming of many channels. Also, at the same time, audience fragmentation across channels is a new reality. Programme ratings have dropped due to this, and today, with so many options available to the audience, there are no cases of programmes reaching double-digit TVRs. Add to this the huge clutter that typically follows high-rated programmes or better performing channels. How does one register impact in an environment of clutter? Should one go for top-rated programmes despite clutter? Should one adjust ratings according to clutter? Should one go for low-viewership, low-clutter programmes? What should be the ideal balance of clutter and viewership? These are some of the questions that play on the mind while looking at this area. Clutter is a function of two things: (a) Ad: Edit ratio of a programme; and (b) actual

number of brands being advertised in the programme. Given these two factors and combined with other factors like viewership, cost, etc., one could take a call.

5. *Programme loyalty levels*: This is yet another way to evaluate programmes. The clutter levels on few programmes being very high is indicative enough that given a good-quality programme, there is an audience to be captured and advertisers to back the programme. The questions now are: Is this audience loyal enough? Can I catch the same person a couple of times so as to drive the message home? Does a soap have higher loyalty than news, or a one-off story, or a film, or a game show, etc.? Programme loyalty actually identifies the core viewers of a particular programme and helps effectively communicate with them. This core audience would perhaps show a higher level of receptivity to the message, perhaps might remember it, and perhaps rate the brand favourably. Therefore, programmes with higher loyalty levels would perhaps deliver the message in a much more effective way. It might not make a dramatic change in the final media plan, but what it really does is that it polishes the final plan. There are a lot of brands on TV, which might require a bit of an explanation. Maybe the consumers don't get the message right the first time, maybe subsequent exposures to the same audience might work towards better message comprehension or an understanding of a new concept, or might just serve as good reminders for brands active round the year. Whichever way one looks at it, it might be a subtle tool to be used to make the advertising work harder. Normally, this analysis could be of use when one is looking at the EF approach to planning, where the goal is to maximize reach at the EF level. It makes sense, then, to reach out to the same audience again and again. Programmes with a higher loyalty level indicate that a higher proportion of its audience is from the previous episode/episodes, and the brand message could be delivered again to this audience. In media jargon terms, there is a higher level of audience duplication with the previous episodes of the programme, and as a result, such programmes are good to deliver high frequency. The reverse logic works when the goal is to maximize reach, where one looks at programmes which have very low loyalty levels and correspondingly lower duplication levels which contribute to building reach. For example a typical soap will have relatively higher loyalty levels as compared to, say, a movie being telecast on a GEC channel.

6. *Viewer volatility*: Another analysis made possible by peoplemeters is the fact that one can track the inflow and outflow of audiences every minute of the programme. Importantly, this also throws up information on where the viewers are coming from and to which channels they are going out. This information is also of subtle use in the channel mix decision. Viewer volatility, for the purpose of our discussion, is defined as the percentage of audience which switches in and out of a programme. The higher this

percentage, the less involved is the viewer in the programme or the channel – and therefore, less likely to see our commercial. Correspondingly, if the viewer volatility is low, it would mean greater involvement with the programme, which enhances our commercial exposure value.

7. *Audience attention spans*: All of us know that people over a period of time have become very impatient, and attention spans have been reduced. This is because there are so many options out there for the viewer to choose from, and if a programme is not good enough to hold attention, people switch to the multiple other available options. Just the way we had discussed the stickiness index when it came to channel selection, this is a similar exercise at a programme level. Here again, we see the cumulative reach of the programme at 1 minute+, and compare it with the cumulative reach where people watch at least say 50% of the programme and develop an index of sorts. The higher the index, the relatively higher the attention spans, and the better chances of our brand communication going through.

   The other way to assess this is to look at the average time a person spends on a particular event (programme). If this scores high on an index, it means that the viewers of the programme are more attentively tuned in, and the likelihood of the advertising message getting noticed is higher.

8. *Cost efficiency/cost per rating Point (CPRP)*: This is a very crucial parameter involved in programme selection. All the aforementioned variables were related to analysis to this area, but this is single-handedly the most important variable used in conjunction with the host of other analyses listed earlier. In simple terms, programmes are compared on cost efficiency as measured by something known as CPRP, and then one looks at programme selection. However, though this might seem a fairly straightforward way of programme selection, it's really not that simple. There are times when the most cost-efficient programme is not necessarily a top-rated programme, and it might deliver a very small audience. At the same time, the highest-rated programme might not feature anywhere on the Top list of most cost-efficient programmes, as it might be very highly priced. So what does one do here? The right mix of absolute rating points and cost efficiency needs to be arrived at. And this will depend upon the brand objectives, budgets, markets, reach and frequency objectives, competitive situation, etc. It is here where judgment and experience come into play. Table 11.8 displays the CPRP of programmes.

Plan Optimization

Every plan has an objective, and it differs from brand to brand and from situation to situation. There are times when reach maximization is the goal, there are other times when frequency maximization becomes a goal, there are still other times when weekly reach maximization at a

TABLE 11.8 Cost efficiency/cost per rating point (CPRP)

Programme	Ratings %	Rate/10 sec	CPRP
A	5.02	250000	49801
B	4.72	240000	50847
C	2.54	200000	78740
D	1.68	50000	29762
E	1.34	48000	35821
F	1.32	50000	37879
G	1.32	60000	45455
H	1.14	100000	87719

Source: Created by the author.

given EF is a goal, and so on. At the end of the day, the goal is to arrive at the most optimized plan that money can buy. One has to look into things like diminishing returns, and one has to worry about incremental reach added by every channel in the mix. Additionally, there is another reality that needs to be kept in mind: not all viewers of TV watch TV with the same intensity. There are some heavy viewers, some medium viewers, and some viewers who watch very little TV. How does the TG stack up into heavy, medium, and light viewers, and how does one optimize deliveries between these three types of audiences? For instance, a TV plan could be delivering 90% reach and an average OTS of 10. But if we break up the deliveries amongst heavy, medium, and light viewers, the plan might deliver 99% reach and 25 AOTS amongst the heavy viewers, a 70% reach and 15 AOTS amongst the medium viewers, and 30% reach and 3 AOTS amongst the light viewers. From here we know that the plan is just not delivering in the right direction. It is easy to deliver higher amongst heavy viewers and more intensity will mean more exposures amongst the heavy viewers. Such issues require a detailed analysis of viewer behaviour, and it might mean making a lot of iterative changes to the plan. One might need to substitute some mass reach channels with niche channels viewed by the light viewers, and try to ensure a more balanced plan delivery across the three types of viewers. To aid media planners in managing the huge complexity of TV viewership data (which is updated weekly), the BARC software also has an optimizer module which helps in maximizing reach or minimizing GRPs for a given reach. It helps create optimized plans based on constraints put in by the planners.

A plan optimizer works with the basic premise of how much incremental reach each spot adds to the plan. The software evaluates the thousands of options available and helps determine the next best spot that could be added to the plan to get the best incremental reach. It modifies a natural plan in two ways:

a. It reallocates budgets across the selected channel mix.
b. It reallocates spots across various dayparts.

Dealing with Sponsorships

Sponsorships have become a very important part of TV planning. Here we will talk of sponsorships purely from a TV planning point of view in terms of programme or event sponsorships and their value to the plan.

At a very basic level, sponsorship means association with a certain programme or event on TV. Three basic types of sponsorships are normally used:

a. *Title sponsor*: Here the brand name becomes a part of the title of the programme itself – for example, Dream 11 IPL, Livon Supermodel, Oppo Roadies, JBL Hustle etc. The name of the programme incorporates the brand name, and whenever the programme is promoted on the channel or through other media, the brand name gets a prominent mention. This is the value that a title sponsor gets. In addition, the title sponsor also gets to air its ad first in the commercial breaks, it gets to block competition to some extent. There can be only one title sponsor for the programme.
b. *Presenting sponsor/co-presenting sponsor*: Here the brand is mentioned as a presenting sponsor. An example of this in action could be 'Odonil Air Sanitizer presents *Kundali Bhagya*'. Here, the brand name is not part of the title of the programme. In all promotions of the programme, the brand is mentioned as the presenting sponsor. The presenting sponsor also gets some preferential placement of commercials within the breaks of the programme. Usually, there is only one presenting sponsor; for example, 'Tresemme presents *Bigg Boss*'. Sometimes there are instances where there is more than one presenting sponsor for a programme. In such cases they are called co-presenting sponsors. For example, 'Maruti Suzuki and Colgate co-present *Indian Idol*', or 'New Zealand vs India, co-presented by Dream 11, Byju's, Maruti Suzuki, Amazon.in, and Kamla Pasand'.
c. **Co-Sponsor/Associate Sponsor/Powered/Co-Powered/Partner**: This is the third level of sponsorship, where the brands are also tagged in the promos and mentioned as co-sponsors or associate sponsors. For example, a programme could be promoted as '*Hero Honda MTV Roadies* presented by Airtel, in association with Pepsi, Colgate, and Horlicks'. Here Pepsi, Colgate, and Horlicks are associate sponsors. Normally there is more than one associate sponsor for most programmes – the number could vary from three to six associate sponsors.

So what's the value that one gets through sponsorships?

a. *Building brand awareness*: Whenever the programme is promoted either on the same channel, or on other channels or other media, the sponsor gets a brand-name mention. This is an important value-add, as it helps in building brand TOMs to some extent.

b. *Reinforcing the key brand message*: With every programme promo, the sponsors get a 4- to 5-second promo tag. This means that the brand's pack shot and the key brand message are also aired as part of the programme. It works like a 4- or 5-second ad. Normally, brands use a pack shot and the end line of the commercial for such promos. An example could be, say, Amul, where in the 4- to 5-second promo tag they might show an Amul product with the line 'The Taste of India' as it appears in the commercial. These work as very good reminders of the brand name and the key brand promise. Because the programme needs to gather viewership, it is promoted across the channel and other channels across various dayparts and usually promoted with a very high frequency. The sponsors ride on this programme promos to build a good frequency at least for the brand name.

c. *Environment fit*: Some brands look at a qualitative fit between the brand promise or values and the programme. For Hero Honda, a bike manufacturer, an association with *MTV Roadies* was not just about promo tags and other sponsorship deliverables; the real value for them comes from the qualitative fit the programme offers to the brand. Or for that matter, consider *JBL Hustle*, which is a rap reality show. The environment fit and the audience connect are the biggest values added to the brand through such a sponsorship.

d. *Value additions to a plain media deal*: Given the values that sponsorship brings to the table in terms of promo tags, normally during the negotiation stage, a couple of sponsorships are thrown in to sweeten the deal or are used as value additions to the deal. More on this when we discuss media buying.

e. *Preferential placement of advertising and competitive exclusivity*: A sponsor normally gets preferential placement of spots in the commercial break – it could be the first spot or the last spot of the break. At the same time, they also get category/competitive exclusivity to some extent. For instance, if Pepsi is the title sponsor for a programme/event, one of the clauses in the agreement could be that Coke and other soft drink category brands put together will not get more than 60% of the inventory given to Pepsi. This gives the brand a chance to stand out from competitive clutter.

Dailies Planning

With 400 million readers, print is one of the most dominant media types used in India along with TV. The IRS reports readership data for 478 newspapers and magazines. Besides these, thousands of other smaller local newspapers are circulated. However, with TV ratings data out every week vs four times a year for print, there's greater dynamism and rigour that goes behind TV planning. The other reason is also that print is far more stable, and readership changes do not happen overnight. At the same time, data is made available on industry trends once every 3 months. Print planning brings its own set of criteria of vehicle selections. We will discuss some primary considerations involved when it comes to taking decisions regarding vehicle selections in print.

a. *Audience fit*: How well the profile of the publication fits in with the target audience profile is the primary consideration in choosing media vehicles. This is much the same as the case in TV planning. This usually requires an analysis of the profile of publications on various demographic parameters. For instance, a plan targeting kids will have a different mix of vehicles vs a plan targeted at women audiences or male audiences. There are many instances, particularly when one is looking at magazine planning, where there are no numbers at times both on readership as well as circulation. In such situations, the environment fit of the magazine becomes the central element of decision making. Usually, these decisions come in play for niche magazines like *Golf Digest*, *Vogue*, *Digit*, and others targeted at a very small but focused audience. Newspapers are normally that much more mass in nature and cater to a wide range of society – typically used by mass products.

b. *Intensity of use of the medium*: Apart from audience fit, with how much intensity the audience interacts with the medium is an important element. Are most of the people spending less time with the medium and are light readers, or are most of them heavy readers? These also give some indication of the level of involvement with the medium and give small directions on the overall impact of communication carried in the medium.

c. *Usage of product and brands*: Print research in India, has one very important edge over other forms of media research – product and brand linkage data is also captured for every respondent. This means that it is possible to understand the readership of a publication title along with category and brand linkage. For instance, one can say that while Publication X has an overall readership of, say, 1,00,000 readers, we can also say that out of these 1,00,000 readers, 50,000 of them use Lux Soap, 20,000 of them use hair dyes, and so on. There are approximately 60 product categories and brands for which data is available. This makes print planning that much sharper and more precise. We can also, for instance, do an analysis and find out what kind of publications heavy users of soft drinks read. Things like frequency of purchase and publications read could be put on a cross tab to analyse purchasing patterns in a particular category and corresponding readership numbers. This is another way how publications could be profiled. In addition, this kind of data helps in better target group selection and definitions. For instance, there are many times when it becomes difficult for a new brand to define a target audience on demographic terms. However, at times, one defines the set of brands that this potential audience would be using. Once that is done, through this, one defines the audience, and then one can work backwards to figure out what core demographic patterns the audience falls into. Vehicle selection in print is that much more definite and sharper as compared to that in any other medium in India because of the availability of product and brand data.

Table 11.9 demonstrates how precision print planning takes place based on the granularity of readership data available.

In Table 11.9 you can see that the ranking of the Top 10 newspapers would change when we define an audience demographically. Newspaper C, which is overall ranked no. 3, moves to the no. 6 rank when we define the audience as Women, 20+ years.

In Table 11.10 you would see, as we change the audience definition to Edible Oil Users, a different ranking emerges. And when we define it more specifically as mustard oil or groundnut oil users, the readership rankings change completely.

Print readership data allows us to precisely define brand users and check the readership against this definition of an audience. It is this data granularity of print that makes it possible for sharper targeting. This kind of data, as shown in Table 11.11, isn't available for TV, radio, or even digital currently.

TABLE 11.9 Overall readership, and readership within a defined TG

Daily	Overall Readership (000s)	Daily	Readership amongst Women 20+ yrs (000s)
A	50000	A	6597
B	40000	B	6401
C	38000	E	5935
D	30000	G	5384
E	20000	D	4128
F	18000	C	4250
G	15000	F	4070
H	14000	N	3081
I	13000	M	2895
J	12000	H	2547

Source: Created by the author.

TABLE 11.10 Readership amongst different category users

Daily	Readership amongst	Daily	Readership amongst	Daily	Readership amongst
	Edible Oil Users (000s)		Groundnut Oil Users (000s)		Mustard Oil Users (000s)
A	44556	E	6831	A	40830
B	37507	K	3249	C	33911
C	34174	M	3022	D	31141
D	26265	B	2763	B	15619
E	19142	H	1702	L	8065
F	17379	F	1668	P	6647
H	12834	I	1449	R	5633
G	13298	U	1407	S	5552
I	12007	J	1341	H	5379
J	11576	O	1289	I	5275

Source: Created by the author.

TABLE 11.11 Readership by brand usage

Daily	Readership amongst Users of	Daily	Readership amongst Users of
	Brand X Groundnut Oil (000s)		Brand Y Mustard Oil (000s)
B	357	C	926
H	218	A	832
F	202	B	421
J	159	Q	393
I	156	P	360
X	118	H	334
Y	115	L	218
A	113	W	218
C	112	D	210
U	108	Z	197

Source: Created by the author.

d. *Position of ads*: Very often when it comes to planning in newspapers, positioning of ads becomes a central area of decision making apart from the other factors. Where the ad is being placed in the paper has a major bearing on the eventual noticeability of the ad, and hence the impact of communication. Does an ad placed on the Sports Page have as much noticeability as compared to that on the Front Page? Readership is captured at a title level for all publications in India. For the last couple of years, section readership is also being captured. Today it is possible to find out the readership of various sections in a newspaper. This has helped to some extent in sharpening planning decisions. Then there is this huge issue of left-hand page vs right-hand page. The dominant belief is that right-hand pages work better as compared to left-hand pages, and buyers try to ensure that the campaign is placed on the right-hand page. Publications too charge a premium to place an ad at a specified position. There is little research available that talks about left-hand- vs right-hand-page effectiveness, and there are no conclusive thoughts on this. Going by data, approximately 60% of ads were placed on the right-hand side and 40% on the left-hand side in India. However, what happens when the reader reads the paper in this fashion – reads the Front Page first, then flips over and reads the Back Page, and then reads the newspaper in reverse order, first the sports page, then the business page, and last pages read are Page 3 and Page 2. What happens to the entire left-hand vs right-hand page logic? A lot of agencies have done their own research in this area and have derived various norms, but there is still no universally accepted standard. The dominant thinking is that Front Page works best followed by Back Page and Page 3. However, within this also, there are options available. Will a Front Page Solus ad work better than a strip ad below the mast head? Will a Top of Column ad work better than an ad somewhere at the bottom of the page? And so on. There are no conclusive answers. A large part of the decision making here is done on the basis of prior experience and available budgets.

e. *Size of the ad*: This is another major area of decision when it comes to planning for print. While in TV, the options are fairly standardized (you have, say, a range from 60 to 45 seconds – 30- to 15-second spot durations mainly), in print, the ad sizes are major factor. Will a full-page ad work better than a half page? Logic says yes because probably a large ad will grab attention faster and may leave a longer-lasting memory trace. However, the flip side is that on a full-page ad, there is no editorial material, and the reader may not spend that kind of time on the page. Therefore, should you take a size that covers probably 65–70% of the page and leave room for some editorial material, so that the page itself becomes slightly more important from a readership point of view? At the end of the day, people read a newspaper mainly to read the news of the day and points of view on various issues facing society. The advertising, though an integral part of the paper, is largely incidental for most readers. While the dominant thought is that larger sizes work better than smaller sizes as it probably helps stand out from the clutter, one can communicate better and give more details about the brand, and so on. Along with size, add the position placement of the ad and it gives a different spin. Will a 60 cc Front Page ad work better than a full page on Page 17? Is a half-page ad on the Back

Page better than a quarter-page ad on Page 3? This opens up a whole lot of permutations and combinations. There are no ready-made answers to this area. Different agencies have done their own reading and noting studies and have arrived at their own thumb rules of what will work best under different circumstances for different categories. However, the most popular positions in India are an Island, or a half page, Solus ads, ear panels, jackets, horizontal strips, vertical strips, and Skybus (horizontal strip below the masthead).

f. *Main issue vs supplement*: Where the ad appears – in the main issue or the supplement – also has a bearing on the kind of impact it has. In India, most newspapers have a main section, and every day of the week there are separate supplements covering different kinds of subject areas such as education, appointments, city entertainment news, women's issues, general interest reading, kids' content, etc. Normally, these supplements are targeted at a certain target group, such as youth, women, kids, etc. From whatever research is available, the readership of supplements is far lower than that of the main issue of the newspaper. The advertising rates for the main newspaper are also higher than those of supplements. They are normally used when either the communication is targeted at a very select kind of audience, or the communication requires a certain kind of editorial environment around it. The City Entertainment supplement like a *Delhi Times* or a *Mumbai Times* has a lot of Page 3 party news, as well as Bollywood, Hollywood, and TV news. Most of the advertising carried in such supplements is largely local retail. Normally, the other supplements (other than the city news section) are common supplements and are usually spread across all the editions of the newspaper. They make great sense for communication targeted at a specific group of people like youth, kids, women, employment seekers, auto enthusiasts, etc. About 80% of all ads in India are placed in the Main Issue and the remaining 20% are placed in supplements. Typically, planners look for a conducive editorial environment which could go with the brand theme, as well as the importance of the position of the ad; of course, budgets and affordability would also play a role.

g. *Geographical flexibility*: This probably is one of the greatest advantages that newspapers as a medium have over others. Advertising can be targeted only to a specific city, and even within that, only to a certain area. There are a lot of advertisers who sell in a particular city only or sell in a particular part of the city. For them, taking the full edition run is wasteful; therefore, flexibility of a newspaper is a great benefit – it gives them targeted reach, minimizes spillovers, and also works out cheaper. Most large newspaper groups have printing setups in such a manner that they are virtually printing 150–200 sub-editions. A sub-edition is a customized local paper and has local relevant news of that area. For instance, the

Kanpur edition of *Dainik Jagran* has nine sub-editions – and each of these sub-editions caters to a different city/district. While the main news is common, there are four pages that keep changing from sub-edition to sub-edition – and each has local news. This has two benefits: to the reader, it gives them local relevant content, and to the advertiser, those local pages become a good option to advertise in the local area. Therefore, rather than buying the full Kanpur edition, a small local retailer in a place like Unnao can place his advertising on the local pages of the Unnao sub-edition and reach out to his audience. Other large newspaper groups like *Times of India*, *Dainik Bhaskar*, and *Hindustan* all follow a similar practice. Brands can leverage this flexibility to their advantage, and also change communication by city if needed.

h. *Quality of reading measures*: This is another factor that at times plays a role in vehicle selection. The various dimensions of quality are: How much time do the readers devote to the newspaper title? How many readers are the sole readers of this newspaper? How much of this readership is at home vs out of home? These are areas that advertisers and planners believe are indicators of the strength of the newspaper title, and also indicate the degree of involvement/loyalty the readers have for the newspaper. The operating logic is that the more involved readers are with the newspaper title, the better the chances of advertising making an impact. Over a period of time, most advertising in newspapers has become tactical of sorts; it is either about announcing a launch, or giving product details, availability or price announcements, or a special consumer offer. Most of the communication has a sense of "immediacy" around it, and therefore response to advertising becomes an important factor while choosing publications.

i. *Clutter*: Just like in TV, even in newspapers, clutter is one of the key factors in deciding a newspaper title. Normally, clutter comes with success. A good and successful/leading newspaper which attracts a large number of readers also attracts many advertisers and normally will have higher clutter as compared to smaller titles. The same thing holds true in the case of TV. A high-rated programme will attract more advertising and will have relatively higher clutter levels. Clutter in print too is dependent upon two key factors: the Ad:Edit ratio of the newspaper and the number of ads. Normally each newspaper works with a basic understanding of, say, a 40:60 Ad:Edit ratio or even a 50:50 ratio. It generally does not go beyond this. Of course, during the festival seasons the ratios get altered a bit, but an overall average is maintained. Most large newspaper groups have set editorial content standards to say that they will carry 100 or 150 items of news and the total editorial content will on an average be of so many words. If there's more advertising, then more pages are added to accommodate this rather than editorial making way for advertising.

j. *Reproduction quality*: Newspapers are printed on newsprint, which varies for different newspapers. It also happens to be one of the key raw material used by a newspaper, and normally accounts for almost 30–40% of the total cost of producing the newspaper. There are various kinds of newsprint available:

- Glazed newsprint
- Standard newsprint

Within these, various kinds of varieties are available, like Russian, Canadian, Chinese, Indian, etc, and the price varies for each based on the GSM (grams per square metre). Most newspapers in India use a mix of Indian and imported newsprint. Typically, imported newsprint is more expensive than Indian newsprint. Basically, the quality of newsprint impacts the quality of reproduction of the advertising. Ads are normally done in colour, but poor newsprint quality can mar the impact of communication. Therefore, a normal check is also done on the reproduction quality of the newspaper. This also becomes one of the measures that help in finalizing the choice of a newspaper title.

k. *Duplication levels*: How many readers of a particular title also read the other titles is another measure used in the selection criteria. If duplication levels between the papers in the plan are high, it means that the communication will be seen by the same number of people and the plan would deliver higher frequency. Correspondingly, if the duplication levels between publications in a plan is low, then the plan would deliver higher reach. Depending upon objectives of the specific campaign, plans are constructed. It is here where duplication levels make a difference to the plan during the plan optimization stage.

l. *Readership of the newspaper*: This is one of the most important criteria used in the selection of a newspaper. The absolute number of readers of a newspaper is a critical determining factor in drawing the consideration list. There are two measures reported by the readership surveys for the readership of a title – average issue readership, and total readership. AIR is an indication of "yesterday" readership of a title and from a planning point of view gives an indication of regular readers. It also means that any ad that one releases in the paper will on an average reach out to that many number of readers. Then there is the measure of total readership, which indicates the cumulative reach of the newspaper. If one releases advertising in a newspaper over a period of time, reach will build up, and eventually the plan will reach out to a much higher number of people than indicated by AIR. Therefore, in planning terms, both AIR and TR have their own relevance. Normally, AIR is used as a currency for trading and TR plays a role in determining the eventual reach of a plan. Table 11.12 shows the Top 10 newspapers in India as per MRUC.

m. *Circulation*: This is another important metric used in publication selection. Circulation indicates the number of copies sold by a publication, and a lot of advertisers who do not understand or believe in the various readership debates tend to use circulation as a key criterion to base their choice. Normally, this method is favoured largely by local advertisers who decide their plans based on their experience in the local market in terms of response, and who do not either have access to or belief in readership data. However, large national advertisers normally base their media decisions on readership and supplement it with circulation data. Largely, it is used to reconfirm the plan selections, and it also helps in understanding the market spread of different editions of a publication. Lots of advertisers have a "Dealer Panel" below their ads which indicates to consumers the outlets where the product is available. Which dealer panel goes in which edition is an important question, and this is normally answered through circulation data. In reality, given the various issues surrounding circulation data (as discussed in the initial parts of the book), circulation data is not a key metric used in publication selection for large national advertisers. Yet, this is an important metric for local advertisers to make their plans. The office of registrar of newspapers for India classifies newspapers into large publications (circulation >75,000 copies), medium publications (circulation 25,001–75,000 copies), and small publications (<25000 copies). The total claimed circulation of publications registered with RNI is 43.99 cr.

n. *Cost efficiency*: While the measure for cost efficiency in TV is CPRP, in print the measure for efficiency is cost per thousand (CPT). This is a very important parameter involved in publication selection. All the previous

TABLE 11.12 Top 10 newspapers in India

000s	Total Readership	Average Issue Readership
Dainik Jagran (Main)	68667	16872
Dainik Bhaskar (Main)	52429	15566
Hindustan (Main)	49890	13213
Amar Ujala (Main)	44196	9657
Malayala Manorama (Daily)	17763	8569
Daily Thanthi	26314	7379
Lokmat (Main)	22343	6285
Rajasthan Patrika (Main)	16333	5863
The Times of India (Main)	17344	5560
Mathrubhumi	12316	4849

Source: IRS 2019 Q4, MRUC.

factors were related to analysis in this area, but this is singlehandedly the most important variable used in conjunction with the host of other analyses listed. In simple terms, publications are compared on cost efficiency as measured by CPT. However, though this might seem a fairly straightforward way of publication selection, it's really not that simple. There are times when the most cost-efficient publication is not necessarily the Top publication, and it might deliver a very small audience. At the same time, the highest-read publication might not feature anywhere on the Top list of most cost-efficient publications, as it might be very highly priced. So what does one do here? The right mix of absolute readership numbers and cost efficiency needs to be arrived at. And this will depend upon the brand objectives, budgets, markets, reach and frequency objectives, competitive situation, etc. It is here where judgment and experience come into play. Normally, CPT calculations are done on readership, but some people do it even on circulation.

o. *Gross impressions mapping*: Just to revisit the concept, one person being exposed once is one impression. There are times when planners use this technique to set media weights for various markets based on their relative importance, and then backwork the cost of the plan. So for instance, one might say that in Delhi and Mumbai, which are P1 markets, one might want to deliver 5 million gross impressions; while for Bhopal and Indore, one might want to deliver 2 million gross impressions, as these markets could be lower in priority. Given this, the plan is worked out to deliver these numbers. It's here that absolute readership comes into play to deliver gross impressions. There are times when planners also benchmark competition and try to assess their intensity in print through the gross impressions delivered in different markets. A simple way to calculate gross impressions is multiply the number of insertions by the readership of the publication within the defined TG in a given market. For example, if there's a print plan for Delhi which has 3 insertions in Publication A (AIR of 1000 within defined TG), 3 insertions in Publication B (AIR of 2000 within defined TG), and 2 insertions in Publication C (AIR of 3000 within defined TG), and the defined target audience for the campaign is Males, SEC ABC, 25+ years, then the gross impressions delivered by this plan are as explained in Table 11.13.

Also, just the way GRPs are normalized, even gross impressions could be normalized to, say, a 240- to 400-square-centimetre ad for newspapers or a full-page ad when it comes to magazines.

p. *Other values, like sampling, innovations possibilities, sponsorships, joint promotions*: Besides the important factors previously discussed, there are planners and advertisers who want to move beyond just buying blocks of advertising in newspapers and magazines. Given the relationship that print titles enjoy with their audiences, it becomes important for any plan

TABLE 11.13 Gross impressions calculation

Daily	Readership amongst Males NCCS ABC, 25+ Years	No. of Insertions	Gross Impressions
A	1000	1	1000
B	2000	2	4000
C	3000	3	9000
Total			14000

Source: Created by the author.

to try to leverage this relationship for the benefit of the brand. It's here where people talk of going beyond just advertising. There are many examples of sampling through newspapers and magazines, where small sachets could be pasted along with the copy of the newspaper or the magazines. Magazines are normally delivered in a plastic bag which could carry different types of samples. Then of course, this entire area of innovations becomes a huge factor in the decision-making grid – the objective is how do we best communicate the brand's proposition to the users and how does one register impact. Then there is this entire area of sponsorships of some relevant editorial columns. Then there are sponsorships of some on-ground properties being executed by publishers. Most publishers do a lot of reader relationship-building exercises, and normally they end up as huge on-ground events where audiences are engaged at a one-to-one level. There are times when brands align with such activities to drive additional mileage.

q. *Content leverage*: Over the last few years, brands have increasingly been showing an interest towards creating branded content in newspapers and magazines. So for instance, a cookery brand might want to create custom recipes and create a branded column in the newspaper or magazine. It could also crowdsource recipes by floating a contest in which the winning recipes get printed in the newspaper/magazine. Sometimes, contextual content is planned for a brand, and the ad is placed on the specified page. For example, an agarbatti brand ad could be placed on a page with contextual editorial content around profiling key shrines in India. Or a page where the city's sanitation problems are being raised, an ad of Lifebuoy soap could be placed, or on an entertainment page, an ad for Lux could be placed. Brands are increasingly looking for contextually relevant content environments to place their ads, as the belief is that there are significant carry-over effects from relevant content to ads. The ability of a newspaper/magazine to create contextual content, and partner content co-creation opportunities, are also becoming important while planning for print.

The preceding were some of the key considerations involved in print planning. There could be a few other criteria based on custom research and on response measurements that help sharpen print planning decisions.

Radio Planning

Radio is one of the big support mediums in India. Till as late as 2000, the industry was completely a government-controlled medium with Vividh Bharti and Primary Channel being the only options available to advertisers. During those days, radio was used largely to cover rural markets or smaller markets where TV and print penetration weren't sufficient enough. Once the industry opened up to privatization in 2001, at least some major towns like Delhi, Mumbai, Bangalore, Kolkata, Chennai, Ahmedabad, and Indore got their own FM stations. Yet it still remained a large-city phenomenon till the second phase of FM liberalization in 2006, when about 91 cities were opened up and over 331 licenses given out to private operators after a stringent round of bidding. This has opened up the industry like never before, and advertisers started looking at this as a different medium altogether. While planning on radio in the earlier days revolved around trying to find out which Primary Channel or which Vividh Bharti station was available to cover which area, and within that the options were very few – one could choose from among three or four different types of programme categories. The decision making was largely based on gut feel or qualitative factors and time band decisions largely taken on the basis of what the IRS or NRS reflected. Not much money was being spent behind the medium, very little data was available on listenership, and there wasn't much of a chance of going wrong with one's instincts on radio planning – therefore, there was no real rigour and time spent planning on radio. The situation has changed now, with multiple stations to choose from, and within a station one has various options in which to make a choice. More than plain spot buys, there are exciting innovations on radio, like contests, listener engagement ideas, RJ mentions, sponsorships, merging on-air and on-ground activations, buzz generation ideas, and so on. Of course, at the same time, industry research on the medium in the form of RAM has come in, and decision making is now being based to some extent on the numbers and listenership patterns being thrown up by RAM. However, the research is still restricted to major towns, and a large majority of the stations are still not being measured. While the medium and research and planning metrics are still in the evolution stage, here I'll run you through some topline factors that are largely being used to make radio plans:

a. *Absolute listenership*: Just as what is reflected as channel reach in TV and readership for a title in print, which reflect the absolute number of people being reached by the channel/title, in radio too, this metric is a good starting point. RAM gives us the reach of each station, indicating the number of audiences covered. This at least gives a good starting point to work out a consideration set and move forward. However, the research is not all conclusive, and given the limitations, a large part of listeners are probably still not captured, and many people in the industry still do not buy into this research. Then there are some stations which have commissioned their own custom research on audience measurement and have been sharing the findings with advertisers and agencies. IRS also captures data on listenership as part of its research, and it gives us broad direction on the audience size of each station. To the station's reach numbers, throw in the cost element, and one can look at some sort of cost-efficiency parameters to help decision making. Table 11.14 shows the top radio stations in key metros.

b. *Profile of listeners*: While the radio industry in India is still in its infancy stage, there is not much product differentiation yet – most radio stations in India are playing contemporary film hits or popular tracks, so to say. Of course, almost all of them have a small mix of local music and retro tracks. Therefore, from a content point of view, there's not much of a differentiation that has largely happened. Yes, a few stations have tried to address a niche audience and have tried to differentiate their product, but largely most stations are targeting a mass audience. The major differentiation,

TABLE 11.14 Top radio stations in key metros

	Last One Week			
000s	*2019 Q1*	*2019 Q2*	*2019 Q3*	*2019 Q4*
Mumbai				
Radio Mirchi FM (98.3)	2712	2647	2719	3280
Red FM (93.5)	2029	2042	2167	2890
Big FM (92.7)	2169	2057	2033	2550
Radio City (91.1)	1770	1716	1802	2489
Fever FM (104.0)	2148	1884	1724	2293
Delhi				
Radio Mirchi FM (98.3)	3717	3395	3189	2815
Red FM (93.5)	3026	3092	2910	2704
Big FM (92.7)	2906	2716	2561	2230
Fever FM (104.0)	2351	2177	2042	1908
Radio City (91.1)	2246	2138	1984	1766

Source: IRS 2019 Q4, MRUC.

though, that one witnesses currently is in the station identity, the packaging of the music, the RJ talk, and what has been described as 'stationality'. This has created a huge degree of differentiation. Given this, each station has its own core profile of listeners, and this helps in taking decisions on which station to include in a plan. Therefore, to a limited degree, people do use this parameter for decision making on radio planning. However, given the fact that most stations are targeting a mass audience, one doesn't see a huge difference in profile of stations.

c. *Daypart listenership trends*: Having selected which station(s) to buy, the next step is to figure out where to place the advertising. This is where RAM data and IRS data are of great help, and one can find out how audiences tune in and out of a station. An important starting point here is the brand's TG and how it interacts with the medium. For instance, for youth, the morning time band (typically treated as prime band) might not be relevant – probably the afternoon or evening band may be more relevant once college gets over. Similarly for the working male or the housewife, there are different time bands that one tends to use.

d. *Moving beyond just spots on air*: In radio planning, planners have moved away from just putting spots on air. There are talks of using the power of the medium – 'interactivity' – and the medium's potential for 'buzz creation' to its fullest potential. In this direction, some innovative use of the medium is being made. 'RJ Mentions' have become an important tool in planning on radio. This does two things – the brand rides on the 'editorial appeal' of the channel and also helps in 'buzz creation'. It could be used during brand launches and promo launches, or to talk a particular feature about a brand, and so on. Beyond this, planners also tend to ride on the interactivity possibilities of the medium. Along with some radio plans, some sort of on-ground activity is planned to drive better consumer connect. Feedback or snapshots from the on-ground activity are put on air to reinforce the brand message and complete the brand's communication. The on-ground activity creates local buzz, and that buzz is then amplified through on-air talk by the RJs. Then there are times when people throw in a contest around the brand or its communication theme where listeners can call in and participate. This too helps in generating a better response to the brand's advertising message. Besides this, there are the usual elements of programme sponsorships that are used on radio.

e. *Other factors*: Given the kind of data that's now available through RAM, the other issues like channel loyalty, clutter levels, audience involvement, intensity of listenership, CPRP too are used at times. However, largely, radio station selectivity is based on geography, absolute reach, possibilities of audience involvement in brand's communication, innovation possibilities, absolute costs, and cost efficiency.

OOH Planning

OOH has always played a significant role in the media mix and typically accounts for around 5% of the overall advertising spends. OOH as a medium has evolved from being just about outdoor hoardings to complete OOH solutions that includes brand signages, retail visibility, mobile LED screens, train branding, street furniture, and a host of other possibilities. However, the biggest problem so far used to be the fact that the outdoor industry was largely very fragmented, not professionally managed, and suffered from lack of accountability and lack of research. These factors actually were a big stumbling block to the growth of outdoor. However, since the 2010s, we see an increasing number of large professional players getting into the medium and some sort of consolidation in the industry. With organized players coming into the fray, some things have changed dramatically for the medium – introduction of professional management, consolidation, more investments in the medium – and therefore more options are available to advertisers. These things will propel the growth of OOH as a medium. Earlier there were ad hoc studies on the medium, and crude reach-frequency models were used to give a broad sense of the numbers. However, due to the nature of the medium and lack of research, most of the conventional planners were not comfortable in planning on outdoor. Yes, they would stop at why the medium is necessary for the brand, which markets are relevant, and how outdoor in the media mix will help magnify the brand's message, and what role outdoor should play in the media mix selected. Beyond this, planning was getting difficult. It is here, where the outdoor players like Portland, Ogilvy Landscape, Primesite, and a host of other professional entities get into the act and take things further. Outdoor planning involves moving beyond using Microsoft Excel, and one has to actually get on ground to get a feel of the medium and actually construct the plan.

There are some basic factors involved in outdoor planning. We'll run through some of the most important factors that influence site selection in outdoor:

a. *Traffic patterns of the city*: Traffic flow patterns of the city help in identifying the key routes for presence. Typically, the route plan helps one in generating both reach and frequency through outdoor. The higher the traffic flow through a particular route, the better the route becomes as an outdoor hoarding location. In the biggest outdoor market of India – Mumbai – one often hears the phrases 'morning traffic' or 'evening traffic', with the former being on your route to office and the latter being on the route to home.

b. *Site location*: Actual location of the site becomes an important factor in influencing site selection decisions. Sites in prominent locations like major traffic crossings normally tend to command a higher visibility and therefore a higher price.

c. *Size and visibility*: How big the site is and how visible it is from a distance are important factors in site selection. The site's angle to the road is another factor that impacts site visibility. A site which is parallel to the road, vs a site that is at an angle to the road, vs a site that is head on over the road – all have different visibility levels. The general rule is, the bigger the size and the better the angle, the better the site visibility – and hence it commands a relatively higher price. Figure 11.3 serves as an example of metro pillars, Figure 11.4 gives an example of a site at an angle, and Figure 11.5 shows a bus shelter.

d. *Lit vs non-lit*: Sites that are lit have a larger audience as compared to non-lit sites as they are visible both during day and night. Normally, lit sites come at a higher price premium as compared to the normal non lit sites. Figure 11.6 shows a lit site.

e. *Clutter*: This also plays an important role in decision making. There are numerous locations within a city which could be important traffic junction points with a large traffic flow. At each of these junctions there are a variety of sites to choose from, and the physical number of sites are huge.

FIGURE 11.3 Example of metro pillars.

Source: Jagran Prakashan Ltd.

FIGURE 11.4   Site at an angle.

Source: Jagran Prakashan Ltd.

FIGURE 11.5   Bus Shelter – Parallel to Road.

Source: Jagran Prakashan Ltd.

FIGURE 11.6   Lit site.

Source: Jagran Prakashan Ltd.

Breaking out from the clutter is an important variable that is considered by outdoor planners. Figure 11.7 shows a clutter of sites.

f. *Absolute cost*: The absolute cost of a site is a very important factor in site selection. This is particularly more so in the case of OOH, as there is no data on site reach and visibility, the prices are determined by market forces, and the benchmarks applied are fairly crude. There are instances when on the same location, five different sites will command different prices. The measures of cost efficiency do not exist as of now, and there-fore price comparisons in outdoor selections are normally done on abso-lute prices – and the operating rule is that bigger, better located sites will command a higher price.

Options in OOH

Moving away from the conventional hoardings, there are a huge number of options available today in the OOH arena. They could be grouped under Traditional OOH, Digital OOH, and Transit. Traditional OOH includes conventional billboards, pole kiosks, bus shelters, etc. Digital OOH includes digital screens at metros, airports, metro stations, etc. Transit media

FIGURE 11.7 Clutter of sites.

Source: Jagran Prakashan Ltd.

includes airports, metros, trains, etc. Some of the most prominent types of OOH options available are:

a. *Conventional billboards*: These are the hoarding billboards that one notices all around. They are the most prominent, and they account for a large part of the OOH plans for most advertisers.
b. *LED screens*: These are fewer in number due to the huge cost of acquisitions. Normally placed outside malls or at important stationery crowd locations, they play out the brand's commercial – it works like a giant TV screen to address large masses of people.
c. *Mobile vans*: These are vans fitted with hydraulic systems which display a billboard. Normally these are used in areas where either the permanent billboards don't exist or they are very expensive. You would find a lot of these trucks parked at the side of a road displaying a message. Additionally, since they are mobile, one could use them to go around the city and change locations daily   this ensures a higher reach.
d. *Railway stations/bus terminals*: This is a huge traffic congregation point and an area with very high footfalls. This is a location that is heavily used by advertisers.
e. *Trains/metros*: Trains as an OOH medium are increasingly being used by brands. Apart from just putting vinyl stickers on the inside and outside of the train, some have even gone ahead with Train branding. Kurkure Express (running between A and B) is a very good example of this. Another example the use of trains as a medium by Airtel, India's leading Telecom brand, which has branded six Rajdhani trains across various locations (Bangalore, Chennai, Howrah, Ahmedabad, Patna, and Mumbai). All six

trains had extremely high-quality vinyl stickers pasted on the exteriors of all the coaches so that they could last through the rigours of rough conditions outside. Inside the coach they had various brand messages, tariff plan sheets, promotions for the various kinds of services, etc., all vinyls displayed at appropriate locations. It did not end here with the display of commercial messages. They went a step beyond by also taking over the housekeeping contract and ensuring that the journey was a wonderful experience. Under this, they provided for air fresheners in all the coaches, set up a regular cleaning schedule of the toilets and floor mopping within the coach, and other such things, which ensured that the passengers get a great journey experience courtesy of Airtel. The look on the faces of the passengers said it all – a brand message displayed on TV or any other form of conventional media would be a transient experience, but here they provided for over 40 hours of interaction with the brand and gave them an experience worth remembering – this is what one can say was true brand engagement. They used the medium's power truly.

f. *Metro stations*: In large metros like Delhi, the metro rail service is a very well-developed network. Stations provide huge visibility not just to commuters, but also to people on the streets crossing a metro station. Metro station branding is available where the station is coloured in the brand colours and the name of the station is integrated with the brand name, amongst several other custom brand deliverables at the station.

g. *Buses*: Just as with trains, buses are used as mediums with bus back panels, side panels, entire bus branding, branding inside the bus, and so on.

h. *Retail signages*: This is another major opportunity area in the OOH space. Increasingly, brands have wanted a permanent space in the point-of-purchase area. A visit to any market area will bear testimony to this. Starting from the name of the shop which is on a branded backlit board, to various types of shelf space branding, custom-branded shelves, other electronic danglers, etc., are all over the shop.

i. *Pole kiosks*: These are again in the conventional domain of OOH advertising. A pole kiosk is a small board placed on the poles of street lights either on the central verge of the road or on the sides. Normally, brands use these to reinforce the brand name or a central brand message given the small size of the board.

j. *Glow cubes*: These are very similar to pole kiosks, except that glow cubes are all backlit, are slightly bigger in size, and are like cubes on which the message could be displayed on all four sides of the cube.

k. *Bus shelters*: These are also in the conventional area of OOH solutions. However, some people have gone beyond and have redone the bus shelter to provide greater comfort to people waiting for a bus.

l. *Garden squares/circles*: In most large towns, there are many traffic intersections which have a garden in the middle of the junction and traffic moves around it. Brands have taken over the maintenance of these gardens and in turn place their brand messages around the garden.

m. *Traffic booths*: These are branded traffic booths from where traffic police manage the traffic. These are customized with a brand name mention and they also mention some safe driving directions such as 'wear helmets', 'don't drink and drive', etc.

n. *Temples*: Some brands have managed to enter temples where direction boards to the temple are branded, the temple gates are branded, and inside the temple, the Arti boards are also branded. Some brands also print small Arti booklets or mantra booklets which the temple priests hand out to devotees.

o. *Police stations/parks/hospitals*: Even these can be branded.

p. *Traffic barricades*: Most towns have police check posts or Octroi check posts at the entry/exit points of the city. To manage traffic, they put up barricades. These barricades also could be branded along with some traffic safety messages.

q. *Entry and exit gates of towns*: A lot of small towns have entry and exit gates which could be branded.

r. *Petrol pumps*: There are some unique opportunities available here too.

s. *Dhabas*: Branding of dhabas on the highways is another unique medium.

t. *Entrance gates of residential localities*: These also serve as an interesting permanent branding option.

u. *Malls and multiplexes*: Here's another big opportunity emerging with the retail revolution that one is currently witnessing. Malls provide a lot of space for branding. Multiplexes also have numerous options for brands.

v. *Public utilities*: The outer walls of public utilities provide another option. The best examples of these can be found in Delhi.

These were some of the major options that are being used today. Apart from these there are numerous other options in the OOH which are being created every day around us. Given the kind of options that are being used here, measurability is a huge issue. While conventional options in OOH could still be measured, there are so many other options available that it is harder to evaluate them – and with every passing day, more such opportunities are being created.

Current Tools and Techniques Used in OOH Planning

While the data available is scratchy, various professional outfits have done their own bit of proprietary research and have collected data on traffic flow patterns, site visibility indexes, site reach numbers, and so on. All of these combined have been used to develop rudimentary models on location selection within a town and some sort of reach frequency estimations for campaigns. Some have developed site simulators where one could place a JPEG image of the outdoor creative on different types of sites and actually see how the creative would look, and what the visibility range would be, and so on. But most of the models are still grappling with the basic issues of which sites to select in the city and what the reach and frequency would be of those sites, and also provide some sort of competitive benchmarking. Plan optimization models are still in the process of being developed. However, a large part of OOH planning is done on the basis of experience, competitive benchmarking, and a judgement about the traffic flow patterns of the city.

Categories that Use OOH

Major categories that use outdoor are hospitals, restaurants, education, OTT, organized retail, real estate, FMCG, financial services, media, telecom, auto, e-commerce, durables, pharmacy, and petroleum/lubricants.

Chapter Summary

Once the media mix has been decided, the next stage is making the actual media plan. This involves translating the strategy into an actionable plan. Choosing media vehicles from several options is quite a task, particularly when each medium has its own currency, and there are different variables that play a role in vehicle selection. Let's understand the process by medium:

1. *TV Planning*:

   - *Genre/Channel Selection*

     - Audience fit: At a macro level, the decision is to look at genres which will be in sync with the audience and markets spelt out in the strategic planning document.
     - The audience's viewing intensity: At times channel mix or genre selections are also done on the basis of what genre and with what intensity the audience is watching.
     - Channel shares: Once a broad genre-level decision is taken, percentage share of viewing each of each channel plays an important part of the decision-making process.
     - Market-level skews for channels: India is a diverse country with different regional languages. Since the 2010s, we've seen regional channels acquiring greater importance in terms of absolute viewership. A lot of brands have necessarily used regional channels to either target a specific geography, or to add to media intensity in a particular region, or maybe cover up the shortfall wherever large national channels fall short in terms of GRPs.

- Cumulative reach and reach build-up: Cumulative reach of the channel and its ability to deliver a quick reach build-up are major variables that are considered in channel selection.
- Channel stickiness: How loyal are the viewers to the channel, or what is the stickiness level of the channel? This also has a bearing on channel selection.
- Audience fragmentation: The higher the degree of fragmentation in the market, the greater the number of channels required to achieve plan reach and frequency numbers. Analysing the extent of fragmentation has an important role to play in the channel mix decision.

- *Programme/Daypart Selection*

  - Absolute viewership: The absolute rating of a programme, or the number of viewers, or a drop-down list of the Top programmes within the selected genre, is a good starting point.
  - Audience profile of the programme: Given the definition of the target audience, one tries to look at an overall profile fit with the programme.
  - Programme viewership vs commercial break viewership: Along with programme ratings, it is also possible to get the viewership rating of commercial breaks within the programme. This data too is of immense use when judging the value of that programme to the media plan.
  - Clutter levels: Clutter levels on TV have increased dramatically over a period of time with the mushrooming of many channels. Add to this the huge clutter that typically follows high-rated programmes or better-performing channels. Planners tend to look at clutter levels and try to balance the TV plan with a mix of programmes.
  - Programme loyalty levels: Programmes with a higher loyalty level indicate that a higher proportion of its audience is from the previous episode/episodes, and the brand message could be delivered again to this audience. It helps in building frequency in the plan.
  - Viewer Volatility: It is the percentage of audience which switches in and out of a programme. The higher this percentage, the less involved is the viewer in the programme or the channel – and therefore, less likely to see our commercial.
  - Audience attention spans: One way to assess this is to look at the average time a person spends on a particular event (programme). If this scores high on an index, it means that the viewers of the programme are more attentively tuned in, and the likelihood of the advertising message getting noticed is higher.
  - Cost efficiency/cost per rating point (CPRP): This is a very crucial parameter involved in programme selection.

- *Plan Optimization*: Sometimes planners have the goal of reach maximization, or frequency maximization, or weekly reach maximization at a given EF. Once a goal is defined, plan optimizers are used to arrive at the ideal TV plan.
- *Dealing with sponsorships*: Sponsorships have become a very important part of TV planning. The following list of sponsorship types talks of sponsorships purely from a TV planning point of view in terms of programme or event sponsorships and its value to the plan:

  - Title sponsor: Here the brand name becomes a part of the title of the programme itself. For example – Dream 11 IPL
  - Presenting sponsor: Here the brand is mentioned as a presenting sponsor.
  - Co-sponsor/associate sponsor/powered/co-powered: In this third level of sponsorship, the brands are also tagged in the promos and mentioned as co-sponsors or associate sponsors
  - Benefits of sponsorships

    - Building brand TOM
    - Reinforcing key brand message
    - Environment fit
    - Value additions to a plain media deal
    - Preferential placement of advertising and competitive exclusivity

2. *Dailies planning*: With 400 million readers, print is one of the most dominant media type used in India along with TV. Here are the primary considerations involved when it comes to taking decisions regarding vehicle selections in print:

- Audience Fit: How well the profile of the publication fits in with the target audience profile is the primary consideration to choose media vehicles.
- Intensity of use of the medium.
- Usage of product and brands: Print research in India has one very important edge over other forms of media research – product and brand linkage data is also captured for every respondent. This means that it is possible to understand the readership of a publication title along with category and brand linkage.
- Position of ads: Very often when it comes to planning in newspapers, positioning of ads becomes a central area of decision making apart from the other factors.
- Size of the ad
- Main issue vs supplement: Where the ad appears – in the main issue or the supplement – also has a bearing on the kind of impact it has.
- Geographical flexibility offered by the vehicle.

- Quality of reading measures: The various dimensions of quality are: How much time do the readers devote to the newspaper title? How many readers are the sole readers of this newspaper? How much of this readership is at home vs out of home?
- Clutter: Just like in TV, even in newspapers, clutter is one of the key factors in deciding a newspaper title.
- Reproduction quality of the advertisement in the newspaper.
- Duplication levels: How many readers of a particular title also read the other titles is another measure used in the selection criteria.
- Readership of the newspaper: The absolute number of readers of a newspaper is a critical determining factor to draw the consideration list.
- Circulation: Circulation indicates the number of copies sold by a publication.
- Cost Efficiency: While the measure for cost efficiency in TV is CPRP, in print the measure for efficiency is cost per thousand (CPT).
- Gross impressions mapping: Planners use this technique to set media weights for various markets based on their relative importance, and then work backwards to calculate the cost of the plan.
- Other values including sampling, innovations possibilities, sponsorships, and joint promotions.
- Content Leverage: The ability of a newspaper/magazine to create contextual content, and partner content co-creation opportunities, are also becoming important while planning for print.

3. *Radio planning*: While the medium and research and planning metrics are still in the evolution stage, the following topline factors are largely being used to make radio plans:

- Absolute listenership.
- Profile of listeners.
- Daypart listenership trends.
- Moving beyond just spots on air: There are talks of using the power of the medium – "interactivity" – and the medium's potential for "buzz creation" to its fullest potential. So things like RJ mentions, contests, on-ground activations tied in with radio, etc., are considered very important in the medium's usage.
- Other factors: Given the kind of data now available through RAM, other issues like channel loyalty, clutter levels, audience involvement, intensity of listenership, and CPRP are used at times.

4. *OOH planning*: Outdoor planning involves moving beyond using Microsoft Excel and actually getting on ground to get a feel of the medium

and actually construct the plan. Here are some of the most important factors that influence site selection in Outdoor:

- Traffic patterns of the city
- Site location
- Size and visibility
- Lit vs non-lit: sites that are lit have a larger audience as compared to non-lit sites
- Clutter
- Absolute cost

Further Reading

Breaking the News Story, BARC India Newsletter, 2018 Vol 1, https://www.barcindia.co.in/resources#thinkwithbarc
Indian Readership Survey 2019 Q4, MRUC, 8 May 2020.
Press in India, 2019–20, RNI.
The Era of Consumer A.R.T., March 2020, India's Media & Entertainment sector, EY & FICCI

12

VEHICLE SELECTION II – DIGITAL MEDIA

Digital Planning

With the ever-increasing Internet penetration, advertisers have begun to look at internet as an important media channel. With over 880 million Internet users in India, the medium has sufficient size and scale for it to be considered seriously.

There are four broad areas of decision making in Internet planning:

- Channel selection – search/social/video/display/others
- Site selection within each of the five channels
- Plan optimization techniques
- Dealing with native/branded content, etc.

The advantage with digital media is its addressability – both in the sense of targeting the right person and, importantly, targeting him/her at the right time. As we're all aware by now, there's a purchase journey every consumer has. In marketing jargon, it's called the funnel, and how a consumer moves from awareness to action and eventually to post-purchase advocacy. Digital, unlike any other media, has this unique ability to talk to people as they move across the purchase journal. So for instance, at the top of the funnel is the need for awareness, and there are specific digital channels like Search, Social, and Display which can help deliver on this count with customized creative communication. As the consumer moves towards the middle of the funnel, he/she is aware, is now actively considering buying, and in all likelihood would show an intent to buy. During this stage, paid search, retargeting, emailing, etc., might be handy. At the bottom of the funnel, the consumer

DOI: 10.4324/9781032724539-12

might be into the act of buying or even recommending the product to others. At this stage, influencer content, user-generated content, blog posts, retargeting (to remind), etc., could be used. Therefore, at every stage of the purchase journey, digital allows one to influence each step with uniquely targeted channels and customized creative.

Let's discuss each of these four broad areas with respect to digital media vehicle selection.

Channel selection: Figure 12.1 depicts the split of digital ad spends across different categories as per the Dentsu Aegis digital report 2022. The report says that 29% of digital advertising budget was spent on social, 23% on paid search, 28% on video, and 16% on display, and the balance of 4% was on others. However, this mix varies across different categories. So for example, the BFSI category spends 37% on paid search (as it works largely on lead generation as a goal), while FMCG spends 31% of its digital budgets on video, while auto and telecom spend 24% and 27% respectively on social.

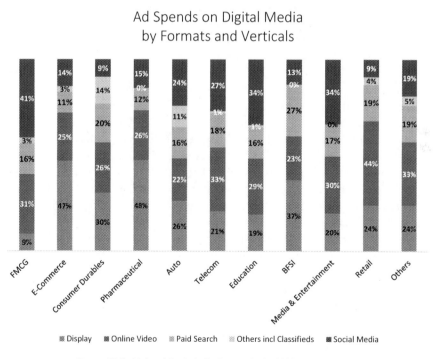

Ad Spends on Digital Media by Formats and Verticals

Source: Digital Advertising in India, Dentsu Aegis, 2022

FIGURE 12.1   Ad spends on Digital Media by formats and verticals.

Source: Exchange4Media, Digital Advertising in India, Dentsu Aegis, 2022

However, there is no standard formula by which one could allocate budgets across these channels. The factors that play a key role in determining the usage of a channel are:

a. *Setting the right objectives*: It is important to first set up the campaign goals in terms of whether it is about generating awareness, sales, leads, or brand building. These goals will play a significant role in determining what mix of search, social, video, or display will one use. So for example if the goal is to generate awareness, then search, display, and social can play a big role. If the goal is lead generation, then search probably will play a greater role; while if it is brand building, then probably social and video would have a greater role to play. It is important to have clarity on how important different parts of the funnel are for the brand. If the top of the funnel is important, then metrics like awareness and saliency become important, and channels like search and display get priority. If the bottom of the funnel is more important, then lead generation and performance marketing parameters become relevant, and the channel drivers for them are prioritized accordingly. This goal setting is clearly aligned with the business objectives, and that's what makes digital such an exciting medium to consider, particularly due to measurability.

b. *Past performance*: It's important for brands to review the performance of search, social, display, and video from their past campaigns. There are enough data points that one would accrue to be able to arrive at a judgement of what worked better than others. This would help modulate plans accordingly and reallocate budgets and efforts. However, one must be careful while evaluating the performance of different channels. Display, for example, might work for longer-term brand building and awareness, but paid search might work for immediate leads. The performance metrics for both might be very different because the consumers across each of the two channels might be at different positions in the funnel. Therefore, comparisons must be made with this caution in mind.

c. *Competitor reviews*: At the same time, a review of the competition also helps one arrive at a balanced mix in terms of usage of search, social, display, and video. This analysis is similar to what one does while planning the media mix for traditional channels like TV, print, etc. One makes a thorough competitive analysis to study where and with what intensity competing brands spend their money, and make their decisions with that knowledge.

d. *Media consumption behaviour of consumers*: It's important to analyse how your audience uses digital media, and how they spend time and navigate across channels. If any particular channel is over-indexed on time spent/users, then it might make better sense to allocate a higher priority to that channel. So, for example, if housewives are the audience and they are clearly over-indexed on watching videos of recipes rather than reading, then one might look at creating a video-led approach to engage better with them. Also one needs to understand which channels are best suited to talk to your audiences. So if one wants to talk to young executives, maybe B2B social media would be a better bet, but if one wants to talk to college going kids, informal social media like snapchat might target them better. Therefore, it's important to study which channel is being preferred by your audience.

e. *Audience buying behaviour*: At the same time, it would be well worth studying how consumers buy in the category, and what the influencer channels are at different stages of the purchase funnel. So for example, if for a youth audience, peer recommendations and reviews are most important at the final stage of the funnel, then it might make sense to use influencer marketing via social channels to drive sales.

Planning on Google

Once the broad channels of search/social/display/video are finalized based on the aforementioned criteria, the next step is the actual plan construction. So typically, within search, it's largely Google where the advertising outlays are planned. Typically one would do a paid search campaign based on keywords relevant to the brand/campaign/consumer need. Google's service Google Ads allows brands to plan their advertising campaigns on the Google platform. As per Google Ads, there are eight steps to planning a campaign on Google:

Step 1: Defining a Campaign Objective

Here one must define campaign goals expressed as generating sales, leads, or website traffic. You could also consider setting goals like product and brand consideration, brand awareness and reach, and Local store visits or promotions.

Step 2: Choose a Campaign Type

Here one chooses between several campaign type options in Google – Search, Display, Video, Discovery, App, Shopping, and Local.

Search Campaigns

These are text ads that are shown to users when they search for a product/solution that matches a brand. This is typically used when one has a goal defined like driving site visits or lead generation. One could create different types of creatives for different geographies or target audiences. So, for example, if someone clicks on Google search for the keywords 'online grocery', then the search engine would list out several online locations where one could find content related to 'online grocery'. However, on top of the search results you will find a few links with the word 'Ad' prefixed to the site name. This is how a search ad would appear.

There are three components to a search ad – a headline ('Get Up To 60% off on Groceries ...'), the site URL (www.getmygrocery.com), and a short text which describes the site content ('Houseful Sale brings Min. 50% Off on 1000+ products along with B1G1 Offers & More. Get Up to 60% Off On Monthly Groceries at Getmygrocery. Buy 1 Get 1 Free on 500...'). Besides this, one can also have ad extensions, which give the user extra information regarding location, price, special offers, apps, or extensions that point to a specific page on the website. In our example, the Fruits and Vegetables hyperlink on the getmygrocery.com ad is an extension, and clicking on it would take the user to the Fruits and Vegetables page on the website. Basically, an ad extension makes the ad work harder.

Display Campaigns

These are display ads which are shown on sites which the customer visits. The Google display network consists of over 2 million sites. It builds on from the search campaign which is typically targeting potential customers who are searching for a product/solution. Once they go a relevant website, the ads shown here might help consumer decision making. You could target a display campaign based on user demographics like age and gender, and their interests. If a brand has created first-party data on people who visit the brand's website or app, the brand could also create a display campaign that targets just these users. Display campaigns are typically used to generate sales leads, create brand awareness and reach, or serve ad reminders to people who have visited your app/website. Figure 12.2 showcases an example of a display ad.

Video Campaigns

These are videos ads that are shown either before the YouTube content plays (Pre-rolls) or in the middle of that content, like a mini ad break. Video campaigns are also placed by Google on sites other than YouTube. These are called Google Video Partners. Video ads are typically used for building brand awareness and for product/brand consideration. While planning a campaign on YouTube, one could choose from the following campaign goals: Sales, Leads, Website traffic, Product and brand consideration, and

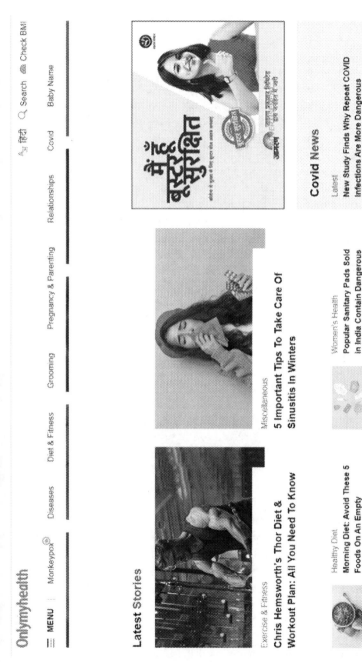

FIGURE 12.2 Example of a display campaign.

Source: Jagran Prakashan Ltd.

Brand awareness and reach. Within these, there are six campaign sub-types that one could select depending upon the desired campaign objectives:

- *Drive conversions*: These are campaigns that are focused on driving sales.
- *Custom video campaign*: In these campaigns, one uses different ad types to customize the campaign for the brand.
- *Video reach campaigns*: These campaigns try to optimize reach. They do this by trying to reach new users through instream skippable or non-skippable ads. Instream ads are shown either before, during, or after the YouTube video.
- *Outstream*: Outstream ads are those video ads that are played on websites other than YouTube. These ads appear alongside content of other non-video websites and play when the page loads.
- *Influence consideration*: These are skippable ads played pre-roll, mid-roll or post roll. The ad plays for 5 seconds, and the viewer has the option to skip the ad. The basic purpose of these is to get users to driver brand consideration amongst users.
- *Ad sequence*: These are a set of video ads that tell a story.

Shopping Campaigns

As the name implies, shopping campaigns are designed to generate sales and leads to either a shop or a shopping website. These campaigns use ads that visually show products with an intention to drive buyers to buy them either from a physical store or an online website. The shopping ads could be linked to the brand's app as well. If this linking is done, then users who click on the shopping ads can get directed to the brand's app. The shopping ads could appear on the search page, the shopping tab, Google Search Partner websites, or the Google Display Network. So if someone searches for the keyword 'Party shoes for men', on the search page, you would see results with images of shoes with their style name, price, and website name. However, if someone clicks the Shopping tab on the search page, then you would see results which would show images of shoes, their style name, website name, and price, and additionally you would see a panel on the left with filters for colours, price, type, brand, etc. These would help one narrow down the search.

App Campaigns

These are campaigns done with a view to drive new app downloads or to increase sales within the app. There are three sub-campaign types within app campaigns:

- *App installs*: This campaign is for generating new app downloads.
- *App engagement*: This campaign is about influencing existing app subscribers to take some action within the app.
- *App pre-registration*: These are campaigns for new apps which are targeted at getting users to pre-register for the app before they are released.

Local Campaigns

These are campaigns that tell potential shoppers when and how they could visit the physical store. These campaigns are usually run on Search, Maps, YouTube, and Google Display Network. These ads give information to prospective shoppers on the address and opening and closing hours and could be used as an option to promote a sale/offer.

If someone searches for 'Jewellery Shops' and clicks on the Maps tab on the search page, the user would see a map with locations marked for different jewellery outlets in the city. On the left there's a panel with names of different jewellers. If one clicks on any jeweller's name, the map would display its exact location. That's how local campaigns appear on the Maps tab.

Smart Campaigns

These are automated campaigns managed by Google for advertisers who are targeting sales and leads. The advertiser creates the ads and sets up the campaign time frame and budgets, and Google does the rest of the campaign optimization. The benefit of this campaign is the ease of setup. The advertiser can also get analysis on campaign performance, the number of calls received for the campaign, actions that users initiated on your ads (either through clicking the ad or on a map). Usually, these are pay-per-click campaigns where the advertiser pays only if someone clicks on the ad.

Step 3: Set a Campaign Budget

The user must specify the campaign budget and the average daily budget. Based on the input, Google will optimize the campaign in such a manner to get you the best results but within the budget specified by you. However, there will be variations in the budget spent daily depending upon search traffic. Therefore, on some days, the amount spent will be lower than the average daily limit specified by you, while on other days it could be higher. Typically in a case of overspend from the daily budget specified, it would normally be 2 times the average specified, while ensuring at the same time that the monthly limit of spending will not be exceeded.

To help you choose and set budgets, Google has two tools:

- *Performance Planner*: This is a tool that uses some basic data from the initial period of the campaign and creates a forecast for campaign performance based on machine learning. So for example, if you have a search campaign, then to use the Performance Planner you need to have the campaign running for at least 3 days and must have received at least three clicks in the last week. Using this data from your initial campaign performance, the tool will forecast the campaign performance. Based on this forecast, you could change your budget level to achieve the desired campaign results.
- *Cost Per Click*: As the name suggests, in this case, the advertiser pays only when someone clicks on the ad. The advertiser can set the maximum cost per click bid. This defines the upper limit the advertiser will pay for the click. One could choose between manual bidding (where the advertiser sets the bids) or automatic bidding (where the Google system automates bid setting to optimize your budgets).

Step 4: Choose Your Bidding

The campaign objective that one sets up in Step 1 is used to set up the bidding focus for the campaign. So if the objective is sales or lead generation, then this goal defines the bidding focus. Bidding, as discussed earlier, could be of two types – manual or automated. An automated bid strategy helps the advertiser achieve the campaign goal within the budget specified in the most optimal manner. This is called Smart Bidding. They use the campaign's initial performance data to forecast overall performance. Types of Smart Bidding strategies are:

- Target Cost Per Acquisition (CPA) is used when the advertiser wants to optimize for campaign goals of conversion (defined as a consumer action). Here, one sets a bid for each conversion.
- Target Return on Ad Spend (ROAS) is used when the advertiser wants to optimize for campaign goals of conversion value, keeping an eye on optimizing return on ad spend. This strategy works on the premise that if the system predicts that a certain conversion is unlikely to be a high-value conversion, then the system will place a lower bid. However, if the system believes that the prospective conversion could be high value, then it would place a higher bid.
- Maximize Conversions is used when the advertiser wants to use the entire budget to just drive conversions.
- Maximize Conversion Value is used when the advertiser wants to focus on optimizing conversion value rather than just drive conversions.

- Enhanced Cost per Click (ECPC) is used to automatically modify manual bids to maximize conversions depending on the likelihood of a click resulting in a conversion.

Step 5: Add Extensions to Your Ads

Ad extensions give the user extra information regarding location, price, special offers, apps, or extensions that point to a specific page on the website. In our example, one such extension is the Fruits and Vegetables hyperlink on the Getmygrocery Ad, which would take the user clicking on it to the Fruits and Vegetables page on the Getmygrocery website. Basically, an ad extension makes the text ad work harder by giving the ad more visibility. It is usually highlighted in blue in a slightly larger font size. Manual extensions can be created by the advertiser, while automated extensions are automatically created by the Google ads system if it predicts that the extension will help improve the ad's performance.

Step 6: Create Ad Groups

In this step one must group all ads of a category together. For example, you could group all ads of clothing accessories together which could be shown to people looking for accessories.

Step 7: Select Your Targeting

In this step the advertiser must select how mass or narrow/specific targeting needs to be. If no targeting is done, then the ads could be shown to anyone, anywhere, and across any type of content. If one defines targeting, then the ads are shown to a narrower group of a more likely audience, in markets that are important and in content contexts that are relevant to the brand. Targeting is of two types:

Audience Targeting

- *Affinity*: Google has created about 80-odd predefined affinity or interest groups like music enthusiasts, football enthusiasts, gamers, news junkies, fashion lovers, etc. These groups are made based on the browsing history of Google users. You could choose to target one or more of these affinity groups, and the display ads will be seen on the sites visited by the affinity groups selected by you.
- *Custom Affinity*: In case you do not wish to target as per the pre-defined affinity audiences, then one can also customise a group of audiences. So for example, if your campaign is about healthy organic food recipes, you might want to use keywords like healthy cooking, organic food, conscious

eating, organic recipes, natural foods, or plant-based diets. You could also add a few websites that healthy eaters are likely to visit – say something like everythingorganik.com or healthyeating.com. The ads will then be targeted to this custom affinity group that one has defined.

- *In-market*: This is targeting consumers who are actively in the buying mode online. They have either bought something and put it into their shopping carts, or they are comparing different products before buying, or they are researching which products to buy. This allows one to talk to audiences further down the funnel who are almost ready to buy or are in the process of buying. This is done by Google in real time, allowing a brand to target a purchase intention.
- *Life Events*: This is targeting consumers based on achieving some life event – say birthday, anniversary, college graduation, getting married, etc. These are times when purchase patterns shift and consumers are in the market for new things.
- *Demographics*: Besides targeting interest groups, one could also target based on consumer demographics like age, gender, and parental status. Google has the following demographic targeting:

  - Age: '18–24', '25–34', '35–44', '45–54', '55–64', '65 or more', and 'Unknown'
  - Gender: 'Female', 'Male', and 'Unknown'
  - Parental status: 'Parent', 'Not a Parent', and 'Unknown'

  One could also combine different demographics and create an audience like, say, Females, 35–44 years for the purposes of the campaign. One could also combine a demographic audience with some affinity groups for sharper targeting. One could also 'exclude' specific audience groups from the campaign. So if you do not want to target males, then while defining your audience, you could specifically exclude the male audience. By doing this, your campaign will not be visible to males.
- *Your Data Segments*: This is based on the first-party data collected by brands on their websites or on their apps. This data could be used by the Google ads system to target people who have interacted with the brand either on its website or on its app.

Content Targeting

- *Topics*: Under this one could specify content contexts for a brand. For example, if the brand is in the domain of organic and health eating, then one could identify topics such as organic eating, healthy eating, organic foods, natural foods, plant-based supplementation, organic recipes, etc. When this is specified, then the Google ads system matches them with the content on websites and pages, and the ads are shown only on websites that match with these keywords.

- *Placement*: Here the advertiser mentions specific websites where the ads have to be placed. This is called manual placements.
- *Content keywords*: This is similar to Topics discussed earlier, except the fact that here keywords are specified for the brand/service/audience and ads are served only to those users who search for these keywords.
- *Display expansion for search*: Here the Google ads system serves ads to users based on automated bidding and smart targeting.

Step 8: Set Up Conversions

This is a post-campaign or live campaign stage where the advertiser gets a report on the number of conversions the ad has created. Conversion is defined as an event that happens after the customer clicks on the ad. Some conversions could be of high value, where the customer goes to the brand's website and purchases something. Some conversions can result in the customer downloading an app. Some conversions could be the customer going to the brand site and filling out a form. This tool helps the advertiser get a view on conversions being driven by the campaign. This helps sharpen the campaign and even make real-time adjustments to the campaign.

Planning for Social through Facebook

Within social, Facebook becomes the key vehicle, and then the other platforms follow. With the largest share of the social pie being with Facebook, let's quickly review the process of creating a campaign on Facebook.

   Setting up objectives: There are three levels of objectives that one could set up on Facebook – Awareness, Consideration, and Conversion. Under Awareness, there are metrics like Brand Awareness and Reach. Under Consideration, there are objectives like Traffic, Engagement, App Installs, Video Views, Lead Generation, and Messages. Under Conversion, there are objectives like Conversions, Catalogue Sales, and Store Visits.
   Audience Selection: Core audiences can be defined based on demographics (age, gender, education, job title, etc.), location, interests, and hobbies of people, behaviour (prior purchases of brand and device usage), and connections (here one could choose to include connections of your audience or ignore them).
   Custom audiences are those that we already know and want to reach out to them through Facebook. This could include first-party databases, or site visitors (Facebook could be set up to target advertising to those people who have visited your site) or talk to app users.

A third way is to talk to lookalike audiences. Here, one defines the desired audience. Based on this definition, Facebook could reach out to people who have similar interests.

Ad Placements: This is about deciding where to place the ads – this could be done by manually selecting, or done automatically by Facebook, in which it places ads across its network comprising Facebook, Instagram, Messenger, and Audience Network. Ads can be placed anywhere on the Facebook News Feed, Instagram feed, Facebook Marketplace, Facebook video feeds on Facebook Watch and the Facebook News Feed, Facebook Search results, in-article, Facebook right column on desktops, Instagram Explore, and Messenger Inbox.

Setting up a budget: You could fix the budget you want to spend and set up a bid for your ad which determines the maximum amount you would pay if someone sees your ad or clicks through.

Set up ad formats: You could choose to do a photo ad, which is image-based, or a video ad. You could create an ad for Stories, which is an immersive brand story, or you could use Messenger for one-on-one conversations with audiences. A Carousal is another format that allows you to showcase 10 images or videos in a single ad, each with its own clickability. Another format is that of a Slideshow, where you could group series of images and set them to animate with some audio. These are usually lighter than videos. For retailers, there's an ad format called Collections, where you could showcase your product image with pricing details, etc. For app developers, there's a format called Playables, which allows the user to see a sneak preview of the app before deciding on downloading.

All along you can track and manage your campaign to see which formats, audiences, devices, locations, and interest groups are more responsive to the campaign, and use these insights to modulate and manage the campaign.

Similarly, one can set up a campaign on Twitter which allows one to set up campaign objectives like awareness – reach, consideration – video views, pre-roll views, app installs, website clicks, engagements, followers, or conversions through app re-engagements. Essentially, Twitter advertising is about awareness, considerations, and conversions. In fact, the ability to target consumers at different stages of the funnel has been a defining feature of the Internet.

Planning for Programmatic

Since both search and social do not have many options, plan allocations to different vehicles are relatively easier, and one does the detailed planning using the ad management suite of services offered by these walled gardens.

Once one gets into display, then one has to deal with a huge number of options. It is not possible to deal with hundreds and thousands of websites individually to place ads. Therefore, this process of ad placements is being facilitated by something called programmatic. This is a technologically driven platform that enables digital inventory planning, buying, and selling across thousands of websites dynamically.

When a user X browses a website, it sends out information to the Supply Side Platform (SSP) to serve an ad to this user. This information about the user and his/her characteristics is captured via cookies. The SSP works on behalf of publishers to sell advertising inventory. Publishers give a floor price (below which they would not sell the inventory) for their inventory to the SSPs. The SSPs in turn interact with multiple ad exchanges, ad networks, and demand side platforms (DSPs) and make the publishers' ad inventory available to a wide set of potential buyers. The major SSPs in India are Sharethrough, Google Ad Manager, MoPub, Wunderkind, OpenX, and PubMatic.

The DSPs act on behalf of the buyers who give out brand briefs in the form of CPM targets, audience to be targeted, kind of browser on which to place ads, geographical locations for placing the ads, and the type of device. Based on this brief, the DSP scans for inventory put out by different SSPs that matches the brand brief. If there's a match (user X is relevant), the DSP places a bid on the available inventory. Similarly, the SSPs will receive multiple bids from different DSPs for the ad targeting user X. The SSP selects the highest bidder and displays the ad on the publisher's website. All of this bidding by DSPs, the evaluation by SSPs, and the transaction take place in real time, and the ad is seamlessly displayed on user X's screen along with the requested page.

While planning for programmatic, one needs to follow the following key steps:

Clear understanding of audiences: This factor can never be under-emphasized. It is a very critical part of the strategy planning process (as discussed in earlier chapters). Who they are, what their digital media consumption is, where they are located, and how they stack up across the entire purchase funnel – these are some of the key analytics done amongst several others.

Setting campaign objectives: Just like what we did for search and social, it's very important to keep campaign objectives at heart before embarking on the programmatic journey. The objectives could be generating awareness, or app downloads, driving traffic to the website, etc. If the objective is to create awareness and generate reach, then the programmatic engine will select sites that have lesser duplications, and ones that have wider reach.

Setting up the Campaign Type: This means getting clarity on what format of digital to use – banners, video, in-app, or native. Banner ads are the ones that are ubiquitous across different websites. They display the brand message and, despite a low click-through rate, are great at helping build reach and awareness. Video ads work better at communicating emotion and product demonstrations. They work well during the consideration stage of the funnel. Native ads are usually text or infographic-driven and usually merge with the content of the website. In-app programmatic ads run on mobile apps.

Identify the right demand side platform (DSP): A DSP is a web-based server that enables advertisers to buy ads across multiple websites. It interacts with the Ad Exchange, scans the available impressions and user characteristics, and places bids on behalf of the advertiser to serve an ad to users that meet their criteria. Beyond just placing ads, the DSPs can track the ads and can help the advertiser optimise their digital programmatic plan. While choosing a DSP, one must consider the number of websites it has access to, targeting capabilities, whether it has mobile and web inventory, the sophistication of its optimization engine, the parameters on which optimizations can be done, etc. Some leading DSPs in India are Amazon Advertising, Adobe Advertising, Google Marketing Platform, StackAdapt, RTB House, Platform.io, IgnitionOne, TubeMogul, SpotX, Verizon Media, and Epom.

Plan optimizations: Plan optimizations on programmatic can be done based on several parameters like clicks, CTRs, video views, viewability, cost, device, browser types, reach, and frequency. Site selections can be done based on affinity, locational, and demographic parameters. One can set up maximum campaign impression limits, daily impression limits, budget, frequency caps for a day or 30 days, even select SSPs, define the kind of audience you would want to reach, define frequency caps (how many times the same user can see the campaign), etc.

Planning for Branded Content and Partnerships on Digital

With digital being ubiquitous, consumers are being targeted and retargeted by multiple brands, which might even be irritating. In the bargain, sometimes even brands that follow ethical targeting methods, and are conscious of consumer advertising fatigue, tend to not get attention. With the rising adoption of ad blockers and the emergence of personalized consumption, getting consumer attention is all the more difficult. With privacy concerns and the glut of fake news, credibility concerns loom large across the digital advertising landscape, making engagement with consumers a challenging task. Smart brands are now not just relying purely on search, social, display, and video – they are going a step ahead and engaging users at a content level.

Branded content and partnerships are now increasingly gaining in importance. A good start on this front is being made by brands targeting niche audiences, as branded content allows them to engage with sharply defined audiences with a minimum spillover. The main considerations while looking at branded content on digital are:

Brand KPIs and objectives: The process begins by getting a clear alignment on brand KPIs. So for example, for an ed-tech client, the main KPI could be driving the theme of learning from home. Based on this theme, one would identify audiences. So in this case the audiences could be children who could be wanting to learn via online classes on the app, it could be parents who would help children take decisions, or it could be mid-career executives working from home who might want to specialize and upgrade their current skillsets.

Brand fit: The content of the site, and the brand theme, tonality, and imagery must have a match. So for example, if it's an education brand which talks about making STEM easy, then possibly websites that talk about STEM education and career opportunities become an option. Or for an auto brand, maybe auto-related sites would have a natural affinity. Therefore, the content of the site and the theme of the brand must complement each other for branded content to thrive.

Custom content creation: For each of the selected audience groups, content needs to be created. Enough care has to be taken to ensure that the brand is not too much in your face – one has to maintain subtlety, else the audience would tune out.

Identifying the right influencers: A large part of branded content is nowadays disseminated by influencers who command following across their social media channels. One needs to identify the right influencer based on the brand fit, influencer credibility, size and quality of the followers, the depth of engagement he/she has with followers, and so on. You could look at the Comments to Views ratio, which could give an indication of the level of engagement. There would be many influencers who have just the numbers, but not the right kind of engagement – it's better to identify and focus on influencers who command credibility and are able to subtly weave in the brand story in their posts. When it comes to influencers, quality metrics matter more than the absolute numbers. For different audience groups, you would need to identify different influencers.

Getting across to the right publisher partners: Reaching out to the right publisher partner network is important. They have content creation capability and could help create branded content that subtly merges with their editorial content on their respective platforms.

Evaluating success: Usually, branded content and partnerships work across every stage of the funnel from awareness to conversions.

However, unlike the rest of digital planning, the focus is on getting the brand story right and bringing it into public conversation. To that extent, the performance metrics work slightly differently here. While the broad reach numbers and impressions are looked at, the core metrics that one should look for are the positive reactions, depth of engagement, etc. – and all will need to be tied in with the brand KPIs to gauge the level of impact. Since there are no fixed evaluation templates, different brands are creating their own playbooks based on experiences.

Chapter Summary

Once the media mix has been decided, the next stage is making the actual media plan. This involves translating the strategy into an actionable plan. Choosing media vehicles from several options is quite a task particularly when each medium has its own currency, and there are different variables that play a role in vehicle selection. Let's understand the process by medium:

1. *Internet planning*: With the ever-increasing Internet penetration, advertisers have begun to look at the Internet as an important media channel. With over 100 million Internet users in India, the medium has sufficient size and scale for it to be considered seriously. The four broad areas of decision making in Internet planning are:

   - *Channel selection*: Channels here mean search, social, online video, and display. The factors considered here are:
     - *Setting the right objectives*: It is important to first set up the campaign goals in terms of whether it is about generating awareness, sales, leads, or brand building.
     - *Past performance*: It's important for brands to review the performance of search, social, display, and video from their past campaigns.
     - *Competitor reviews*: At the same time, a review of the competition also helps one arrive at a balanced mix in terms of usage of search, social, display, and video.
     - Media consumption behaviour of Consumers: It's important to analyse how your audience uses digital media, and how they spend time and navigate across channels.
     - Audience buying behaviour: At the same time, it would be well worth studying how consumers buy in the category and the influencer channels at different stages of the purchase funnel.

   - *Plan optimization on Google Search*: Google Ads allows brands to plan their advertising campaigns on the Google platform. This takes inputs from the user on brand objectives, budgets, demographic targets, geographies, etc., and helps create a custom plan and provides a dashboard to manage the campaign. There are three types of Google Ads:

- *Search campaigns*: These are text ads that are shown to users when they search for a product/solution that matches a brand.
- *Display campaigns*: These are display ads which are shown on sites which the customer visits, usually bought based on an auction. Where your ad is displayed is a function of the Ad Rank which is based on the Quality Score (as discussed earlier), and the maximum CPC you are willing to bid.
- *Video campaigns*: These are video ads that are shown either before the YouTube content plays (pre-rolls) or in the middle of the content, like a mini ad break.

- *Planning for social through Facebook*: Within social, Facebook becomes the key vehicle, and then the other platforms follow. Here's a quick overview of the process of creating a campaign on Facebook:

- *Setting up objectives*: There are three levels of objectives that one could set up on Facebook – awareness, consideration, and conversion.
- *Audience selection*: Core audiences can be defined based on demographics, location, interests and hobbies of people, behaviour, and connections.
- *Ad placements*: This is about deciding where to place the ads – this could be done by manually selecting, or done automatically by Facebook where it places ads across its network comprising Facebook, Instagram, Messenger, and Audience Network.
- *Setting up a budget*: You could fix the budget you want to spend, and set up a bid for your ad which determines the maximum amount you would pay if someone sees your ad or clicks through.
- *Set up ad formats*: You could choose to do a photo ad, which is image-based, or a video ad. You could create an ad for Stories, which is an immersive brand story, or you could use Messenger for one-on-one conversations with audiences.

- *Planning for programmatic*: Beyond search and social, one has to deal with hundreds and thousands of websites individually to place ads. This process of ad placements is being facilitated by something called programmatic, a technologically driven platform that enables digital inventory planning, buying, and selling across thousands of websites dynamically. When a viewer X browses a website, it sends out information to the Supply Side Platform (SSP) to serve an ad to this viewer.

This information about the user and his/her characteristics is captured via cookies. The SSPs in turn interact with multiple ad exchanges, ad networks, and DSPs and make the publishers' ad inventory available to a wide set of potential buyers. While planning for programmatic, one needs to follow the following key steps:

- *Clear understanding of audiences*: Who they are, their digital media consumption, their geographical location, and where they stand in the purchase funnel – these are some of the key analytics done amongst several others.
- *Setting campaign objectives*: Just like what we did for Search and Social, it's very important to keep campaign objectives at heart before embarking on the programmatic journey.
- *Setting up the campaign type*: This means getting clarity on what format of digital to use – banners, video, in-app, or native
- *Identify the right DSP*: A web-based server that enables advertisers to buy ads across multiple websites, a DSP interacts with the Ad Exchange and scans the available impressions and user characteristics and places bids on behalf of the advertiser to serve an ad to users that meet their criteria.
- *Plan optimizations*: Plan optimizations on programmatic can be done based on several parameters like clicks, CTRs, video views, viewability, cost, device, browser types, reach, and frequency. Site selections can be done based on affinity, locational, and demographic parameters.

- Planning for branded content and partnerships on digital: With the rising adoption of ad blockers and the emergence of personalized consumption, getting consumer attention is all the more difficult. Smart brands are now not just relying purely on search, social, display, and video – they are engaging users at a content level. A good start on this front is being made by brands targeting niche audiences as branded content allows them to engage with sharply defined audiences with a minimum spillover. The main considerations while looking at branded content on digital are:

  - *Brand KPIs and objectives*: The process begins by getting a clear alignment on brand KPIs.
  - *Brand fit*: The content of the site, and the brand theme, tonality and imagery must have a match.
  - *Custom content creation*: For each of the selected audience groups, content needs to be created.
  - *Identifying the right influencers*: A large part of branded content is nowadays disseminated by influencers who command following

across their social media channels. One needs to identify the right influencer based on the brand fit, influencer credibility, size and quality of the followers, the depth of engagement he/she has with followers, and so on.

- *Getting across to the right publisher partners*: They have content creation capability and could help create branded content that subtly merges with their editorial content on their respective platforms.
- *Evaluating success*: Usually, branded content and partnerships work across every stage of the funnel from awareness to conversions. While the broad reach numbers and impressions are looked at, but the core metrics that one should look for is the positive reactions, depth of engagement, etc. – and all will need to be tied in with the brand KPIs to gauge the level of impact.

Further Reading

Denstu Aegis, *Digital Advertising in India*, 2022.

Facebook Ads, https://en-gb.facebook.com/business/ads

Google Ads Help, https://support.google.com/google-ads/

Novatska, Kate, "How to Set Up Your First Programmatic Ad Campaign in 3 Simple Steps", *Epom*, October 2019 https://epom.com/blog/programmatic/how-to-create-your-first-programmatic-ad-campaign-in-3-simple-steps

"The Era of Consumer A.R.T.", March 2020, India's Media & Entertainment sector, EY & FICCI.

"The Ultimate Guide to Programmatic Advertising", Bannerflow, 2021, https://www.bannerflow.com/inspiration/ultimate-guides/programmatic-advertising/

13

MEDIA BUYING

The media buying area of the media business has fast evolved into a truly exciting era over the last decade or so. Today with a few unruly thousand options available, the art and science of media buying is gradually coming of age. It's a specialized function in organized set-ups, and as much rigour is involved in the buying process as one puts in the planning area. The function has evolved from buying the cheapest to adding value to the brand. In the world of media buying, there are three main stakeholders:

- The media
- The advertisers
- The media agency specialists

Each of these groups has their own pulls and pressures, and that what makes the discipline very exciting. Let's understand the mindsets of each of these three sets before progressing further.

The Media

Multiple options targeting different audiences are being launched constantly. Each media brand has extensions and has developed the ability to talk to different types of audiences – be it kids, women, men, etc. At the same time, while there is huge competition across most media types and within most markets, we have seen instances of monopolistic situations being created. With the increasing aggression amongst media players, one believes that soon monopolies will be a thing of the past. We have seen it in TV, where Zee used to dominate the 90s while Star has dominated the 2000s, and over the last

DOI: 10.4324/9781032724539-13

decade, we've seen channels and networks in a see-saw of ups and downs. But now with serious competition stepping in from digital TV, and OTT, the traditional TV market has suddenly changed complexion. The same is the case with print, where every market/state had its dominant daily. Gradually, competition stepped up, and most dailies ventures out of their 'home states', so to say. Today one sees large players like Bennet & Coleman, HT Media, Jagran Group, and Bhaskar Group emerging as the key players in this arena. The same is also the case with radio, with 331 licenses being given out in the second phase of liberalization – with small markets having multiple frequencies, and the large markets having a problem of plenty. In the outdoor area, new formats are being launched every day. Cinema has changed and moved away from just the option of playing a film or showing a slide; some remarkable progress has occurred here, ranging from product placement within the film as part of the storyline to branding of the hall itself. With digital acquiring critical mass, the erstwhile media platforms have now got new wings. Every large TV network now has its own OTT service, be it Sony LIV from Sony, Voot from Colors, Zee5 from Zee TV, or Disney Hotstar from Star. Add to this several standalone OTT services we have available. Audiences now have the power to control what they watch and when they watch. And a plethora of ad-free environments are also available. Similarly, most newspaper titles now have their own apps, websites, e-paper sites, digital editions, WhatsApp editions, email listings, Facebook pages, etc. – all these platforms have extended the reach of newspapers and magazines. Digital OOH services are still at the nascent stage but are catching up rapidly as advertisers warm up to the numerous opportunities offered by digital OOH. Likewise, most large radio station networks also have their own web radio stations.

While industry measurements are there in the form of readership, viewership, and listenership research, there is a belief that there's still a long way to go. While this is at times used as a currency in the buying process, there are times when one wants to move away from these measures of efficiency. The pressures here are of a different type. Each media wants to have a larger share of the pie; the product is perishable, with a huge number of options; each has invested a huge amount of capital to run the business; each believes that they understand their audiences best and that this cannot be captured by any research; each carries the power of the editorial content; some are monopolies while most are not. All these change the relative equations of strength in the media buying process.

The Advertisers

The advertiser is concerned about cutting through the clutter of jargon and delivering the right message to the right consumer when he/she is in the right frame of mind. They understand the power of volume buying. All of them want the budgets to work harder and look towards consolidating their media spend with one agency partner rather than scatter their budgets. They seek to drive value through controlled cost efficiencies and through sponsorships. It's an important area of decision making for them as Media Spends account for a huge part of the marketing budgets. They seek to drive critical brand success parameters like – TOM, Spon, trial rate, repurchase rate, purchase intentions, etc., and the regular media jargon of GRPs, reach, frequency, clutter, efficiency, etc., are just that – jargon – but essential ingredients that help them achieve their eventual objectives for the brand. Absolute cost, cost efficiencies, and return on investment (ROI) are things that are high on their agenda, and they expect both the media planning and buying functions to deliver on that. Then of course, a critical decision is to swim through the maze of media options available and arrive at a final list of vehicles which fall within their benchmarks of absolute costs and cost efficiency parameters. There are many instances where advertisers are directly involved in the media negotiation process to drive tangible efficiencies. Their objectives from the media buying part of the discussions are very different from the media owners' objectives from the buying process.

The Agency

The agency plays the most vital role in the buying process. Media owners are driven by higher absolute spend and higher market share, while the advertiser is driven by the eventual objectives of sustaining brand visibility and boosting trial and repurchase rates, or generating favourable brand imagery, and at the same time wanting to derive huge efficiencies from the media buying process. With the objectives of these two elements being in completely different directions, the agency is the one that usually aligns them to some common objectives. There are times when they get the advertiser to understand the media point of view, and times when they get the media to see the advertiser point of view. However, from a buying point of view, the bottom line is how well one is managing the overall absolute cost and what efficiencies they drive from the various media buys. Smart media owners who attempt to understand advertiser concerns, and align their thinking to deliver value to the brand, are the eventual winners. The agency's concern is to deliver the best to help achieve brand objectives and at the same time maintain an overall balance between absolute cost and relative cost efficiencies.

Each of these three main constituents to the buying process approaches the negotiation table with different mindsets. At the heart of all this are the brand objectives and a finite budget which work as the controls. It's this mix of different objectives of the parties involved and the operating constraints that make this process that much more an exciting part of the media decision making process. We will now look at the key factors that influence buying decisions across various types of media.

Across a range of categories, there are different advertisers who buy into different channels depending upon their objectives and budgets. They buy into multiple genres of channels and publications, buy into multiple options within the same genre, and so on. Not all of them might be the most cost-efficient buys or the cheapest buys. If this were true, all advertising would be polarized either to the cheapest media option available or the most cost-efficient media available. A lot of factors go into buying – factors like absolute rate, cost efficiency, genre fit with TG, sponsorship opportunities, ROI, competitive considerations, reach build, impact generation capability, innovations, etc. At times, one would wonder whether there is a method to this madness. Few would agree, but the evolved buyers have a method and have moved beyond just the Rate/sqcm or CPRP mode, so to say. A popular myth about media buying is that it's all about volume. Given this, consolidation of buying is the way to go. However, the way our market is structured, the unwritten code is that all deals are client-specific and not agency-specific. This means that if a media owner has given a specific rate to an agency handling Brand X, then that rate is valid and applicable only for Brand X. The agency cannot use the same rate for Brand Y, which it also handles. Yes, there are exceptions where some sort of arrangements happen between the media and the agency, where there is a basic agreement on a base price, and then there are variations in the final rate depending on the client. Therefore, the unit of consolidation is the advertiser, not the agency.

The second myth around media buying that many would like to believe is that it is about effective rate (ER). This is an important parameter, but not the only factor. If this were true, all advertising would be polarized to the cheapest option available in media. But that's not the case. I'm reminded of reading something interesting long back on this factor. When John Glenn, who went back to space at the age of 77, was asked whether he was afraid about his journey into space, he replied that the idea was not half as scary as the thought that every component of the rocket had been bought by NASA's procurement department at the lowest tender price!

A third dominant myth about buying is that it's all about cost efficiency – how many GRPs my money can buy on Option A vs Option B. Again, this is not entirely true. On TV you might get the best CPRP in the time band from 12 am to 5 am – but is it going to work? Another dominant myth is that media buying is about applying pressure on the media. The more 'ruthless' you are as a buyer, the better the deal you 'extract'. Frankly, even this does not work. The best deals emerge where the buyer and seller work together to deliver true value to the brand. Till the time the buyer and seller believe that they are sitting on opposite sides of the table, it is about negotiation only. But when they come together as true partners, they deliver true value for the brand and help achieve brand objectives in a far more efficient manner.

One last myth I'll leave you behind with is that media buying is about 'who blinks first'. Frankly, the person who is underprepared will invariably always blink first. Therefore, it is absolutely critical to do your homework before you get into the negotiation process. Just as in any other field, the one with better preparedness is the one who wins the game in the long run. However, what is this homework all about? It would vary marginally for different types of media, but the operating rules remain pretty much the same. Media buyers must do a fair amount of homework to get the best value (not just the best rate) for the brand. We developed something known as a media buying worksheet, which helped tremendously in the final negotiation process and delivered added value to the brand. This is like a negotiation strategy. Some key factors that are part of the strategy are given below.

Initial Pre-Buy Analysis

Given the fact that planning and buying are not sequential processes – both go hand in hand most of the time – a large part of the analysis done during final vehicle selection also serves as a good foundation for the media buyer to base the buying decisions on. This is done largely to get the consideration set of channels or vehicles, key time bands or page positions, or properties to target and to get some sense of the budgets available across different options. Some of the key analysis variables are:

a. For TV/radio

1. Channel share analysis across dayparts
2. Cumulative reach build of channels
3. Cumulative reach build at 1 min + vs 5 min + to study stickiness
4. Weekday vs weekend viewing pattern
5. Top properties/time bands across channels
6. Break performance vs programme performance
7. Clutter levels across channels
8. Benchmarks for activity on the channel
9. Value of promo tags

b. For dailies/magazines

1. Readership options within the genre
2. Time spent on reading
3. Duplications
4. Cost efficiency as on market rates
5. Circulation analysis
6. Top properties that could be targeted

7. Clutter levels across (ad:edit ratios)
8. Benchmarks for activity
9. Other opportunities – sampling/innovations, etc.

Demand Supply Equation

a. *Inventory sales analysis*: This would involve an analysis of how much inventory is being sold by the channel across various dayparts in the case of radio and TV. This would throw up the weaker and stronger time bands, and gives the buyer a sense of which timeslots one could target. The same analysis could be done for other media like dailies and magazines based on the advertising volume sold by pages for dailies and number of pages sold for magazines. Or one could do it for specific positions too – how many days in a year the Front Page of a newspaper is vacant with no advertising vs a back page, and so on. Also, a page-wise inventory analysis on newspapers would show up the 'weaker pages' which have little or no advertising, and one could look at targeting some of these spaces. But what this analysis does is that when you are sitting with the media partner, you are well aware of that partner's relative strengths and weaknesses and can use some of these to help structure a better deal. However, more often than not, I have observed that the negotiation game tilts in favour of the buyer because that person is normally better prepared on this front as compared to the seller.
b. *Inventory utilization ratio*: This is an analysis which is typically done in the case of TV/radio, where the upper limit on the inventory is more or less standardized as it is governed by the telecast rules. The norm in India is generally 10–12 minutes of airtime per hour that could be used to air commercials. The gap between the inventory available and inventory sold is what one tries to evaluate. This will throw up the relatively weaker timeslots and the relatively stronger timeslots. This analysis gives a fair idea of the gaps in the demand-supply equation which could be used to the buyer's advantage. Similarly in the case of print, most papers follow an ad:edit norm. An analysis of this would clearly throw up the relative strengths and weaknesses of the title concerned. This knowledge could be used as a very powerful tool in the negotiation process.
c. *Seasonality of sales*: A third analysis under this section is the seasonality of sales. Here one attempts to find out during which times of the year inventory sales are lower and to identify the weak points or the 'chinks in the armour', so to say. A knowledge of this puts you in a tremendous position of advantage in the negotiation process.

Category Competitive Considerations

a. *Advertising market share analysis*: While the demand supply equation analysis was at a macro level, we now move into more specific analysis.

The idea is to determine the market share of different media vehicles for the category under consideration. For instance, if one is working on the refrigerator category, one looks at the overall category advertising levels and finds out the relative market shares of each vehicle within this. This gives a fair idea of how competitively the channel/station/title is placed within the refrigerator category. For example, say the category spends 100 crores on TV as a medium. Within this, the market share of Star Plus may be, say, 23%, and the market share for Star News may be, say, 3%. A similar analysis could be done for print and other media. This information tells us how the channel is placed as far as this category is concerned. A vehicle with a lower market share will be more vulnerable vs a vehicle which commands a dominant market share in the category. This knowledge becomes absolutely critical to the buyer and has a major bearing on the negotiation process.

b. *Importance of category to the media vehicle*: This is another analysis which throws up something interesting – what percentage of a channel's inventory is dependent on the category under consideration? Taking our example of the refrigerator category forward, we would try to find out the proportion of the total inventory sold by a channel that is contributed by the refrigerator category. If this percentage is higher, it indicates that the channel's dependence on the category is high. A similar analysis could be done across any other media type. This knowledge could be used as a very interesting negotiation tool. My personal buying experience has been that with underprepared salespeople, this knowledge throws them off guard completely. And the media buying process is also at some level a game of wits. The attempt is to do homework in which you study the strengths and weaknesses of the person sitting across and take the discussion forward the way you want to.

c. *Relative importance of the advertiser to the media vehicle*: Here the attempt is to find out how important the advertiser is to the channel, station, daily, or other media vehicle. If the advertiser who the buyer is representing accounts for a large part of the channel's business, then one enters the media buying table in a position of strength. If the advertiser in question accounted for a marginal share of the concerned channel's inventory, then it would not matter much. The idea is to understand the degree of dependence and the importance of the advertiser to the channel. The unwritten rule is that the greater the dependence, the better the buyer's negotiating power, and the lesser the dependence, the greater the leverage the seller has. This knowledge too plays a significant role in the media buying process.

Other Factors

a. *Year/month closing dates*: The fact that all media salespeople have targets is not a secret. These targets get higher every year, and this exerts a certain degree of pressure on the sales teams. This pressure also brings about a certain eagerness to close deals quickly so that the needle on target achievement moves. There are certain critical times of the month towards the month-end, or during quarter-end or year-end, where there is a rush to close deals to achieve targets. A knowledge of these times can be subtly used to enhance the deal from a buyer's point of view.

b. *Relative strength of media vehicle in office*: If a particular media sales office for a particular channel, daily, or other media is strong in a particular city, the pressure levels are of a different type. For instance, if for Channel X, the Delhi office is the highest revenue-generating office within their network, then the pressures on them are of a different type. One needs to understand the degree of this pressure and play the game accordingly.

c. *Relative standing of the individual concerned*: The standing of the salesperson in his/her organization, his/her unique traits and degree of preparedness – these are important softer aspects of the media negotiation strategy. Every salesperson works with a certain strategy. It is important to decode the salesperson's strategy and then proceed accordingly with the buying process. Sometimes when you see an empowered sales team, it might make sense to work with junior executives on the sales team. One needs to understand the situation and play his/her cards accordingly. At the end of the day, human beings are involved in the process of buying, and every individual brings a unique mindset/style of working. The better we understand this, the better we're placed in the buying process.

d. *Relationship*: This is an oft-repeated word in both the agency side and the media sales side. Over a period of time, as previously stated, with human beings involved, some relationships get forged. Some very good equations happen between the buyer and seller, and sometimes it's a love-hate relationship scenario. There are some equations in which people don't see eye to eye, and some in which both the buyer and the seller bend backwards to make the deal happen. A degree of comfort between the buyer and the seller always make the proceedings a bit easier as compared to an absolutely cold relationship between the two. Organizations across both the agency business and the media business tend to work towards establishing good equations with the other partners.

Delivering Value to the Brand

a. *Innovation possibilities*: There are media organizations which display a lot of flexibility to go beyond just selling airtime/sqcm and try to create true brand impact through innovations of various types. At the same time, there are media organizations that are bound by too many conditions and do not display that kind of flexibility. One thing that clearly stands out across most deals is how much value one is willing to add to the deal to make the communication work that much harder. We're increasingly seeing examples of media organizations taking a brief and creating innovations that work.

b. *Going beyond*: We're increasingly seeing a trend of most media organizations developing capabilities in other types of media – say, activations, OOH, mobile value-added services, etc. Today there are many examples where media organizations are taking brand briefs and coming back with a complete integrated media solution to deliver brand impact. Most of the larger groups in media have developed expertise in the other forms of media apart from their core business of print, TV, or radio. In future, we certainly see an increasing drift towards deals of this kind. Media having the capability to do this stands at a greater advantage as compared to 'single-play' media.

Understanding the Economics of Media

The relevance of the rate card is fast receding in the Indian market, and discount percentage from the rate card is no longer relevant. With so many options to choose from, the level of competition is so high that one sees all sorts of deals and rates floating around. No one is really able to assess the bottom of the market. In such a scenario, media organizations are attempting to study the economics of the media business to analyse what really should be the price one should pay. The attempt is to work towards a 'cost upward' rather than a 'rate card downward' way of negotiating. However, this is a very difficult task, as different kinds of media organizations work with different business models, and it would be near impossible to get to the bottom. However, the fact that there is an increasing consciousness on this front itself is a huge step forward. As more media organizations become public companies, that much more information will be available about an organization's financial health, and we will increasingly see discussions veering around this area in the future.

Putting all of these factors into one format gives us something that we named as the buying worksheet. During the time we developed it, it was a must-do before sitting at the negotiating table. This sheet should be prepared for each media vehicle. Figure 13.1 demonstrates an example of the summary for a TV channel.

The above was a description of the kind of homework that a buyer must put into the media buying process, and must take care of some of the softer aspects of the issue.

Other than the aforementioned, the buyer also needs to look at considering strategies like a rate freeze, share incentives, growth incentives, exclusive buys within a network, and so on. A rate freeze is an agreement between a media buyer and a media seller that the rates given at the start of the year remain frozen irrespective of whether the viewership/listenership/readership/

Buying Worksheet

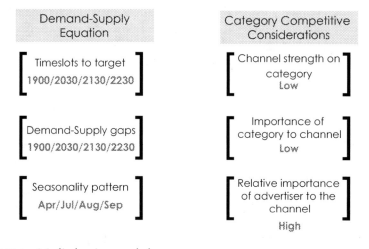

FIGURE 13.1   Media buying worksheet.

Source: Created by the author.

UVs of the media vehicle increase during the course of the year. Sometimes, some buyers give a longer term and a higher value commitment and incorporate a rate freeze clause. This helps the buyer save on media inflation costs. Incentives are another part of buying tactics. The buyer could give a guarantee that the share of spend/duration/space in a particular media vehicle would be higher than its competitive set. In return for a higher market share, the media seller gives a certain incentive (discount) to the media buyer. Sometimes incentives could take the form of growth in ad spends. The buyer could commit that the brand would spend, say, 30% more on the media vehicle as compared to the previous year. In return, he would expect a higher discount, and also a rate freeze. Also, sometimes the buyer could commit to a large media network that they would buy into all their properties. In return, the media owner offers a discounted deal for the network. Today, large media groups have presence across a range of media like TV/print/digital/radio. By giving a consolidated network deal, the seller is assured of revenue, while the buyer gets an advantage on advertising rates and also some value-adds. These are all negotiation tactics that are employed in various combinations.

Given the proliferation of digital, a lot of brands are now looking at performance marketing. Here, the arrangement is that the media remuneration to the media seller is based on the brand achieving some pre-defined benchmarks like unit sales, market shares, brand awareness scores, etc. The arrangement works like this: The buyer approaches the seller and says that they would pay say something like 60% of the media cost upfront. Based on brand performance metrics like unit sales in a particular market, the balance money would be paid. So if 70% of the target is achieved, the buyer would pay the seller 70% of the balance budget. If the targets are over-achieved, then there's an incentive which would be paid. This grid and the parameters are pre-determined and agreed by both the buyer and the seller. To the advertiser, it works like performance-linked media payments. Some large, established advertisers often invoke this in media conversations. However, there are some limitations to this as well. The fundamental assumption that this goes by is the fact that advertising is a powerful force and consumers act on the basis of the ads they see. However, in reality, the media owner would argue that his job is to take the message to the consumer. How the consumer processes the information is not in anyone's control. What if the competitor's price is better? What if the distribution is an issue? What if the reader/viewer has already bought into the category and doesn't want to buy immediately again? What if the buyer postpones the purchase? There are a lot of grey areas in this, but some interesting experiments are taking place, and brands are setting up success parameters based on these experiments.

There are various ways of buying, and each buying situation throws up something unique. As an overarching objective, the first goal is to secure an overall cost-efficient buy (expressed as CPRP or CPT across various types of media), and the second is to maintain a tab on the overall cost. Post this come in the issues of impact, innovations, sponsorships, branding, etc. At times, given the dynamic nature of the process, buying and planning is taking place simultaneously. While the planner works on what kind of intensity is required and optimizes the plan to arrive at the right mix of media to deliver brand objectives, he/she also simultaneously works out options – just in case one is not able to buy the required media vehicle within the broad cost allocated towards it. For instance, in a TV plan, one at times considers the option of taking cricket. Given the genre, the rates and ratings could fluctuate given various situations. The CPRPs might be high, and at times the absolute cost might go through the roof. Alternate plans are made to figure out what happens if mass channels are taken to replace cricket. Then evaluations are done for both options before finalizing one. This is also the case with print. People typically tend to work with options – they could be from the same medium, or from other mediums as well. Therefore, the buying and planning process is happening at the same time, and given the final deal and evaluations, the plans get closed. So the sequence could be that the first stage is planning with a couple of options, the second stage is buying, the third stage is evaluation of comparative deals and their impact on the overall plan, and the fourth stage is finalizing the plan.

Most deals have some or the other element in them which help close the deal. It could be a quick response sometimes, or it could be adding in a little value-add like a contest within the same budget, or it could be a pure opportunistic buy. There are times of distress sale too, where the channel is wanting to get rid of unutilized inventory at the last minute. There are times when budgets are limited and one can afford to buy only one channel, and people pit one against the other. Likewise, in every deal, there is some or the other element/hook, which makes it work. Given the fact that human beings are involved in the process, there are many different approaches to the process. Some are individualistic, some are part of a large systemic approach, while some are completely based on relationships. I will try to explain a few dominant models:

The White Collar Model

This model is normally based on reasonable numbers and a thorough quantitative analysis. Normal buys are for high-ticket media items and are very CPRP-led in their approach. The buying here is on very professional terms and hence not very opportunistic. Media buyers rely more on the volume of media as a key negotiating tactic.

The Home-Grown Model

Closest to the ground, and since it's their own money they spend, the decisions are that much more calculated. They want to make their money work very hard, and in spite of smaller volumes as compared to the MNCs, they tend to drive good bargains. Advertisers don't find much relevance in media research numbers and go largely by gut-feel-led decisions across most media. They are extremely opportunistic and calculative. They believe in relationships and most times come to the fore on distress selling. While volume of business is low, because of their relative isolation, they at times get away with very good bargains. To the media owners, these are an important set of advertisers as put together they account for a huge volume of business.

Evaluating TV Deals

There are a couple of ways of evaluating deals here. After having arrived at a consideration set of channels, deals are worked out and then a relative evaluation is made to select the final channel. The evaluations work largely on the following parameters:

1. Deal CPRP
2. Rate/10 sec
3. Value-adds

Deal CPRP analysis is typical starting point for mass channels like Star Plus, Zee, Sony, and Colors, and you could even include other smaller niche channels. Tables 13.1–13.6 showcase examples of typical deals on channels X, Y, and Z and their evaluations.

Table 13.7 shows the comparison across the three channels.

Here too, the analysis stops at giving the CPRPs of the three deals. Further to this, some people do actual reach and frequency builds and see the

TABLE 13.1 A typical deal on channel X

Programme Category	Duration (sec)	Rate/10 sec (Rs)	Value (Rs)
A	450	180000	8100000
B	1250	15000	1875000
C	750	0	0
D	1000	0	0
Total	3450		9975000

Source: Created by the author.

TABLE 13.2 Deal evaluation, channel X

Programme Category	Duration (Sec)	Avg Rating	GRPs (10 sec)
A	450	11.8	531
B	1250	6.2	775
C	750	2.8	210
D	1000	0.4	40
Total	3450		1556
Cost	9975000		
GRPs	1556		
CPRP	6411		

Source: Created by the author.

TABLE 13.3 A typical deal on channel Y

Programme Category	Duration (sec)	Rate/10 sec (Rs)	Value (Rs)
Events	400	100000	4000000
A	400	160000	6400000
B	600	0	0
C	600	0	0
D	400	0	0
E	2000	0	0
F	300	0	0
G	2000	0	0
Total	6700		10400000

Source: Created by the author.

TABLE 13.4 Deal evaluation, channel Y

Programme Category	Duration (Sec)	Avg Rating	GRPs (10 sec)
Events	400	3.7	148
A	400	6.7	268
B	600	3.7	222
C	600	2.7	162
D	400	1.2	48
E	2000	1.0	200
F	300	4.0	120
G	2000	3.0	600
Total	6700		1768
Cost	10400000		
GRPs	1768		
CPRP	5882		

Source: Created by the author.

TABLE 13.5 A typical deal on channel Z

Programme Category	Duration (sec)	Rate/10 sec (Rs)	Value (Rs)
A	390	250000	9750000
B	390	100000	3900000
C	1560	58500	9126000
D	1500	5000	750000
E	6000	2000	1200000
F	1560	2000	312000
Total	11400		25038000

Source: Created by the author.

TABLE 13.6 Deal evaluation, channel Z

Programme Category	Duration (Sec)	Avg Rating	GRPs (10 sec)
A	390	17.4	679
B	390	5.6	218
C	1560	2.8	437
D	1500	0.8	120
E	6000	1.1	660
F	1560	0.5	78
Total	11400		2192
Cost	25038000		
GRPs	2192		
CPRP	11423		

Source: Created by the author.

TABLE 13.7 Deal comparison

Channel	GRPs	Cost (Rs)	CPRP
X	1556	9975000	6411
Y	1768	10400000	5882
Z	2192	25038000	11423

On this basis, one might decide on a combination X + Y

Or

One might say, let us go with Z but reduce campaign period

Source: Created by the author.

comparisons between the options available. In addition to this, one looks at the sponsorships and other value-adds that the channel has to offer.

Deal Evaluation Criteria for a Mass Channel

1. CPRP (cost efficiency)
2. Absolute cost (because budgets are limited)
3. Absolute GRPs (a certain minimum is required to achieve campaign objectives)
4. Reach-frequency builds (to assess reach build-up and frequency generated – again, to ensure the reach and frequency numbers are enough to achieve campaign objectives)
5. Proportion of big-ticket/prime-time properties (important from a brand saliency point of view, and also from a reach build perspective)
6. Value of sponsorships and other value-adds

However, the evaluation criteria change marginally when we look at niche channels. Niche channels by definition are targeting a certain niche audience, and hence the TVR numbers are not huge. They are usually added to the channel mix to add frequency, to add some incremental reach to the plan, to connect to the TG targeted, and to address the lighter viewers of TV (in some cases). Since the viewership numbers of individual programmes are not high, so to say, buying on such channels is done normally on time bands rather than on individual programmes. Typically, the day is divided into 5 dayparts – morning, afternoon, evening, prime, late-prime. Buying is usually done across these 5 dayparts, and one looks at the overall channel to deliver rather than at individual programmes. The deals too are here devised accordingly and sellers also sell by time bands. Normally the deals here are what you might call ROS or RODP. ROS is Run on Schedule, and it means that if there are 20 spots to be aired in a day, they would be equally spread out over an 18-hour period beginning at 0600 hrs and ending at 2400 hrs. Run of Daypart, or RODP, is slightly different. Here, the dayparts during which the spots have to be aired are fixed. For instance, one might want to air 6 spots during the morning time band (usually defined at 0600–1200 hrs), and 12 spots during prime time (usually defined as 1900–2300 hrs). In this case, 1 spot per hour will be aired during the morning time band and 3 spots per hour will be aired during prime time. The deal here is to air spots on a certain time band irrespective of the programme being aired.

Deal Evaluation Criteria for Niche Channels

1. Rate/10 sec
2. Absolute spends
3. GRPs/CPRPs (have a small role here, but whatever it's worth)
4. Distribution of spots across dayparts (how much prime time component is there in the deal?)
5. Cumulative reach build speed (how quickly does the channel's cumulative reach build?)
6. Sponsorships and value-adds

Additionally, there are times when buyers/planners have to make a choice between programmes on a mass channel. Most channels categorize their programmes depending upon viewership or time-band ad have five to six broad categories of programmes. In a deal typically, they offer a certain volume of seconds of airtime across a couple of categories depending upon the deal brief. For instance, Star Plus may have a top-tier programme group of, say, five programmes, and as per the deal, say 500 seconds can be used in the top-tier category. Here, the planner needs to choose from amongst a couple of programmes, or one might want to go with all programmes in the category. The typical ways of evaluating programmes is done on the basis of some criteria.

Evaluating Big Format Properties on TV

TV in the early 21st century has come up with big format properties like the IPL, the IIFA Awards, big singing and dancing reality shows, or shows like *Big Boss* and *Khatron Ke Khiladi*. Also, we've seen the rise of sporting leagues for sports like football, hockey, kabbadi, and wrestling, which are promoted very heavily across different media. These are mounted as big opportunities for advertisers – not just from a sponsorship point of view, but from content integration, brand presence on ground, viewer interactive contesting, and several other opportunities. These properties are first evaluated on whether there is a brand fit with the property. This, in fact, becomes a huge first determinant of whether the brand would be interested in evaluating the property.

Sometimes, brand fit is also seen from the point of view of not just content theme, but also whether the brand ambassador is part of the show. So for example, if Salman Khan is the brand ambassador of a hosiery brand and is also the host of *Big Boss*, then does it make sense for the brand to sponsor *Big Boss*? Sometimes the timing of the property also determines whether to associate with it or not. So if a brand is being launched, and at the same time a big media property is being launched, then it could make sense for the brand to ride on the media property. Sometimes, a media channel launches a big property with big investments and puts a huge marketing effort to ensure its success; then too (in such high stakes game), it becomes an important criterion in deciding to sponsor the property because of the huge salience the brand would get.

Usually, in such large format deals there are several elements which are evaluated by media buyers. So other than FCT, there are programme promos, contests, on-ground promotions, product placements, commentary mentions, graphic elements during telecast, etc. So the buyer while evaluating will put a value to each of those elements. In addition, the buyer will also evaluate the value a brand gets from the cross-media promotion of such properties. For instance, if the IPL is promoted in print, how much mileage would a sponsor get through this? Similarly, every element of the promotion plan is evaluated separately to understand the value the brand would derive. This evaluation forms the basis of negotiation for large format properties.

Programme Selection Criteria

1. Viewership rating.
2. Cost per rating point (CPRP).
3. Commercial break vs programme rating.
4. Clutter level of advertising within the programme.
5. Programme loyalty levels – how many people come back again to watch subsequent episodes of the programme. At times the objective might be to maximize frequency, and in this case it might make sense to have a mix of programmes that have high loyalty levels. This would ensure that you could have the same set of people exposed multiple times to your communication.
6. Volatility ratios – sometimes people also check the inflow and outflow of audiences from a certain programme or a daypart. The higher this number, the lesser the likelihood of your communication being noticed. This is normally done at a macro channel level, but some people also analyse the channel-switching behaviour during certain key time bands or programmes.
7. Audience attention spans – here normally one tries to find out what percentage of a programme's viewers are involved with the programme.

Therefore, a filter like 'people who watch 50% or more of the programme' is used. Here, one looks at the overall programme TVR within the defined audience and then evaluates the percentage of people who watch, say, 50% or more of the programme. This gives them an indication of 'programme stickiness', which is used to fine-tune decision making. Sometimes, people do a cumulative reach of 1 min + on the programme, compare it with the cumulative reach at 50%+, and then arrive at an index. Whichever way you look at it, the idea is to find out what percentage of the audience is involved with/attentive to the programme. The higher this index, the better the chances of effective communication.

8. Programme environment fit with the brand.

Evaluating Print Deals

Evaluation of print deals is relatively simpler as compared to TV, given the fact that print research is not available as frequently as TV, and the factors involved are fewer. Also, there is relatively greater stability in the medium as compared to the volatile nature of TV.

Criteria for Evaluating Print Deals

1. *Cost per thousand*: This is a measure of the cost efficiency of the publication. One could do this analysis in two ways – CPT on Readership, or CPT on Circulation. This is one of the broader ways of selection of vehicles within the medium.
2. *Absolute rate*: Given the high cost of advertising in print, the absolute rate assumes a huge significance. There are times when planners/buyers compare it with the rate card rates to see what kind of discounting is there. However, given the steep rise in rates in print, the relevance of the rate card in print is fast diminishing. Therefore, people are moving away from discounting and comparing relative rates of publications with the relative readership or circulation figures, and then arrive at some kind of a benchmark.
3. *Relative positions*: This assumes a huge significance in print buying. Where the ad is placed has a huge bearing on its noticeability. There are certain positions like the Front Page, Back Page, and Page 3 or even the Sports Page which are preferred locations. A deal which has a higher component of ads placed in premium positions will be seen differently from a deal which has a random placement of ads.
4. *Innovations*: This is another major area in print advertising where brands look at some sort of innovations to get the advertising noticed. There are numerous kinds of innovations. The most common ones are Text Wrap (where some elements of the ad jut out of the ad and the editorial content is text wrapped around the element), changing the colour of the editorial

font, size and position innovations, and gatefolds. Innovations play a significant role in deal evaluations.

5. *Branding/sponsorship values*: Print lends itself to flexibility in this area. Here an editorial column can be created to suit the overall category, and the brand sponsors the column. For instance, a recipe column can be created which is branded by an edible oil brand, a hair care column can be created which is branded/sponsored by a shampoo brand, and so on. The column is custom designed to integrate the brand theme or communication message so that the brand gets extended association in a relevant environment. This also give the brand the opportunity to move out of conventional advertising and leverages the power of editorial to appropriate the category. Over a reasonably sustained time period, these develop as unique brand properties which can be leveraged in multiple ways. For instance, all the branded-recipe edit columns could be put together to create a booklet which could be distributed with the newspaper or the magazine, or contests could be linked where cookery contests could take place offline and the winners and their recipes are featured in the newspaper/magazine. Increasingly, the print medium is moving in these directions to generate extra value for brands, and to allow brands to connect better with their audiences.

The preceding were a few top-line methods on evaluation of print deals. Many other factors could play a role in decision making depending upon unique situations.

Evaluating Radio Deals

Radio planning, after the onslaught of private FM, has changed complexion dramatically. During the early days, we had the Primary Channel and the Vividh Bharti service. Radio planning in those days was about finding out which markets needed radio support. There used to be a fixed rate card for various timeslots/programme categories, and the plans were made on that basis. Once industry privatization took place during 2000–2010, radio planning and buying changed forever. Suddenly, there were so many things one could do with the medium. The biggest strengths of the medium were its local nature and instant audience interactivity. Apart from airing just spots on radio, there were a lot of other things one could do with the medium – things like airing a contest and give instant gratifications to callers, RJ mentions, branding of shows, on-ground brand activation linked back on air with participant feedback, sponsorships, etc. However, a problem with the industry has been its measurability. For some time there was no research on the medium, and decision making was based on one's individual understanding of the relative standings of channels or on the basis of ad hoc research that was done. Now with RAM coming in, a fair bit of data is available. But with over 90 cities and over 300 stations across India, a large majority of them have yet to come under the ambit of RAM. However, the IRS does cover some basic information at the station level, such as listenership, place of listening, daypart listenership, demographic profile, etc. Therefore, decision making on radio largely is still based on qualitative parameters and individual understanding/ad hoc research or past experience with a station.

Criteria for Evaluating Radio Deals

1. *Rate/10 sec*: This is a major factor that's used given the fact that not too much research is available on the medium. Therefore, the absolute rate of station A vs that of station B still is a major factor in taking a final decision. Then there are some benchmarks that people have for evolved markets like Delhi, Mumbai, Bangalore, and Indore, where stations have been in operation for over 7–8 years now. Those rates are used as some sort of benchmarks.
2. *Cost per thousand*: Cost per thousand listeners is another way to benchmark the efficiency level of various stations. There are benchmarks that one can develop for the markets covered by RAM. Then there's IRS, which tells us the listenership base of various radio stations in the other towns. The CPT benchmarks of some major markets then help one arrive at some sort of rates for the other markets.
3. *Value additions*: While the first two criteria were quantitative parts of the deal evaluation, a large part of the deals on radio are being led on things that are not inventory led. Programme sponsorships are a major part. A second major direction most radio stations have taken is that they have integrated on-ground activation with playbacks on air. This has advertisers really excited. For instance, for a particular campaign, the radio station puts up a small stall/arena near a mall/shopping area and gets people to participate in various kinds of small contests related to the brand – and the RJ on road calls in live to the station and gets some of the on-ground participants to talk to the RJ on air about the experience, etc. Then there are on-air contests where listeners call in and play a contest on air and win prizes from the brand. Today, radio stations have set up creative teams that not only help you create your commercial spot, but also will ideate on the brand and come up with solutions that go just beyond airing spots. It is things of these kinds that are swaying the major deals on radio.

Evaluating Outdoor Deals

The OOH medium has changed dramatically from what it was in the 2010s. Multiple new formats have come in, and the medium has moved far ahead of being just about billboards. Technology has brought in immense possibilities.

However, the biggest problem for the medium is twofold – the industry is largely unorganized, and measurability is still a worry. While one can see signs of consolidation happening all around with some large corporates getting into the business, we're far from a happy situation. It would still take a while to arrive at a common currency for buying in the OOH space. OOH buying and planning is a specialized space, and different organizations have evolved their own models of planning, optimizing, and evaluating an OOH plan.

Criteria for Evaluating OOH Deals

1. *Site location*: Where the site is located determines its price. A site at a prominent crossing or a major traffic route will command a higher rate as compared to a site which has lesser traffic going past. Every city has its traffic flow pattern, and OOH specialists try to understand that and arrive at a pricing benchmark. However, there is no uniformity in the pricing. There are times when there are six sites at the same location, and the prices for each could vary. Most OOH agencies have developed location optimizers which help identify the 'hot spots' of the city.
2. *Site visibility*: How visible the site is from a distance is another factor that is considered. Various kinds of models are floating around – some measure the height from the ground, the angle to the road, and visibility from a distance and arrive at a site visibility index, while others don't even care to look at this. OOH specialists have different kinds of models, and buyers normally look at this as one of the factors in evaluating a deal on OOH.
3. *Size*: Large format site vs small format site is another factor in the decision-making process.
4. *Lit vs non-lit*: A lit site normally has a longer life than a non-lit site. This is another area of decision making.
5. *Absolute rate*: This of course is another major factor.
6. *Cost efficiency*: At times people compare cost efficiency on the basis of Cost/sq ft of Plan A vs that of Plan B and arrive at some sort of decision.
7. *Reach–frequency*: Some OOH players have evolved their own models of evaluating plans with give an indication of reach and frequency generated by a plan. At times these are used to arrive at a final plan and help take a decision.
8. *Previous experience*: A large part of the decision making is done on the basis of experience. Prior experience on what works and what does not work plays a handy role in arriving at decisions.
9. *Other formats*: There are the conventional billboard formats, and besides this, there are multiple other formats – branding on trains, inside buses, bus panels, petrol pumps, sign boards, direction boards, traffic barricades, inside malls and multiplexes, shop boards, toll collection booths, etc.

Many formats are being developed, and a comprehensive measurement system has yet to take place.

Internet

Buying on Search

Media buying on search is largely based on bids; therefore a bidding strategy becomes important. Here are some of the key aspects you should consider while planning the bidding strategy on Google:

1. *Aligning bid strategy based on campaign goals*: As per Google, here are the key goals one should consider while bidding:

   - If you want consumers to take direct action and your focus is on conversions, then Smart Bidding is recommended. Smart Bidding is optimized bidding based on machine learning which takes into account user behaviour and context to predict possible conversions. You could optimize on cost per action, return on advertising spend, bids to maximize conversions, maximize conversions value (sales, profit margins, etc.) bidding, or enhanced CPC (this tries to keep the average CPC below the maximum limit you set manually). In Smart Bidding, the bid optimization control is given to Google. While it saves time for the advertiser and is useful for new advertisers to the digital medium, it is important for you to track the success of your campaign and take direct control of optimizations for best results.
   - If you want to maximize clicks and drive traffic to your website, then you must consider the Cost Per Click bid strategy. You could opt for an automated bid strategy, where you set the budget and leave the rest to the Google Ads system to optimize. Alternately, you could opt for a manual bid strategy, where you manually put up bids for your campaign elements. Based on your experience, you could keep modulating the bid.
   - If you are targeting awareness and visibility, then you could look at Target Impression Share (it attempts to enhance visibility for your ad by trying to place it on the Top or some other prominent position) or a CPM strategy where you pay for the ads that get shown, or tCPM (Target CPM) where you decide how much you want to pay for every thousand impressions (it's good for budget control), or a vCPM (Viewable CPM) strategy where you set the highest budget you can pay for every thousand impressions viewed.

2. *Manual CPC bidding*: This is the most common method used where you can specify the maximum price you would pay if someone clicks on your

banner. Here, based on your business parameters, you could set up an amount which could roughly be the cost of per-customer acquisition, and use it with some back calculations to arrive at it. So for example if you eventually need 100 customers to buy, then based on your prior experience you could say that for this you would need, say, 500 to actively consider, and maybe 2000 to show interest by clicking through. Based on the brand budgets, you could then arrive at the maximum cost you could spend per person. Or you could take the help of the Google bid simulator and see different what-if scenarios to fix your budget. Also be aware that for your ad rank to go up, your maximum bids must be competitive.

3. *Enhanced CPC*: Here the Google Ads system will optimize the manual bids set by you based on your campaign's previous performance, and lead you to better conversions.

4. *Cost per view bid*: This works for video, where you specify the maximum CPV. You pay only when the viewer either sees at least 30 seconds of your ad, or interacts with the ad. Just like CPC bids, you could set up the maximum you would pay per view.

5. *Bidding on impressions*: Here the bid is placed on the impression being delivered. This is used typically in awareness campaigns, where one is not necessarily targeting conversions.

Bidding strategy, therefore, is largely coming from the campaign objectives. Typically for conversions, one would look at cost per action strategy; for awareness, you could look at bidding by impressions; for video, you would use a cost per view strategy. Then there are options of manually controlling the bids and modulating your campaign, or leaving it to the Google Ads system to optimize the campaign for you within the constraints you specify.

Buying on Social

When it comes to buying on social media like Facebook, there are two dominant strategies – reach and frequency buying, and auction buying.

Reach and frequency buying: This is typically used for campaigns targeting brand awareness, driving traffic to a website, app installations, or even conversions. Here the buyer can set the reach and frequency benchmarks and have a complete control on the plan deliveries. The ads can be placed on Facebook and Instagram in this way. The Facebook Ads Manager is a tool that helps you set up the campaign and track the progress. You could set up Frequency Caps, set up a schedule, and identify ad placement positions. This works almost like in traditional media. You could optimize the plan, and the plan deliveries are predicted in advance. You could maximize either reach or frequency depending upon the desired objectives.

Auction buying: Auction buying works similar to the way it is in Search. There's greater choice and flexibility, but the results are not as predictable as they are when one does reach and frequency buying. There are ways to optimize the campaign based on objectives. You could control pricing, scheduling, targeting, placement, and formats, and optimize the plan to achieve campaign objectives. The ads can be placed across Facebook, Instagram, Messenger, and Facebook Audience Network (this comprises apps). Essentially, the Facebook Audience Network is used to extend campaign reach by reaching out to people beyond Facebook and Instagram. Facebook Network ads also come at a lower cost as compared to Facebook and Instagram, and one can run Native Ads (designed to fit your app seamlessly), Full-screen ads, banner ads, rewarded video ads and playable ads (used for gaming apps where the user can play and experiment before downloading the app).

Buying on Programmatic

Programmatic is about delivering the right message to the right consumer at the right time, possibly in the best context, and at the best possible price. All of this facilitated by technology (DSP at the buyer's end and SSP at the seller's end). The key factors behind programmatic buy are:

Alignment with campaign objectives: At the centre of every programmatic buy are the brand objectives – awareness, traffic, sales, conversions, etc. While some campaigns could work with a simple CPM target, others would work better with cost per action or a cost per view target depending upon the objective.

Audience understanding: It's important for the buyer to understand what stage of the funnel one is on. At the same time, a deep analysis of the audience set is very critical to be able to direct the messaging in contexts that are favoured by the audience. The deeper the audience understanding, the better the targeting and the greater the likelihood of campaign success.

Other aspects: Programmatic is about efficiency in digital media buying. While this is an important benefit, the buyer must be careful about working with the right DSPs. At the same time, buyers need to be careful about ad fraud, brand safety, and the need to create their own standards for viewability while optimizing their buy. One of the important prerequisites for the buyer is to be agile and be able to modulate the buy depending upon the results. One must be clued on to which creative formats are delivering results and phase out the ones that are not; even the budget must be flexible depending upon the response.

Evaluating Value-Adds

Value-adds are now almost part of every media deal. A value-add is nothing but an extra offering by the media seller to the media buyer. It helps the media seller up-mark a premium to the media vehicle, and to the buyer it offers an opportunity to get extra mileage for the brand. Value-adds come in different forms. Sometimes, the TV channel might offer sponsorship of some key properties. This helps extend the brand saliency because whenever the programme is promoted, the promo tag of the brand is also aired. Similarly, if it's a print property like a column sponsorship in the newspaper, the brand gets highlighted wherever the column is promoted. On TV and radio, sometimes the seller might offer bonus spots, meaning that for every 1000 seconds you buy on the channel/station, you would get 100 seconds of free airtime which will be used by the brand during a specified time band. Similarly, a newspaper could offer bonus space which could be used on some specified section/page.

Sometimes TV/radio stations could give a value-add by fixing the position of the ad in the break. So for instance, while the commercial break could have 10 spots being aired, the media seller could give a value addition by committing to airing 50% of all the spots of the brand concerned first/last in the commercial break. Sometimes, they could also fix the commercial break sequence and say that all spots of the brand would be in the first commercial break of the programme. Similarly, a newspaper could commit that a certain number of ads would be fixed on the first page or the last page of the newspaper, or on an early right-hand page. A magazine could commit to placing the ad in the first 25 pages of the magazine, or on the covers – to enhance brand visibility.

TV sellers could also give value-adds in the form of scrolls or aston bands. An aston band/scroll is like an animated banner that appears at the bottom of the screen while the programme is on. It could be a static banner or a dynamic banner. Sometimes a value-add could come in the form of a contest which is organized by the TV channel, radio station, newspaper or magazine, or the website. The contest is promoted by the media owner, and the brand gets a mention in all promotion and publicity of the contest. Sometimes TV/radio stations offer deals by spreading the spots across different time bands. So for instance of the split of spots between prime time (1900–2300 hrs), and non-prime time (0700–1900 hrs) is 50:50, a value addition could be done by changing this ratio to, say, 60:40 in favour of prime time.

Another interesting value-add that is now a regular feature of a lot of deals is content integration and in-programme placement. So for example, a TV channel could offer a value-add to a car brand by saying that all cars used in the TV serial would be of their brand. This would mean a subtle product placement in the programme. Also sometimes, the brand could be integrated in the storyline of the programme.

Sometimes, value-adds could be added in the form of ground sponsorship of some event being organized by the media company. It could be in the form or sampling opportunities offered to the brand, and so on.

Checklist for the Media Buyer: Things that He/She Must Know

1. *Alignment on audience*: The media buyer is an integral part of the media process, and therefore it is very important that there's alignment all through. The buyer must understand the advertising objectives, brand strategy, brand positioning, competitive scenario, the target audience, detailed psychographic profiles of the audience, primary audience vs secondary audience, etc. This would enable the buyer to look for the right qualitative fit of genres, programmes, channels, and environments where the brand message could be brought alive. Also, it would help the buyer identify media opportunities which could be leveraged for the brand. For instance, if one has an understanding that the audience is very health conscious, then one would evaluate opportunities with media vehicles that are either targeted at health-conscious people, or they have content which could appeal to health-conscious people. The media buyer could evaluate possibilities of creating customized branded content within the right editorial environment. Likewise, the media buyer would look at planning the buy differently if he is talking to people who are self-confessed foodies. In this case, one would look at a completely different kind of editorial context in which to place ads.
2. *Alignment on markets*: Then, there are some important information points that are mandatory for the media buyer to understand. The buyer must know the geographical markets to be targeted, and the prioritization of these markets. The buyer must also understand the rationale for the market prioritization, and must understand and appreciate different media targets set for each market depending on its priority. This would naturally guide the buyer to consider media opportunities in higher-priority markets. Media 'isolatability' also becomes important for buyers to consider this – particularly when the markets are very sharply defined.
3. *Campaign mandatories*: The other critical input that the buyer needs is information on media mix and the rationale for selection of each type of media. It is important that the buyer is briefed on the budgets that have been allocated for each media type. The buyer must also know the creative units – size of ads, number of edits, duration, languages, etc. Also, sometimes, different creative pieces have different objectives – therefore, it's important for the buyer to be completely aligned on media objectives by market, and even by creative (wherever applicable). The other mandatory information includes the campaign duration, any

change in campaign weights by seasonality, etc. Sometimes brands have short-term promotional offers, and the buyer must be aligned to these critical dates.

4. *Alignment on media targets/media selections*: It's important for the buyer to understand the media selections made in terms of media mix, programmes, genres, channels, platforms, etc. It's also important to understand plan targets in terms of reach, frequency, and GRPs across different markets.

5. *Scope for creativity/innovations*: There must be some latitude for the media buyer to explore ways and means to think creatively and create innovations for the brand which would help extend the brand message or deliver it more powerfully. The buyer could look for existing properties in media which have a good thematic fit with the brand, or could even work with media partners to create contextual content in which the brand's message could be placed. The psychographic profile of the audience and any consumer insight or research become critical inputs for the buyer. With the kind of clutter that's prevailing in the media environment, the ability to think creatively often becomes the differentiator between a good campaign and a great campaign. Every second brief nowadays from brand marketers places a special premium on creativity and innovation in media.

Other Tasks of the Buyer

1. *Monitoring plan implementation*: It's the responsibility of the buyer to ensure that the plan is executed as per schedule. Therefore, every execution plan is closely monitored. Sometimes, some spots are dropped on air, or some ads don't get printed in some editions of the newspaper, or are missed on some radio stations. The buying team keeps a track of this very closely and attempts to take a 'make-good' immediately while the campaign is on. Sometimes, the spots get truncated (like for example in live telecasts of cricket, the break between overs is short, and sometimes an ad is truncated because the live feed begins), or sometimes in newspapers, the ad has not appeared in the specified position, or the colour reproduction of the ad is not good. In such cases, again the ads have to be 'made good' during the campaign period itself. Sometimes, the brand's tag line is not carried in the promo tag, the ads don't appear first in the break (if promised), etc. Therefore, monitoring the campaign becomes a very important part of the media buying function. Also, the plan's reach-frequency deliveries are monitored weekly to make mid-course corrections (if required) to ensure that the plan targets are met. Also all sponsorship entitlements are monitored on an ongoing basis.

2. *Post-buy analysis*: While daily monitoring of the campaign is done, at the end of the campaign, a thorough post-buy analysis is done to check

whether the targeted plan deliveries were achieved or not. Also checked are some efficiency measures like CPRP targets, performance-measurement targets (in case of performance-linked deals), and so on. An in-depth analysis of the media mix is done to understand which media over-delivered and which media under-delivered, and the reasons for both. Also, the competitive activity is tracked alongside to assess how the brand performed versus its competition, and the level of clutter during the campaign. These are important learnings which are taken on board while planning the next campaign.

Overall, media buying is one of the most exciting areas of the business. With a lot more media options coming in, this will continue to be so. As a function, it's as challenging an area as planning is. Today in most agencies, the planners also double up as buyers. Some agencies have set up separate teams of buyers. Today, the buyers and planners work in very close coordination to deliver value to the brand, be it in terms of extending the life of the brand communication through an innovative media deal which creates a lasting brand impact, or in terms of identifying opportunities for brands much in advance.

Many factors go behind a media buy – quantitative and qualitative. There are buyers who buy media like they are buying vegetables in a 'mandi', and there are buyers who do a huge degree of homework before entering into the process. Both methods have their own virtues. There are times when the largest volume commitment will not get you the lowest possible rate. There are umpteen instances of small isolated local advertisers getting away with some very good deals, whereas large-volume deals go at a higher unit price. At times, it does appear like a strange business. Eventually, it's about the attitude that an individual brings to the discipline.

Chapter Summary

Today, with a few unruly thousand options available, the art and science of media buying has truly evolved and is gradually coming of age. It's a specialized function in organized set-ups, and as much rigour is involved in the buying process as one puts in the planning area. The function has evolved from buying the cheapest, to adding value to the brand. In the world of media buying, the three main stakeholders are the media, the advertisers, and the media agency specialists.

The Media

The media marketplace is getting ever more crowded with serious competition stepping. The traditional TV market has changed with the entry of digital TV and OTT. The traditional print market has changed with newspapers venturing out of their "home" states. Radio has seen a lot of action with 331 FM licenses being given out in the second phase of liberalization. In the outdoor area, new formats are launched every day. Cinema has changed and moved away from just the option of playing a film or showing a slide. And with digital acquiring critical mass, the erstwhile media platforms have now got new wings. Every large TV network now has its own OTT service, along with several standalone OTT entities. Most newspaper titles now have their own apps, websites e-paper sites, digital editions, WhatsApp editions, email listings, Facebook pages, and so on. The market is just warming up to digital OOH, and most large radio station networks also have their own web radio stations. Competitive intensity is at an all-time high, with each competitor wanting a larger share of the pie.

The Advertisers

The advertiser is concerned about cutting through the clutter of jargon and delivering the right message to the right consumer when he is in the right frame of mind. They understand the power of volume buying. All of them want the budgets to work harder. Absolute cost, cost efficiencies, and return on investment (ROI) are high on their agenda, and they expect both the media planning and buying functions to deliver on that. Their objectives from the media buying part of the discussions are very different from the media owners' objectives from the buying process.

The Agency

The agency plays the most vital role in the buying process. It is focused on managing the overall absolute cost and driving efficiencies from media buys. The eventual winners in this process are smart media owners who attempt to understand advertiser concerns and align their thinking to deliver value to the brand. The agency's concern is to deliver the best to help achieve brand objectives and at the same time maintain an overall balance between absolute cost and relative cost efficiencies.

Key Factors that Influence Media Buying Strategy

1. *Initial pre-buy analysis*: The initial analysis is focused around reach numbers, profiles, channel shares, reach build-up, loyalty levels, clutter levels, duplications, innovation opportunities available, etc., for each of the media vehicles in the consideration set.
2. *Demand supply equation*: In this analysis one looks at inventory sales analysis of different media options to study their strengths and

weaknesses. Along with this, buyers also apply inventory utilization ratios and seasonality analysis to understand how different media options stack up.

3. *Category competitive considerations*: The idea is to determine, for the category that you are operating in, the market share of the respective vehicles. It's important to analyse the vehicle's dependence on the category for advertising. Additional analysis is done to find out how important the advertiser is to the channel/station/daily/other media vehicle. If the advertiser whom the buyer represents accounts for a large part of the channel's business, then this is a position of strength while negotiating a media buy.

4. *Other factors*: Other factors like monthly/quarter closing dates, relationship between the buyer and seller, relative standing of the media office concerned, etc are some of the softer nuanced elements that play a role in the media buying strategy.

5. *Delivering value to the brand*: Here one looks at innovation possibilities and other types of media, such as activations, OOH, mobile vas, etc. Today there are many examples where media organizations are taking brand briefs and creating a complete integrated media solution to deliver brand impact.

6. *Understanding the economics of media*: With so many options to choose from, the level of competition is so high that one sees all sorts of deals and rates floating around. No one is really able to assess the bottom of the market. A buyer armed with the knowledge of media costs and economics is always better prepared.

Evaluating Media Deals across Types of Media

Here are the key factors that are used to evaluate media deals:

1. Evaluating TV deals

   - Deal CPRP
   - Rate/10 sec
   - Value of sponsorships and other value-adds
   - Reach–frequency builds
   - Distribution of spots across dayparts

2. Evaluating print deals

   - Cost per thousand
   - Absolute rate
   - Relative positions
   - Innovations
   - Branding/sponsorship values

3. Evaluating radio deals

- Rate/10 sec
- Cost per thousand
- Value additions

4. Evaluating outdoor deals

- Site location
- Site visibility
- Size
- Lit vs non-lit
- Absolute rate
- Cost efficiency
- Reach–frequency
- Previous experience
- Other formats

5. Buying on search

- Aligning bid strategy based on campaign goals: If you want to consumers to take direct action and your focus is on conversions, then Smart Bidding is recommended. If you want to maximize clicks and get traffic for your website then you must consider the cost per click bid strategy. If you are targeting awareness and visibility, then you could look at target impression share, or a CPM strategy where you pay for the ads that get shown, or tCPM where you decide how much you want to pay for every thousand impressions, or a vCPM strategy.
- Manual CPC bidding: This is the most common method used, where you can specify the maximum price you would pay if someone clicks on your banner.
- Enhanced CPC: Here the Google Ads system will optimize the manual bids set by you.
- Cost per view bid: This works for video where you specify the maximum CPV.
- Bidding on Impressions: Here the bid is placed on the impression being delivered.

6. Buying on Social

- Reach and frequency buying: This is typically used for campaigns targeting brand awareness, driving traffic to a website, app installations, or even conversions.
- Auction buying: This works similar to the way it is in Search. There's more choice and flexibility, but the results are not as predictable as they are when one does reach–frequency buying.

7. Buying on programmatic

- Alignment with campaign objectives
- Audience understanding
- Other aspects, including working with the right DSPs, being careful with regard to ad fraud and brand safety, and creating their own standards for viewability while optimizing their buy

Checklist for the Media Buyer

- Alignment on audience
- Alignment on markets
- Campaign mandatories
- Alignment on media targets/media selections
- Scope for creativity/innovations

Key Tasks of a Media Buyer

- Monitoring plan implementation
- Post-buy analysis

Media buyers and planners work in very close coordination to deliver value to the brand, whether by extending the life of the brand communication through an innovative media deal which creates a lasting brand impact, or by identifying opportunities for brands well in advance.

Further Reading

Ads.Google.com, https://support.google.com/google-ads/answer/9121108
Facebook Business Help Centre, https://www.facebook.com/business/help/654484604719506?id=842420845959022

14
MEDIA MARKETING

The media industry in India is rapidly undergoing a transformation with digital acquiring critical mass. Several changes are happening simultaneously in the media environment, from the way people consume media, to the way advertisers look at media, to how media planners and buyers think about media, and how media research companies look at measuring media. It's in these contexts that media marketing needs to be understood.

Changes in Media and Entertainment Dispersion and Consumption

The good news is that more people will consume more media. At the same time there will be more content producers than ever before. This will be aided by more platforms for dispersion of news. Audience fragmentation is the most likely fallout of this phenomenon. We're seeing how linear TV will compete with digital TV, how print will compete with social media and other digitally powered news platforms, how radio will compete with web radio, how cinema will compete with OTT players, and how the Internet will compete with itself with ad blockers and the privacy regulations around the world. Many of these stories will be played out over the next 2–3 years as of this writing. Probably, media has reached its peak level of complexity – my sense is that those next 2–3 years will give ample directions on way forward – but I see the media ecosystem moving towards simplicity.

DOI: 10.4324/9781032724539-14

Changes in Media Planning

With mass individualized media consumption happening simultaneously across multiple media, media planning will have to struggle with the challenges of gaining audience attention. The battle will no longer be about SOV and reach – it will shift to how much attention we are able to hold of our audience and translate that attention into business gains for advertisers.

And attention will be at premium. With so much media multitasking, our cognitive functions will be sub-optimal. The truth is that we cannot properly multitask. Female, or male, humans can only focus on one cognitive function at a time. Yes, we can flick quickly and easily between tasks, but when we do that, we're still performing only one function at a time, whether it is reading, listening, viewing, or talking. In fact, genuine multitasking is not only impossible, but when we attempt it, it can significantly affect our ability to remember and focus.

From a planning perspective, the trend to target multi-screening millennials should be approached with caution. It might be better to look for moments when the recipient's concentration levels are higher. And that brings us to *context* – this will become the sweet spot for media planning – to draw attention in the right context. So media solutions will move towards finding out opportunities to layer a combination of contextual and behavioural solutions to achieve maximum effect.

Changes in Media Buying

As a direct fallout of the changes in media planning, buying will have to move out of the transactional mode and get into the mode of identifying opportunities for grabbing audience attention in the media environment. Also necessarily, they will need to look at picking and buying multiple media simultaneously, as in an idea-driven media planning world, the idea will have to reign supreme – the platforms may become irrelevant. That means they will also need to make the apples-and-oranges comparisons between different media types. And that brings us to the media research challenge.

Changes in Media Research

Digital has blurred all sorts of boundaries – not just geographical boundaries, but boundaries between individual media as well. The same media content got repurposed, repackaged, and redistributed across different platforms and devices – in a sense extending the long tail of media content. With the long tail now accounting for a significant share of time and attention, we have a situation where a large part of media consumption will go unmeasured. Add to this the fact that these new platforms are spawning new media behaviour.

This creates questions of measurement that need to be tackled very differently from our traditional methodologies.

On the other hand, marketers have broken out of silos – they are planning idea-driven, cross-platform campaigns that frequently mix traditional media with PR activities, sponsorships, events, product placements, and other forms of promotion. But research is still operating in silos of individual media. We have TV research separately, we have print research separately, and so on for each individual media. And seldom are all these "siloed" media on the same page.

The economics of yesterday were created for measuring eyeballs, reach, and awareness. Today, marketers have moved towards targeting multiple niches and in a dialogue mode with consumers. The media currency was created for trading, but that will increasingly become a smaller part of the overall game. Research will need to emerge out of silos and create metrics for 'decision making' rather than just 'trading'. However, given the way things are going where we are still trying to get on top of our game in traditional individual media-centric research, I doubt whether we will see any dramatic move towards a 'media research renaissance' movement anytime soon. I see these media research silos digging deeper.

Looking at the media industry from a macro lens, one could view three key pillars of the industry:

- Content creation
- Content distribution
- Audience monetization

Historically, media organizations held a monopoly of sorts on content creation. They were the specialist content creators. They understood audience tastes and created content accordingly, or they created content to lead on new audiences. But this sole monopoly of content creation was upended by the rise of digital platforms which democratized content creation. Today, everybody is a content creator. That includes the numerous millions of bloggers scattered around the world who create content based on their interest and worldviews. They are able to find like-minded people who subscribe to their point of view. Then there are millions of video creators who have opened their own YouTube channels, created video blogs, are on platforms like TikTok, and several others. Then there's the huge swathe of opinions that float on social networks and personal chat sites like WhatsApp, Telegram, Signal, Snapchat, etc. With so much more content being created, the domain of content creation is being disrupted by digital like never before. Here, we aren't discussing the quality of content or the credibility of the content. These are contentious issues in a world that's awash with fake news, privacy concerns, and the supposed threat posed by big tech to legacy media.

The earlier model of content distribution was fairly straightforward. The content creators created content, and the distribution arms took over to ensure that the content reaches its intended audience. In the case of TV, there were cable operators who laid out a complex web of wires and carried the content from house to house. This was later upended by DTH, where we see the urban landscapes now dotted with little satellite dish 'umbrellas' that sent TV signals direct to home. This was then further upended by digital TV subscriptions via telecom lines. While all this was happening, we also saw the transformation of the 'idiot box' to 'smart TV'. We now have a surfeit of OTT apps bypassing everything, and talking one on one with consumers to access video content on demand. Similarly, in print, we see how the circulation teams ensured a door-to-door delivery of the newspaper. This comfortable model was disrupted by news aggregators and the rise of platforms which enabled people to access news on their phones on the go to either read e-paper editions, watch live news feeds, or get news alerts as they went about their day. They no longer need to wait for the newspaper the next day. We now have the new age distributors like social media and search engines – between these two agents, they account for almost two-thirds of visitors getting through to any content online. Then there are platforms like Twitter, Instagram, Flipboard, LinkedIn, Storify, Blendle, etc. To top it up, we have aggregators and various chat sites that now carry information. With this, digital platforms have disrupted the content distribution pillar of legacy media.

That brings us to the third piece in the story – the audience. They now have options to choose from. As a result of these options, this audience is now fragmented across thousands of media vehicles. Historically, when the options were limited, the audiences naturally gravitated towards a few large media titles/channels and the media owners were able to monetize these audiences through advertising, which formed a critical part of media revenues and sustained their business models. But with increasing fragmentation, audience monetization became slightly more difficult.

Therefore, over the last decade and a half, we've seen the erstwhile media business model being disrupted across every pillar – content creation, content distribution, and the resulting audience monetization. Instead, media is now in different stages of re-inventing these models. As per the E&Y–Ficci report ("The Era of Consumer ART", 2020), the media industry is realigning itself from the verticalized segmentation of the industry which comprised distinct segments like TV, print, radio, digital, OOH, and cinema to a new segment-agnostic horizontal model which is based on multi-platform aggregation, distribution, and consumption with ability to collect and analyse end-customer data. This new segment-agnostic model comprises content producers, content aggregators, content distributors, and content platforms and devices. This new model is based on how different media entities focus on direct contact with their consumer. In this model, everyone cooperates with everyone, and everyone competes with everyone for audiences and revenues.

In this brave new media world, one can no longer take for granted that the content that has been created will automatically find its way to consumers. In this world, the task of the media entity does not end with content creation and distribution; they now have to actively think from the lens of how to get the content 'discovered' in a time when the consumer has an array of choices and wields control on what they consume and where. Therefore, more than content distribution, it's content promotion that assumes centre stage for media organizations. One has to not only create great content, but also ensure 'content discoverability'. So from a TV perspective, there are over 900 channels and thousands of hours of content – how does one ensure that their content is visible to people? This becomes the biggest marketing task for media brands. If the content is promoted well and is 'discoverable' by a significant mass of people, then the chances of monetizing that audience are higher. Great content could be residing on the channel, but if it is not discovered, then one wouldn't be able to monetize with it. Similarly, in print, there could be a great piece of journalistic writing on page 13, but if readers are not made aware of this, then the purpose of the story is lost.

At the same time, audiences must not be seen as just pure headcounts to be monetized. Media brands now need to reach out to their audiences and establish direct connections with them. Not only do we need to acquire audiences, but we need to retain them adequately enough, give them content that's relevant to them, adapt/repurpose content for different platforms and devices for ease of consumption, and monetize them adequately. This is not possible unless we establish deep connections with our audiences. The deeper the connection, the more engaged they are, and the better we're able to monetize their attention. In fact, media titles that engage deeply with their audiences are able to provide greater context and a better environment for brands to advertise. At the same time, given privacy concerns, one must ensure the highest possible ethical standards in collecting and using audience data.

While we see media organizations moving towards a segment-agnostic model, it is important that brand consistency is maintained. A siloed approach to building media brands wouldn't work. The audience is consuming our content seamlessly across platforms and devices, and it is imperative that we also create seamless brand experience for the consumers. Long-term brand building is about establishing deep connections with one's audience, and the foundation for such connections must be based on what the brand truly stands for. There are some unique characteristics of media brands that set them apart from other traditional product categories. Media brands are intangible. They work on our hearts and minds and shape our opinions. They have different distribution cycles. Some are live round the clock, some ask the audience to pause and spend time. Media brands are live. Everyday there's new content on TV, on radio, or in the newspaper, but the brand that brings this to the audience is the same, and the audience would engage more deeply if the consumption experience is seamless. So if there's a newspaper brand that the audience follows because of its crisp layout, great headlines, and huge credibility, then it is imperative that these values are reflected even on the website of the newspaper or on the app. Therefore, the key challenges for media brands are:

- How to manage brand consistency when the carrier remains constant, but the content changes on an everyday basis.
- Rising clutter within media and fragmentation of audiences
- Erasing of boundaries – in the new scheme of things, everyone competes with everyone

Key Assets of a Media Brand

1. *Content creation skill.* Media brands have the core capability to create content. This is a key asset which could be leveraged to appeal to a large audience base, and also to create custom content for brands.
2. *Stars of the content.* These include actors in TV shows, writers of content in newspapers and magazines, and RJs. They are content icons who are a pull factor to draw in audiences.
3. *Our network and its offline advantages.* Media brands like newspapers and radio stations have physical presence on ground in terms of offices and distribution setups. This offline network brings in huge advantages. It helps media brands keep a close ear to the ground, and it is able to customize content for local markets. At the same time, they have deep connections with local communities which could be leveraged for different brands. The network also helps local media to have great relationships with local civic authorities, local administration, and civil society. These relationships make it easier for brands to co-partner with newspapers to contribute to civic issues or community development programmes.
4. *Our brand credibility as the messenger.* Established media brands lend credibility. In today's day and age, where fake news abounds, local legacy media brands are a first choice because of the credibility factor. Trust becomes a fundamental differentiator particularly amongst news brands.
5. *Our distribution capability.* Both on-ground and online, this is a huge factor. The on-ground distribution ability gives local media a distinct advantage in terms of forging deeper community relationships. It also gives us 'feet-on-street' which could be leveraged for brands in terms of sampling, product promotion, etc.

6. *Our audiences and their profile.* There are two very important determinants to monetize an audience base. The first is the absolute size of the audience. A large audience base is a preferred choice for brands that need mass reach. At the same time, the profile of the audience also matters. If one has a higher proportion of its audience as NCCS A and B, then it becomes a potential media vehicle for brands that are targeting upmarket homes. Or, if a media brand has a high proportion of its audience as women, then brands targeting women would prefer to use it as an advertising vehicle. Similarly, youth brands would prefer media brands that have a higher proportion of young people.

7. *The advertising environment we create.* In the earlier chapters we have discussed the importance of context and how critical it is for brands to be placed and seen in the right context. If as a media brand, we're able to create a great editorial/content environment, the audiences would engage better and would be loyal, and this provides a great environment for brands to talk to such audiences.

8. *Innovation opportunities.* Does the media brand offer opportunities for innovation? In a highly cluttered, fragmented, and attention-deficit media world, brands are finding it difficult to navigate and communicate adequately enough with consumers. They are looking for ways and means to beat through the clutter and create opportunities for the brand to stand out. Therefore, the ability of media brands to create opportunities for innovation becomes a key factor. Also, media brands understand their audience best and are best placed to create the right innovation opportunities for advertisers.

9. *The reach we provide.* Media brands provide reach, which is a critical requirement for advertisers who are targeting mass reach or want to reach out to specific kinds of audiences. The ability of media to provide reach (either mass or targeted) is a key in monetizing the business.

10. *The markets we cover.* The geography covered by a media brand matters. There are large media brands that cover say the entire Hindi belt (Hindi General Entertainment TV channels like Star Plus, Zee TV, Sony, Colors, etc., or newspaper brands like *Dainik Jagran* and *Dainik Bhaskar*), and they become good choices for brands that want to talk to the Hindi belt. Similarly, there are some media vehicles that cater to a specific state or a city. These become important to advertisers who want to target specific geographies. Then there are some media like large newspapers and radio station networks that provide geographical flexibility to advertisers. They could pick and choose select geographies in which to advertise, or they could change their communication for different markets. Therefore, the markets covered and the flexibility that one offers to brands, provide another huge advantage for media brands.

Audience for a Media Brand

A media brand has two kinds of audience:

- *Business-to-Consumer (B2C)*: The person who consumes the content. It could be a reader of a newspaper or a magazine, a viewer of TV or OTT service, a listener of a radio station, or a visitor of a website or an app. The key objectives behind talking to this audience are:

  - To acquire new readers or listeners or viewers.
  - To engage with them deeply enough so that we're part of their consideration set and the first pick up (in case of a newspaper), or the go-to channel for entertainment (in case of TV or OTT), or the first on dial (in case of a radio Station), etc.
  - To ensure that they spend the maximum time with the media brand. The more time they spend, the greater their engagement.
  - To ensure that they consume the media brand frequently. Having a large set of loyal returning readers or viewers is a key factor in driving monetization.

In order to fulfil these objectives, it is important that we point the audience to the great content that we are creating. This is where content discoverability and content promotion play a big role.

- *Business-to-Business (B2B)*: This comprises advertisers (which could be brand managers, product managers, marketing managers, or CEOs), media planners, and media Buyers. These are the audiences that may or may not be consuming the concerned media, but that evaluate media vehicles for their efficacy in reaching out to consumers. Take the example of a newspaper brand like *Dainik Jagran*. It is circulated in the Hindi belt, but the B2B audience is in large cities like Mumbai, Bengaluru, or Delhi, and they may not be reading the newspaper. Or consider a brand like Sun TV, which is a Tamil TV channel. For such brands, the B2B audience in Mumbai/Delhi might not be consuming the vehicle, and therefore it becomes important to talk to this audience so that they consider the media vehicle in the media plan. However, at the same time, there are B2B audiences who are also readers/viewers of a media vehicle. For example, the brand manager of a local brand in Tamil Nadu might also be a viewer of Sun TV. However, despite this, one needs to talk to this brand manager both as a viewer and as an advertiser – we need to cater to two different need states. The key objectives behind talking to this audience are:
- To communicate our strength in terms of audience numbers and profile of audience so that the media brand is favourably considered as part of the media plan

- To communicate the unique advantage that the brand has in terms of content creation
- To communicate the network strength of the media brand
- To communicate the innovation possibilities that one could explore with the media brand
- To communicate consumer and market insights
- To demonstrate geographical coverage
- To demonstrate relative competitive positioning
- To communicate special B2C consumer connect initiatives which demonstrate the media brand's scale, stature, and power
- To communicate content highlights so that brands are able to see thematic connections with the content
- To announce sponsorship opportunities for large format properties/Ips

To help understand media marketing, it would be best to examine case studies that have been implemented across TV, print, digital, and radio over a period of time.

CASE STUDY 1:   BRAND POSITIONING CAMPAIGN OF A NEWS CHANNEL

This case considers brand positioning of a news channel in the crowded TV news market in the backdrop of the pandemic. The channel has used its news anchors as brand ambassadors.

Aaj Tak Sabse Tez Campaign

In the backdrop of the pandemic, where myths and misinformation were rampant, Aaj Tak created a campaign that sought to establish the channel as one that stood for truth without any sensationalism. Aaj Tak had always relied on humour as a creative strategy for brand building, and this campaign too was in the same vein. This campaign cast their news anchors as protagonists in the advertising campaign aptly titled 'Aaj Tak Hai Toh Sach Hai'. The campaign films touched on themes like sensationalism, cherry-picking convenient truths, rumours, and intrinsic bias.

The Khabristan ad highlights how the channel stood as a watchdog for truth, the Achaar Gully ad talks about no exaggeration of news. The Afwaah ad establishes the channel's credibility as it verifies every news story before airing it, and the Sach ka Band ad is a funny take on how people can clearly differentiate between rumours and real news. Another ad, Zara Jhuk ke, clearly states that Aaj Tak believes in straightforward reporting without any political leanings.

CASE STUDY 2:   LEVERAGING AN EVENT WITH A SOCIAL MESSAGE BY A NEWS CHANNEL

This case describes how a news channel takes on the task of creating awareness about an important social message on hygiene. They've used an interesting device to spread this message during the Kumbh Mela.

Aaj Tak Changing Rooms (Safai Ki Dhun)

Aaj Tak takes the Safai Ki Dhun to the Kumbh Mela, the world's largest confluence of humanity. With millions of people thronging the mela, the need for hygiene was absolutely critical. As a response, Aaj Tak installed special changing rooms on the Ghats of the river Godavari at the Nasik Kumbh, which in addition to being of great utility to the pilgrims also subtly spreads the message of cleanliness with an innovative approach through sensor-activated musical messages. The campaign also assumed greater significance given the PM's call to launch the Swachh Bharat Abhiyan.

The entrance of these changing rooms was equipped with sensors which played the Aaj Tak "Safai ki Dhun Bathroom ko chun" jingle the moment someone entered these rooms, thereby encouraging them to use toilets rather than going to relieve themselves in the open.

Alongside the hygiene initiative, India Today Group also hosted the India Today Safaigiri Singathon & Awards. Cleanliness Champions across 13 categories, selected through a rigorous jury process, were felicitated by the PM. The day was also marked by a Safai Singathon with singers and musicians performing through the day.

CASE STUDY 3:   MARKETING TIE-UP FOR A FILM PROMOTION

Here's a case that describes how a channel leverages its content creation strength to create customized videos for film promotions. The following two examples are brilliant in terms of execution, and they drive value for both the viewers and the filmmakers.

Barfi Campaign

Aaj Tak partnered the makers of the film *Barfi!* and shot a promo with the film's lead actor Ranbir Kapoor. The promo, incorporating cutting-edge technology, captured some of the biggest events in recent times, and Ranbir Kapoor was juxtaposed in the frames of these historic moments in politics, sports and entertainment in his *Barfi!* avatar. Some of the moments include Anna Hazare's movement, India winning the Cricket World Cup, A.R. Rahman receiving the Oscar, the F1 race in India, the Commonwealth Games, Atal Bihari Vajpayee meeting Musharraf and the royal wedding of Prince William. It was a humorous, sweet, and out-of-box idea that connected with viewers across television and social media.

Chennai Express Campaign

Aaj Tak partnered with the Hindi movie *Chennai Express* during its promotion drive. It shot promos featuring Shah Rukh Khan for its show 'Halla Bol'. The co-branded promos under the brand 'Aaj Tak Chennai Express' featured Khan and announced the special daily segment on the channel to viewers. The segment highlighted issues affecting people in various cities. It intended to become a medium for the public to raise these issues and to highlight them to the respective authorities. The promos featured Khan in a train, urged people not to adjust to what they see around them, exhorting them to push for change.

CASE STUDY 4: CREATING BRAND SALIENCE BY LEVERAGING ELECTIONS

Here's a case that describes how a campaign was created by leveraging local folk music to generate awareness for election-related programming on the channel.

Hello Kaun Song Launch for Bihar Elections

Objective: The Bihar Assembly Elections 2020 were being held during the COVID pandemic. The goal was to register the message of tuning into Aaj Tak for news on elections in a quirky but interesting way. The idea was to create an election anthem leveraging the popularity of Bhojpuri music in Bihar. The song was sung by Ritesh Pandey, a Bhojpuri superstar who had delivered several hit songs including 'Hello Kaun'. The song was a 'digital-only' launch by the popular Bhojpuri actor and politician Manoj Tiwari. The song was streamed across popular platforms like Gaana.com and Saavn. It was promoted to Symbian devices through messages and WhatsApp to other devices. Additionally, the song was launched on radio. The channel also dedicated a show with the same name where viewers could call to ask their questions and the caller tune was 'Hello Kaun'.

Impact: The song became an instant hit with a listenership of approximately 1.2 million across Gaana and Saavn and close to 5 million in listenership overall.

CASE STUDY 5: EDUCATING CITIZENS ON RESPECTING OTHERS

This campaign (the logo of which is shown in Figure 14.1) is another interesting example of programme promotion on the channel. The campaign had an important social message at its core, had interactivity built into it, and gained immense popularity while drawing in viewers for the programme.

Mera Swabhimaan

In the wake of incidents where guards, cab drivers, etc., were mistreated by people, Aaj Tak initiated a campaign which focused on their stories in their prime time show *Black & White*. The campaign sought to educate citizens on valuing the self-esteem of blue-collar workers and initiating public conversations around the theme.

The social awareness campaign, titled 'Mera Swabhimaan', was hosted by hosted by Sudhir Chaudhary, garnering over a million views on the day of its launch with over 35,000 tweets within 2 hours of the launch. In the first 5 days of its launch, the interactive campaign had over 25,000 submissions from around India. Celebrities and influencers from all walks of life supported the campaign.

Aaj Tak's initiative was a wonderful example in demonstrating how a news brand leveraged its platform to help curb social malaises.

FIGURE 14.1   Mera Swabhimaan campaign, Aaj Tak.

Source: TV Today Network Ltd.

CASE STUDY 6: CELEBRATING LITERATURE AND ARTS

Art and culture is an important aspect of our lives. This campaign (the logo of which is shown in Figure 14.2) is a fantastic example of how a channel can leverage its strength to celebrate art and culture.

Sahitya Aaj Tak was conceptualized by Aaj Tak as an event to connect people closely to culture and the world of Hindi literature. It's a festival unlike any other that brings together the biggest names in Indian literature, including scholars, poets, writers, musicians, actors, authors, and artists. Amongst the largest literature festivals of the country, it also featured political leaders and film stars.

The festival was promoted through print, social, digital, TV, outdoor, and radio. Over 2,00,000 people registered for the event, and the footfall was 1,00,000+ over 3 days. In addition to the on-ground audience, millions also participated in the show online.

FIGURE 14.2 Sahitya Aaj Tak campaign, Aaj Tak.

Source: TV Today Network Ltd.

CASE STUDY 7: AN EXAMPLE OF A B2C INITIATIVE FOR A NEWSPAPER BRAND

This generation is upfront about their responses to an adult world they reject. As they chart their own course, making sense of the world, they are inventing their systems of codes, values, and mores in the process.

This campaign was about accelerating this mood by reminding young people about what they could achieve, and what they should care about. It was about how a news media brand could play its part in inspiring the next generation of leaders, activists, and citizens – to inspire children to expand their circle of concern, to view the world from a new perspective, and to realize their incredible power to usher change.

Sanskarshala by Dainik Jagran

Getting young readers is a challenge for newspaper brands not just in India, but across the world. The challenge was to reignite *Dainik Jagran*'s role as the conscience keeper, and create content that would attract young readers to the newspaper.

Dainik Jagran decided to lead the change from being the carrier to corrector, and from reporting on 'value erosion' to resurrecting 'value system'. Thus was born the initiative – Jagran Sanskarshala. The word *Sanskarshala* means 'School of Values'.

A Sanskarshala page was created in *Dainik Jagran* that spoke about moral value education for contemporary times. The campaign wrote on topics like gender equality, respecting diversity, selflessness, right use of language, etc. Stories were written for children containing a moral message. Experts, school principals, and children were invited to write for the Sanskarshala page. This page broke the shackles of negativity and included stories of hope, positivity, and optimism with a message for the younger generation and their guardians. The campaign partnered with schools and children and asked them to follow the Sanskarshala pages every day. Through this, *Dainik Jagran* played the role of a teacher of moral values, and the Sanskarshala initiative became a platform for preparing a future full of aware, responsible, and confident young citizens.

Here's a case that demonstrates this. This case was adjudged "Best in South Asia" at the INMA (International Newsmedia Association) Global Media Awards in 2020.

The Generation That Could Save Us

'The eyes of all future generations are upon you. ... Right here, right now is where we draw the line' – thundered Greta Thunberg.

This is the generation that can look at the world and its problems and believe they can solve them. This is the generation that doesn't freeze in the face of overwhelming stress. No, our children are not in a crisis – maybe, this could be the generation that saves us.

Leading Them on Their Path

Be it a 13-year-old Canadian water activist Autumn Peltier, who told the UN it was time to 'warrior up'; or a 17-year-old Malala Yousafzai, who secured education for girls in Pakistan; or a 7-year-old Bana Alabed, whose document drew world attention to the plight of children stuck in the middle of conflict; or a 13-year-old Alexandria Villasenor, a climate change activist – all these children remind us that our next generation is more self-aware, compassionate, and committed. This might just be our best hope for the world of the future.

The current generation of children is upfront about their responses to an adult world they reject. They are charting their own course to make sense of the world around them. They are inventing their systems of codes, values, and mores in the process.

It was high time that media reminded young people about what they could achieve, about what they should care about, what change they could bring about, and just make them realize their incredible power. It was time *Dainik Jagran* played its role in inspiring the next generation of leaders, activists, and citizens who could create a positive emotional footprint, and improve quality of life for all.

Hierocles, the ancient philosopher, said we're surrounded by concentric circles. The innermost circle of concern surrounds our own self, followed by family, neighbours, fellow city-dwellers, countrymen and, finally, the human race. Moral progress meant moving members of outer circles to the inner ones.

This was Sanskarshala – a campaign to inspire children to expand their circle of concern, to view the world from a new perspective and realize their incredible power in creating a better world. Figure 14.3 showcases the programme's launch.

Objectives

- Create newspaper content that strikes conversations with children and stirs a debate on modern value systems
- Highlight 'intrinsic' values which underpin increased social and environmental concern, and motivate children to act in line with this concern
- Position *Dainik Jagran* as a newspaper that steers public towards socially desirable goals

FIGURE 14.3 Sanskarshala campaign, *Dainik Jagran*.

Source: Jagran Prakashan Ltd

Execution

It was a multi-sensorial content campaign that blends into the daily lives of millions of children. Therefore, "Total Immersion" was what we aimed at through the following:

- *Read*: There were 866 stories of value-based editorial content were printed on specific topics like gender equality, respecting diversity, and selflessness.
- *Watch*: Nine animation films conveyed the story to children. Special screenings in schools were done for 4,00,000 children.
- *Listen*: All stories were converted into audio stories.
- *Debate*: A total of 812 students participated in 390 debates in 2 weeks across 30 cities – arguably the largest debate ever held in the country on moral dilemmas.
- *Live*: A total of 912 school morning assemblies were converted to Sanskarshala assemblies (covering 8,35,395 students), where the newspaper stories were read and children enacted the stories.
- *Institutionalize*: Several schools incorporated Sanskarshala content into their curriculum. The stories became comprehension passages in language classes – newspaper content made it to the class notebooks of children.
- *Inspire*: A total of 157 children took up peer-to-peer education projects and relayed the Sanskarshala content to 15,508 underprivileged children.
- *Expertise*: A total of 99,365 children attended 254 workshops and webinars conducted by experts.
- *Curate*: A comic book was created with the stories, and 20,000 copies were placed in 927 school libraries, potentially reaching 1.1 million children.
- *Partner*: School principals brainstormed to finalize Sanskarshala content.

Campaign in Numbers

- A total of 1.4 million children participated directly
- Campaign reached 70 million readers of *Dainik Jagran*.
- Digital reach of 5.8 million
- Animation films shared in 914 hyper-local WhatsApp groups of students, parents, and teachers, potentially triggering a massive chain of views.

Impact on Brand

- *Strong brand parameters:* Dainik Jagran had the highest brand awareness and satisfaction. It was the most preferred and recommended brand.
- *Highest on intention to read*: outscoring competition by 1.48x.
- *Brand imagery*: The brand scored the highest on parameters of youthfulness, trust, innovativeness, seriousness, helping people become better citizens, and the newspaper readers looked forward to.

CASE STUDY 8:   USING A NEWSPAPER TO SPREAD THE MESSAGE OF WATER CONSERVATION

It is estimated that 40% of India's population won't have access to drinking water by 2030. Water stress is more than a hydrological issue, as usage is shaped by human behaviour. It was imperative that citizens took responsibility.

It's customary in Indian culture to serve a glass of water to guests. This campaign attempted to change this practice by advocating serving a 'Half Glass of Water'. Along with several other measures, *Dainik Jagran* enlisted the support of 1757 restaurants to serve only half glasses to all guests. The campaign saved 15 million litres of water in 56 days, with a potential to save about 100 million litres annually. This is a perfect example of how a newspaper could leverage its strength and activate the community to bring about change.

Dainik Jagran - A Glass Half Full

Countdown to Day Zero

India is undergoing the worst water crisis in its history, announced Niti Ayog, a government thinktank:

- It is estimated that 600 million Indians face 'high to extreme water stress'.
- It is also estimated that 200,000 die each year because they can't get clean water.
- By 2030, water availability will be half of what India needs.
- The thinktank predicted that up to 6% of GDP could be lost to extreme water scarcity.
- In India, 21 major cities could exhaust their groundwater supplies within two years affecting 100 million people. Several smaller cities are teetering on the edge.
- By 2030, 40% of the population will have no access to drinking water.

Put another way, millions of Indians could be too thirsty, or sickened by contaminated water, to study, work, or live.

In part, the problem is population: India has about 17% of the world's people but just 4% of the world's freshwater resources. Analysts also blame poor management by government, corruption, and endemic pollution of existing water sources, as well as a reliance on inefficient crops and farming methods.

Water Matters

Water stress is more than just a hydrological issue, as usage is shaped by human behaviour. While policy took its own course, it was imperative that citizens too played their part. *Dainik Jagran* stepped in to find solutions leveraging the power of community. We stepped out with the belief that water problems won't go away by themselves; rather, they'll worsen, unless communities intervene. Saving water is a global project, and all Indians should join – every effort will count.

Water specialists stress on three "Rs": Reduce, Reuse and Recycle. Given the current groundwater situation and the lopsided demand-supply equation, our solution relied on the 1st R – Reduce. It was imperative to shift the narrative to water conservation.

Campaign idea: Serve just half a glass water to guests at homes and hotels instead of the customary full glass of water.

Objectives

- Mobilize community to conserve water
- Create next-generation change leaders
- Demonstrate that *Dainik Jagran* stands for community

Bringing the Campaign Alive

It is customary in Indian culture to serve a glass of water to guests. *Dainik Jagran*'s campaign attempted to bring about a change in this practice. The campaign's message was "Use Half Glass of Water"

Reaching 35 million people through water patrons: The campaign partnered 'Hotel and Restaurant Association of Northern India' and asked 1757 hotels and restaurants to serve half a glass of water to all guests.

Appointed 2,92,042 student water heroes: They spread awareness in their localities to spread the word on serving half a glass of water to guests.

Water engineers to the rescue: A total of 1654 citizens called a toll-free number and reported problems of leaky taps or pipelines, and the engineers would fix the leaks.

Mainstreaming the issue: A total of 132 pages of newspaper content set the agenda for water conservation.

Cause Promotion

- The water conservation pledge was taken by 87,272 people.
- There were 40 street theatres talking to 4560 people.
- There were 2063 water conservation workshops attended by 493,934 people.
- We created an advertising campaign to promote the cause.

- Door-to-door rallies, signature campaigns, painting competitions, and club meetings connected 32,535 people.

The Campaign in Numbers

During the 56-day campaign, we saved 14.8 million litres of water. Conservatively, the annual economic impact of this could be over Rs 900 million, saving almost 100 million litres.

- A total of 1757 restaurants saved 3.5 million litres water during the campaign (23 million litres annually).
- Water Heroes saved about 11.3 million litres during the campaign (73.6 million litres annually).
- Complaints addressed by Water Engineers, saving 71 million litres/day!
- We connected with 36.2 million people directly through the campaign.
- Campaign message reached out to the 70 million readers of *Dainik Jagran*.

Impact on Brand

As per research, *Dainik Jagran* had:

- Highest Top of Mind awareness
- Highest scores on the following brand image parameters:

    - This brand is the market leader
    - This newspaper is innovative
    - This newspaper makes me a better citizen
    - This newspaper comes up with relevant campaigns
    - I participate in the various activities conducted by this newspaper

Source: Brand Study, December 2019

CASE STUDY 9:   B2C: CREATING A BRAND IP FOR A MEDIA BRAND

In a cluttered newspaper market, *Dainik Jagran* created a film festival to speak to new audiences and present a different side of theirs to the world. The festival (the logo of which is shown in Figure 14.4) was positioned as 'Good cinema belongs to everyone'.

FIGURE 14.4 Jagran Film Festival campaign.

Source: Jagran Prakashan Ltd.

This integrated marketing campaign reached 300 million people through a mix of digital media and conventional media, and created native content in the newspaper. The event was packaged and promoted as a huge magnet that it earned media worth Rs 250 million through its sheer size, scale, and uniqueness. This is a great example of how newspaper media could create an event IP that generated content and helped build brand salience in a cluttered media market.

Jagran Film Festival

Dainik Jagran created a film festival to speak to new audiences and present a different side of its brand to the world. A traveling film festival running across 18 cities was an unheard-of event in India. They re-invented the film festival model to appeal to markets that otherwise weren't the usual choices for film festivals. The festival's positioning too resonated with the brand ethos of *Dainik Jagran*, the largest newspaper in India with 70 million readers. In a cluttered newspaper market, they had to be decisively different and had to operate at a scale that befitted their stature as the industry leader.

Campaign objectives:

- Reinvent the way conventional film festivals are organized
- Increase brand awareness
- Create a buzz around the festival

It was a multi-layered marketing campaign that used a mix of digital media along with innovative use of conventional media and created native content within the newspaper.

Brand building: The festival was positioned as "Good Cinema" for everyone.

Size and scale: The festival hired 76 screens across 18 cities and organized 444 cinema screenings in a span of 3 months.

Worldwide interest: The festival received 4800 film entries from 37 countries, 36 languages. A preview panel of curators sat through and sifted from this gigantic list to curate the content for the festival.

Multiple side events: Through the festival, 144 events were organized including masterclasses, panel discussions, in-conversations with stars, Q&A sessions, and a summit on 'The Future of Cinema'.

Marketing associations: The festival collaborated with eight brands/platforms to enhance its reach.

Unique newspaper content: The newspaper editorial celebrated a collective social art and created debates, conversations, and an atmosphere.

Results

Newspaper as the Agent of Culture

The campaign helped create over 100 full pages of newspaper content that initiated conversations around contemporary issues in society and how cinema shapes culture.

Impact-Driven Media Strategy Reaching 300 Million

The campaign was promoted through releasing 200 ads in newspapers, 4133 radio spots, 3500 Instagram stories and Facebook posts, 572 TV spots, and 105 cinema ads, along with 350 billboards, and it used Influencer marketing channels.

Through the campaign, 180 short videos were created and boosted through 200 hyperlocal WhatsApp groups.

- The campaign reached 70 million readers of *Dainik Jagran*.
- An OOH campaign was mounted with over 350 sites.
- The digital reach of the festival was 150 million on external platforms.
- Social media reach through JFF platform was 105 million.
- Video views of the festival touched 65 million.
- A digital engagement totalled 1 million.
- The campaign engaged 50 influencers to spread the word on the festival through their channels.
- The campaign reached 20 million through radio.

Earned Media Worth Rs 250 Million

- A total of 18 TV channels aired content about the festival.
- A total of 746 digital media platforms wrote about the festival, generating 160 million impressions.
- A total of 71 publications wrote about the festival.
- Celebrities attending the festival tweeted.

High Points

- On-ground we created a festival environment.
- An audience footfall of 55,000 attended the festival.
- The festival premiered 37 films.
- The film industry joined in, as 125 film personalities participated in the festival.
- Three hundred international delegates attended the festival.

Revenue Generated

- The campaign generated a revenue through sponsorships and ticket sales.

Impact on Brand

Highest on awareness: Dainik Jagran had the highest Top of Mind awareness with 50.9%. The next brand had a TOM of 23.3%. *Dainik Jagran* also ranked highest on satisfaction, preference, intention to read, and recommend.

Brand imagery: Dainik Jagran scored the highest on key brand imagery parameters:

- "This newspaper is the market leader"
- "This newspaper is innovative"
- " I look forward to getting this newspaper"

CASE STUDY 10:   CREATING VALUE FOR A BRAND BY LEVERAGING PRINT + DIGITAL PLATFORMS

This is an interesting case where a news media brand created a platform that leveraged both its online and offline assets to create value. The programme generated unique content that resonated with its readers across both online and offline platforms and resulted in appreciable gains in terms of audience numbers.

My City My Pride

My City My Pride was a branding campaign with a sole purpose to increase brand awareness, recall, and engagement. Jagran.com designed and launched My City My Pride with the following objectives:

- Increase user traffic on the site by at least 20% from 10 cities in the core Hindi heartland.
- Build online communities for Jagran.com on social media platforms (Facebook), which helps the brand to have user communities from its core markets.
- Increase the engagement (page views) on the site by at least 10% from the 10 targeted cities in the core Hindi Heartland.
- To reach 100 million impression for the overall campaign over a 3-month period.
- At least 15,000 in registrations for the campaign.

Execution

- A dedicated microsite was launched for the campaign.
- City-based issues were highlighted on the site.
- Videos related to round-table conferences, which were attended by local administrators, influencers, decision makers, and citizen forums, were posted on a microsite.
- The results of the ratings were published and promoted along with a City Liveability Report, which published city ratings around the five pillars.
- Articles and advertisements of the campaign were carried in *Dainik Jagran*.
- Over 700 stories were published on the microsite.
- The campaign was promoted on outdoor and radio.
- Influencers and administrators were involved in the campaign.
- Ten public forums were conducted.
- Fans participated in the campaign on social media.
- Ninety roundtable conferences were organized to discuss city issues.

Results

- 25% growth in Jagran.com users
- 3–4% overall growth in user for overall news and information category
- 18,237 total registration

CASE STUDY 11: SACH KE SAATHI - COUNTERING FAKE NEWS ONLINE

In an era of multiplicity of information sources leading to misinformation and fake news, the normal tendency for people is to look for anchors of trust. In the online world, under the garb of personalization, echo chambers are being created, and opinions are being polarized. As a response to this issue, a fact-checking site was launched by Jagran New Media which not only did fact checking, but also conducted several workshops to create a pool of fact-checking champions.

Vishvas News is a fact-checking initiative of Jagran New Media and is certified by the International Fact Checking Network. In less than two years of its launch, Team Vishvas News has published 2000+ fact-checked articles in 11 languages (Hindi, English, Urdu, Punjabi, Assamese, Tamil, Telugu, Malayalam, Marathi, Gujarati, and Odia) on its website. Team Vishvas News has done some extraordinary work and also was featured in different Indian and International publications as well.

COVID-19 articles by Vishvas News have also been featured in the list of Alliance Database on Poynter website which unites more than 100 fact-checkers in 45 countries and includes articles published in at least 15 languages.

Apart from getting featured in different news reports in Indian media, Vishvas News is also associated with IFCN to manage its Fact Check bot in the Hindi language and as a third-party fact-check partner of Facebook in India in four languages – Hindi, Urdu, Punjabi, and Assamese. It is a part of the world's top-rated fact-checkers on the WhatsApp FAQ page to help users to counter COVID-related and other misinformation and is in process to launch its own Fact Check bot in association with WhatsApp and Meedan (third-party firm). Vishvas News is also associated with World Health Organization (WHO) and Press Information Bureau (PIB) through a WhatsApp group to counter COVID-related misinformation.

To take the idea forward, a programme called 'Sach Ke Saathi' was launched. Under this, fact-check training sessions were organized to directly reach out to people by creating a pool of Super Champions and Champions.

CASE STUDY 12: THOUGHT LEADERSHIP BY A DIGITAL NEWS BRAND

The pandemic had devastating consequences on every aspect of our existence. However, hope, tenacity, and optimism were the key values that helped us tide over this. Rebuilding our lives post pandemic was a key task. This campaign was mounted by Jagran.com to celebrate the stories of resilience in India. Very topical and relevant, the series not just inspired citizens to rise and rebuild, but it also generated unique content for the site, leading to great audience engagement.

Rising above the Pandemic by Jagran New Media

Overview

A marquee thought leadership initiative of Jagran New Media and Facebook, the Rising India campaign (https://www.jagran.com/search/jeetegabharat; its logo appears in Figure 14.5) aims at throwing light over the innovative practices happening on the ground from all across the country and pertaining

FIGURE 14.5 Rising India campaign.

Source: Jagran Prakashan Ltd.

to all walks of life so that people at large could effectively cope up with the challenges thrown upon by the COVID-19 pandemic. The series of special stories underscores how people at every possible level, from rural hinterland to the shining metros of this fast-growing country, are trying to bring positive changes to the society and people who need them. The series is also a chronicle of India's rise as a prosperous country, as it also reflects how far we have moved ahead in terms of growth, prosperity, cohesion, and ultimately as a nation. The series includes success stories of all sorts, including successful developmental initiatives of people who hardly have learnt any management lesson to those whose innovative social and scientific ways and means helped India win the war against the vicious cycle of the pandemic that engulfed almost the entire country and rattled all like anything. The story series does suggest how rich in ideas the rural people can be when it comes to rescuing people in trouble, bringing smiles on the faces of the sufferers and thinking out of the box when needs strike the door. This series is a unique combination of ideas of different shades and hues.

Results

The Rising India campaign brought expected results, inspiring a lot of people to strive for positive changes, especially in the wake of the COVID pandemic, which halted life like never before in the history of humankind. The series brought good works into the light, specifically the unsung heroes who selflessly and tirelessly work for the betterment of the society. The positive and constructive changes brought before the world, through stories in dozens, inspired millions of people, who appreciated the campaign through messages, mails, and letters. Readers across the generations liked the campaign as it ignited their passion to do something good for the society they belong to. When people were reeling under severe distress because of the corona pandemic, this series of highly inspiring stories gave them much-needed hope and respite that there are also a lot of people who think selflessly and yearn to do something for society. This campaign also nourished the long-cherished Indian ethos of community welfare, bringing people together to work for a common cause. Countless stories of people serving others when in need, rejuvenated the fast declining humanitarian value system.

The first phase of the campaign started in May 2020, with 2,87,377 impressions and 8670 engagement on Twitter and a Facebook reach of 29,70,055, while the second part of the campaign which started in December, got 1,02,272 impressions and 4452 engagement on Twitter and a Facebook reach of 56,64,103 and engagement of 71,594.

CASE STUDY 13: CREATING A SOLUTION FOR A BRAND THROUGH RADIO

This is a case about how Radio City created a solution for a brand and connected it with a very contemporary local issue of pollution faced in North India every year post Diwali. The campaign was called 'Shield Your Lungs'.

Objective

While most people are aware about the rising pollution in Delhi City every year during Diwali, least did they know how to protect themselves from its harmful effects. With the campaign Dettol Siti Shield #Shieldyourlungs, the aim was to ride on (a) the Diwali festival and (b) the Smog Event that became the prime talk of the town during the season, hence sensitizing the people and making them ready to combat the smog season with Dettol Siti Shield that protects them from dangerous smog particles.

Execution

- Radio city along with Dettol City Shield associated with two more eminent radio stations to create an awareness campaign that was just not educative but interactive too. The campaign ensured that every person in the city was 'Smog Ready'.
- Major radio disruption with radio-jocks across three prominent radio stations hearing weird noises of coughing and sneezing across their shows for one whole day. Post creating fear, RJs from all the three stations came together to find out the reason of these sounds and revealed how smog in Delhi led the city's health to deteriorate; these sounds were actually a depiction of the same.
- This was followed by exclusive Dettol Siti Shield mask unboxing and sharing USPs of the product to make them smog ready. The activity culminated with an on-ground activity where RJs spread awareness about smog and breathing hazards and, through interesting fun-filled activities, educated people about Dettol Siti Shield's offering and advantage.

Results

The disruptions and communication throughout the campaign were noticed by many. The client was extremely happy as many people learnt the adverse effects of smog and understood the effectiveness of the Dettol Siti Shield mask. It resulted in an appreciable sales growth of Dettol Siti Shield post the campaign time.

CASE STUDY 14: B2C CAMPAIGN DEMONSTRATING THE POWER OF RADIO

This is a brilliant and powerful case of how Radio City demonstrated the power of radio. It describes a campaign that went full tilt in helping find a missing boy within hours of reporting.

Concept

There are some things that you can plan and some you can't.

On a usual Saturday afternoon RJ Yuvi received an unusual call. A howling Arun Tyagi pleaded him to help find his 13-year-old son Yuvraj, who went missing two days earlier from Agra. Yuvraj was last spotted at a metro station as per the CCTV footage (Faridabad), where a hassled schoolboy (possibly Yuvraj) was trying to cross the metro line by foot. Unlike any other radio campaign, planning this one was not possible. RJ Yuvi, without losing on time, put the fader up for a live public service announcement (PSA). The only plan of action was to get the boy back ASAP.

Execution

On August 26, 2017, RJ Yuvi was doing his show (City Da Gabru) and during a caller interaction received a call from a father who was trying to find his son in Delhi.

- On Air:

  - RJ Yuvi did live PSAs throughout the day.
  - Listeners joined in to support from all corners of the city.
  - Delhi police shared last spotted report on air.
  - The father's plea was aired and details about the boys shared again and again.

- Digital

  - Post Yuvraj's reunion with his family, celebs like Daler Mehndi, Sangram Singh, Harbajan Singh, Kuwar Virk retweeted the Radio City post congratulating the Tyagi family.

CASE STUDY 15: CREATING IMPACT THROUGH RADIO

Here's another example of how Radio City created a highly localized campaign and used its RJs to spread the message of good health at a ground level. It's a great example of community connect by a radio station.

Dhara-Zara Sa Badlav

Objective
Dhara wanted to spread the message that a little change can bring contentment in our lives and in the lives of others. While Dhara wanted to promote health with the use of the right oil in the right way, we thought of taking forward Dhara's 'Zara Sa Badlav' initiative of good food to people who do not get to eat it through a most innovative campaign.

Execution
The campaign was executed in the scorching heat of June where Dhara cooking oil along with Radio City installed 4 Dhara Community Fridge, across various Resident Welfare Associations (RWAs) of the city. The societies readily took care of the mechanism, provided electricity, and happily contributed food during the campaign period.

Results
- By the end of the campaign, 10 more Community Fridges were adopted by RWAs and commercial places in Delhi NCR after this campaign. They pledged to keep food in them all year round and feed the needy.
- The MLA for the Alaknanda area, Mr Saurabh, came to visit the Dhara Community Fridge and appreciated the simplicity of the idea and the huge impact it is bringing in the society.
- Every day, hundreds of people were fed through these Dhara Community Fridges as many people changed their habit and started feeding people around.

Chapter Summary

The media industry in India is rapidly undergoing a transformation with digital acquiring critical mass. Several changes are happening simultaneously in the media environment, including the way people consume media, the way advertisers look at media, how media planners and buyers think about media, and how media research companies look at measuring media. It's in these contexts that media marketing needs to be understood.

With mass individualized media consumption happening simultaneously across multiple media, media planning will have to struggle with the challenges of gaining audience attention. In an attention-deficit era, context will become the sweet spot for media planning – to draw attention in the right context. So media solutions will move towards finding out opportunities to layer a combination of contextual and behavioural solutions to achieve maximum effect. As a result, media buying will have to move out of the transactional mode and into the mode of identifying opportunities for grabbing audience attention in the media environment. The big challenge, however, is for media research to emerge out of their silos and create metrics for 'decision making' rather than just 'trading'. The economics of yesterday were created for measuring eyeballs, reach, and awareness; today, marketers have moved towards targeting multiple niches and in a dialogue mode with consumers.

The media business model has been disrupted across every pillar – content creation, content distribution, and the resulting audience monetization. Instead, the media industry is realigning itself from the verticalized segmentation of the industry – which comprised distinct segments such as TV, print, radio, digital, OOH, and cinema – to a new segment-agnostic horizontal model based on multi-platform aggregation, distribution, and consumption with ability to collect and analyse end-customer data. In this model, everyone cooperates with everyone, and everyone competes with everyone for audiences and revenues.

As media organizations move towards a segment-agnostic model, it is important that brand consistency is maintained. A siloed approach to building media brands wouldn't work. The audience is consuming our content seamlessly across platforms and devices, and it is imperative that we also create a seamless brand experience for the consumers. In this context, key challenges for media brands are:

- How to manage brand consistency when the carrier remains constant but the content changes on an everyday basis.
- Rising clutter within media and fragmentation of audiences
- Erasing of boundaries, as in the new scheme of things, everyone competes with everyone

Key Assets of a Media Brand

- *Content creation skill.* This is a key asset which could be leveraged to appeal to a large audience base.
- *Stars of the content.* These are content icons which are a pull factor to draw in audiences.
- *Our network and its offline advantages.* This offline network helps media brands keep a close ear to the ground and enables them to customize content for local markets.

- *Our brand credibility as the messenger.*
- *Our distribution capability.* Both on-ground and online.
- *Our audiences, their size, and their profile.* These are two very important determinants in monetizing an audience base.
- *The advertising environment we create.*
- *Innovation opportunities.*
- *The reach we provide.*
- *The markets we cover.*

Audience for a Media Brand

A media brand has two kinds of audience:

- *B2C*: The person who consumes the content. The key objectives behind talking to this audience are:
  - To acquire new readers or listeners or viewers
  - To engage with them
  - To get them to spend more time with the media brand
  - To ensure that they consume the media brand frequently

- *B2B*: The advertisers (it could be brand managers, product managers, marketing managers, or CEOs), media planners, and media buyers. The key objectives behind talking to this audience are:
  - To communicate our strength in terms of audience numbers and profile of audience
  - To communicate the unique advantage that the brand has in terms of content creation
  - To communicate the network strength of the media brand
  - To communicate the innovation possibilities that one could explore with the media brand
  - To communicate consumer and market insights
  - To demonstrate geographical coverage
  - To demonstrate relative competitive positioning
  - To communicate special B2C consumer connect initiatives
  - To communicate content highlights
  - To announce sponsorship opportunities for large format properties/ IPs

Further Reading

https://www.afaqs.com/media-briefs/54924_barfi-salutes-aaj-tak
https://bestmediainfo.com/2020/10/aaj-tak-dials-into-bihar-elections-with-the-launch-of-hello-kaun-song/

https://www.campaignindia.in/video/aaj-tak-boards-chennai-express-with-shah-rukh-khan/419215

https://www.exchange4media.com/industry-briefing-news/aaj-tak-takes-the-safai-ki-dhun-to-the-kumbh-mela-61852.html

https://www.exchange4media.com/marketing-news/aaj-tak-celebrates-20-years-of-sabse-tez-style-with-new-campaign-111202.html

https://www.npr.org/2019/09/23/763452863/transcript-greta-thunbergs-speech-at-the-u-n-climate-action-summit

"The Era of Consumer A.R.T.", India's Media & Entertainment sector, EY & FICCI, March 2020.

15

ADVERTISING BUDGET SETTING

The budget setting decision is fairly complex, as there is no one right method, so to say. One is never certain that the budget that you have arrived at is 100% right. It is just like any other investment decision – and it is important to put in the same rigour as one would put for all other investment decisions. While the effects of advertising are difficult to measure, prudence tells us that there are various impacts of advertising – some are long term in nature while others are short term. Apart from just impacting the end consumer, it also galvanizes the trade and helps improve efficiencies in other areas of marketing. The long-term effects of advertising work by maintaining brand imagery, keep the brand in the frame of mind of consumers, lend credibility to the brand, and give consumers a sense of trust. The short-term impacts work by bringing the brand forward in the consideration set, serve as reminders at the time of purchases, create an acceptability about price changes, and communicate specific brand promotions.

The starting point for budget setting comes from the brand objectives. This could be understanding in terms of volume or market share targets for the brand, the degree of competitiveness in the category, pricing, distribution, and eventually what the brand needs from advertising. At different lifecycles of the brand, the requirements from advertising differ. The early part of the lifecycle focuses more on generating awareness, while the latter part is more about maintenance and overall salience. The important thing is to keep in mind the long term and short term marketing objectives of the brand. The second important aspect is the marketing budget. How much money has been allocated for marketing itself is a good starting point. At this stage people do comparisons like Advertising to Sales ratios over the last couple of years, compare it with other brands in the category, and try to make sense of

DOI: 10.4324/9781032724539-15

some numbers or a range in which the budget could be fixed. Here one does market share and share of voice (SOV) comparisons vs movement on awareness scores or sales movements, etc., and of course one looks at the absolute level of spend with comparison to other competing brands in the category. Another thing that goes on at a parallel level while taking decisions is the expected outcome from advertising, be it in terms of sales or awareness. For this one needs to do a bit of a historical analysis of advertising Input and the resultant impact output to establish some sort of a trend. This is done for your own brand, and one looks at examples of other successful brands within the category or in similar categories. Then of course, the process is also a bit iterative. It is important to have an understanding of media costs. A critical input is about ascertaining the level of advertising exposure that can be bought at what cost. Whether this is enough for the brand is another area that needs attention. Whether this level of media exposure is enough to withstand competitive clutter, and whether it rises above the basic threshold level of advertising, etc., are some of the iterations that need to be done while freezing the final budget.

There are several ways to arrive at a budget. While there is no one golden rule, different situations demand different approaches. A few have a wide acceptability, but that doesn't undermine the value of other approaches. Some require a lot of data analysis to arrive at budgets, while some operate almost as simple thumb rules.

Different Methods of Setting Budgets

Advertising to Sales (A:S)

This is one of the most common and popular methods of deciding advertising budgets. Put simply, the advertising budget is arrived at as a percentage of the sales turnover expected for the year. This is a fairly easy method to use once the percentage has been determined. At the same time, it's fairly easy to defend – you are matching the A:S ratios of competition. Therefore, by default, brands with higher volumes will get higher budgets as compared to smaller brands. However, the most important point is arriving at the percentage of sales that needs to be set aside for advertising. Chances are that a new brand with a low sales target actually might need a much higher budget than the one that is arrived by using the A:S ratio followed by the category. The method is not useful in these cases. At the same time, the method tends to ignore advertising effects on sales. Here, sales will determine advertising and not the other way round. One might tend to overspend using this method, or one might miss out on opportunities, or one might just overlook the real needs of the brand. At times, it might give an unrealistically low budget.

There are times when during a sales decline, the brand might need a higher level of advertising – under this method, declining sales comes with declining advertising budgets, thus aggravating the problem further. Another aspect that the method would not take care of is that it completely ignores product margins. Even in the same category, different brands operate at different scales and have different business models and a very large player might operate on a very different level of margin as compared to a smaller player. Advertising gives a more efficient return on investment (ROI) where margins are high as compared to a brand with lower margins. The A:S method does not work effectively in such cases. Just as underspending is an issue, large brands tend to overspend under this method. A very large brand with a dominant market share in the category could do with a slightly lower level of advertising, but here, the A:S method might lead them to overspend.

Yet, in spite of all the shortcomings, this is a fairly popular method of budget setting used across the world. The starting point for this is to correctly estimate sales and advertising budgets of competing brands in the category over a period of time and this should give a range in which to operate. It is important that the estimates taken are fairly accurate or as close to reality as possible. A:S gives a certain comfort as one is benchmarked with what the other brands in the category are doing, and it helps in maintaining a certain kind of control on the advertising expense – and the accounting part of the business is content with an automatic cost control mechanism. Therefore, it is important to weigh the situation, understand brand needs and then apply judgment on whether A:S benchmark for other brands in the category will work for you or not.

Advertising to Margin (A:M)

Here, instead of the A:S approach of taking a certain percentage of sales as the advertising budget, one takes a certain percentage of the gross margin. Gross margin is defined as revenue less variable costs. Most of the issues that arise with A:S also arise with this method. However, this goes a little beyond – it allows brands to link advertising with the margin and therefore tends to work better as an overall control variable from a financial point of view. But the same issues of overspending or underspending, or ignoring brand requirements, or missing out on opportunities might arise here too. Again, the data collection here is that much more difficult. Even to get accurate data on sales is a problem – this method requires one to find out the variable costs as well. Given data accuracy, this method will work just as well as the A:S ratio method. However, because of the difficulties in accurately estimating revenues and variable costs of competing brands, this method is not very popular.

Per Unit Allowance

Under this method, the sales volume is estimated, and an amount is fixed per unit of sale for advertising. This seems like a very simple method, though the applicability of this, I suspect, would be rare. It's got the same problem as the previous two methods – how does one determine what is the right amount to be allocated per unit?

Other Allowances

Just like the per unit allowance, a fixed sum is allocated per unit. The unit could be defined as number of people in the demographically defined target group, or the number of retail outlets distributing the brand, or in other ways. This again is a relatively simple method, but the problems are similar to the ones we have previously discussed.

Inertia

If it ain't broke, don't fix it. If everything seems to be working fine, why mess with it? This is the philosophy behind this method. If last year's budget was okay, plan on similar lines again. This is a simple and a practical method. However, it ignores media inflation and changes in the media environment.

Media Inflation Multiplier

This method moves a step forward from the last method. Normally, it is used in conjunction with the Inertia method, except that this also takes care of media inflation. For instance, if a 1000 GRP/month plan last year cost us Rs 2 cr, what will it cost this year to get the same level of media exposure? It might work out to, say, 2.2 cr. This takes care of media inflation. Another way is to say, I maintained a 20% SOV in the category. This year too, we need to maintain the same SOV levels. One estimates the GRP levels of the category based on the previous few year's trends and arrives at a certain GRP level that might help maintain our SOV at 20%. The plan is costed out, and you arrive at a budget. This is a very common and a practical method, and it takes care of advertising effects given media inputs.

Competitive Considerations

This is another very common method of benchmarking budgets in media. One studies competitive spending patterns over a period of time and arrives at a trend. Based on this, one could determine whether one would want to match competition spend levels or alternately look at targeting an SOV which would match market share for the brand. This is a fairly easy and practical method of budget setting. It is completely focused on the level of competitive activity in the market. Easy to defend as the benchmarks are very clear.

Task/Objective Method

Here we begin with the advertising and marketing objectives and then lay down in specific measurable terms what it would take to achieve this task. It could mean laying down a Brand Top of Mind Awareness goal, or a specific percentage increase in sales, etc. Here advertising is seen as a critical input to help achieve a certain task, and money is put against specific measurable goals. This is then checked for affordability, and suitable modifications are made. This works in cases where the role of advertising is well defined. It is, however, important to ensure that the goals are something realistic that advertising could possibly achieve, and one must be able to establish the link between advertising and the goal specifically. Importantly, since this is working towards achieving a certain task, measurability is an important aspect that needs to be taken care of. One of the applications of this method could be along with the Effective Frequency method of media weight setting. For instance, let's say that to achieve a certain advertising task, it would take 60% reach at an Effective Frequency of 5+. This translates into, say, 1000 GRPs. The cost of buying 1000 GRPs is then the budget.

However, this media goal should be clearly aligned with the role that advertising will play in achieving the eventual task. Another application of this method could be in a situation where say the objective is to make 50% of the non-users aware of our brand. You also might know through some research that it takes Rs 1 cr to make 10% aware and Rs 2 cr to make 15% aware, and so on. But with what degree of confidence can one say this all the time? Yes, sometimes given one's experience you intuitively know that a certain kind of budget will result in a certain level of impact. But in general, one needs to put the task in perspective and see what it would take to change consumer behaviour, or perceptions. Research of course can play a very important role here. This is one of the methods that is used in conjunction with some of the other methods that we have discussed here. Advertisers usually begin by laying down certain objectives to be achieved by advertising, and the question that is asked is, what would it take to achieve these objectives? This normally sets the tone for all budget setting exercises.

Affordable

This is another simple way to arrive at a budget. How much can the brand really afford to spend on advertising basis the current financial position of the brand/company. This is simple and avoids risk, but at times can give unrealistically low budgets. At times this might throw up a budget that is very low, and it might be just too thinly spread or probably can buy just a few weeks of presence, or probably is enough just to cover a few markets. Here, one needs to get the market priorities right to be able to do justice to some part of the market. However, this comes from pure brand financials and gives a certain starting point for discussion. At least it gives a minimum level. From here, we layer this method with an advertising task or benchmark with competition, arrive at some sort of a realistic budget, and, hopefully with due adjustments in the marketing budget, one is able to arrive at a final budget for the brand.

Share of Voice–Share of Market

This is again a very simple method. We plot market shares against SOV levels of competing brands and see a pattern in that. Against this, we put our brand budgets and see where we stand. It helps us decide the brand budgets in a competitive framework. The problem again is in getting accurate estimates of competing market shares. However, with retail audit data available, one can make a fair comparison on this front. John Philip Jones speaks about under-spending/profit taking brands (those who have a share of voice lower or equal to their market share) and overspending/investment brands (those who have a share of voice higher than their market share) (Jones, 1990). Essentially, he's talking about ESOV (excess of SOV over market share). So usually, brands in the early stages of their lifecycle have a lower market share, and they punch above their weight in SOV terms to build salience and market share. At the same time, legacy brands with dominant market shares could afford to keep slightly lower SOVs as compared to their market shares.

Modelling

This is a very technical method of laying down budgets. Given the huge degree of complication involved, it requires a lot of relevant statistical experience to handle this. Under this method, one needs to gather data on sales, market shares, prices, distribution, advertising expenditures, packaging, positioning, product formulation changes, etc., for relevant competing brands in the category. Using this information, one or more mathematical equations are formed which fit the sales observations, given the data on advertising and other factors.

This process of modelling helps us think through assumptions and inputs and in understanding the interplay of various factors in the sales outcome. It helps us summarize important data which could be of use elsewhere in the marketing process. A what-if kind of analysis at least allows us to look at various possible scenarios, and to this if practical judgment is applied, one can get fairly good results from this process. At the same time, it is just a theory based on certain assumptions. The real world might be very different. What interplay of forces results in sales is something that we're trying to get at based on some assumptions. All that we observe is association and not causality with any definite degree of conviction. Normally, modelling is expected to give you directions for the short term. Long-term advertising effects are ignored. Given the fact that modelling relies on the assumed interplay of marketing forces, there is always this danger of using just the output of the model to work out a final decision on budget setting. At times, this might backfire, and it's absolutely critical to balance the assumptions and the final output of the model with a real-world reality check in terms of competitive benchmarking and some other methods of budget setting.

Experimenting

As the name suggests, this is about doing a small-scale experiment and then after understanding the results, implementing the same thought across a much larger area. It's a little bit like test marketing, where we isolate a certain market and give it concentrated inputs and closely study the impact on brand movement in terms of sales, perception, awareness, etc. Research, therefore, becomes a critical part of such experiments, as it would help in giving a fair assessment of the impact of the media inputs. The flip side is that experiments consume some amount of time and money. At the same time, they are just enough to help take short-term steps, as long-term effects of advertising do not show up in a short window of experimentation.

Another major problem with the method is that the market selected for experimentation should be completely media isolated to get a correct understanding of the situation. At the same time, sometimes competitive activity in the selected test market area can play havoc with the plans. We see very few instances of test marketing nowadays. Normally, at times people follow what is known as a 'phased roll-out plan' where the learnings from Phase 1 of brand/communication launch are taken into account while planning Phase 2, and so on.

Critical Inputs

The preceding section listed some methods of setting budgets in different kinds of situations. However, in each you would have noticed that there was nothing definitive about any of them. All of them involved a certain level of marketing judgement to arrive at the final budgets. The methods described are only starting points. Depending upon the people and the pressures involved in the budget setting process, budgets could be talked up or down. There are times when advertisers look at multiple methods to cross-check a certain hypothesis or use a combination of methods. There is this degree of 'considered judgement' used in arriving at the final budgets. The most common are the A:S ratios and competitive benchmarking. Affordability is also a major criterion – it's tough to think that decisions would be taken without looking at this factor. Modelling too is being used, but by a sophisticated few.

Greater complexity to the decision is added when one is dealing with umbrella branding advertisers, where there is a range of products under the same brand name. For instance, say a brand like Lux is operating in the popular soap, premium soap, shampoo, conditioner, face wash, and shower gel categories. All the brands ride on the name Lux. Should one treat them as different brands or as a single brand and how does one estimate the rub-off of one brand's advertising on the other brands? Here, strategic calls have to be taken based on management expectations from the individual brands and contributions, to finally arrive at some lead brand for advertising and also allocate a certain proportion to the product range.

Another factor that adds complexities is the launch of a new brand. What thumb rules should one follow? Should one necessarily benchmark within the category or look at what brands across other categories have done? Should you follow the targeted share of market and fix a SOV basis that, or look at the experimentation method?

There is no one ideal method to arrive at budgets. Different situations demand a different method of looking at decision making in this area. However, the critical inputs that go behind budget setting decisions are:

a. Estimating competitive spends and SOVs
b. Data on market shares and volume trends of competition
c. An understanding of the media environment and costs and inflation rates
d. Understanding of markets and their prioritization
e. Understanding the operating business model of the brand per se – this would be important to keep a reality check
f. Understanding the impacts and effects of advertising – long term and short term
g. Understanding of brand marketing objectives and eventual long-term brand objectives
h. Understanding of consumer buying behaviour patterns

All of these combined with experience are the ingredients that go behind arriving at the final budget.

While there are no ideal situations in this world, there are some indicative steps towards arriving at a final campaign evaluation:

a. Campaign plan – agreeing to the strategy for the campaign
b. Agree on metrics for evaluation – How does one intend to evaluate the campaign?

c. Campaign monitoring – continuous monitoring of sales, panel data, etc.
d. Post-campaign evaluation – an actual evaluation of campaign effects

Budgets are impacted by both internal priorities and external changes. Internal priorities include value of the brand in the portfolio, distribution strengths, margins, and so on. Then, there are external factors like competitive scenario, spends by competing brands, pricing movements, macro factors affecting demand, and so on. The decision on advertising budgets is based on a complex interplay of factors that one must consciously consider.

Figure 15.1 details the list of Top 50 advertisers in India as per the *Pitch Madison Advertising Report 2022*. According to this report, the top 50 advertisers account for about 38% of the total ad spend in India.

Chapter Summary

The budget setting decision is a fairly complex decision, as there is no one universally accepted right method to be used in all circumstances.

There are several ways to arrive at a budget. While there is no one golden rule, different situations demand different approaches. There are a few which have a wide acceptability, but that doesn't undermine the value of other approaches. Some require a lot of data analysis to arrive at budgets while some operate almost as simple thumb rules.

- *Advertising to Sales (A: S)*: This is one of the most common and popular methods of deciding advertising budgets. Put simply, the advertising budget is arrived at as a percentage of the sales turnover expected for the year.
- *Advertising to Margin (A:M)*: Here, instead of taking a certain percentage of sales as the advertising budget, one takes a certain percentage of the gross margin.
- *Per Unit Allowance*: Under this method, the sales volume is estimated, and an amount is fixed per unit of sale for advertising.
- *Other Allowances*: As with Per Unit Allowance, a fixed sum is allocated per unit.
- *Inertia*: This method is about going with the previous year's plan.
- *Media Inflation Multiplier*: Used in conjunction with the Inertia method, except that this also takes care of media inflation.
- *Competitive Considerations*: In this commonly used method, one benchmarks media spends with the competition.
- *Task/Objective Method*: Here we begin with the advertising and marketing objectives and then lay down in specific measurable terms what it would take to achieve this task.

Rank in 2021	Rank in 2020	Gain/Loss in Ranks	Advertisers	Range in Crs
1	1	0	Hindustan Unilever	3500 – 3700
2	3	1	Amazon Online India	2000 – 2200
3	14	11	Dream 11	1200 – 1400
4	2	-2	Reckitt	1100 – 1300
5	9	4	BYJU's	1100 – 1300
6	4	-2	Procter & Gamble	800 – 1000
7	5	-2	Reliance Industries	800 – 1000
8	26	18	Google	700 – 900
9	8	-1	Mondelez	700 – 900
10	6	-4	ITC	500 – 600
11	7	-4	Maruti Suzuki	500 – 600
12	18	6	Phone Pe	500 – 600
13	NA	New	Upstox	500 – 600
14	37	23	My 11 Circle	500 – 600
15	22	7	Life Insurance Corp Of India	450 – 550
16	15	-1	Coca Cola India Ltd	450 – 550
17	NA	New	CRED	450 – 550
18	30	12	L Oreal	400 – 500
19	10	-9	Godrej Consumer Products	400 – 500
20	12	-8	Colgate Palmolive India	400 – 500
21	11	-10	Hero Motocorp	400 – 500
22	24	2	Asian Paints	350 – 450
23	NA	New	Vimal Pan Masala	350 – 450
24	13	-11	Glaxo Smithkline	350 – 450
25	27	2	Facebook	350 – 450
26	19	-7	Samsung	350 – 450
27	28	1	Hyundai Motor	350 – 450
28	NA	New	Netmed	250 – 350
29	44	15	MPL (Gaming)	250 – 350
30	NA	New	Policybazaar	250 – 350
31	NA	New	Unacademy	250 – 350
32	NA	New	Whitehat Education	250 – 350
33	29	-4	Tata Motors	250 – 350
34	NA	New	Swiggy	250 – 350
35	NA	New	Netflix	250 – 350
36	NA	New	Kamala Pasand	250 – 350
37	43	6	Emami Limited	250 – 350
38	46	8	Apple Computer	250 – 350
39	NA	New	Skoda Auto	250 – 350
40	31	-9	Marico	250 – 350
41	21	-20	Pepsi	200 – 300
42	25	-17	GCMMF (Amul)	200 – 300
43	NA	New	Havells	200 – 300
44	17	-27	Nestle	200 – 300
45	23	-22	VI (Vodafone Idea)	200 – 300
46	36	-10	TVS Motors	200 – 300
47	34	-13	Honda Motorcycle	200 – 300
48	40	-8	AMFI	200 – 300
49	NA	New	Coin Switch Kuber	200 – 300
50	NA	New	Coin DCX	200 – 300

FIGURE 15.1   Top 50 spenders in India.

Source: Exchange4Media, *Pitch Madison Advertising Report 2022.*

- *Affordable*: How much can the brand really afford to spend on advertising basis the current financial position of the brand/company
- *Share of Voice–Share of Market*: In this method, market shares are plotted against SOV levels of competing brands. The trend from here is used to decide the brand budgets in a competitive framework.
- *Modelling*: Under this method, one plots data on sales, market shares, prices, distribution, advertising expenditures, packaging, positioning, product formulation changes, etc., for relevant competing brands in the category. Using this information, one or more mathematical equations are formed which fit the sales observations, and based on this, budget decisions are taken.

There is no one ideal method to arrive at budgets. Different situations demand a different method of looking at decision making in this area. However, the critical inputs that go behind budget setting decisions are:

a. Estimating competitive spends and SOVs
b. Data on market shares and volume trends of competition
c. Understanding of the media environment and costs and inflation rates
d. Understanding of markets and their prioritization
e. Understanding the operating business model of the brand per se
f. Understanding the long-term and short-term impacts and effects of advertising
g. Understanding of brand marketing objectives and eventual long-term brand objectives
h. Understanding of consumer buying behaviour patterns

All of these combined with experience are the ingredients that go behind arriving at the final budget.

Further Reading

Broadbent, Simon, *The Advertising Budget*, Lexington Books, 1988.
Exchange4Media, *Pitch Madison Advertising Report 2022*.
Jones, John Philip, "Ad Spending: Maintaining Market Share", *Harvard Business Review*, 1990.

16

MEDIA BRIEFING

This is the one document that sets the ball rolling in the media planning and buying process. It is the quality of the brief that determines the final outcome of the media strategy and plan. The more information one gets at the start, the better it is for the plan. Many times one tends to simplify the brief by giving just the budget and markets. If this is the only input, imagine what the output would be – pure Excel worksheets with many plan optimizations, and you choose one that's probably giving you the best CPRP or the highest reach, whatever the case might be. A media brief is the most important document that guides the planner and helps determine the course of direction for the media plan. A brief is not a 2-minute conversation on the phone, or an instruction to cost out a media plan, and it is certainly not a guessing game.

A media brief is a formal document, carefully prepared in conjunction with the communications brief. It provides all the information to ensure your consumers have the best opportunity to see your advertising. It's a starting point for dialogue, and it ensures we start with a quality benchmark.

Information That a Brief Should Have

While there is no formal structure, and briefing formats differ from agency to agency, largely they try to extract similar information. I will highlight some of the information that should be ideally in the brief and will also discuss the value of that information and its usage and impact in the planning/buying process. The following are a few top line information areas that should be part of a media brief.

DOI: 10.4324/9781032724539-16

Business and Marketing Objectives

This is virtually the foundation of the plan. It is absolutely critical for the planner to understand the objectives of the brand. With this piece of information, the media objective of the plan is also tuned towards helping achieve the final brand objective. In the absence of this, a media plan becomes just a costing exercise where one is evaluating different kinds of plans, optimizing and arriving at a couple of plans to choose from. If the objectives are clear, they set the tone for all decisions in the media planning process. One can understand that it's difficult to crux a 10-page-long marketing document to a few lines which clearly capture the essence of the marketing objective. But this is the most critical input required for a media plan. Often the outcome of the plan is determined by this one single factor. There are times when a marketing objective could be written in defined quantifiable terms such as increasing market share to a certain percentage, or about selling a certain volume of units of the brand, and so on. At the same time, non-quantifiable objectives could be set, and these could be things like to increase consumer base, to convert medium users to heavy users of the brand, to increase the morale of the sales force in the face of competitive launches, to upgrade image perception of the brand, and so on. Say the objective is to regain lost volumes and achieve last year's market share for a certain brand. In this case, one of the central objectives of the media planning process could possibly be to find out markets where volumes have dropped and market share setbacks have been suffered by the brand, and correspondingly map it with competitive activity across each market. Importantly, the focus would be to identify and prioritize markets most efficiently, set media tasks for each market, and then proceed with the plan. Here, the pivot of the plan will hinge on how the markets have been identified and prioritized and tasks defined for the brand in each market. Then the rigour is followed through in audience selection – is there a certain section of the brand's audience that has impacted the dropping volumes – and special effort is made to address this sub-section of the audience. From a timing point of view, a sales trend analysis could be done in each market to find out the dips in the curve and find out if there are specific times of the year when sales have tapered off and probably one might need to step up presence during these times given the category seasonality and buying habits of the audience. The same logic would go through to the media weight-setting process where one identifies market by market what kind of media weight input was given by us vs the competition, the markets higher on priority to get a differentially higher media weight, and so on. Therefore, each element of the media strategic planning process is being aligned to deliver the marketing objectives – be it audience selection and focus, market selection and prioritization, or timing and weight of advertising. And the key endeavour is to understand the drops in volume and market share specifically with respect to related media decisions, and to work specifically on them.

Then there are times when the objectives are absolutely flat. For instance, an objective could be to maintain broad national coverage and maintain saliency levels as usual. This is a very macro objective and will guide media thinking at an overall level. One might compromise on the odd geographical pocket here and there, but largely the goal is to maintain national presence. There's not much to guide the planner here. Therefore, the more vague the objective, the greater the chances of a media plan being turned into a macro costing and budgeting exercise.

This single factor literally decided which direction the media thinking has to take. Once done, the plan and buying will automatically flow from here.

Set Expectations

This is a reality check of sorts. It opens up a dialogue to discuss what's achievable and what's not. It helps put the task in perspective and gives an overall direction. It helps if the media planning team is in complete sync with the marketing team on the brand challenges and expectations out of this activity.

Set Measurable Deliverables

Are there any specific measurable deliverables for the brand? It's a bit like setting up media KPIs which give clarity on assessing whether the plan has delivered or not, and what are the learnings going forward. It could be specified in terms of sales outcome, a brand awareness outcome, or lead generation. At times, one even might be very specific in terms of media weights and scheduling weeks too at this stage.

Timing

When does the campaign need to be on? Are there specific points in time when seasonality effects take place and it's important for the brand to be active in media? What's the sales value of each week in the year, and how does one look at targeting the maximum number of weeks' activity for the brand? Answers to these questions will enable better scheduling decisions. It would also help to plan and identify appropriate media opportunities which could be leveraged for the brand.

Budget

This is an important input, as it has a bearing on the scale of the media plan and on the media buying process. As we have discussed in the chapter on advertising budget setting, it is important to understand not just the absolute budget, but also how the budget was arrived at.

Market Situation and Competitive Scenario

What's the marketing and the competitive brand scenario, what's the brand task, and what is media supposed to achieve? These are important questions to be answered in a media brief. They would provide inputs that would help benchmark the level of activity. As you would have seen, this input can help in arriving at a better media weighting decision.

Consumption Patterns

Are there any clues on consumer buying and consumption patterns? Is it possible to share any sales/research data which could be of help? This has implications on scheduling, media mix selection, programme/vehicle selection, what time of day, etc. Are there any clues which could help the campaign stand out?

Target Audience

Who's the target audience? Detailed demographic and psychographic information is key. Is there any market segmentation technique used by the brand? Are there any specific user groups that need to be specially targeted? The better the insights available on this front, the richer is the final plan. In fact if the brief could share highlights from any consumer research, it would give a lot of leeway to the planning team to understand the audience. In fact, the more detailed information available on this front, the better the plan would turn out to be. It would help planners identify the right media mix and genre mix and even help in creating innovative ideas to better communicate with the audience.

What's the Change Required?

This has a direct bearing on the media weight levels of the brand. This would in essence be a distillation of the brand's marketing objectives in one single phrase. It would give the planner a clear action point to derive media objectives, and align the entire strategy and plan with the brand's objective.

Branding/Communication Idea

This has importance to the extent that media can help the central communication idea come to life. This opens up doors to think innovative media solutions for the brand. It could help identify genres with the best fit, identifying the right editorial and contextual environments, and identify opportunities for content marketing.

Creative Formats/Campaign Type

These are some of the other mandatory information that needs to be part of the brief.

Markets

What are the key markets for the brand, and is there any prioritization in place from a marketing point of view? For each market, one also needs clarity on how the prioritization has been arrived at. This would help align the media targets based on respective market priorities, and accordingly allocate budgets.

Available Research

Is there any form of research that could be shared with the media team? It could be brand track research, or awareness tracking programme research, etc. A better understanding of the market situation through this will help in arriving at a better brand solution.

The preceding were some of the basic points in a media brief checklist. Other factors too could be considered across various types of categories. But the fundamental idea is to share information with the media planning team in such a manner that the goals of the marketing team and the media planning team are completely aligned. The more information that is shared, the better the media people will understand the brand, and hopefully the brand solutions that emerge from here.

It is easy to give a very straitjacketed brief which has the TG definition, markets, and budget and creative formats. But the real winners are those who leave latitude for creativity. An inspiring brief works like a catalyst and truly helps the media plan go beyond the mathematical deliverables of reach, frequency, and CPRP.

There are times when due to reasons of confidentiality, not too much information is shared with the agency partners. In such cases, while some mandatory information is critical to make a media plan, one needs to take the onus/initiative to understand the category/brand through information available in the public domain, competitive information, custom research, and so on.

Chapter Summary

A media brief is a formal document, carefully prepared in conjunction with the communications brief. It provides all the information to ensure your consumers have the best opportunity to see your advertising. It's a starting point for dialogue and it ensures we start with a quality benchmark.

Information that a brief should have:

- Business and marketing objectives
- Set expectations
- Set measurable deliverables
- Timing
- Budget
- Market situation and competitive scenario
- Consumption patterns
- Target audience
- The change that is required
- Branding/communication idea
- Creative formats/campaign type
- Markets
- Available research

The fundamental idea behind briefing is to share information with the media planning team such that the goals of the marketing team and the media planning team are completely aligned. An inspiring brief truly helps the media plan go beyond the mathematical deliverables of reach, frequency, and CPRP.

17

ORGANIZATIONAL STRUCTURES IN MEDIA

The Indian media industry boasts of several large players. There are media entities that span across media, and there are media entities that are present only across one or two types of media. The governing structures of some large organizations differ from that of some smaller organizations. At the same time, there are different structures that one sees in similar-sized large organizations. Before getting into the details of their structuring, here's a list of media types that we will discuss in this chapter:

- TV media organizations
- Print media organizations
- Internet media organizations
- Radio organizations
- Outdoor media organizations
- Media agency
- Digital agency

TV Media Organizations

a. General Entertainment Channel Organizational Structure
   A typical large general entertainment channel has the following major departments:

   - Business Leads
   - Sales
   - Admin
   - Finance

DOI: 10.4324/9781032724539-17

- Legal
- HR
- IT

Figure 17.1 gives and illustration of the super-structure at a typical general entertainment channel.

There are some large TV networks which are present across languages and different genres. In those cases, they could have language/genre cluster heads depending on the scale of operations.

Then there are sub-structures within each. The major divisions are those of the Business Heads and the Sales Head. The other divisions are usually centralized at the corporate level, with a few people at each of the branches.

The Business Head is responsible for content creation and marketing for the channel. He/she is supported by sub-heads for each individual function, as shown in Figure 17.2.

Content Team: Responsible for creating/sourcing content. There are three teams under the Content Head, each responsible for fiction, non-fiction, and digital.

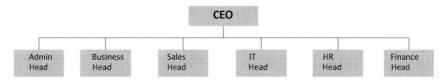

FIGURE 17.1   Macro organizational structure of a GEC.

Source: Created by the author.

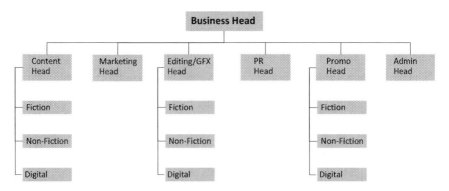

FIGURE 17.2   Business organizational structure of a GEC.

Source: Created by the author.

Marketing Team: Responsible for channel marketing. This includes above-the-line and below-the-line activities, content promotions, marketing tie-ups/associations, and publicity.

Editing/GFX Team: As the name suggests, this team is responsible for editing the content, creating graphics, and adding the channel identity to the content created.

Promo Team: This team is responsible for creating the promos for the content created. These programme promos are used to promote the programme across the channel during the ad breaks.

PR Team: This team is responsible for generating PR for the channel and the programmes.

Admin Team: This team takes care of general office administration across all the teams previously mentioned.

Since a large part of the revenues for a TV channel is generated through advertising, the Sales Team is a fairly large sub-team in a general entertainment channel. The key role of this team is to generate advertising revenue through the following:

- Selling advertising inventory.
- Selling programme sponsorships.
- Creating brand solutions. Here the team works closely with a brand to create a customized advertising solution.
- Brand associations.
- Prospecting for ad-funded programming (here they work in close coordination with the Content Team).

Figure 17.3 gives an example of how a typical sales department structure works for a general entertainment channel.

b. **News Channel Organizational Structure**

A typical large news channel network has the following major departments:

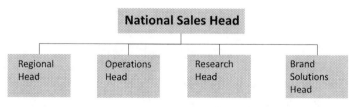

FIGURE 17.3   Sales structure of a GEC.

Source: Created by the author.

- Editorial
- Revenue
- Distribution
- Marketing
- Finance
- On-air promotion
- Technical/broadcast/Ops
- HR
- IT
- Digital – social, digital rev, digital editorial, SEO, syndication, marketing/acquisition

Figure 17.4 gives a view of the superstructure in a large TV news network.

There are sub-hierarchy structures under each of these departments. The size of teams usually would vary depending upon the scale of operations. The functions of the major departments are as follows.

Editorial

Editorial is responsible for creating the news bulletins and other news-related shows. This is a major department in a news channel and has a large sub-structure, as depicted in Figure 17.5.

Input

- Responsible for collecting news
- In touch with news agencies, reporters, news bureaus, and stringers
- Responsible for programme conceptualization and provides story ideas to the output team which produces the programme
- Collects viewer feedback and coordinates guests for live talks/debates on the channel

Assignment

- Works in close coordination with the Input Team.
- Responsible for execution of the Input Team's idea, and therefore largely takes care of technical execution of programmes

FIGURE 17.4 Superstructure of a news channel.

Source: Created by the author.

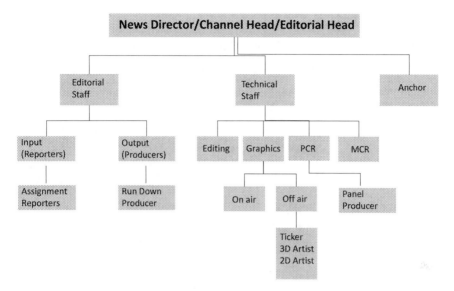

FIGURE 17.5 Editorial structure of a news channel.

Source: Created by the author.

Output

- Usually one of the largest teams within the Editorial Department
- Creates news packages based on the information from the Input Team
- Rewrites information from the Input Team

PCR (Production Control Room)

- Responsible for composing the final programme to go on air

MCR (Master Control Room)

- The technical hub for the channel, and the final point before the image, sound, and live action is transmitted on air

Marketing

- Responsible for ratings analysis, research, trade, and consumer engagement

Distribution

- Responsible for managing channel distribution via all DTH and cable platforms
- Handles subscriber revenue and carriage fees
- Manages international distribution of the channel

Other Support Functions:

- Admin, Finance, Legal, HR, and IT are the other support functions which are essential to the smooth running of operations.

Print Media Organizations

Most large print media organizations have the following departments:

- Editorial department
- Advertising department
- Circulation department
- Brand/marketing department
- Production department
- IT department
- Finance department
- HR department
- Scheduling department
- Stores department
- Legal department
- Administrative department

Editorial Department

The editorial department is responsible for creating content for a newspaper. It is headed by an Editor. The editorial department has two main wings – Input Team and Output Team. The Input Team is responsible for gathering news through reporters, correspondents, and special correspondents. Their main task is to collect news. They report in to the Bureau Chief. All reporters discuss the news collected with the Bureau Chief. He/she also decides which reporter will cover which news event. The approved story then goes to the Input Editor. His/her main responsibility is to work closely with the Bureau Chief and add value to the stories coming in from the Bureau Chief. Besides this, the Input Editor is also responsible for ideation. They also ensure that the news piece that goes to the Output Team has been properly verified. Another important member of the input team is the photographer, and he/she reports in to the Bureau Chief.

The news moves from the Input Editor to the Output Desk. The head of the Output Desk is the Output Editor. He/she assigns the incoming news pieces to different desk editors who edit the news and improve the quality of the writing. The people who work under the Output Editor are the Sub-Editors, Deputy Chief Sub-Editor, and Senior Sub-Editors. Once they edit a piece of news, the final copy is sent to the Output Editor for approval. The Output Editor then assigns a page to the news item. From the respective

FIGURE 17.6 Editorial structure of a newspaper.

Source: Created by the author.

page, in-charges will adjust the size/layout of the news based on the space available on the page. Once the page is ready, the Output Editor approves the final page for printing. Besides this, the Output Editor also keeps a watch on the news items that arrive from news agencies such as Press Trust of India (PTI) and Asian News International (ANI).

The Photo Desk is in charge of the photos that would get printed in the newspaper and also checks the caption mentioned on each photo. The Photo Desk's responsibility is to provide photos to the Output Desk as per their requirement. Besides this, the Photo Desk also keeps track of the photos that are available from the news agencies, and use them wherever appropriate.

The Editor is in charge of both the Input Desk and the Output Desk. He/she is responsible for planning the newspaper, and based on their guidelines, the Input and Output Desks do their work.

Different newspapers have different structures and designations, and there could be variations in levels. Depicted in Figure 17.6 is one editorial structure which depicts a typical newspaper operating across two states. A similar structure is replicated across other states, and the levels and designations could vary depending upon the size and scale of the newspaper operations.

Advertising Department

As we're aware, the revenue model of newspapers in India is an advertising-driven model. Hence, the advertising revenues form a substantial part of the revenues of a newspaper organization. In every newspaper organization, there is an advertising department with a primary role of generating advertising revenues. Revenues are generated through two primary methods:

- *Space selling*: This comprises the selling of advertising space.
- *Solutions selling*: This comprises creating a bespoke solution for advertisers in the form of a co-branded event which is executed on ground and promoted through the newspaper.

There is a hierarchy within the advertising department that's optimized to generate revenues. At the top of the hierarchy is the Sales Director, who usually has two National Heads reporting to him/her. In large newspaper organizations, they make a broad business division of printing centres and business offices. Printing centres are those places from where the newspaper is printed, and the printing centre offices typically look after revenue generation from advertisers and local agencies who are located in the city or nearby districts in which the particular edition is distributed. Business offices are those offices that are located in cities where the newspaper is not printed out of. Business offices look after revenue generation from corporate advertisers and media agencies located in those cities.

The National Head for Business Offices has four Zonal Heads reporting in to him/her. Each Zonal Head will have a number of Advertising Managers depending upon the size of the business. Each Ad Manager will have ad executives under him/her depending on the size of the business. Each Ad Manager is usually allotted a set of categories for which he/she is responsible. Sometimes an Ad Manager is given a set of key clients across categories. Sometimes, there are Ad Managers who are given the task of new business development. In some large organizations, some Ad Managers are entrusted with generating advertising revenues through solution selling. This could involve content generation, events, contests, etc. The number of Ad Managers and executives in a particular zone will depend on the size and scale of the business.

The printing centres follow a similar format, except that instead of Zonal Heads, they have State Heads or Area Heads. Under State/Area Heads, they have Ad Managers for each city. Under the Ad Managers there are Ad Executives. Here too, the number of Ad Executives in a particular city will depend on the size and scale of the business.

Figure 17.7 shows a broad organizational structure of the Advertising Department.

Brand/Marketing Department

Large newspaper organizations have a centralized brand team at the head office or a large office, and local brand managers across each city. The Central

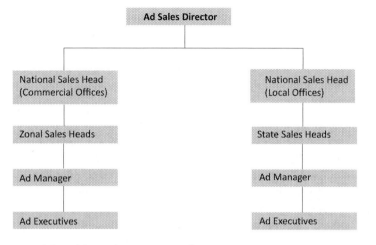

FIGURE 17.7 Advertising sales structure of a newspaper.

Source: Created by the author.

FIGURE 17.8 Brand/marketing structure of a newspaper.

Source: Created by the author.

Brand Team is further divided into four to five teams, with each team taking the responsibility of managing the brand in different geographic areas, as demonstrated in Figure 17.8. The size of the team is dependent on the geographical area covered by the newspaper. The brand team's main responsibility includes the following:

- Ensuring adequate brand awareness across every city where the newspaper is distributed
- Ensuring salience amongst B2B audiences (media planners, media buyers, CMOs, etc.) in cities where the newspaper is not circulated

- Managing brand programmes for to maintain and enhance reader loyalty, gain new readers, and ensure content discoverability
- Manage all brand research and communication
- Create and execute engagement programmes with readers

Circulation Department

The circulation department's primary role is to ensure that the copies of the newspaper reach the doorsteps of readers. However, above and beyond this, over a period of time, the circulation department's mandate has increased to include maximizing circulation sales amongst audiences that can be monetized by advertising. India has always followed a low newspaper cover price model, but things have been changing in recent years, with newspaper companies trying to increase cover prices. As a result, the circulation department is moving forward with a net circulation profit mindset. Besides this, the circulation team also plays a role in building readership numbers.

As seen in Figure 17.9, the circulation team is led by a Circulation Head, who has Region Heads reporting into him/her. Under the Region Heads are Area Heads, followed by PSM Heads. Then there is the Field Sales Team, and teams that look after the particular unit's MIS, and there's a team that handles night despatch at each centre.

The number of Region Heads and Area Heads under them could vary depending on the geographical scale of operations of the newspaper company.

> *Region Heads* have both strategic roles and operational roles. Strategically, their role is to maintain competitive positions in their region, ensure readership growth, maintain revenues and profitability in the region, and maintain relationships with trade networks. In large newspaper organizations, the Region Head could be looking after multiple states.
>
> *Area Heads* have an operational role in their area and look after multiple cities.
>
> *Unit/City Heads* have an operational role and are in charge of respective cities.
>
> The *Field Sales Team* is the operations team which is involved in ground activations and results.
>
> The *City MIS Team* maintains backend data at the city level and maintain ABC records.
>
> The *City/Unit Night Despatch Team* is responsible for dispatching the newspaper. They take responsibility for loading of vehicles once the newspaper is printed and packed, ensure proper labelling, coordinate taxi operations, and confirm all vehicles are available at the right time. They check printing quality and ensure that despatch timings are strictly maintained. They serve as the gatekeeper for any delay in the system.

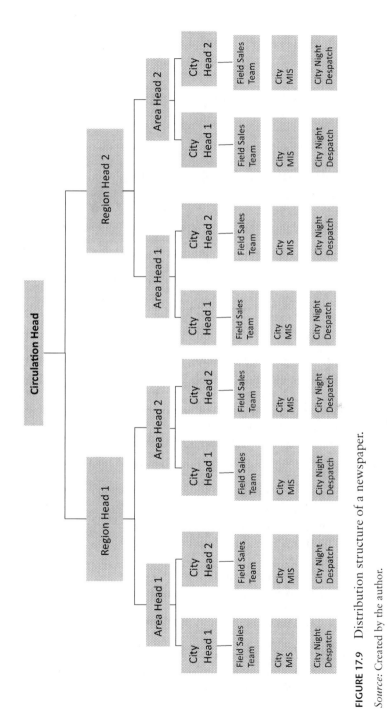

FIGURE 17.9   Distribution structure of a newspaper.

Source: Created by the author.

Production Department

The production department in a print organization has the primary function of ensuring the printing of the newspaper. While doing so, they have to minimize downtime and maintain a consistent quality of printing. The key five sub-divisions within this department are heads who maintain systems, software, electrical works, quality control, and press.

IT Department

The IT department plays an important role in most media organizations nowadays. Typically, the senior-most position in the IT department, the Chief Technology Officer (CTO), reports in to the CEO. His/her main role is to evolve the strategic roadmap and drive enterprise change through IT by enabling or integrating business with IT to reduce costs, maximize efficiency, and achieve business goals.

The CTO works with GMs (with teams reporting to them) who head different areas like Database Administration, Applications, System and Process Architecture, DR and BCP, and Data Centre/Cloud Availability.

Finance Department

This department is headed by a Chief Financial Officer. He/she is assisted by a team of people who maintain the finances of the company. In case it's a listed company, they are responsible for maintaining investor relations as well. In large media organizations usually, there is a central finance team, and at each location/office, there are individual finance managers who take care of individual office financial requirements. The department is responsible for:

- Managing books of accounts
- Managing billings and invoicing
- Managing a company's cash flow
- Maintaining investor relations
- Manage the funds of a company
- Manage payments of taxes
- Budgeting, financial analysis, and forecasting
- Help in raising funds when required

Legal Department

It is usually a centralized team which comprises people with a legal background. They are responsible for managing legal compliances and authorizing legal contracts signed by the company officials. They also liaison with other legal firms who represent the company in various courts of law.

Scheduling Department

This department is in charge of scheduling the ads that have been booked. They essentially keep a record of the advertisements that are scheduled for publishing in the newspaper. Once a release order is received from a media agency to release an advertisement on behalf of their client, the scheduling department enters the details of the ad in a central system. This has details like name of advertiser, name of brand, size of the ad, the editions where the ad has to be published, the position/page number where the ad has to be published, the date on which the ad has to be published, and the advertising rate for the advertisement. The local city scheduling department enters the details, which then go into a central system where the central team plans the pagination and placement of ads in the newspaper.

Human Resources Department

The HR department is responsible for the well-being of the employees. They take care of on-boarding of new employees, training, payroll management, finalizing Key Result Areas (KRAs), managing the employee appraisal process, employee development, and recruitment. The HR function is similar to what one would see in other organizations as well.

Stores Department

This department keeps the inventory of all assets of the company. They manage and maintain the newsprint and all the raw material bought by the company.

Administrative Department

The administrative department takes care of the general administration of the establishment. In large media organizations, there are usually state heads/area heads who are responsible for the general administration of the state/area. Under them, we have local unit heads/managers who are in charge of respective cities/units. They usually take care of the general functioning of the local team. They are responsible for effective coordination amongst all departments in their local office.

Internet Media Organizations

This is one of the fastest-growing mediums in India. There are several players in this market, each with a different structure and offering. Most organizations in this domain are fairly young and evolving quickly as they adopt to business and regulatory challenges. For a large digital media owner, they have the following departments:

- Revenue
- Content
- Product
- Customer Acquisition
- Technology
- Marketing
- Business Intelligence
- Support

  - Human Resources
  - Finance and Legal
  - Administration and Commercial

Figure 17.10 outlines the organizational structure of a fairly large Internet media owner. The number of departments and the hierarchy down the levels could vary depending upon the size, scale, and nature of the business. Each department has a Head and is supported by teams consisting of managers and executives under them.

Revenue Team

This team takes care of the following:

- Direct sales

  - Identifying, pitching, and closing ad sales deals with agencies and direct advertisers
  - Responsible for acquiring new clients and growing the existing clients.
  - Cultivate a pipeline of business opportunities

- Network sales

  - Google DFP for prime inventory
  - Other network partners for house inventory

- Branded content

  - Solution-oriented innovative approach for direct clients
  - Creating content that is directly linked to a brand, allowing consumers to make a connection with it
  - Ideating new solutions in digital for incremental sales
  - Video brand solutions – developing and creating new ideas for all formats, including video solutions, graphics, social media, and innovations, with responsibility to get it produced for the client

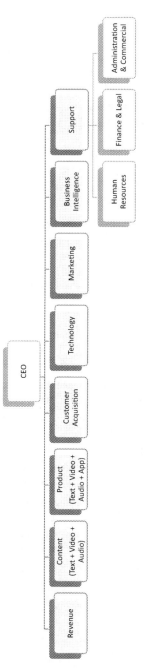

FIGURE 17.10 Superstructure of a typical large Internet media publisher.

Source: Created by the author.

Content Team

This team is responsible for:

- Developing content strategy aligned with the business goals of the organization
- Collaborating with marketing and design teams to plan and develop site content, style, and layout
- Creating and publishing engaging content
- Editing, proofreading, and ensuring qualitative content online
- Developing an editorial calendar and ensuring that content team is in line with the business strategy
- Ensuring compliance with law (e.g. copyright and data protection)
- Staying up-to-date with developments and generating new ideas to draw audience's attention

Product Team

This team is responsible for:

- Developing the core positioning and messaging for the product, including web and video
- Ensuring the product supports the organization's overall strategy and goals.
- Managing product profitability and commercial success – owning the business case
- Customer/user research – setting a product's vision, strategy, and roadmap to ensure that products are strategically planned and managed.
- Supporting the Sales Team in delivering a monthly revenue forecast
- Managing all aspects of in-life products, including feedback, requirements, and issues for all properties
- Continuous evaluation and validation of the product vision to anticipate and address changing business and user needs
- Participation in daily scrum meetings, planning, weekly reviews, and retrospectives
- Monitoring market changes and trends to assess competitive positioning and opportunities for strategic product enhancements.
- Working with sales, marketing, and support teams to ensure revenue and customer satisfaction goals are met.

Customer Acquisition Team

This team is responsible for:

- Setting the strategy for acquisition across paid earned and owned media to drive overall customer growth through new innovation and current optimization

- Taking the lead on identifying new opportunities to test and trial, and to set the strategy and plan as required (tactically and longer term)
- Overseeing delivery of high-quality, on-brand, response-driving campaigns, to acquire new customers to agreed targets across paid, earned, and owned media
- Overseeing the budget and creating a rigorous process for analysis, working with the Data Analytics Team
- Ensuring the right technology, tools, and enablers are in place for campaign measurement
- Constantly challenging and optimizing the media mix and campaign performance to achieve business KPIs
- Initiating and overseeing campaign test and learn activity to ensure the most efficient campaigns are being delivered, including landing page testing, creative and format testing, and message testing
- Developing a high-performing, driven team that consistently exceeds targets
- Working with Research for ongoing improvements through customer feedback and insight

Technology Team

This team is responsible for:
- Development
  - Troubleshoots, fixes defects, and extends the functionality of existing websites, systems, applications, mobile apps, and content management systems
  - Follows established processes and uses tools and technologies that are consistent with existing solutions, infrastructure, and support capabilities
- Design
  - Collaborate with product management and engineering to define and implement innovative solutions for the product direction, visuals, and experience
  - Conceptualize original ideas that bring simplicity and user friendliness to complex design roadblocks
  - Create wireframes, storyboards, user flows, process flows, and site maps to effectively communicate interaction and design ideas
- Infrastructure
  - Proactively manage devices and networks in an agile and adaptable way
  - Identify threats to your network, responding promptly to mitigate their impact
  - Reduce downtime by carrying out repairs more quickly

Marketing Team

This team is responsible for:

- Developing the annual marketing plan and strategy, implementing activities for successful launch of B2B and B2C campaigns
- Working on tactical communication for marketing campaigns
- Publishing and promoting monthly Comscore communication
- Acting as a support for planning and execution of IPs with the respective stakeholders
- Liaising closely with the corporate brand team for special campaigns and PR

Business Intelligence Team

This team is responsible for:

- Implementing methods of tracking and measuring effectiveness of online activity and reviewing reporting tools to ensure optimum efficiency in conjunction with technical team
- Managing additional marketing research requirements (in house and via third parties) to enhance stakeholder data and information
- Performing regular activity tracking analyses and recommending actions to improve open rates, click-through rates, and conversion rates.
- Providing data-driven insights to grow existing and new users
- Providing comparison and insight into reports provided by third parties e.g. online advertising reports, Google AdWords, etc., to ensure consistency of reporting and identify opportunities
- Designing and developing reports for other teams to assist in monitoring the use of and responding to their various online activities
- Interpreting, questioning, and interrogating a wide range of data and information using various software tools

Support

The following three teams fall under this department:

- Human Resources
  - Enabling scalable and sustainable organization culture to deliver business goals
  - Planning manpower and budget to support business objectives
  - Hiring best talent in line with the business goals and budget
  - Identifying learning and development needs and implementing L&D programs
  - Developing and creating SOPs and KRAs to drive performance and productivity

- Creating brand image through social media presence such as Glass-door and LinkedIn
- Finance
  - To enable budget performance through audit, strategy, and compliance
- Administration and Commercial
  - To devise system, process, and cost structures towards an efficient work environment

Radio Organizations

FM radio came into its own in the early 2000s when the first phase of licensing opened. Radio has over 225 million listeners in India and has the ability to relay localized messages. While usually it is used as a support medium to amplify the main campaign on TV and print, FM radio stations have gone beyond and offer an integrated solution to brands. There are about 1100-odd operational radio stations in India, of which there are over 360 private FM stations covering about 100 cities. There are more than 220 million radio listeners in India, making it a fairly large medium. Figure 17.11 showcases how a large national radio network is structured.

The structure depicted in Figure 17.11 is of a large Pan-India network. This is a more centralized structure, with the corporate office playing a larger role, and local zonal offices to take care of radio stations within the zone. Figure 17.12 shows how a typical sub-structure operates within a particular zone.

Following is an overview of the key departments and their functions.

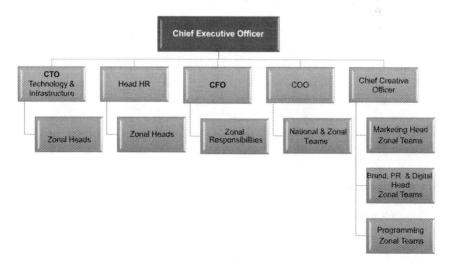

FIGURE 17.11 Superstructure of a large radio organization.

Source: Created by the author.

FIGURE 17.12 Zonal structure of a large radio organization.

Source: Created by the author.

Programming

The zonal programming head reports to the Chief Creative Officer/ Programming Head. The key functions of the local programming team are:

- Content innovations
- On-air reach
- Supporting revenue as per the target
- On-air and online product monitoring
- Support in garnering special innovations and digital revenue

Marketing

The zonal marketing head reports to the Corporate Head of Marketing. The team's key functions are:

- Building brand saliency and credibility in local markets
- Digital content amplification
- Terrestrial content amplification
- Digital content marketing
- Sales support
- Managing barter revenues

Brand Communication and PR

These positions report to the Corporate Marketing Head. The key responsibilities are:

- Driving reach and views on the radio station's IPs
- Creating concepts and creatives for online promotion of programming IPs across social media platforms, internal, and trade

- Building 360-degree campaign promotions for digital + programming IPs
- Driving reach and building community
- Brand building

Digital Media

With competition slowly emerging in the form of streaming services, most large private FM networks have set up their own web radio stations. Digital divisions have been set up in such networks to promote digital content. Figure 17.13 outlines how a typical digital set-up within a radio network looks like.

Digital Client Solutions Team

This team is responsible for:

- Content syndication
- Quality ideation in digital integration
- Creative client pitches, ideas, and innovations

Content Head

The Content Head takes care of:

- Upgradation of website content and overall product
- New IPs (digital + programming)
- Achieving the content syndication revenue targets

Product Head

The Product Head is responsible for:

- Revenue support
- Product development in terms of podcasts/games
- Preventive measures against bugs

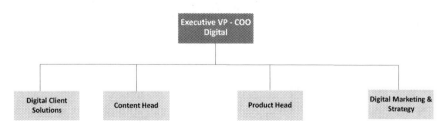

FIGURE 17.13 Digital sub-structure of a large radio organization.

Source: Created by the author.

Digital Marketing and Strategy Team

The Digital Marketing and Strategy Team is responsible for:

- Driving reach and views on the IPs of the radio station
- Driving reach and building community
- Brand building
- Online ideation and execution of digital + programming IPs via social media
- Initiatives for influencers and alliances

Sales

The Zonal Sales Head reports in to the CEO or Corporate Sales Head. The department is responsible for:

- Revenue and collections
- Generating sponsorships for station IPs
- Driving higher effective rates
- Digital solutions
- Agency focus
- Driving higher volume share
- Creating new business avenues in government

Other Support Departments

The Tech and IT Team is responsible for:

- Broadcast and IT
- Processing automation across functions
- Digital focus

The Human Resources Team is responsible for:

- Talent acquisition
- Succession planning
- Driving HR automation
- Managing the statutory compliance
- Cultural excellence
- Employee retention
- Managing the HR Budget

Finance and Legal is responsible for:

- Cost management
- Financial accounting, MIS, statutory audits
- Taxation matters
- Legal and secretarial matters

Administration is responsible for:

- Administrative cost effectiveness
- Budget preparation
- Collections
- Statutory compliance

The lists in this section describe an indicative structure of a large pan-India network of radio stations. There are different structures adopted by different organizations of the same scale. Then there are some small players in the industry with either a single station or a group of channels within a state – they operate with different structures depending upon their size and scale.

OOH Organizations

OOH also accounts for about 5% of the advertising spends in India. OOH is highly fragmented, with both organized and unorganized players running the industry. This includes traditional OOH, transit media, digital OOH, wall paintings, ambient media amongst other formats. A highly localized medium, OOH is usually used by real estate, local retail, media, FMCG, and financial services. Currently, digital OOH and transit media are growing rapidly. Brands usually are present on OOH for its salience, immediacy, quick local reach build-up, and ability to localize messaging. The medium suffers due to lack of measurement, yet it offers several advantages. There are several large outdoor agencies in India. Figure 17.14 outlines the typical structure of an OOH agency.

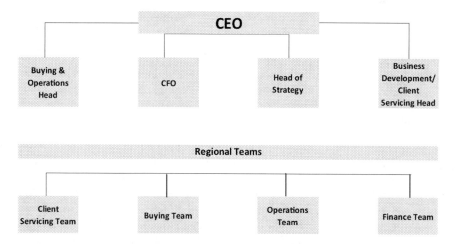

FIGURE 17.14 Organizational structure of an OOH agency.

Source: Created by the author.

While Figure 17.14 shows a setup of a typical large agency, there are some other agencies that have structured their business around profit centres. Under this, the Regional Head in each region is a profit-centre head.

The roles and responsibilities of key people are:

a. *Buying and Operations Head National*

- Buying across territories through regional teams
- Volume deals with partners
- Rate benchmarking
- Execution and monitoring of campaigns through regional teams

b. *Business Development/Client Servicing Head National*

- New business development
- Maintaining relationships with existing clients
- Keeping clients abreast of new media or digital opportunities in the OOH space
- Providing solutions to meet campaign objectives
- Formulation of service-level agreements (SLAs) with clients

c. *Strategic Planning Head National*

- Providing mix and reach of OOH mediums to achieve campaign objectives
- Planning innovations
- Conducting research where required

d. *Operations Team at regional level*

- Campaign implementation, including printing and mounting of sites
- Campaign monitoring and reporting

e. *Client Servicing Team at regional level*

- Maintaining existing client relationships
- Delivering on SLAs
- Preparing campaign execution reports
- Flagging any issues on campaign implementation

Media Agencies

Media agencies work as the intermediaries between the advertisers and the media. A media agency performs the critical functions of media planning, media buying, and media operations on behalf of an advertiser. It handles client relations and manages the entire media mandate from planning media strategy, to creating media plans, to executing plans, to tracking the campaign, evaluating the campaign performance, and managing the billings and payments to media. With new-age digital platforms coming in, during the early 21st century, large media agencies have extended themselves to create digital divisions, data science teams, and technology development teams to assist advertisers navigate the digital medium. In India, there are a few large agency networks:

Group M: It comprises individual full-service agencies like Mindshare, Mediacom, and Wavemaker. A specialist agency, Essence, uses analytics and technology to help marketers grow businesses. M/Six is an agency for building integrated, bespoke, and in-housed teams. Xaxis specializes in using technology, data, and expertise to make programmatic media more effective and efficient. Choreograph is another recently launched (April 2021) specialist data products and technology company, helping advertisers with data management and usage to fuel brand growth. Motion Content is a specialist agency that helps fund, develop, produce, and distribute original and third-party licensed content. Kinetic is a specialist agency in the Out-of-Home advertising arena.

IPG Media Brands: It comprises individual full-service media and marketing solutions agencies like UM (Universal McCann) and Initiative Media. Besides this, it has a performance marketing and ecommerce agency, Reprise; a media barter and capital programs agency, Orion; a media marketplace intelligence and media investment agency, Magna; a specialty activation services in OOH agency, Rapport; and an original, branded, and performance content agency in Mediabrands Content Studio. The IPG Media Lab identifies and researches innovations and trends in media.

Denstu Aegis Network: It comprises a media full-service independent agency Carat, an integrated communications solutions agency, dentsuX; a specialist agency, iProspect, which is focused on performance-driven brand building in the digital domain; a specialist digital agency, isobar; two OOH specialist agencies, Posterscope and Milestone Brandcom; a content-solutions agency, The Storylab; a programmatic specialist agency, Amnet; and a hybrid digital agency, WatConsult, which helps brands connect and co-create with their target customers.

Madison Media: It comprises specialist full-service media agencies Madison and Mediacom (a JV with WPP); HiveMinds, a full-service digital marketing agency; two specialist OOH agencies, MOMS and Platinum OOH; an integrated experiential solutions agency, Madison Turnt; a rural marketing agency, Anugrah Madison; a Sports Marketing and Management agency, PMG, that works on syndicated columns, sports content, sports celebrity management, and events related to sports; a specialist agency focused on leveraging opportunities in football, – The Football Edge; a specialist mobile marketing agency, Madison Xurpas; a data analytics agency, Madison Business Analytics; and two PR agencies, Madison PR and Brandcomm PR.

As you can see, these are large agency networks with different scales and specializations. Therefore, organizational structures for all of them would vary depending on network priorities and strength of individual specialist agencies within the network. Figure 17.15 illustrates an example of the broad organization structure of a typical full-service media agency that provides media planning and buying services to advertisers.

A typical full-service agency services several advertisers simultaneously. Usually agencies create special client teams with resources drawn from different specialties to service a particular brand. The size and diversity of this team would vary depending on the size of the brand business and its specific requirements. A typical media team for an advertiser would comprise the following:

- *Business Team*: This team is responsible for managing the overall business of the advertiser. It understands the media brief, creates an overall media strategy, debriefs the Planning and Buying Teams, coordinates the execution of the campaign, and remains the single point of contact for the advertiser.
- *Planning Team*: This team is responsible for creating media plans as per the agreed media strategy and goals. They are responsible for optimizing media plans and creating innovation opportunities for the brand.
- *Buying Team*: This team is responsible for buying media based on the brief and the plan. They negotiate with several media houses to secure the best deals for the brand. They identify sponsorship and innovation opportunities for the brand. They are responsible for campaign execution, and monitoring and ensure that the set media targets are achieved for the brand.
- *Digital Team*: This team takes care of the digital planning and execution for the brand.
- *Other specialists*: These could include a performance marketing resource, a content marketing resource, or a brand solutions resource – all depending on the advertiser's requirement.

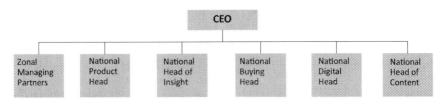

FIGURE 17.15 Broad organization structure of a typical full-service media agency.

Source: Created by the author.

Other support functions at the agency include:

- HR
- IT
- Admin
- Legal
- Finance

In the case of large networks, these are normally centralized functions with some resources from each of the aforementioned departments at individual business units.

Digital Agencies

Digital agency is a 21st-century phenomenon. And then came social media, which really took over the marketing world in the second decade of the 21st century. There are three kinds of digital agencies.

- Those that started as a website/SEO agency, and hence were great in technology. They started flexing their arms in the world of marketing with social media.
- Those that started as a mainline agency and flexed their arms in the world of technology.
- Boutique social media agencies that started as social media.

Till the late 2010s, digital was looked upon as a support structure for marketing. Brands used to think print, radio, and TV, and digital was used to propagate the message. New campaign thinking on digital was kept to small topical events and activities. However, for the last few years thinking has started to move to digital. Print, radio, and TV follow what digital is doing and are used as amplification and reach driver channels. Digital drives the core brand thought and its manifestations for most brands.

Figure 17.16 showcases a structure of a typical digital agency in India. The structure varies based on the expertise of the agency and the key focus. Some agencies have a more varied social media team, while others may have a more exhaustive ads and performance marketing team. Yet others may have a larger and specialized technology team.

The Content Team takes over to write all the informatory content, and the designers have to coordinate accordingly. Further, the work moves ahead to the development and is later followed by the assurance of the quality. Once the collaterals are done, the complete marketing of the brand starts under SEM (Search Engine Marketing) and digital ads.

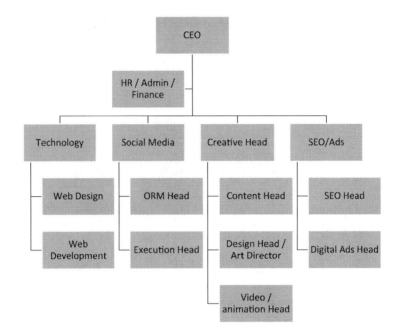

FIGURE 17.16   Structure of a typical digital agency in India.

Source: Created by the author.

The execution in digital agencies is built around collaboration. Between the senior members of the content or design team with the junior, between servicing, content, design, technology, and execution, between the planners and the creators, and so on. While digital is all about the ability of customers to be able to work offline, we sincerely believe that digital agencies themselves can't work offline. If you ask a junior writer to work in silo, quality suffers. If you give the same task to a senior, cost suffers. Every piece of the puzzle across various departments has to constantly be involved in refining and ensuring all is functioning as designed, more so than in any tech or other environment.

When the option of working from home was introduced after the COVID-19 pandemic, professional communication got highly dependent on emails. It became very problematic for digital agencies to have all the conversations via email. A communication gap occurred in between, and thus it started becoming hectic to coordinate with every department on every disagreement.

The pandemic made the management of different firms realize the value of the digital world when the human population was caged in boundaries. The

Founders and CEOs had their eyes on the digital world like never before to look over the progress of their employees and clients from time to time. Today, when the world stands between the banter of working from home or working from the office; it needs to be understood that digital agencies need coordination between the team members. It also results in the resistance of overwork and greater efficiency.

As a response, digital agencies are now moving towards a matrix approach for implementation:

- *Research* will source information on relevant issues which are trending on social/ mainstream media on a real-time basis, 24 x 7.
- *Content* will be created using inputs from Research aligned to the strategy and position of the party on the core issues.
- *Creative* will work on inputs from content and create material across the various platforms, using humour, pathos, urgency, etc., as required to create maximum emotional impact.
- *Social Media* will decide on the relevant platform for each issue depending on the suitability/compatibility of the issue vis-à-vis the platform.

Figure 17.17 describes how Research becomes absolutely critical for a digital agency.

Figure 17.18 discusses a digital agency's roadmap to renewing their focus on content like never before.

Figure 17.19 outlines the creativity process changes at a digital agency in the new post-pandemic environment.

Figure 17.20 describes the rising importance of the social media platforms – the right issue, the right audience, the right platform.

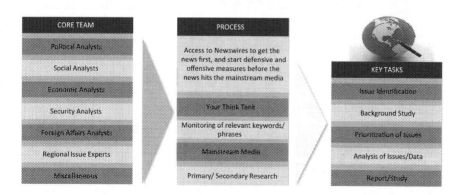

FIGURE 17.17   Criticality of the research function for a digital agency.

Source: Created by the author.

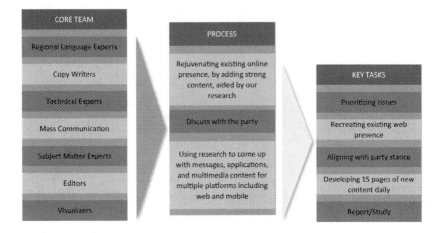

FIGURE 17.18 Content structure of a digital agency.

Source: Created by the author.

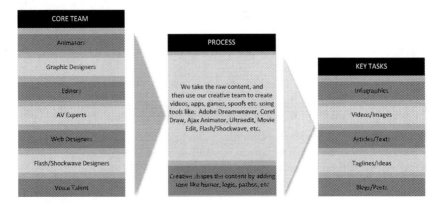

FIGURE 17.19 Creative structure at a digital agency.

Source: Created by the author.

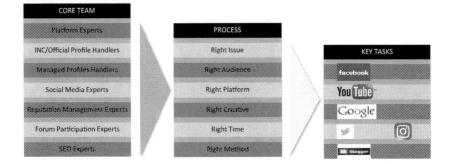

FIGURE 17.20 Social media structure at a digital agency.

Source: Created by the author.

Chapter Summary

The Indian media industry has several large players across different domains of print, TV, Internet, radio, OOH, and the media and digital agencies. There are some large media conglomerates like BCCL, Zee, Star, Jagran, Bhaskar, etc., who have a presence across multiple types of media. There are pure play players who operate only in one domain of media. Then there are large media agencies that have presence with divisions that cater to specific media types such as digital, OOH, analytics, sports, events, PR, and so on. So there's no one defined structure that operates across the industry. Different organizations based on their scale of operations have created structures that enable the efficient running of business.

Here's a broad overview of the key departments across media organizations:

TV Organizations (General Entertainment Channels)

a. *Content Team*: Responsible for creating/sourcing content.
b. *Marketing Team*: Responsible for channel marketing. This includes above-the-line and below-the-line activities, content promotions, marketing tie-ups/associations, and publicity.
c. *Editing/GFX Team*: This team is responsible for editing the content, creating graphics, and adding the channel identity to the content created.
d. *Promo Team*: This team is responsible for creating the promos for the content created. These programme promos are used to promote the programme across the channel during the ad breaks.
e. *PR Team*: This team is responsible for generating PR for the channel and the programmes.
f. *Admin Team*: This team takes care of general office administration across all the other teams.
g. *Sales Team*: The key role of this team is to generate advertising revenue.

TV Organizations (News Channels)

a. *Editorial*: Responsible for creating the news bulletins and other news-related shows. Under the editorial function there are sub-divisions like Input, Assignment, Output, PCR, and MCR.
b. *Marketing*: Responsible for ratings analysis, research, trade, and consumer engagement.
c. *Distribution*: Responsible for managing channel distribution via all DTH and cable platforms, subscriber revenue, and carriage fees
d. *Other support functions*: Admin, Finance, Legal, HR, and IT are the other support functions which are essential to the smooth running of operations.

Print Media Organizations

a. *Editorial department*: The editorial department is responsible for creating content for a newspaper. Headed by an Editor, the editorial department has two main wings – the Input Team and the Output Team.

b. *Advertising department*: Their role is to generate advertising revenues through space selling and solutions selling.

c. *Brand/Marketing department*: The Brand Team's main responsibility is to ensure brand saliency amongst B2C and B2B audiences, creating and executing brand IPS, and managing all brand research and communication.

d. *Circulation department*: The circulation department's primary role is to ensure that the copies of the newspaper reach the doorsteps of readers.

e. *Production department*: The production department in a print organization has the primary function of ensuring the printing of the newspaper.

f. *IT department*: The major role is to evolve the strategic roadmap and drive enterprise change through IT by enabling or integrating business with IT to reduce costs, maximize efficiency, and achieve business goals.

g. *Scheduling department*: This department is in-charge of scheduling the ads that have been booked. They essentially keep a record of the advertisements that are scheduled for publishing in the newspaper.

h. *Other support functions*: The other supporting departments are Finance, Legal, Human Resources, Administration, and Stores.

Internet Media Organizations

a. *Revenue Team*: This team takes care of direct sales, network sales, and branded content.

b. *Content Team*: This team is responsible for planning and developing site content, style and layout, editing, and proofreading.

c. *Product Team*: This team is responsible for developing the core positioning and messaging for the product, managing product profitability, managing customer/user research and providing sales support.

d. *Customer Acquisition Team*: This team is responsible for driving customer growth.

e. *Technology Team*: This team is responsible for troubleshooting, fixing defects, and extending the functionality of existing websites, systems, applications, mobile apps, and content management systems.

f. *Marketing Team*: This team is responsible for managing B2B and B2C campaigns and planning and execution of Ips.

g. *Business Intelligence Team*: This team is responsible for tracking and measuring effectiveness of online activity and review reporting tools to ensure optimum efficiency in conjunction with technical team.

h. *Support*: The key support functions are Human Resources, Finance, Administration, and Commercial.

Radio Organizations

a. *Programming*: The key functions of the local programming team are to ensure quality on-air content and create content innovations which could be leveraged to generate revenues.

b. *Marketing*: The team's key functions are building brand saliency, content amplification, and content marketing.

c. *Brand Communication and PR*: This team is responsible for creating and executing brand Ips, and for brand building.

d. *Digital Media*: This team is responsible for promoting digital content of web radio stations.

e. *Sales*: This department is responsible for revenue and collections, generating sponsorships for station Ips, and driving new revenue opportunities.

i. *Other support departments*: The major support functions in a radio organization are Tech and IT, Human Resources, Finance and Legal, and Administration.

Out-of-Home Organizations

a. *Buying and Operations Team*: It is responsible for buying inventory, rate benchmarking, and execution and monitoring of campaigns.

b. *Business Development Team*: It is responsible for new business development and maintaining relationships with existing clients.

c. *Strategic Planning Team*: This team is responsible for providing mix and reach of OOH mediums to achieve campaign objectives, innovations, and research.

d. *Operations Team*: Responsible for campaign implementation, monitoring, and reporting.

e. *Client Servicing Team*: Responsible for maintaining existing client relationships, and prepare campaign execution reports.

Media Agencies

a. *Business Team*: This team is responsible for managing the overall business of the advertiser and remains the single point of contact.

b. *Planning Team*: This team is responsible for creating media plans as per the agreed media strategy and goals.

c. *Buying Team*: This team is responsible for buying media based on the brief and the plan.

d. *Digital Team*: This team takes care of the digital planning and execution for the brand.

e. *Other specialists*: These could include a performance marketing resource, a content marketing resource, or a brand solutions resource – all depending on the advertiser's requirement.

f. Other support functions at the agency are HR, IT, Administration, Legal, and Finance.

Digital Agencies

Digital agencies in India follow several different kinds of structures. However, with increasing scale and the post-pandemic scenario, digital agencies have started approaching businesses with different operating models. The key departments here are:

- *Research*: Research will source information on relevant issues which are trending on social/mainstream media on a real-time basis, 24 x 7.
- *Content*: Content will be created using inputs from Research aligned to the strategy and position of the party on the core issues.
- *Creative*: Creative will work on inputs from content and create material across the various platforms, using humour, pathos, urgency, etc., as required to create maximum emotional impact.
- *Social Media*: Social Media decides on the relevant platform for each issue depending on the suitability/compatibility of the issue vis-à-vis the platform.
- *Technology Team*: Takes care of web design and development.
- *SEO Team*: Responsible for search engine optimization (SEO).
- *Implementation Team*: Responsible for campaign execution and monitoring
- *Client Servicing*: Manages client relationships.
- *New Business*: Looks for new revenue opportunities.
- *Support functions* like Finance, Administration, HR, and Legal.

Further Reading

Dentsu: https://dentsu.in/
Group M: https://www.groupm.com/businesses/
IPG Media: https://www.ipgmediabrands.com/our-brands/
Madison Media: https://www.madisonindia.com/about-us

INDEX

Pages in *italics* refer to figures and pages in **bold** refer to tables.

Printed in the United States
by Baker & Taylor Publisher Services